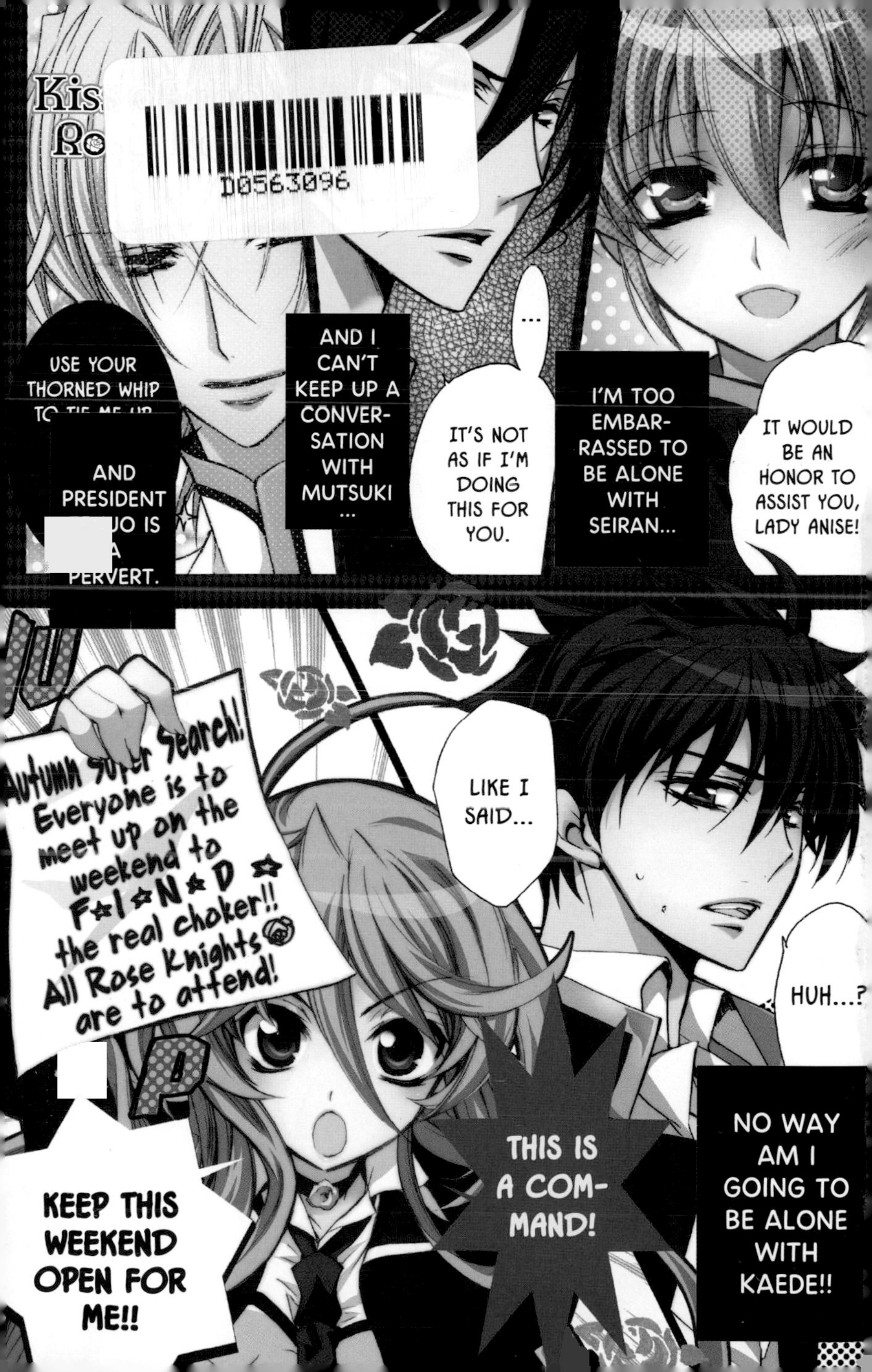
IT WOULD BE AN HONOR TO ASSIST YOU, LADY ANISE!
I'M TOO EMBARRASSED TO BE ALONE WITH SEIRAN...
...
IT'S NOT AS IF I'M DOING THIS FOR YOU.
AND I CAN'T KEEP UP A CONVERSATION WITH MUTSUKI...
USE YOUR THORNED WHIP
AND PRESIDENT
JO IS
A
PERVERT.
LIKE I SAID...
HUH...?
NO WAY AM I GOING TO BE ALONE WITH KAEDE!!
THIS IS A COMMAND!
Autumn Super Search! Everyone is to meet up on the weekend to F☆I☆N☆D☆ the real choker!! All Rose Knights are to attend!
KEEP THIS WEEKEND OPEN FOR ME!!

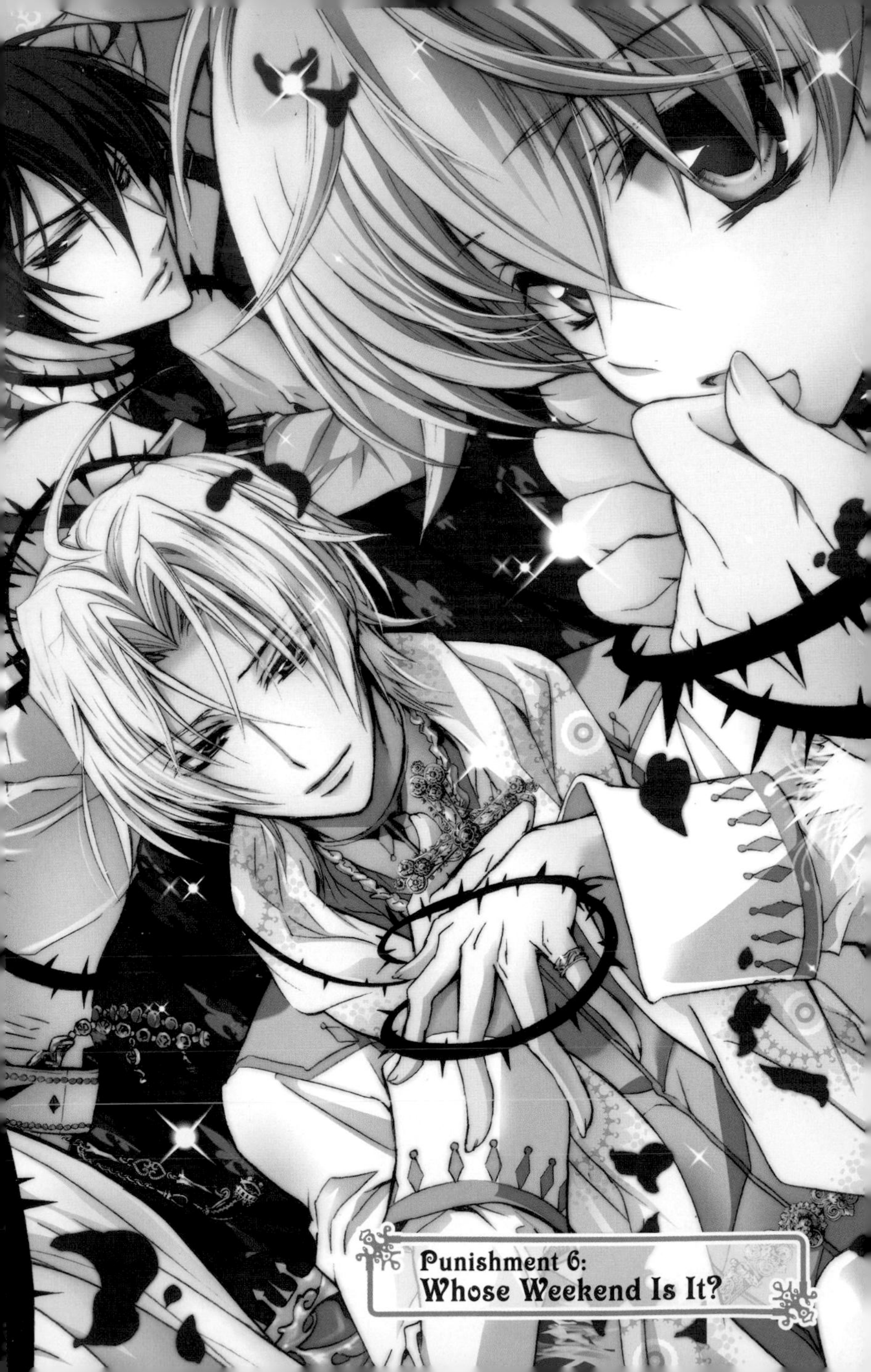
Punishment 6:
Whose Weekend Is It?

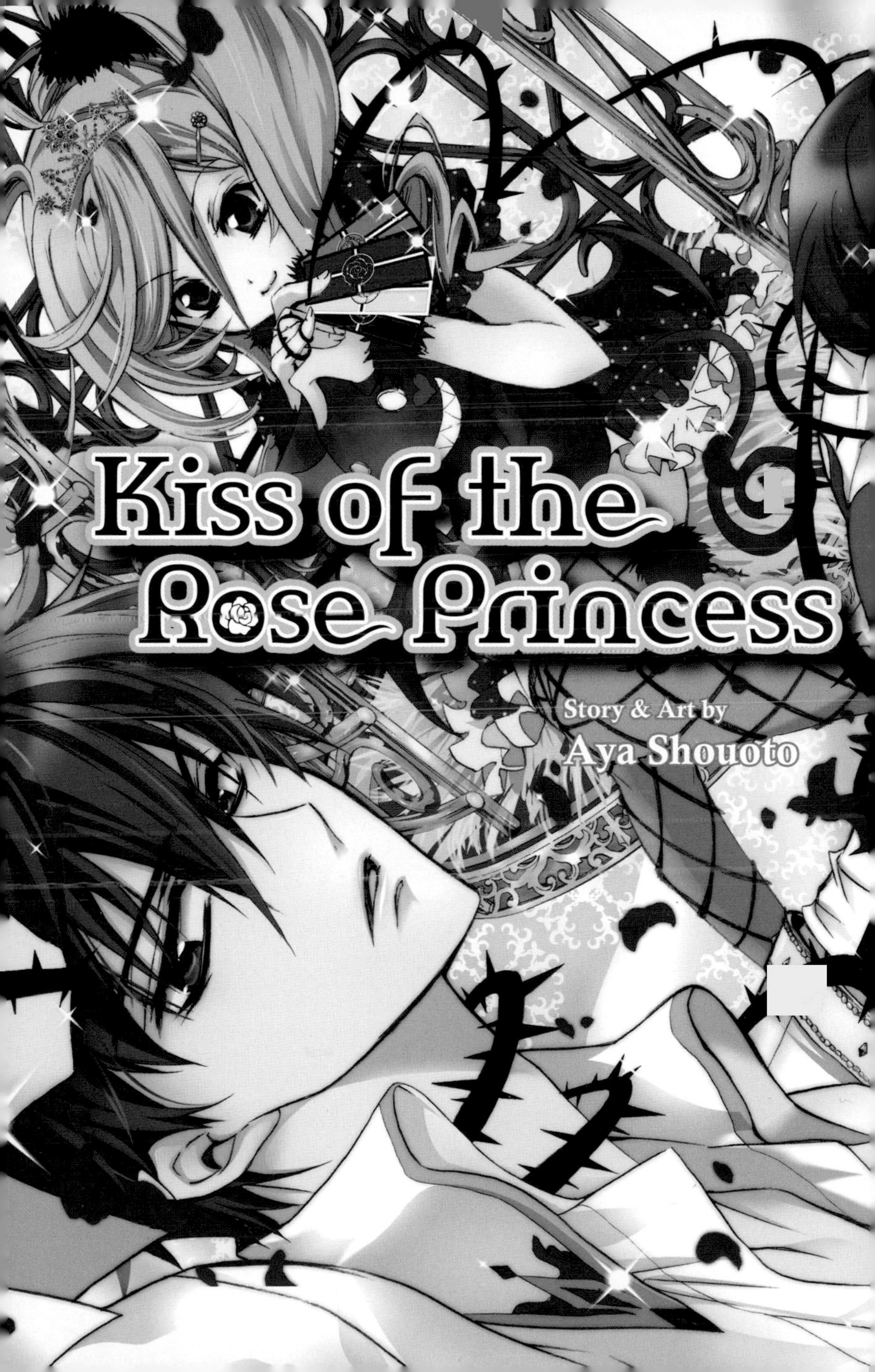
Kiss of the Rose Princess
Story & Art by
Aya Shouoto

Kiss of the Rose Princess

Contents

Characters

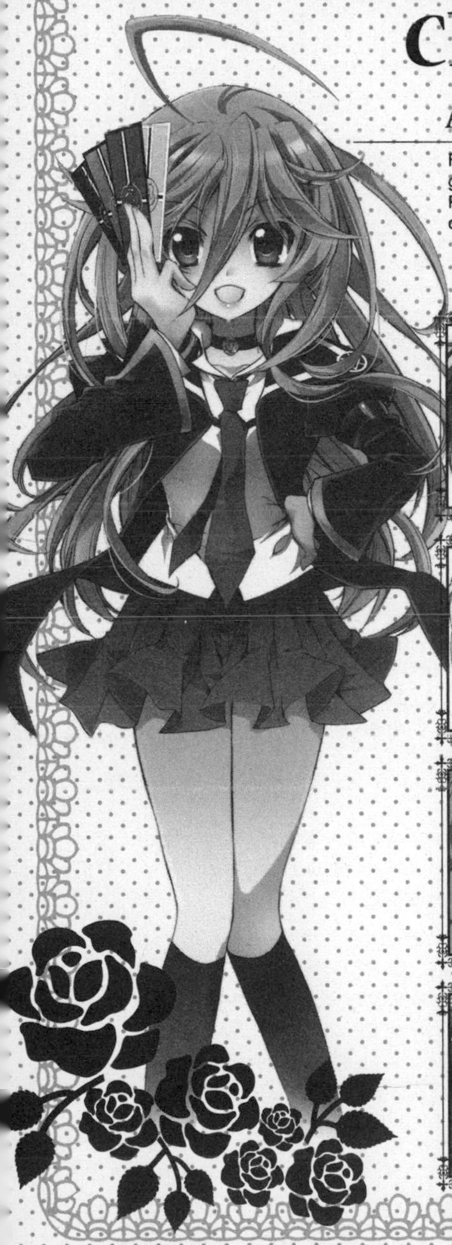

Anise Yamamoto

First-year at Shobi Academy. She's a strong-willed girl who dreams of one day finding and dating her Prince Charming.♥ She dislikes being the center of attention.

Rose Knights

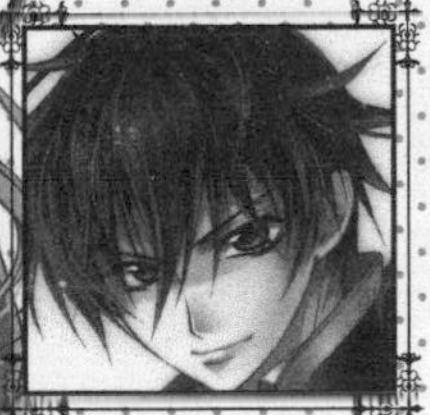

Kaede Higa (Red Rose)

Anise's classmate. He's an excellent athlete who often teases Anise.
Specialty: Offence

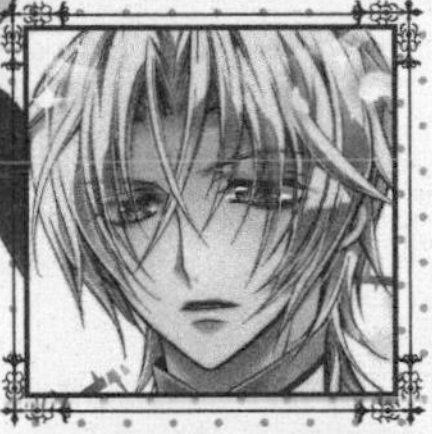

Mitsuru Tenjo (White Rose)

Third-year and Student Council President. He is revered by both male and female students. Super-rich.
Specialty: Healing, Defense

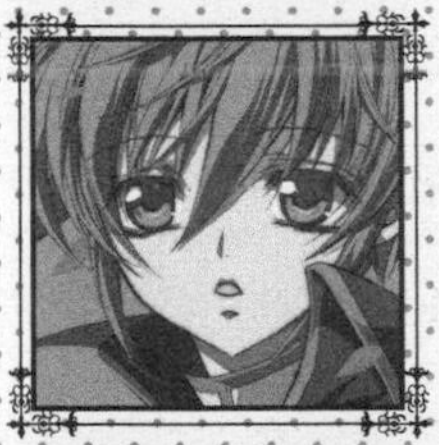

Seiran Asagi (Blue Rose)

First-year. This boy is cuter than any girl at school, and he doesn't know he's the school idol. He's well-versed in a wide range of topics.
Specialty: Alchemy, Science

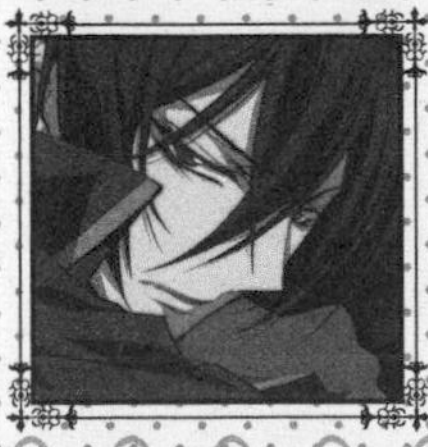

Mutsuki Kurama (Black Rose)

Second-year. There are many frightening rumors about this mysterious student. Apparently he lives in the basement of Tenjo's house.
Specialty: Discovery, Capture

Itsushi Narumi
(Classics Teacher)

He is the most knowledge-able about the "Sovereign," her "Rose Knights," and the "Rose Contract" that binds them...

Ninufa (Guardian)

The guardian who has been protecting the cards since ancient times.

Schwarz Yamamoto

Anise's father. It seems he had a motive in putting the rose choker on Anise.

Kiss of the Rose Princess   Story Thus Far

High school student Anise Yamamoto loses the choker given to her as a talisman by her father. He warned her that a truly terrifying punishment would befall her if she ever took it off... A mysterious creature appears before Anise and gets her to kiss four cards. This causes the Rose Knights to appear before her, asking for her command. The four Rose Knights also happen to be the most popular boys at school! All Anise wants is a peaceful life at school, so at first she wonders if this is her punishment. But the real punishment is closing in on her...

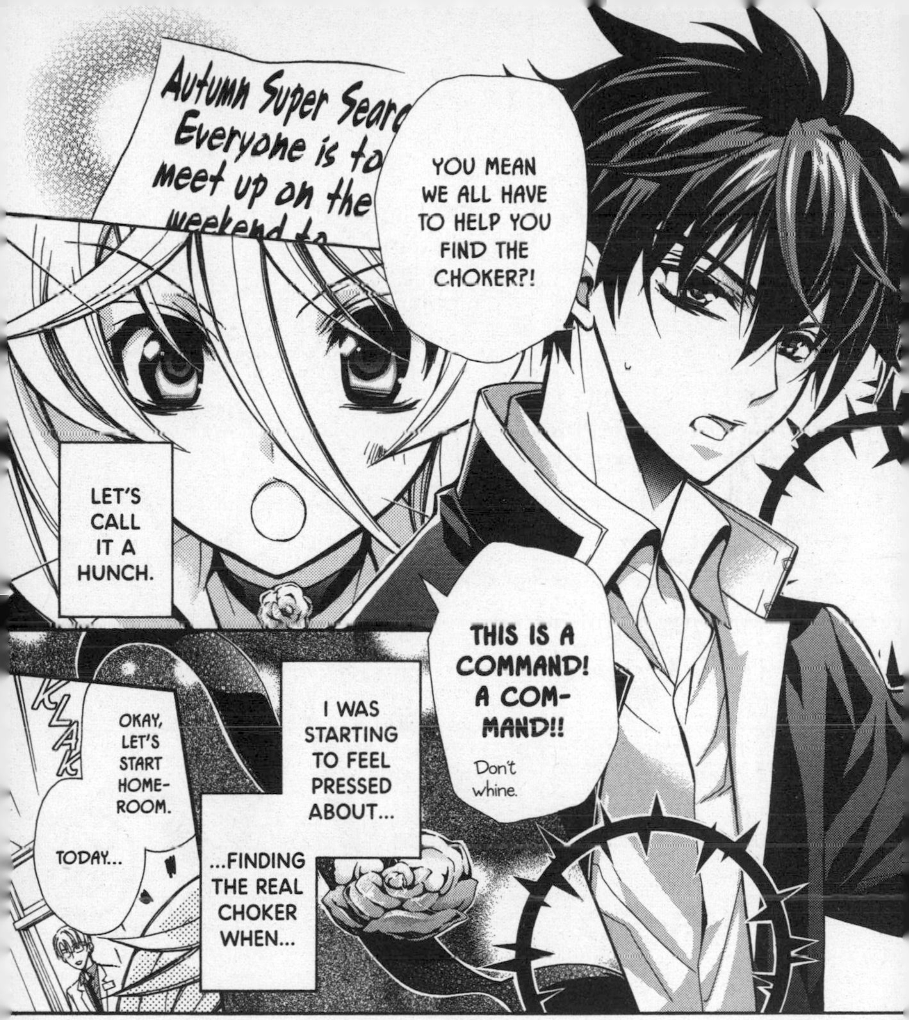
YOU MEAN WE ALL HAVE TO HELP YOU FIND THE CHOKER?!
Autumn Super Searc
Everyone is to
meet up on the
LET'S CALL IT A HUNCH.
THIS IS A COMMAND! A COM-MAND!!
Don't whine.
I WAS STARTING TO FEEL PRESSED ABOUT...
...FINDING THE REAL CHOKER WHEN...
OKAY, LET'S START HOME-ROOM.
TODAY...
KLAK

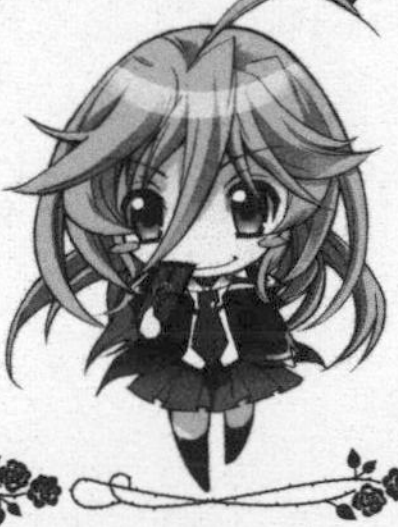

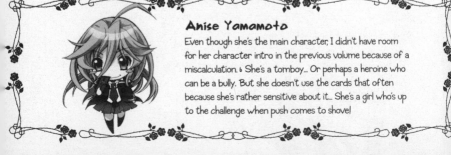

Anise Yamamoto

Even though she's the main character, I didn't have room for her character intro in the previous volume because of a miscalculation. ♭ She's a tomboy... Or perhaps a heroine who can be a bully. But she doesn't use the cards that often because she's rather sensitive about it... She's a girl who's up to the challenge when push comes to shove!

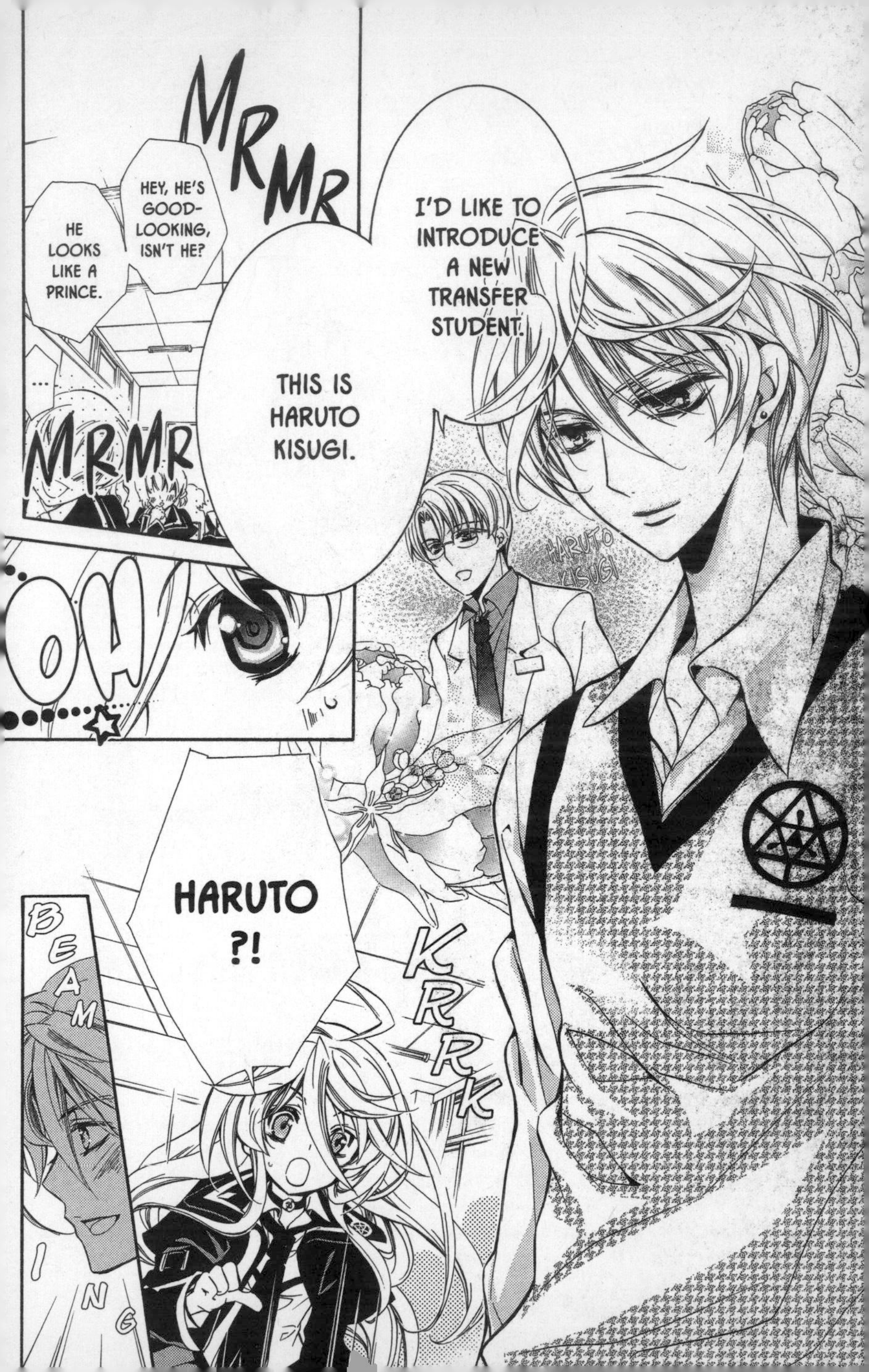
I'D LIKE TO INTRODUCE A NEW TRANSFER STUDENT.
THIS IS HARUTO KISUGI.
HARUTO KISUGI
MRMR
MRMR
HEY, HE'S GOOD-LOOKING, ISN'T HE?
HE LOOKS LIKE A PRINCE.
...
MRMR
OH
HARUTO ?!
KRRK
BEAMING

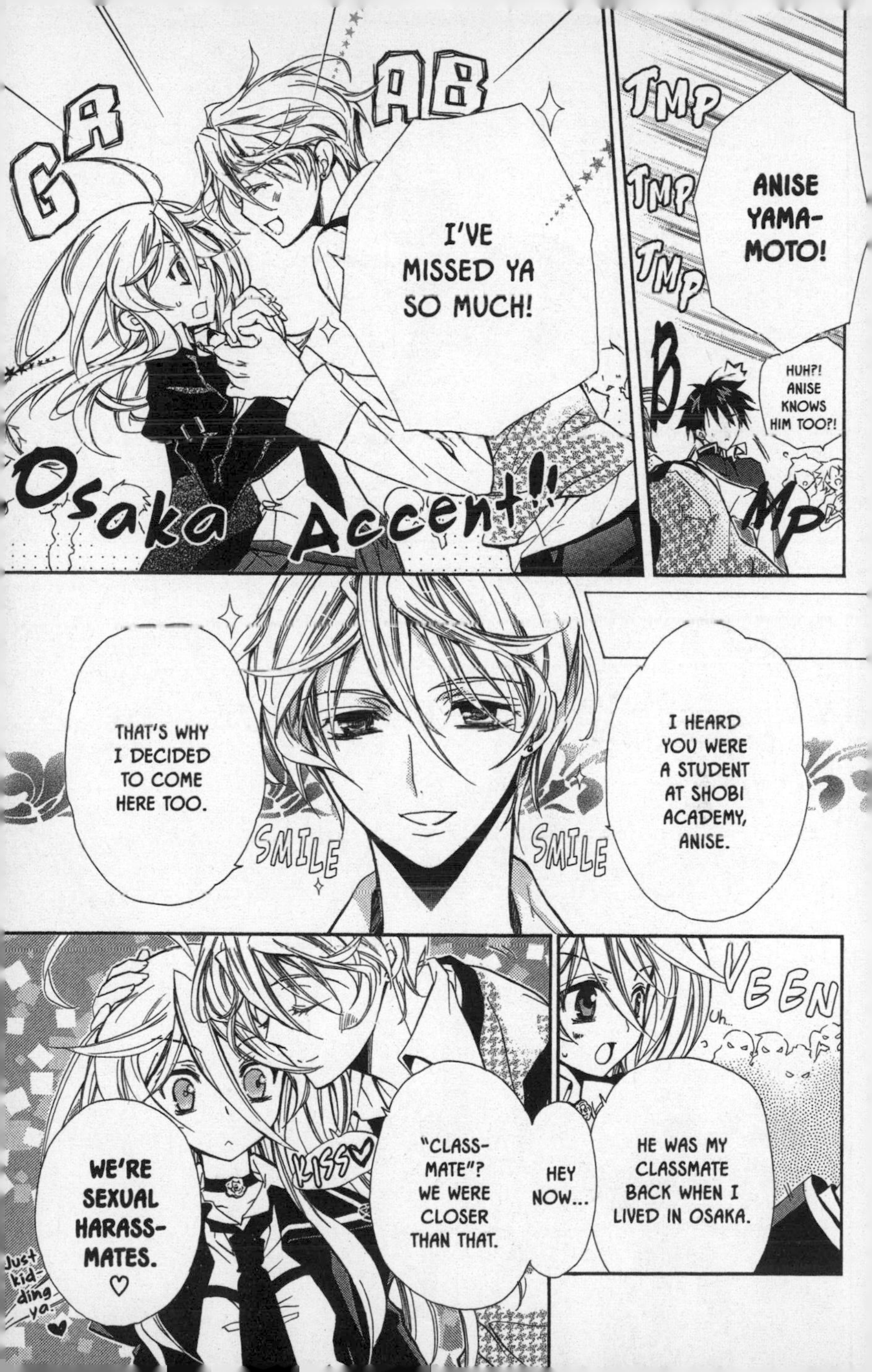
TMP
TMP
TMP
ANISE YAMA-MOTO!
B
HUH?! ANISE KNOWS HIM TOO?!
MP
GR
AB
I'VE MISSED YA SO MUCH!
Osaka Accent!!
I HEARD YOU WERE A STUDENT AT SHOBI ACADEMY, ANISE.
SMILE
SMILE
THAT'S WHY I DECIDED TO COME HERE TOO.
VEEN
Uh..
HE WAS MY CLASSMATE BACK WHEN I LIVED IN OSAKA.
HEY NOW...
"CLASS-MATE"? WE WERE CLOSER THAN THAT.
KISS♡
WE'RE SEXUAL HARASS-MATES. ♡
Just kid-ding ya. ♥

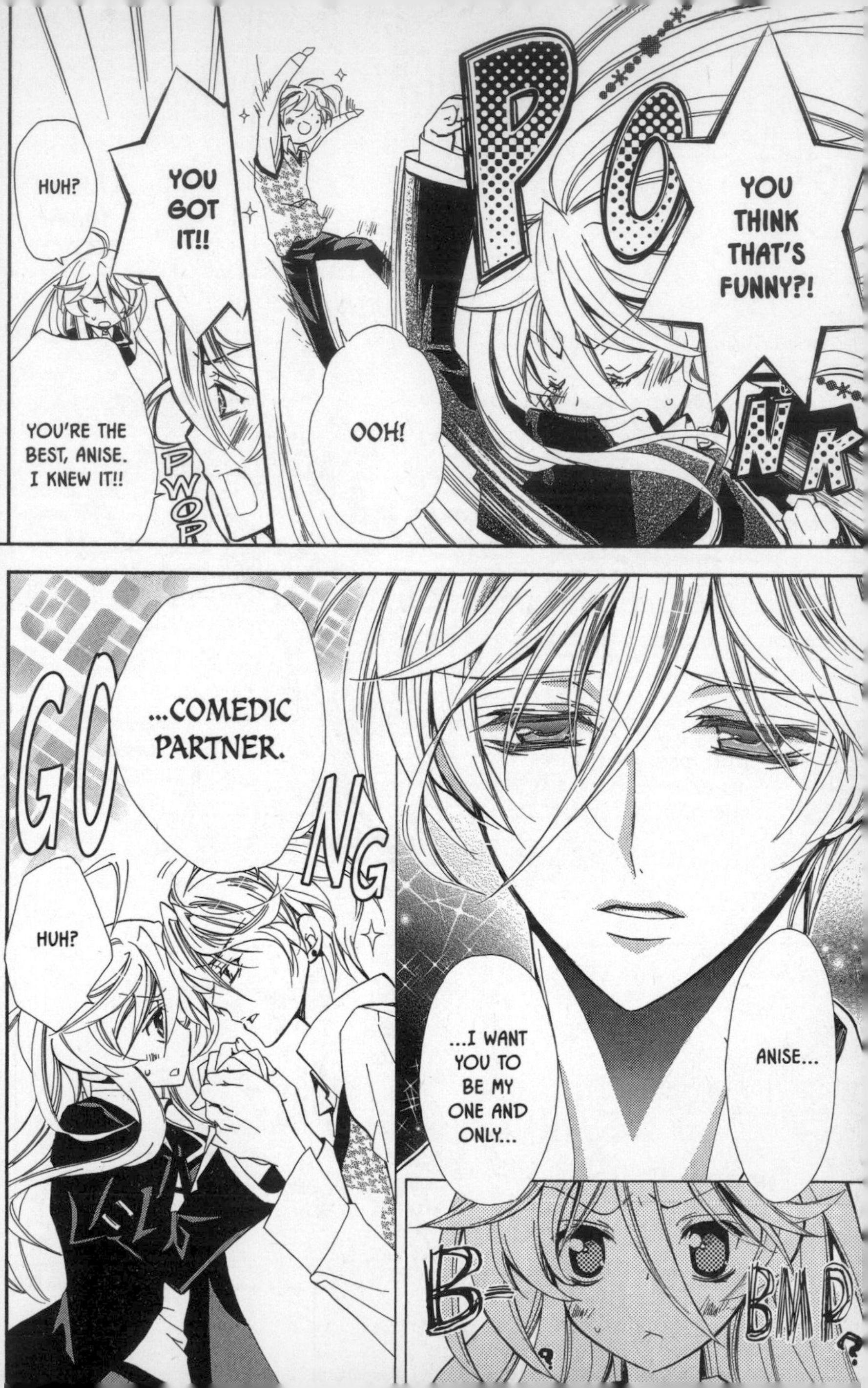
YOU THINK THAT'S FUNNY?!
PONK
OOH!
YOU GOT IT!!
HUH?
YOU'RE THE BEST, ANISE. I KNEW IT!!
PWOP
ANISE...
...I WANT YOU TO BE MY ONE AND ONLY...
B-BMP
...COMEDIC PARTNER.
GONG
HUH?

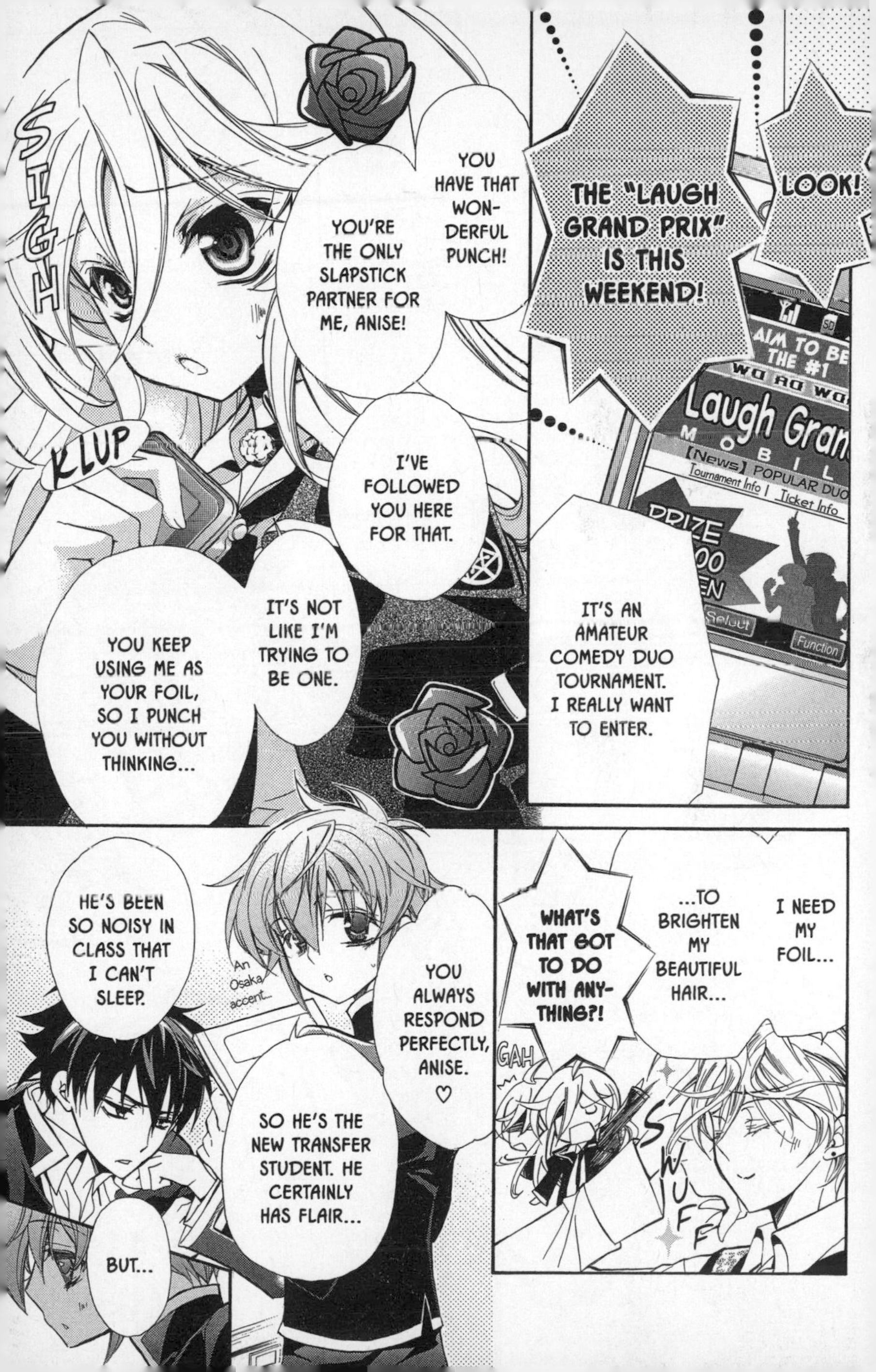
LOOK!
THE "LAUGH GRAND PRIX" IS THIS WEEKEND!
AIM TO BE THE #1
【News】 POPULAR DUO
Tournament Info | Ticket Info
PRIZE
Function
IT'S AN AMATEUR COMEDY DUO TOURNAMENT. I REALLY WANT TO ENTER.
YOU HAVE THAT WON-DERFUL PUNCH!
YOU'RE THE ONLY SLAPSTICK PARTNER FOR ME, ANISE!
SIGH
KLUP
I'VE FOLLOWED YOU HERE FOR THAT.
IT'S NOT LIKE I'M TRYING TO BE ONE.
YOU KEEP USING ME AS YOUR FOIL, SO I PUNCH YOU WITHOUT THINKING...
I NEED MY FOIL...
...TO BRIGHTEN MY BEAUTIFUL HAIR...
WHAT'S THAT GOT TO DO WITH ANY-THING?!
GAH
SWUFF
YOU ALWAYS RESPOND PERFECTLY, ANISE. ♡
An Osaka accent...
HE'S BEEN SO NOISY IN CLASS THAT I CAN'T SLEEP.
SO HE'S THE NEW TRANSFER STUDENT. HE CERTAINLY HAS FLAIR...
BUT...

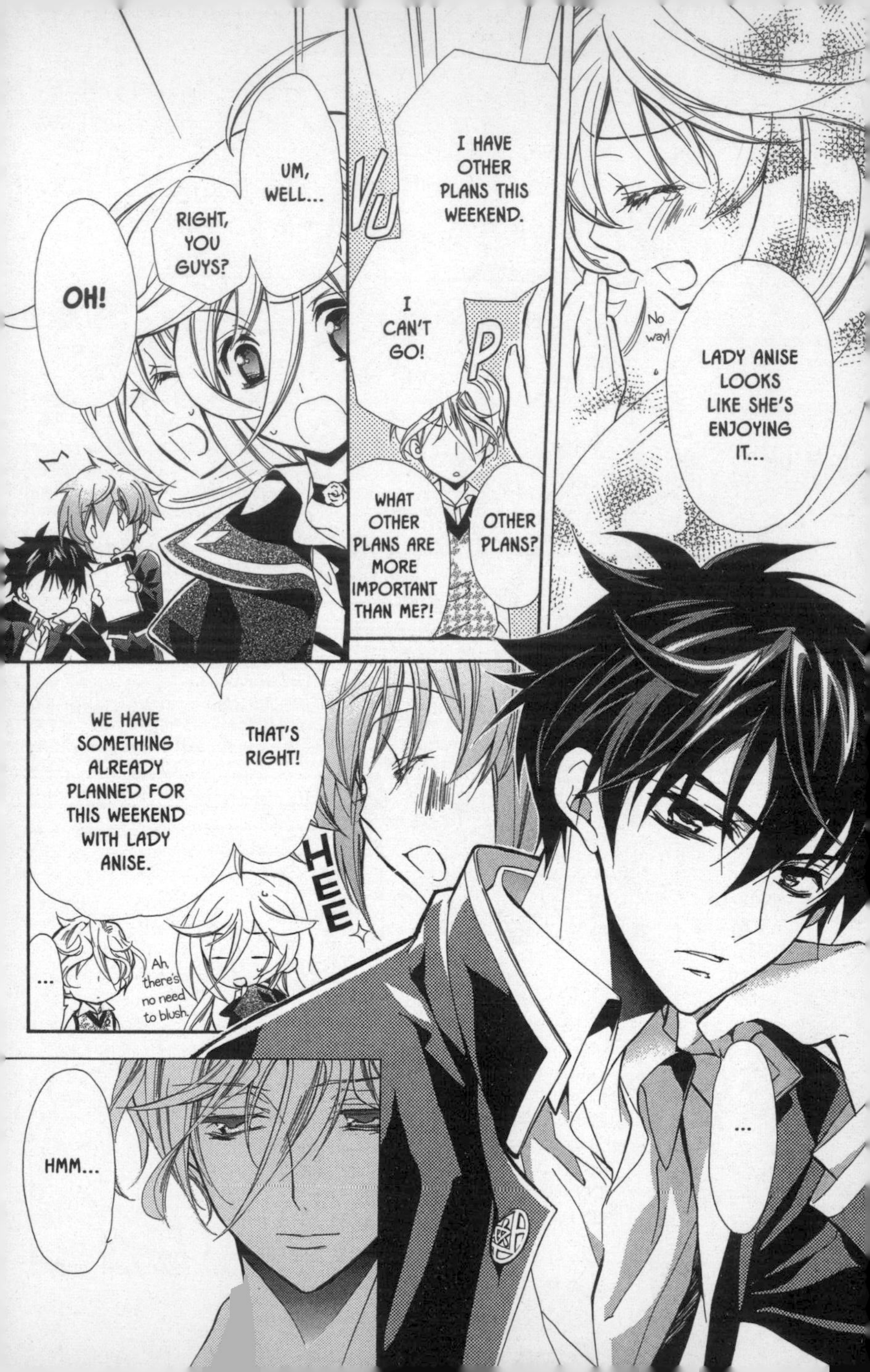
LADY ANISE LOOKS LIKE SHE'S ENJOYING IT...
No way!
I HAVE OTHER PLANS THIS WEEKEND.
VU
I CAN'T GO!
P
OTHER PLANS?
WHAT OTHER PLANS ARE MORE IMPORTANT THAN ME?!
UM, WELL...
RIGHT, YOU GUYS?
OH!
...
THAT'S RIGHT!
WE HAVE SOMETHING ALREADY PLANNED FOR THIS WEEKEND WITH LADY ANISE.
HEE
Ah, there's no need to blush.
...
HMM...

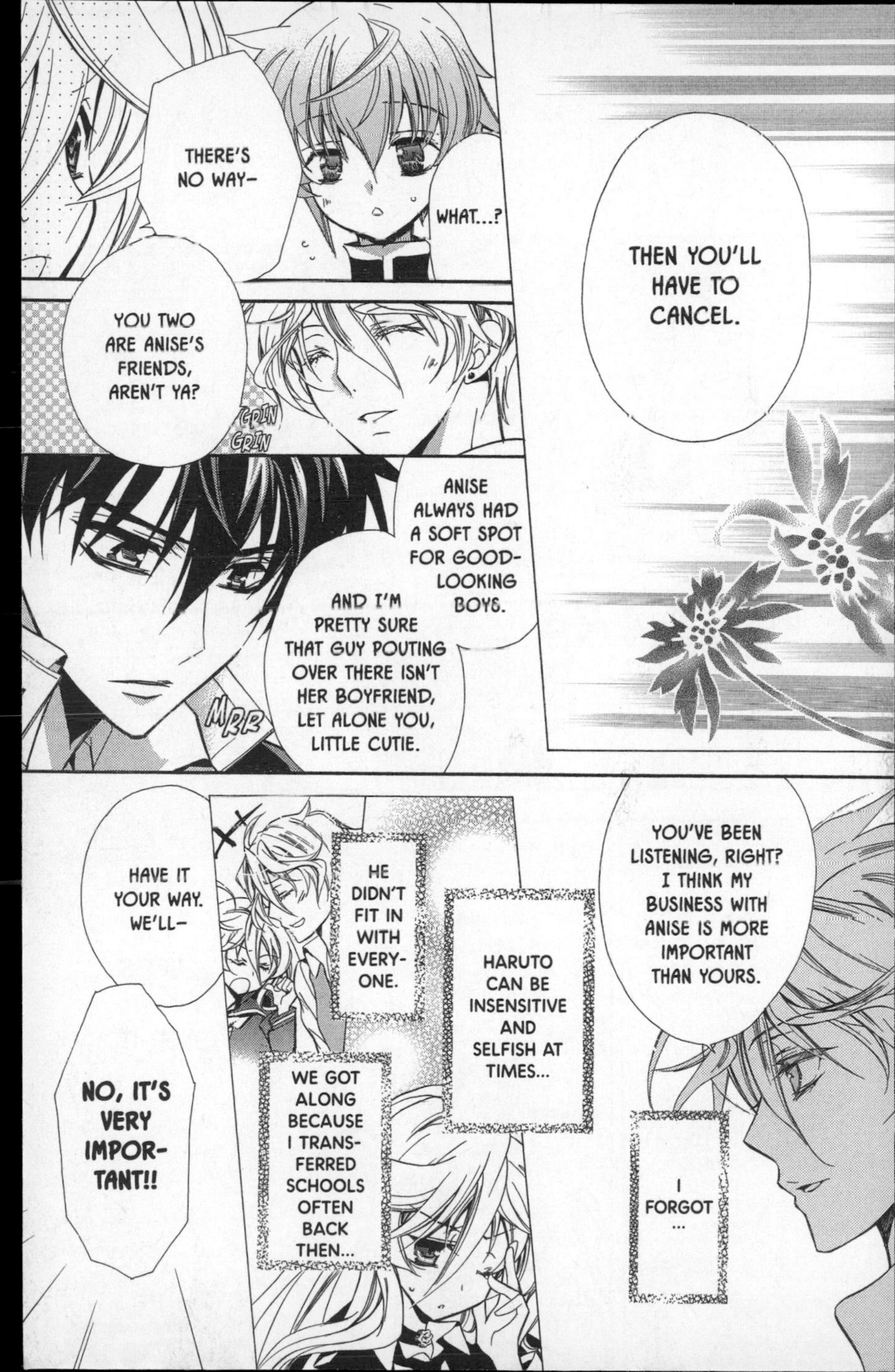
THEN YOU'LL HAVE TO CANCEL.
WHAT...?
THERE'S NO WAY-
YOU TWO ARE ANISE'S FRIENDS, AREN'T YA?
GRIN GRIN
ANISE ALWAYS HAD A SOFT SPOT FOR GOOD-LOOKING BOYS.
AND I'M PRETTY SURE THAT GUY POUTING OVER THERE ISN'T HER BOYFRIEND, LET ALONE YOU, LITTLE CUTIE.
MRR
YOU'VE BEEN LISTENING, RIGHT? I THINK MY BUSINESS WITH ANISE IS MORE IMPORTANT THAN YOURS.
I FORGOT...
HARUTO CAN BE INSENSITIVE AND SELFISH AT TIMES...
HE DIDN'T FIT IN WITH EVERY-ONE.
WE GOT ALONG BECAUSE I TRANS-FERRED SCHOOLS OFTEN BACK THEN...
HAVE IT YOUR WAY. WE'LL-
NO, IT'S VERY IMPOR-TANT!!

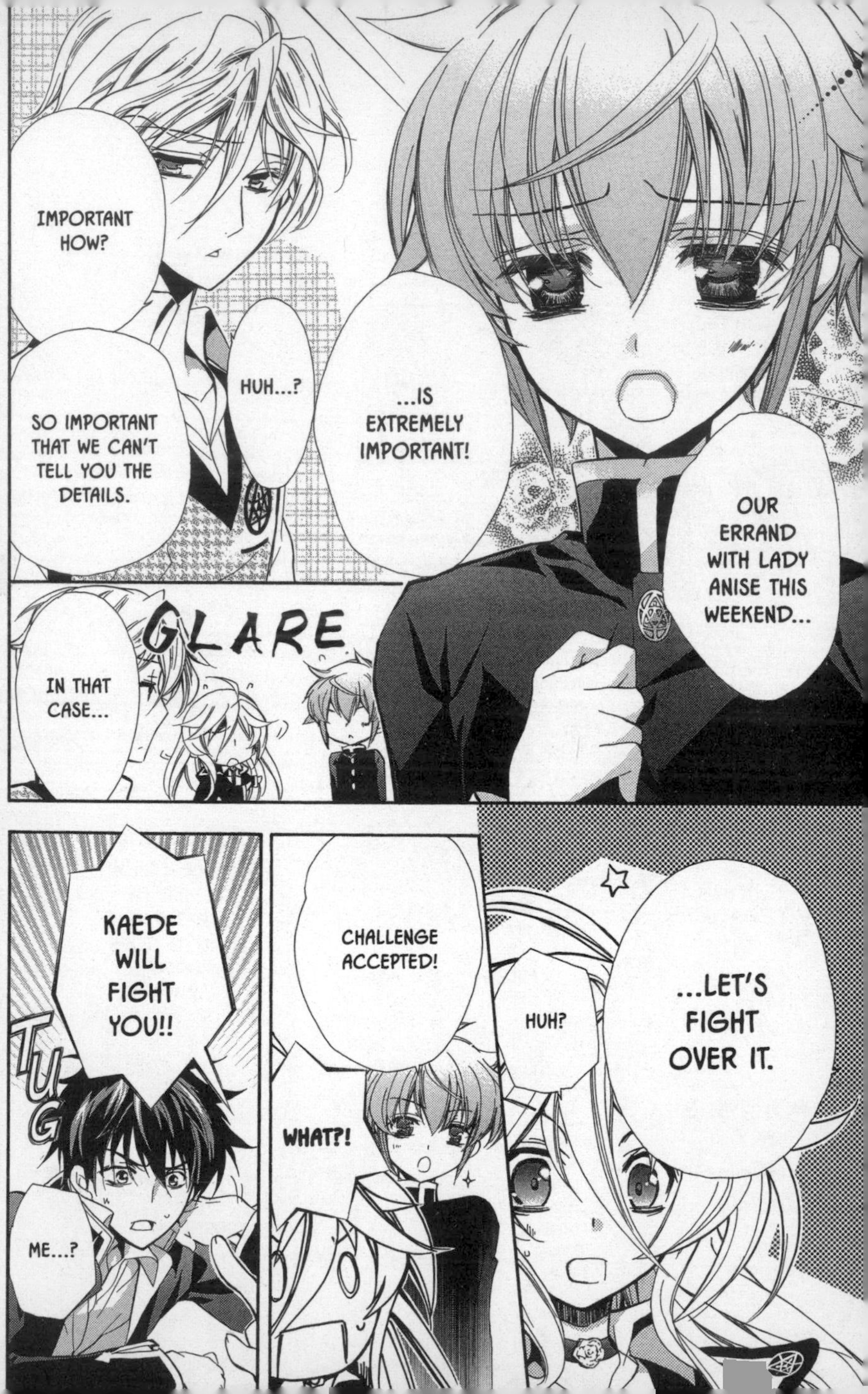
OUR ERRAND WITH LADY ANISE THIS WEEKEND...
...IS EXTREMELY IMPORTANT!
HUH...?
IMPORTANT HOW?
SO IMPORTANT THAT WE CAN'T TELL YOU THE DETAILS.
GLARE
IN THAT CASE...
...LET'S FIGHT OVER IT.
HUH?
CHALLENGE ACCEPTED!
WHAT?!
KAEDE WILL FIGHT YOU!!
TUG
ME...?

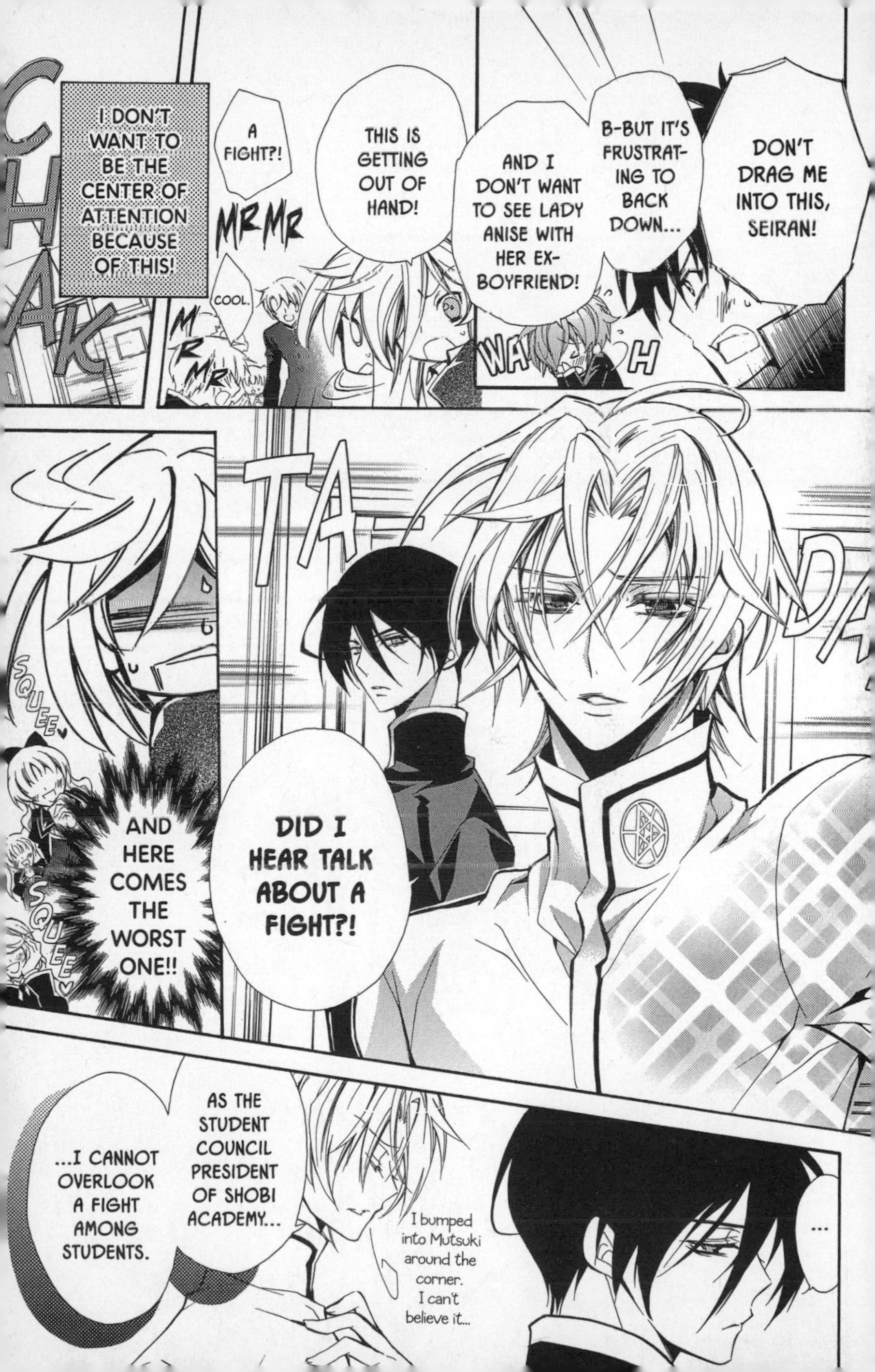
DON'T DRAG ME INTO THIS, SEIRAN!
B-BUT IT'S FRUSTRAT-ING TO BACK DOWN...
AND I DON'T WANT TO SEE LADY ANISE WITH HER EX-BOYFRIEND!
THIS IS GETTING OUT OF HAND!
A FIGHT?!
MRMR
COOL.
MRMRMR
I DON'T WANT TO BE THE CENTER OF ATTENTION BECAUSE OF THIS!
CHAK
DA
TA-
DID I HEAR TALK ABOUT A FIGHT?!
AND HERE COMES THE WORST ONE!!
SQUEE
SQUEE
...
I bumped into Mutsuki around the corner. I can't believe it...
AS THE STUDENT COUNCIL PRESIDENT OF SHOBI ACADEMY...
...I CANNOT OVERLOOK A FIGHT AMONG STUDENTS.

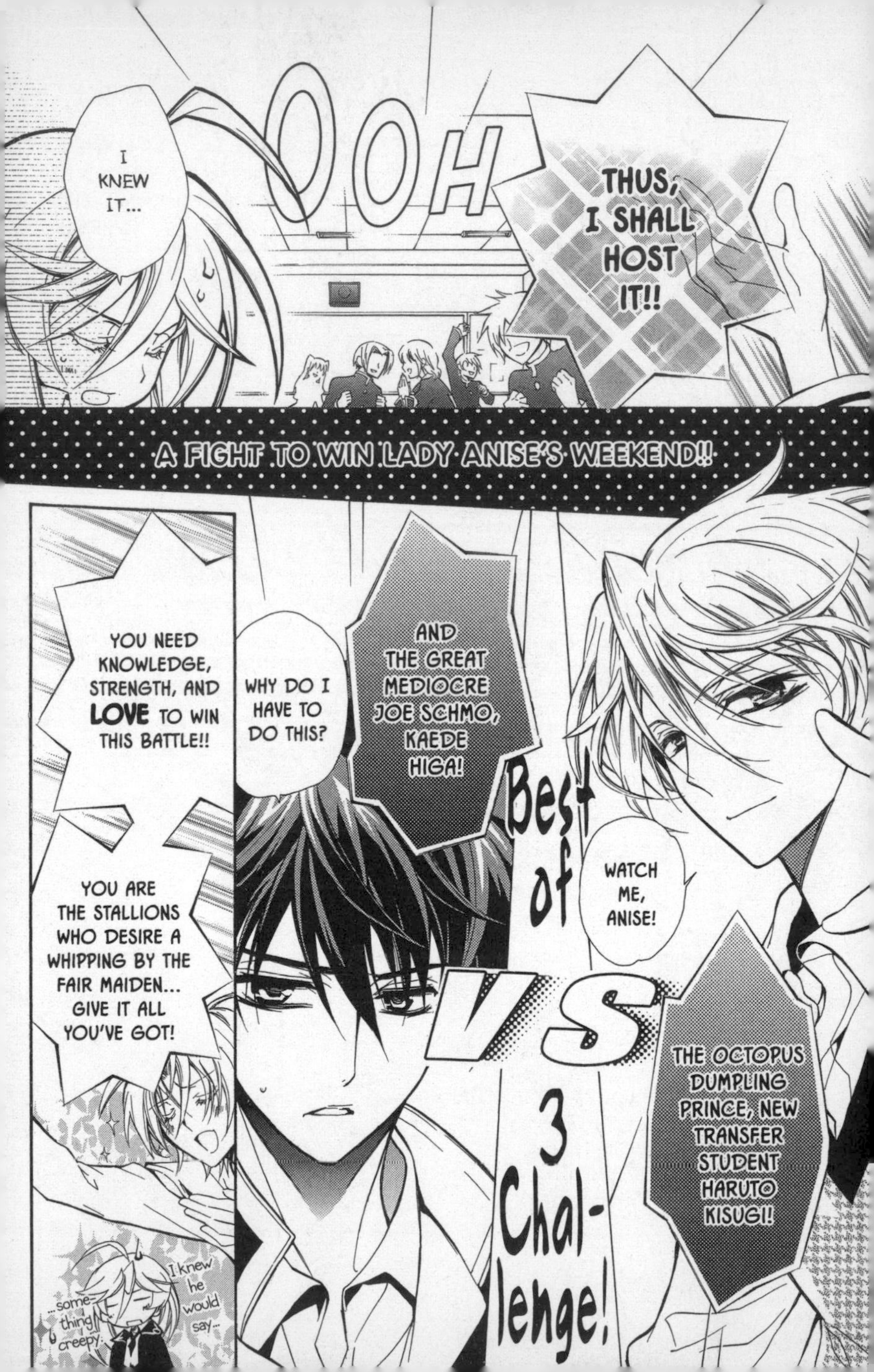
THUS, I SHALL HOST IT!!
OOH
I KNEW IT...
A FIGHT TO WIN LADY ANISE'S WEEKEND!!
WATCH ME, ANISE!
THE OCTOPUS DUMPLING PRINCE, NEW TRANSFER STUDENT HARUTO KISUGI!
Best of
VS
3 Chal-lenge!
AND THE GREAT MEDIOCRE JOE SCHMO, KAEDE HIGA!
WHY DO I HAVE TO DO THIS?
YOU NEED KNOWLEDGE, STRENGTH, AND **LOVE** TO WIN THIS BATTLE!!
YOU ARE THE STALLIONS WHO DESIRE A WHIPPING BY THE FAIR MAIDEN... GIVE IT ALL YOU'VE GOT!
I knew he would say...
...something creepy.

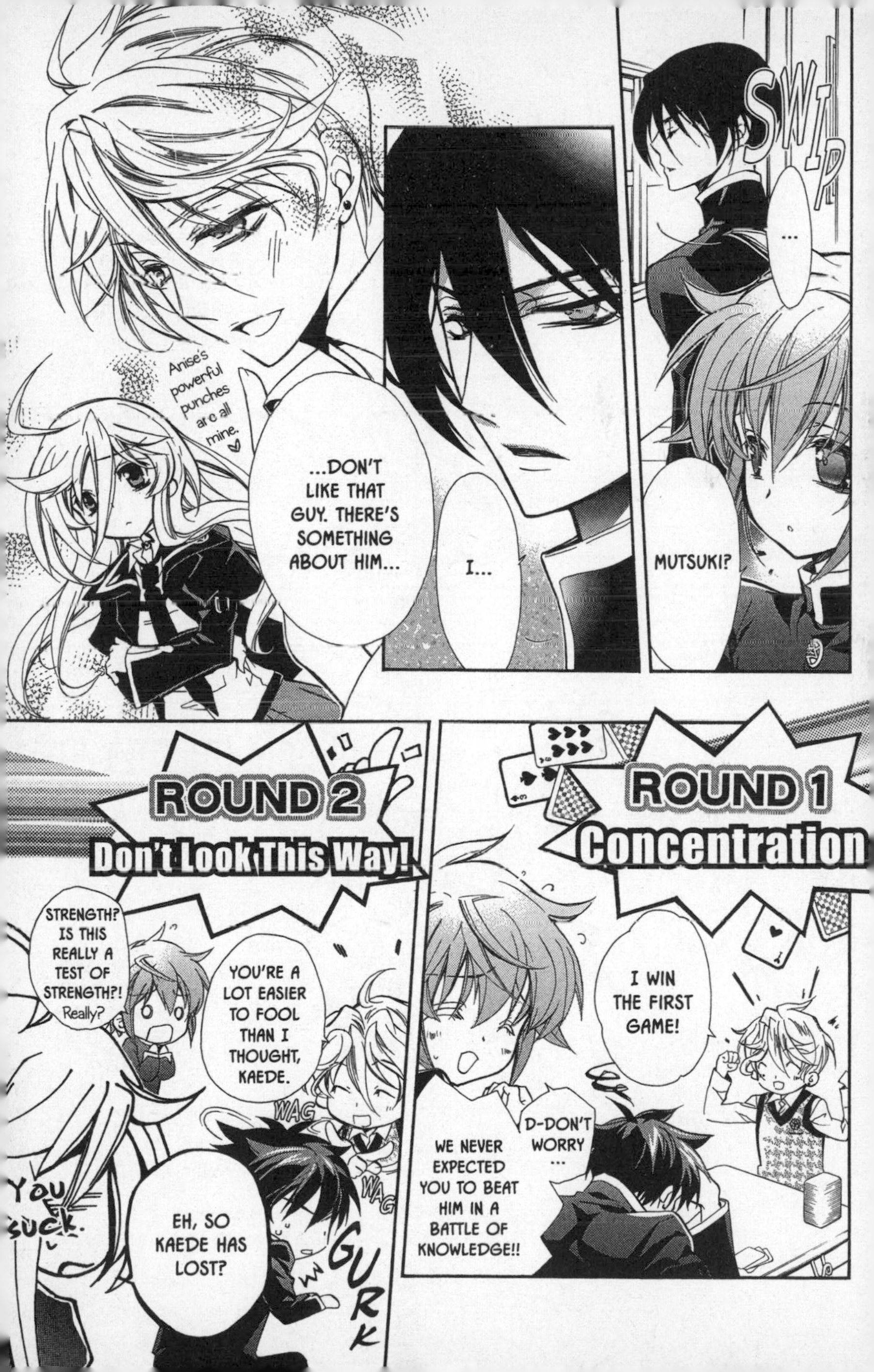
SWIP
...
MUTSUKI?
I...
...DON'T LIKE THAT GUY. THERE'S SOMETHING ABOUT HIM...
Anise's powerful punches are all mine.
ROUND 1
Concentration
I WIN THE FIRST GAME!
D-DON'T WORRY ...
WE NEVER EXPECTED YOU TO BEAT HIM IN A BATTLE OF KNOWLEDGE!!
ROUND 2
Don't Look This Way!
YOU'RE A LOT EASIER TO FOOL THAN I THOUGHT, KAEDE.
STRENGTH? IS THIS REALLY A TEST OF STRENGTH?!
Really?
WAG
WAG
EH, SO KAEDE HAS LOST?
GURK
YOU SUCK.

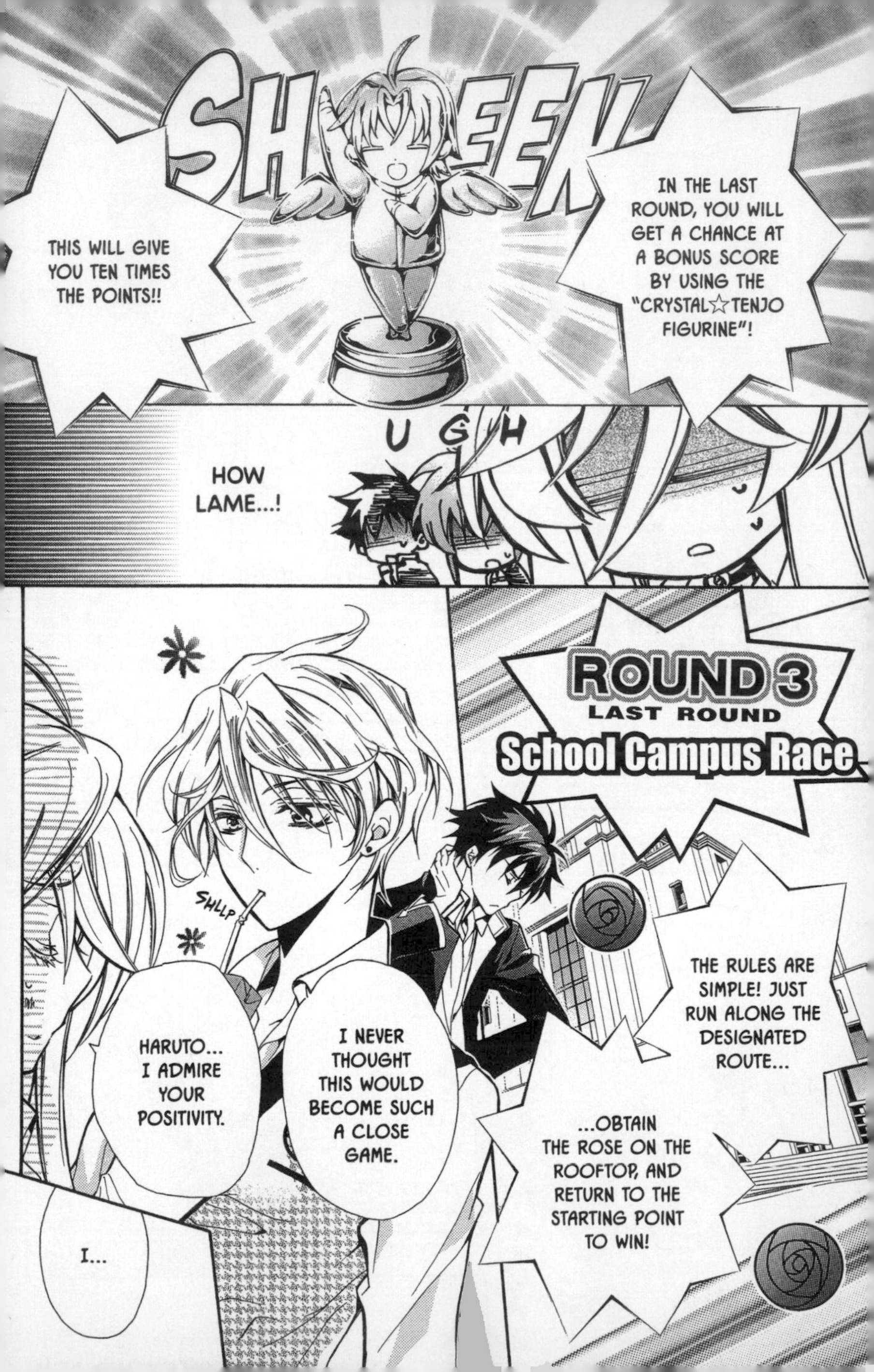
IN THE LAST ROUND, YOU WILL GET A CHANCE AT A BONUS SCORE BY USING THE "CRYSTAL☆TENJO FIGURINE"!
THIS WILL GIVE YOU TEN TIMES THE POINTS!!
UGH
HOW LAME...!
ROUND 3
LAST ROUND
School Campus Race
THE RULES ARE SIMPLE! JUST RUN ALONG THE DESIGNATED ROUTE...
...OBTAIN THE ROSE ON THE ROOFTOP, AND RETURN TO THE STARTING POINT TO WIN!
SHLLP
I NEVER THOUGHT THIS WOULD BECOME SUCH A CLOSE GAME.
HARUTO... I ADMIRE YOUR POSITIVITY.
I...

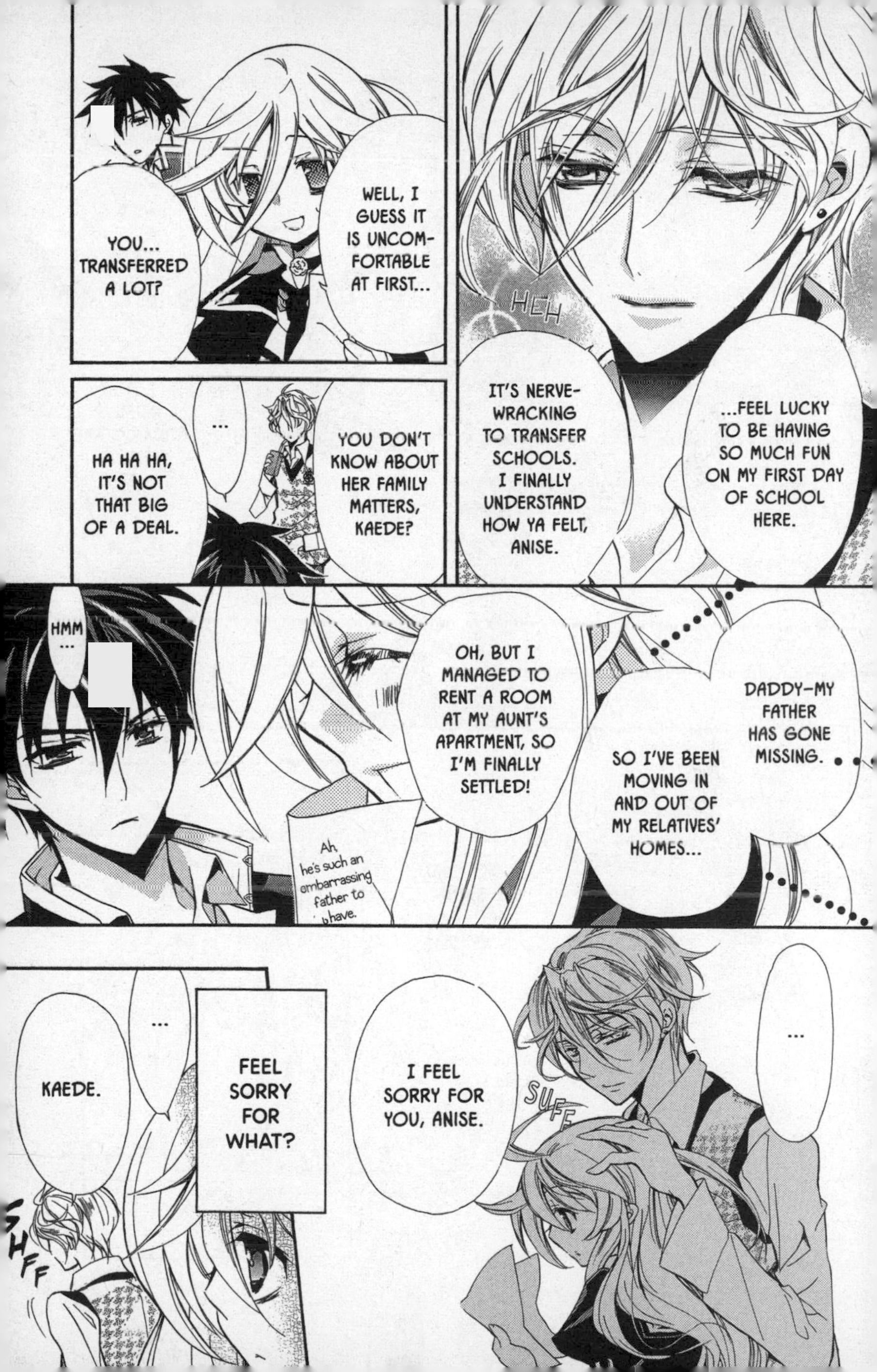
HEH
IT'S NERVE-WRACKING TO TRANSFER SCHOOLS. I FINALLY UNDERSTAND HOW YA FELT, ANISE.
...FEEL LUCKY TO BE HAVING SO MUCH FUN ON MY FIRST DAY OF SCHOOL HERE.
WELL, I GUESS IT IS UNCOM-FORTABLE AT FIRST...
YOU... TRANSFERRED A LOT?
YOU DON'T KNOW ABOUT HER FAMILY MATTERS, KAEDE?
...
HA HA HA, IT'S NOT THAT BIG OF A DEAL.
DADDY—MY FATHER HAS GONE MISSING.
SO I'VE BEEN MOVING IN AND OUT OF MY RELATIVES' HOMES...
OH, BUT I MANAGED TO RENT A ROOM AT MY AUNT'S APARTMENT, SO I'M FINALLY SETTLED!
Ah, he's such an embarrassing father to have.
HMM...
...
SUFF
I FEEL SORRY FOR YOU, ANISE.
FEEL SORRY FOR WHAT?
...
KAEDE.
SHFF

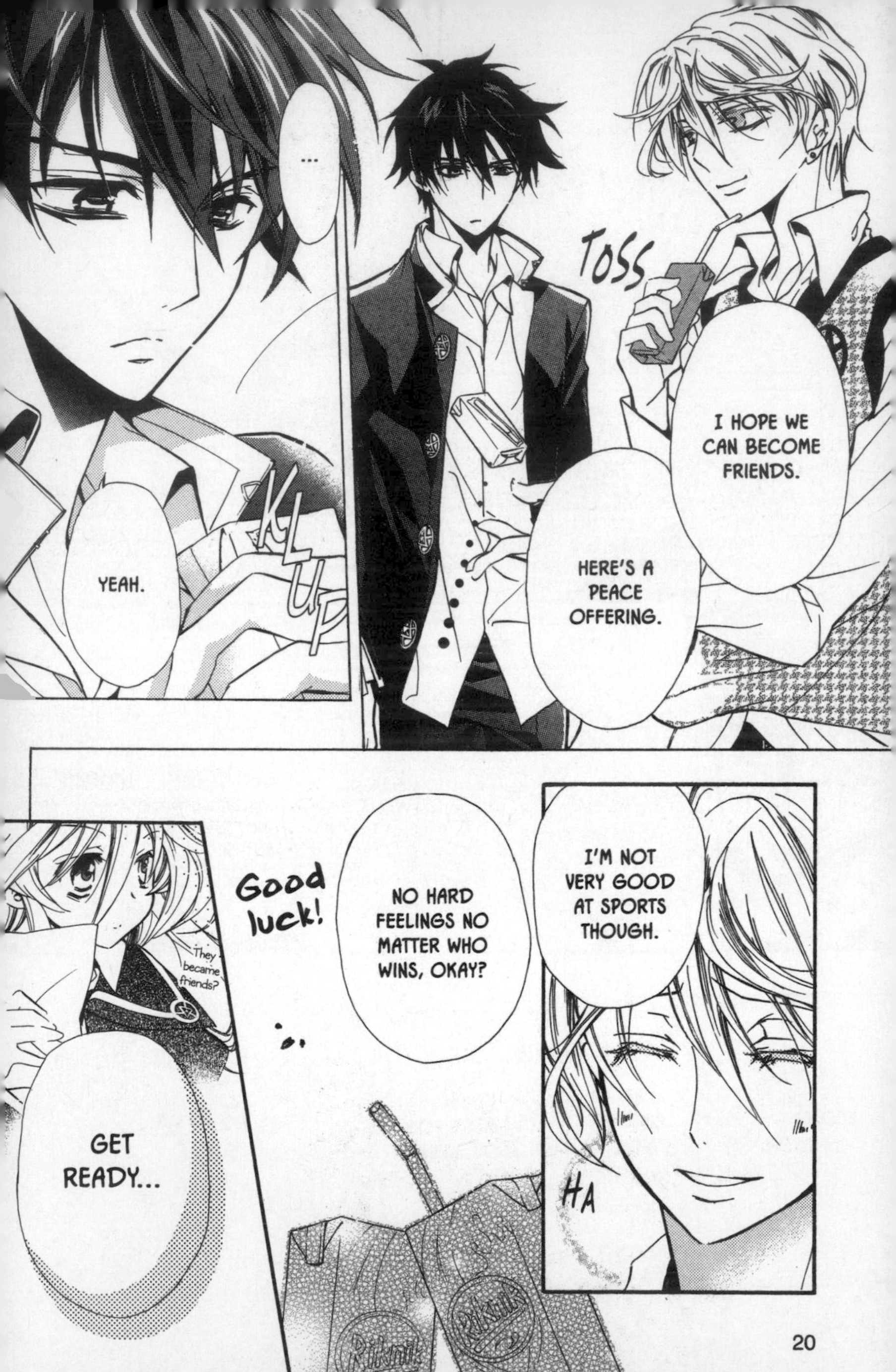
TOSS
I HOPE WE CAN BECOME FRIENDS.
HERE'S A PEACE OFFERING.
...
KLUP
YEAH.
I'M NOT VERY GOOD AT SPORTS THOUGH.
HA
NO HARD FEELINGS NO MATTER WHO WINS, OKAY?
Good luck!
They became friends?
GET READY...

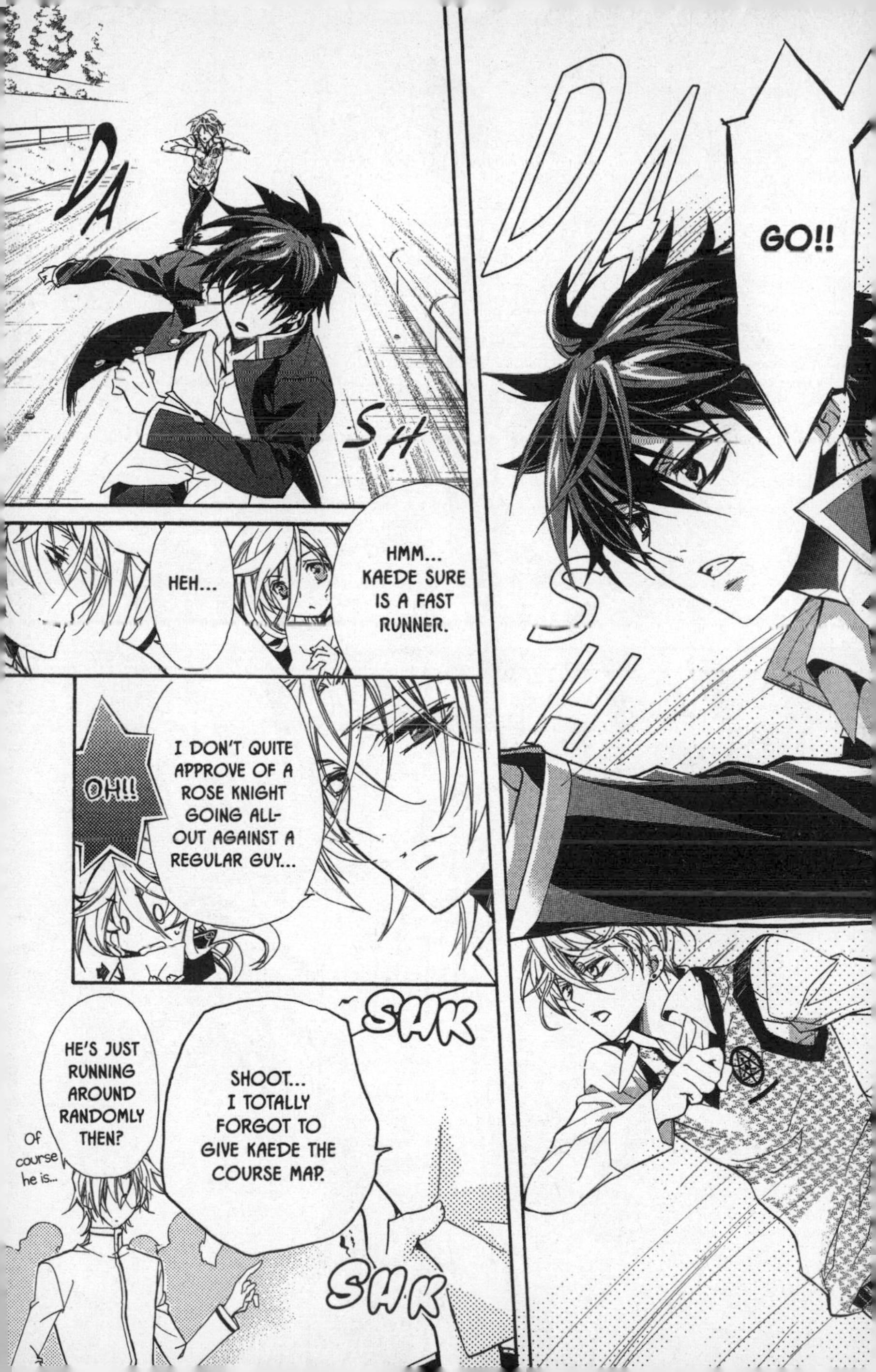
DASH
GO!!
DA
SH
HMM... KAEDE SURE IS A FAST RUNNER.
HEH...
I DON'T QUITE APPROVE OF A ROSE KNIGHT GOING ALL-OUT AGAINST A REGULAR GUY...
OH!!
SHK
SHOOT... I TOTALLY FORGOT TO GIVE KAEDE THE COURSE MAP.
HE'S JUST RUNNING AROUND RANDOMLY THEN?
Of course he is...
SHK

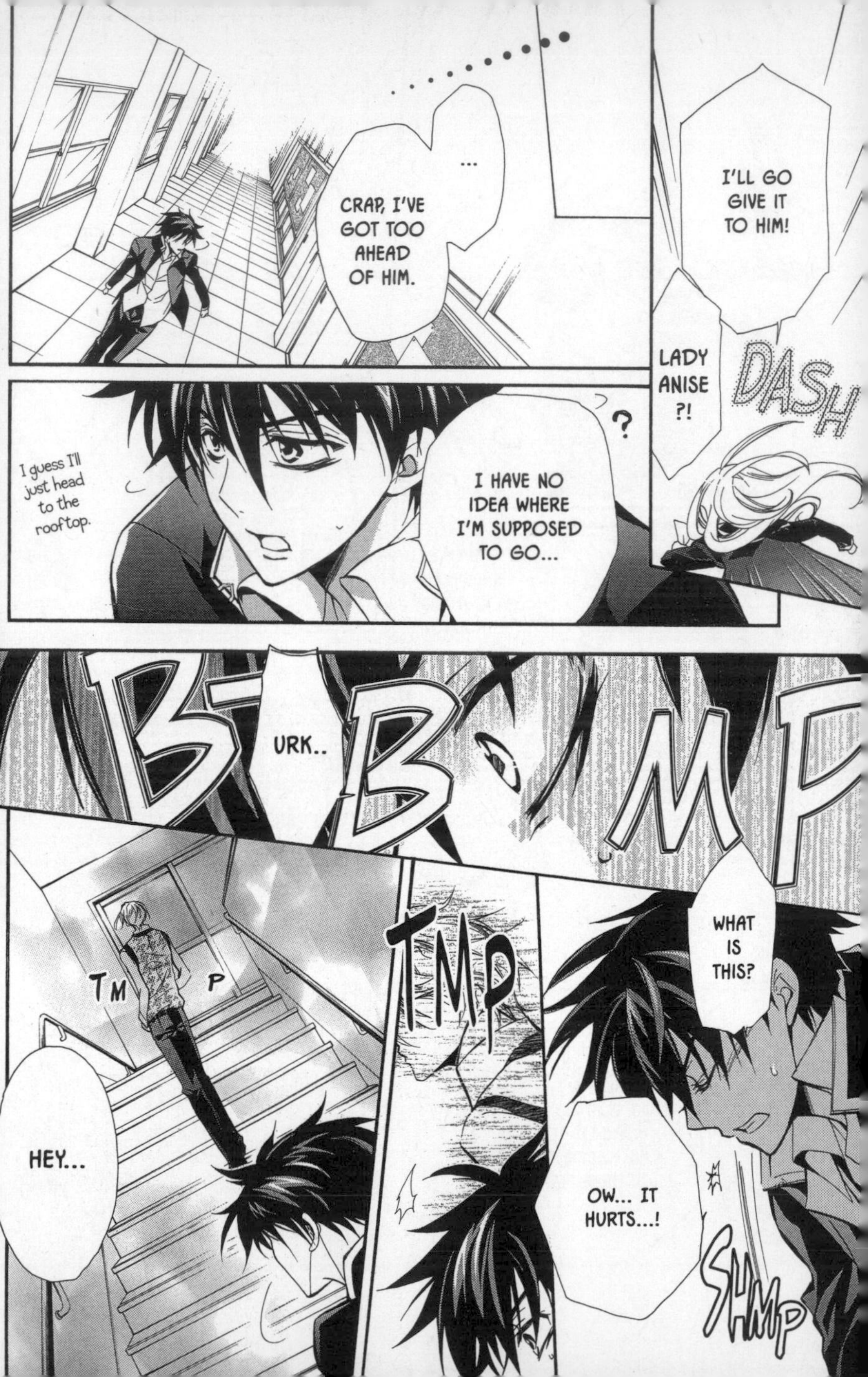
I'LL GO GIVE IT TO HIM!
LADY ANISE ?!
DASH
...
CRAP, I'VE GOT TOO AHEAD OF HIM.
?
I HAVE NO IDEA WHERE I'M SUPPOSED TO GO...
I guess I'll just head to the rooftop.
B-BUMP
URK..
WHAT IS THIS?
OW... IT HURTS...!
SHMP
TMP
TMP
HEY...

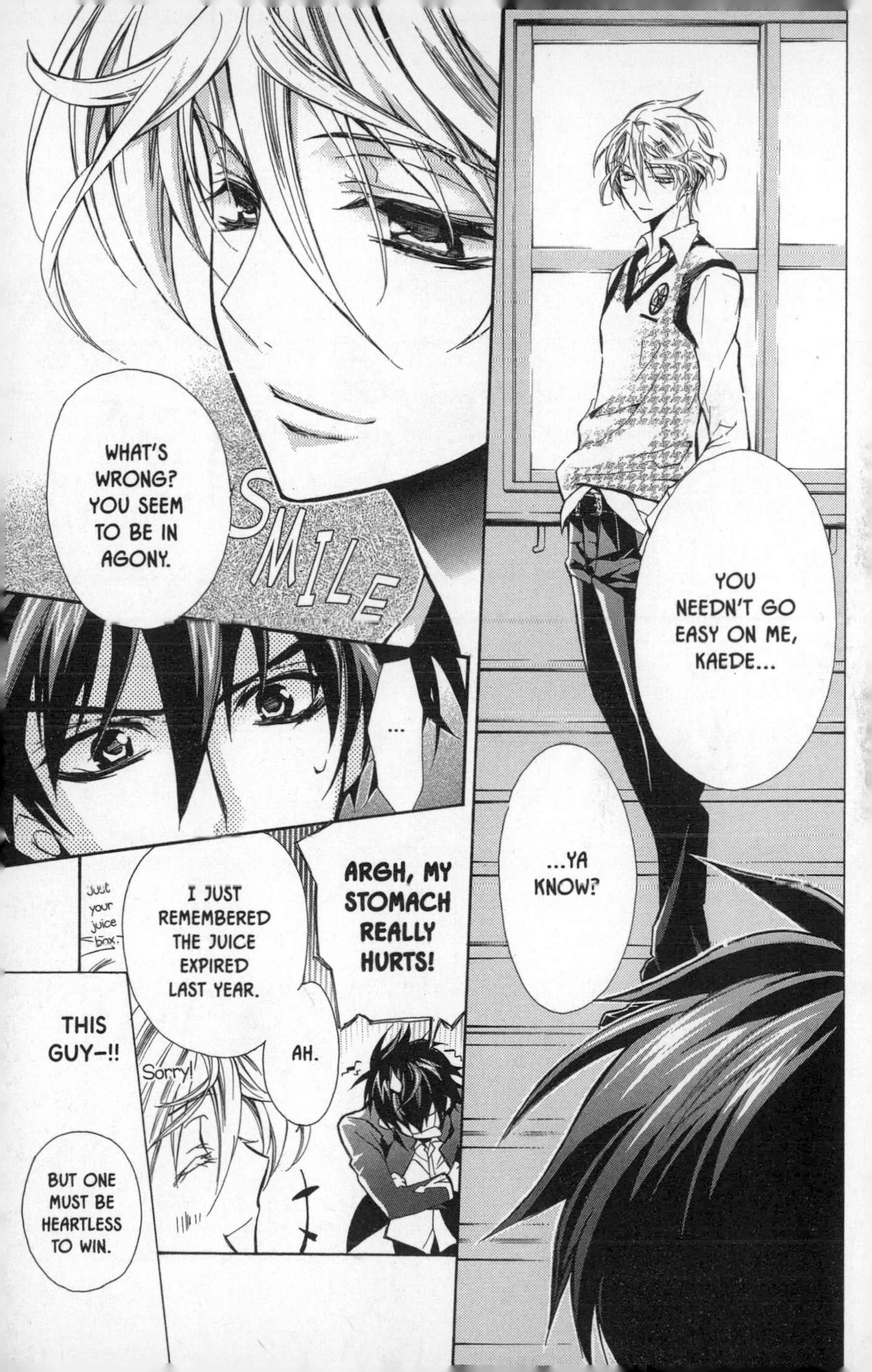
YOU NEEDN'T GO EASY ON ME, KAEDE...
...YA KNOW?
WHAT'S WRONG? YOU SEEM TO BE IN AGONY.
SMILE
...
ARGH, MY STOMACH REALLY HURTS!
I JUST REMEMBERED THE JUICE EXPIRED LAST YEAR.
Just your juice box.
AH.
Sorry!
THIS GUY—!!
BUT ONE MUST BE HEARTLESS TO WIN.

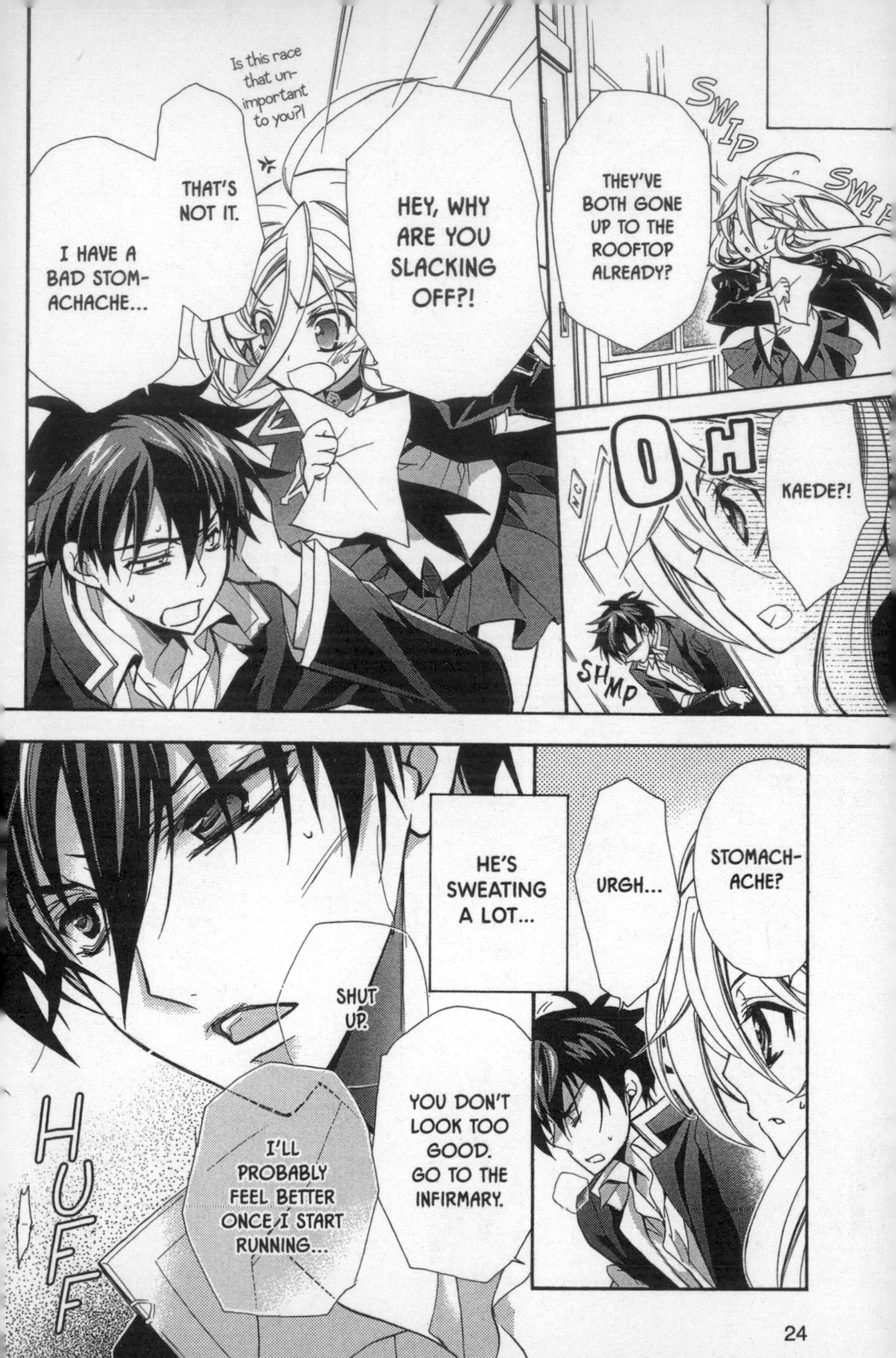
SWIP
SWIP
THEY'VE BOTH GONE UP TO THE ROOFTOP ALREADY?
OH
KAEDE?!
SHMP
HEY, WHY ARE YOU SLACKING OFF?!
Is this race that un-important to you?!
THAT'S NOT IT.
I HAVE A BAD STOM-ACHACHE...
STOMACH-ACHE?
URGH...
HE'S SWEATING A LOT...
YOU DON'T LOOK TOO GOOD. GO TO THE INFIRMARY.
SHUT UP.
I'LL PROBABLY FEEL BETTER ONCE I START RUNNING...
HUFF

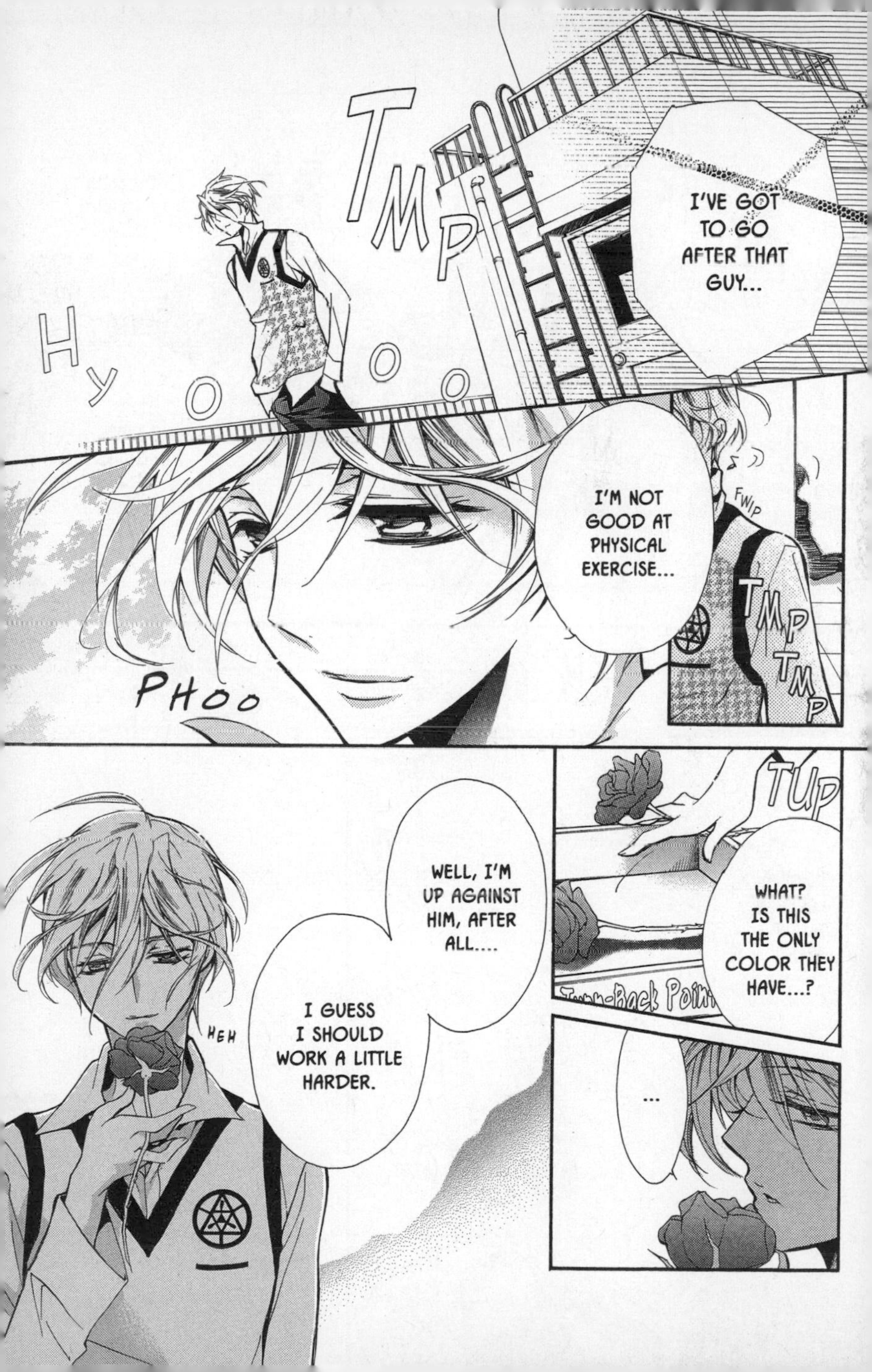
I'VE GOT TO GO AFTER THAT GUY...
TMP
HYOOOO
FWIP
TMP TMP TMP
I'M NOT GOOD AT PHYSICAL EXERCISE...
PHOO
TUP
WHAT? IS THIS THE ONLY COLOR THEY HAVE...?
...
WELL, I'M UP AGAINST HIM, AFTER ALL....
I GUESS I SHOULD WORK A LITTLE HARDER.
HEH

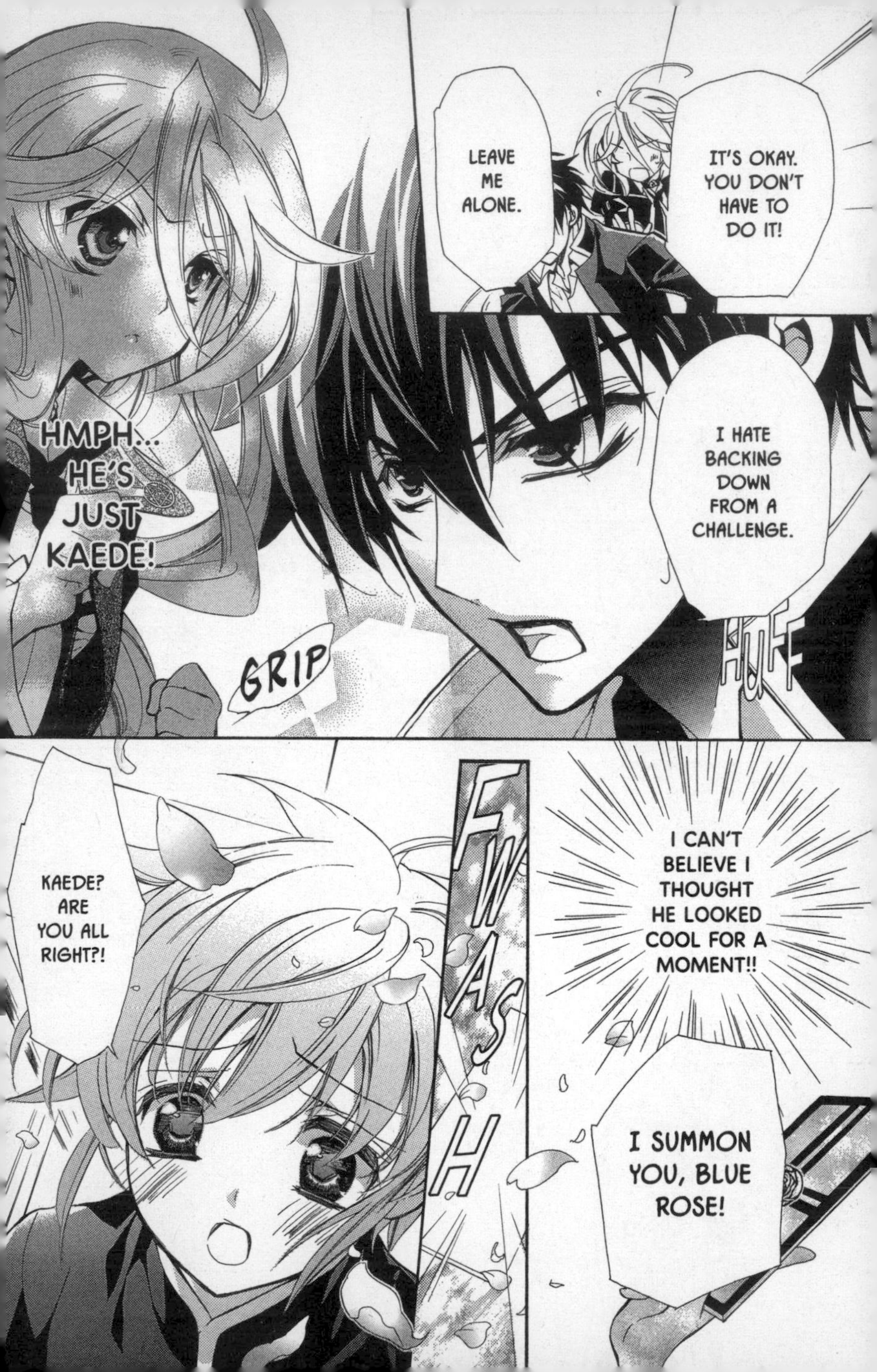
IT'S OKAY. YOU DON'T HAVE TO DO IT!
LEAVE ME ALONE.
I HATE BACKING DOWN FROM A CHALLENGE.
HUFF
GRIP
HMPH... HE'S JUST KAEDE!
I CAN'T BELIEVE I THOUGHT HE LOOKED COOL FOR A MOMENT!!
I SUMMON YOU, BLUE ROSE!
FWASH
KAEDE? ARE YOU ALL RIGHT?!

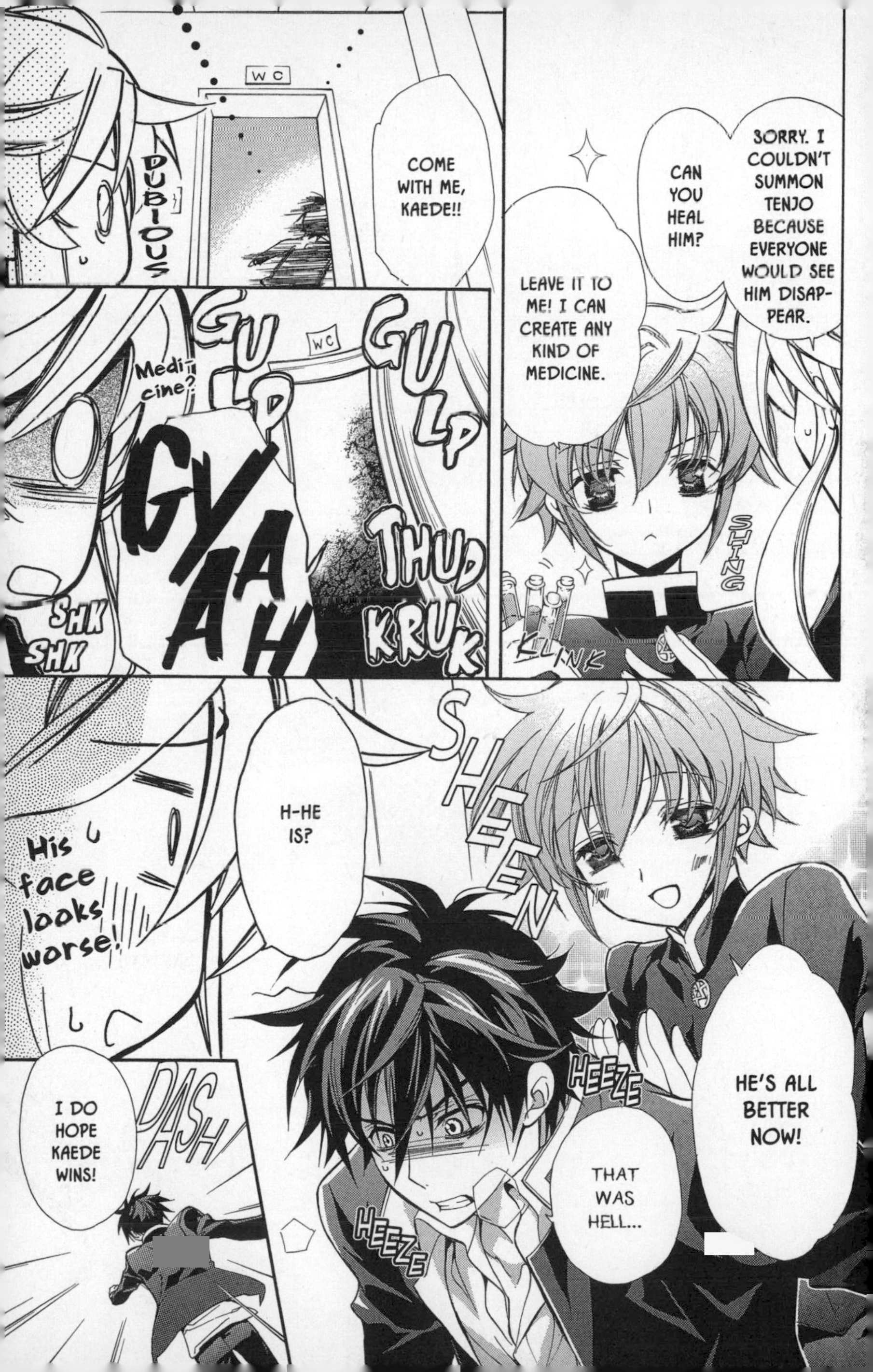
SORRY. I COULDN'T SUMMON TENJO BECAUSE EVERYONE WOULD SEE HIM DISAPPEAR.
CAN YOU HEAL HIM?
LEAVE IT TO ME! I CAN CREATE ANY KIND OF MEDICINE.
SHING
KLINK
COME WITH ME, KAEDE!!
DUBIOUS
WC
GULP
GULP
WC
Medicine?
GYAAAH
THUD
KRUK
SHK SHK
SHEEN
HE'S ALL BETTER NOW!
H-HE IS?
His face looks worse!
HEEZE
THAT WAS HELL...
HEEZE
I DO HOPE KAEDE WINS!
DASH

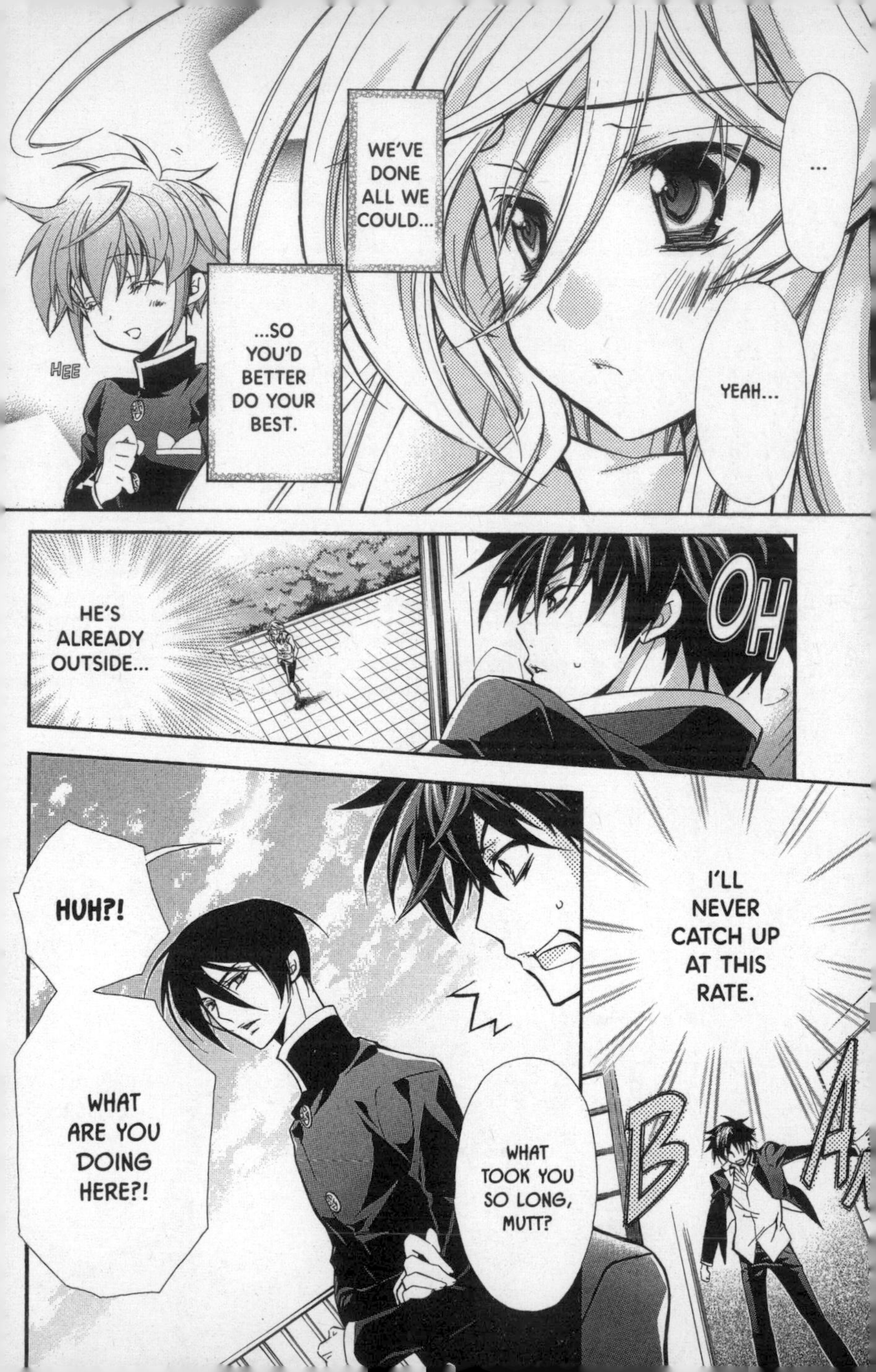
...
WE'VE DONE ALL WE COULD...
YEAH...
...SO YOU'D BETTER DO YOUR BEST.
HEE
OH
HE'S ALREADY OUTSIDE...
I'LL NEVER CATCH UP AT THIS RATE.
BA
WHAT TOOK YOU SO LONG, MUTT?
HUH?!
WHAT ARE YOU DOING HERE?!

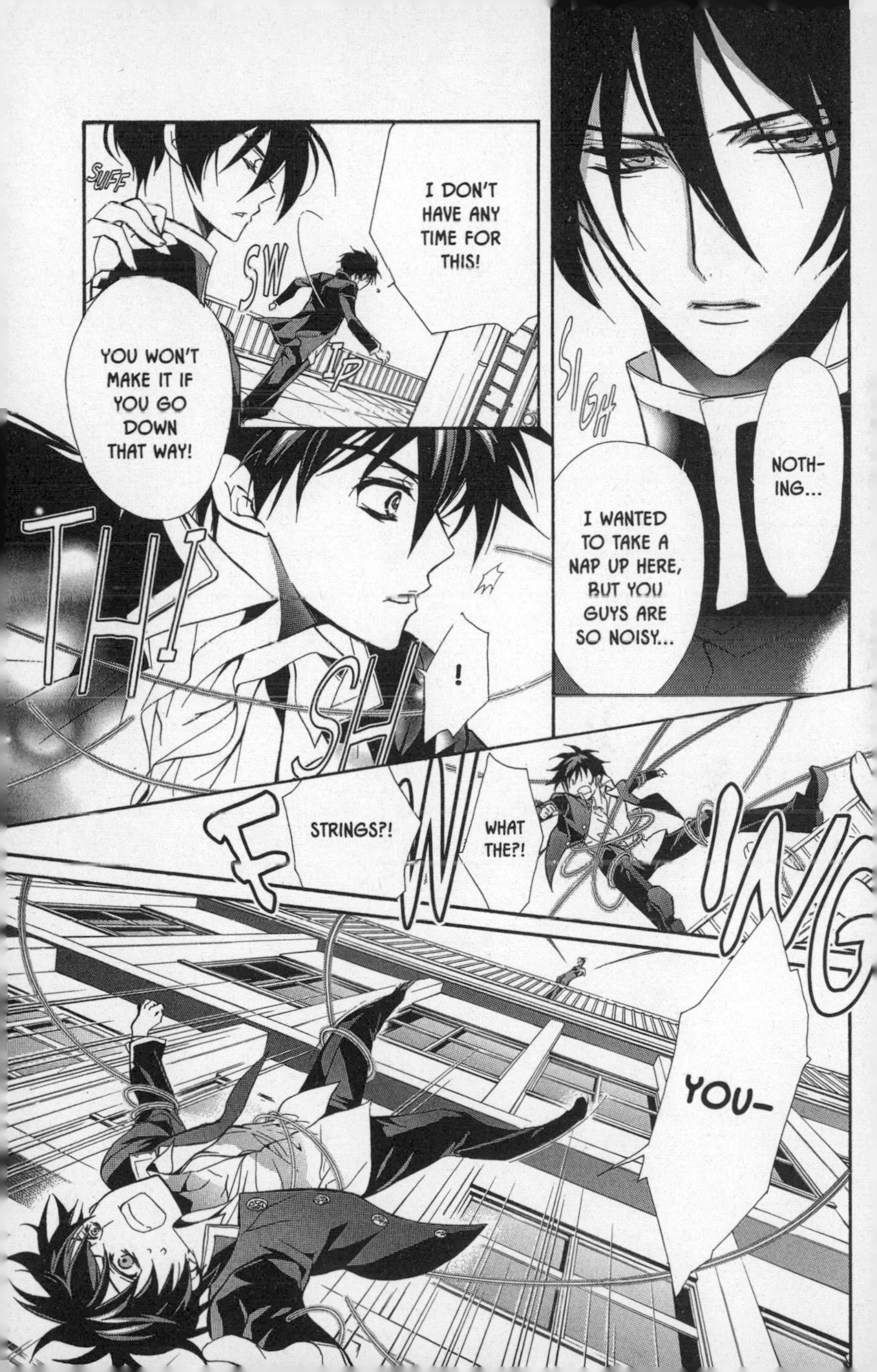
SIGH
NOTH-ING...
I WANTED TO TAKE A NAP UP HERE, BUT YOU GUYS ARE SO NOISY...
I DON'T HAVE ANY TIME FOR THIS!
SUFF
SW
IP
YOU WON'T MAKE IT IF YOU GO DOWN THAT WAY!
!
SH
THI
WHAT THE?!
STRINGS?!
ING
N
F
YOU–

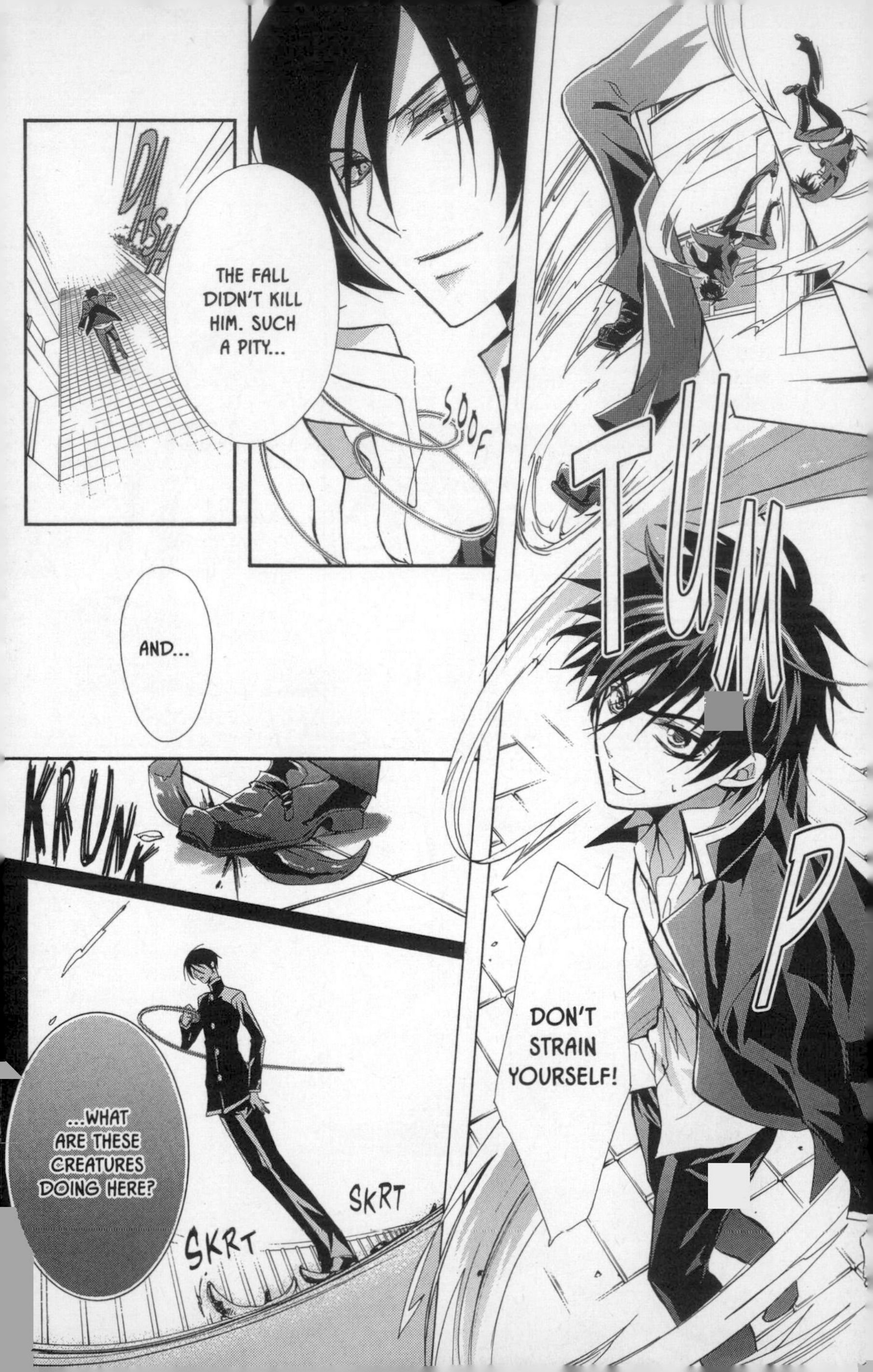
TUMP
DON'T STRAIN YOURSELF!
SOOF
THE FALL DIDN'T KILL HIM. SUCH A PITY...
DASH
AND...
KRUNK
...WHAT ARE THESE CREATURES DOING HERE?
SKRT
SKRT

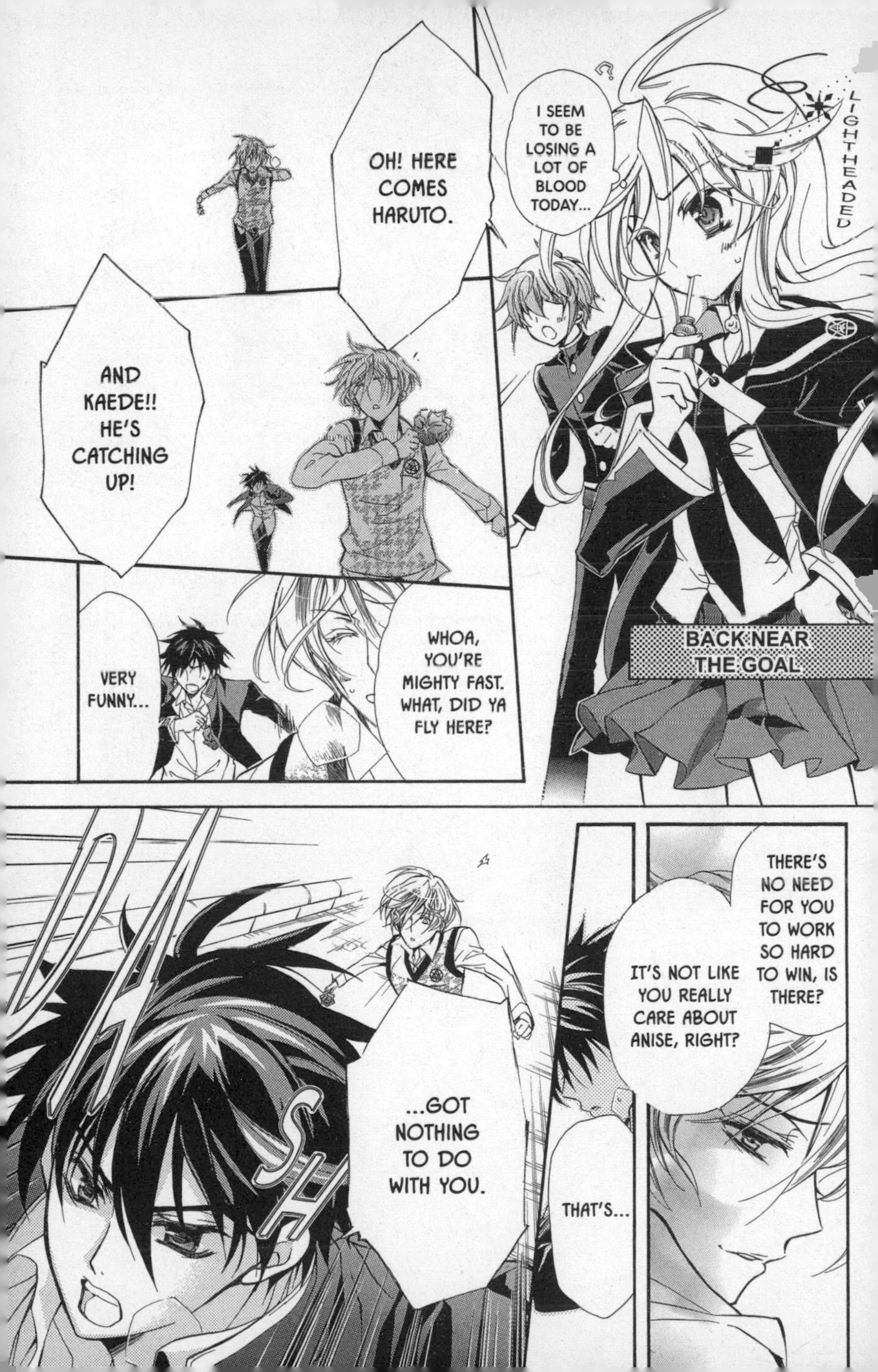
LIGHTHEADED
I SEEM TO BE LOSING A LOT OF BLOOD TODAY...
BACK NEAR THE GOAL
OH! HERE COMES HARUTO.
AND KAEDE!! HE'S CATCHING UP!
WHOA, YOU'RE MIGHTY FAST. WHAT, DID YA FLY HERE?
VERY FUNNY...
THERE'S NO NEED FOR YOU TO WORK SO HARD TO WIN, IS THERE?
IT'S NOT LIKE YOU REALLY CARE ABOUT ANISE, RIGHT?
THAT'S...
SH
...GOT NOTHING TO DO WITH YOU.

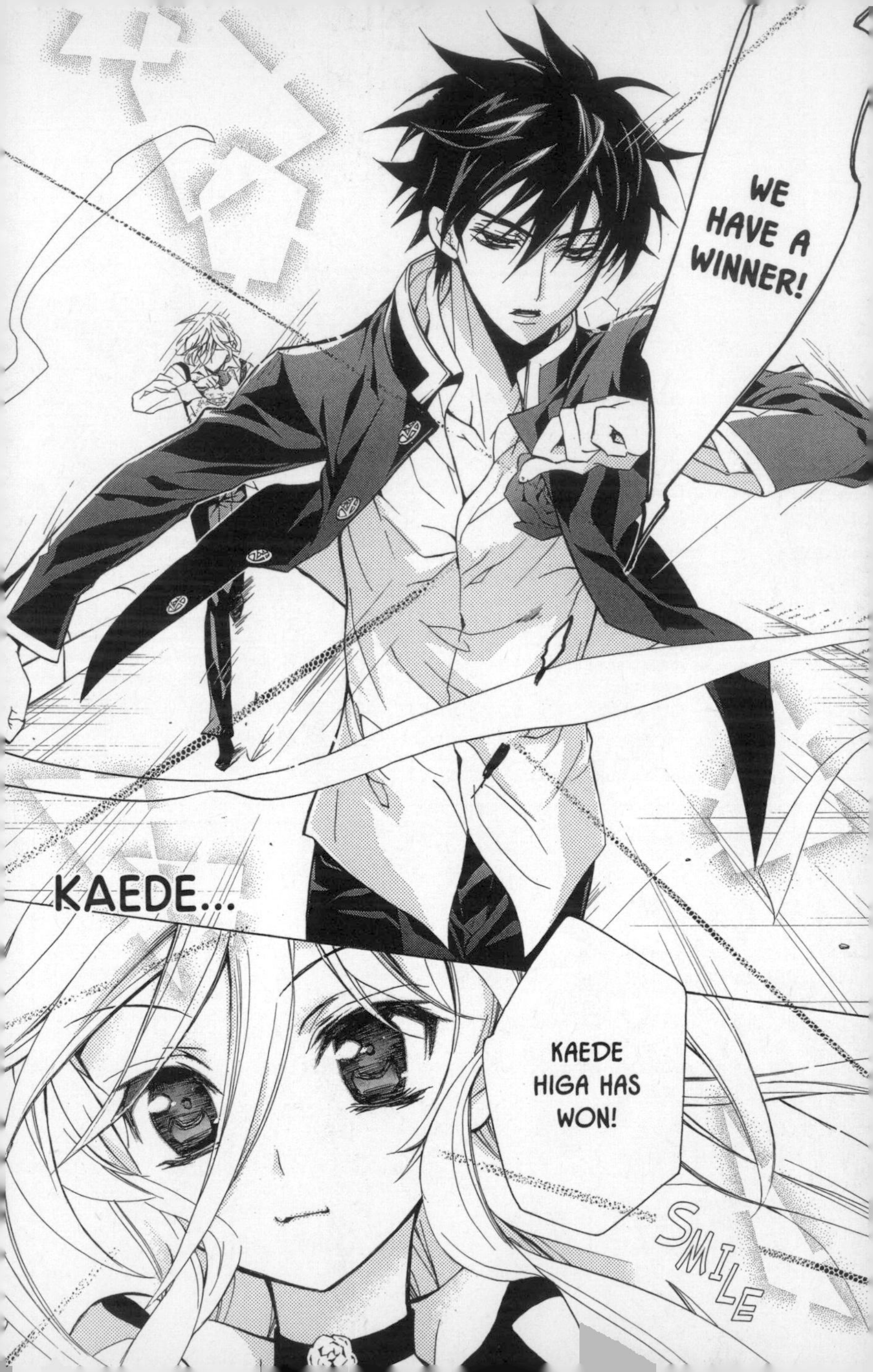
WE HAVE A WINNER!
KAEDE HIGA HAS WON!
KAEDE...
SMILE

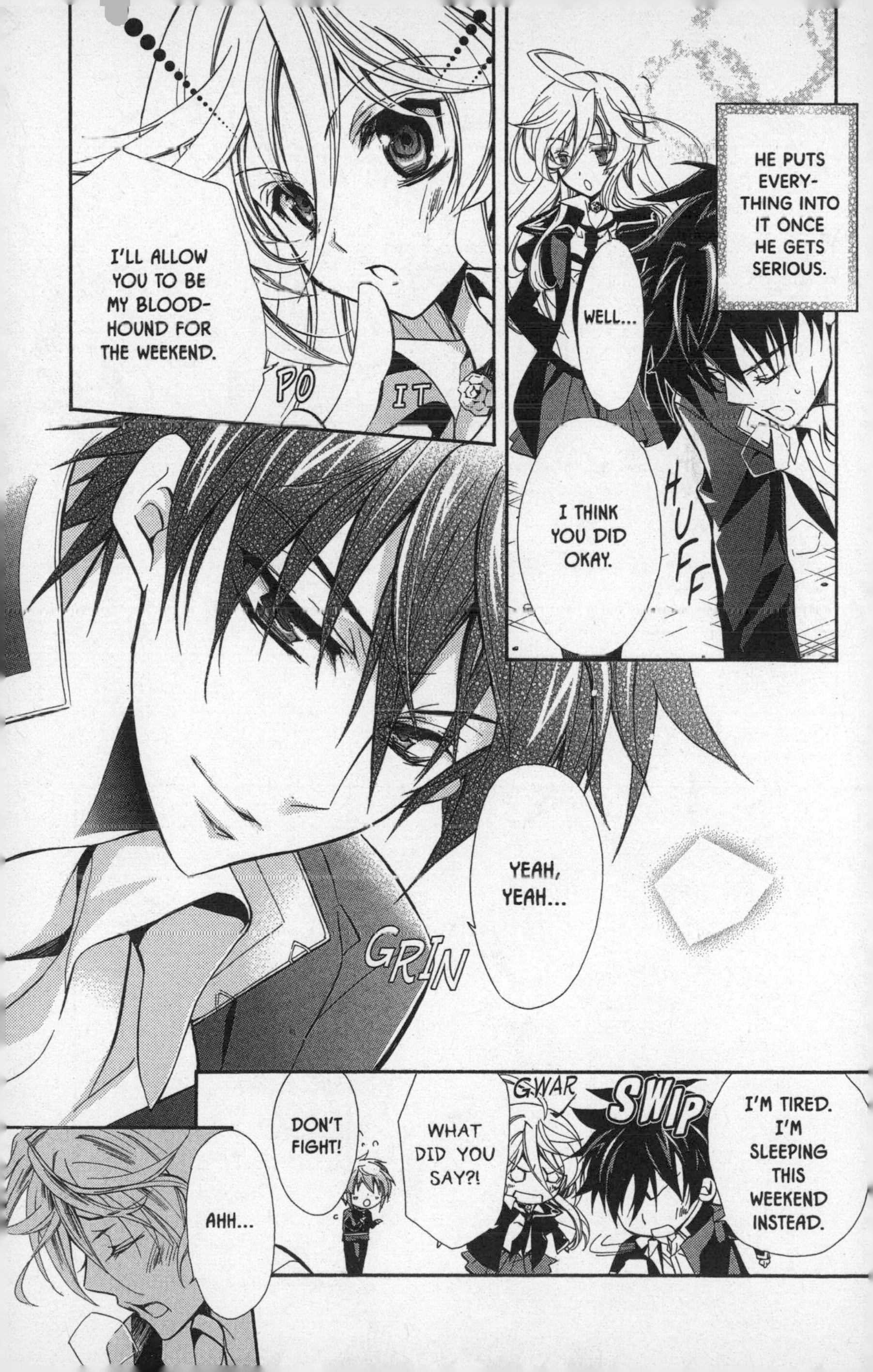
HE PUTS EVERY-THING INTO IT ONCE HE GETS SERIOUS.
WELL...
I THINK YOU DID OKAY.
HUFF
I'LL ALLOW YOU TO BE MY BLOOD-HOUND FOR THE WEEKEND.
PO IT
YEAH, YEAH...
GRIN
I'M TIRED. I'M SLEEPING THIS WEEKEND INSTEAD.
SWIP
GWAR
WHAT DID YOU SAY?!
DON'T FIGHT!
AHH...

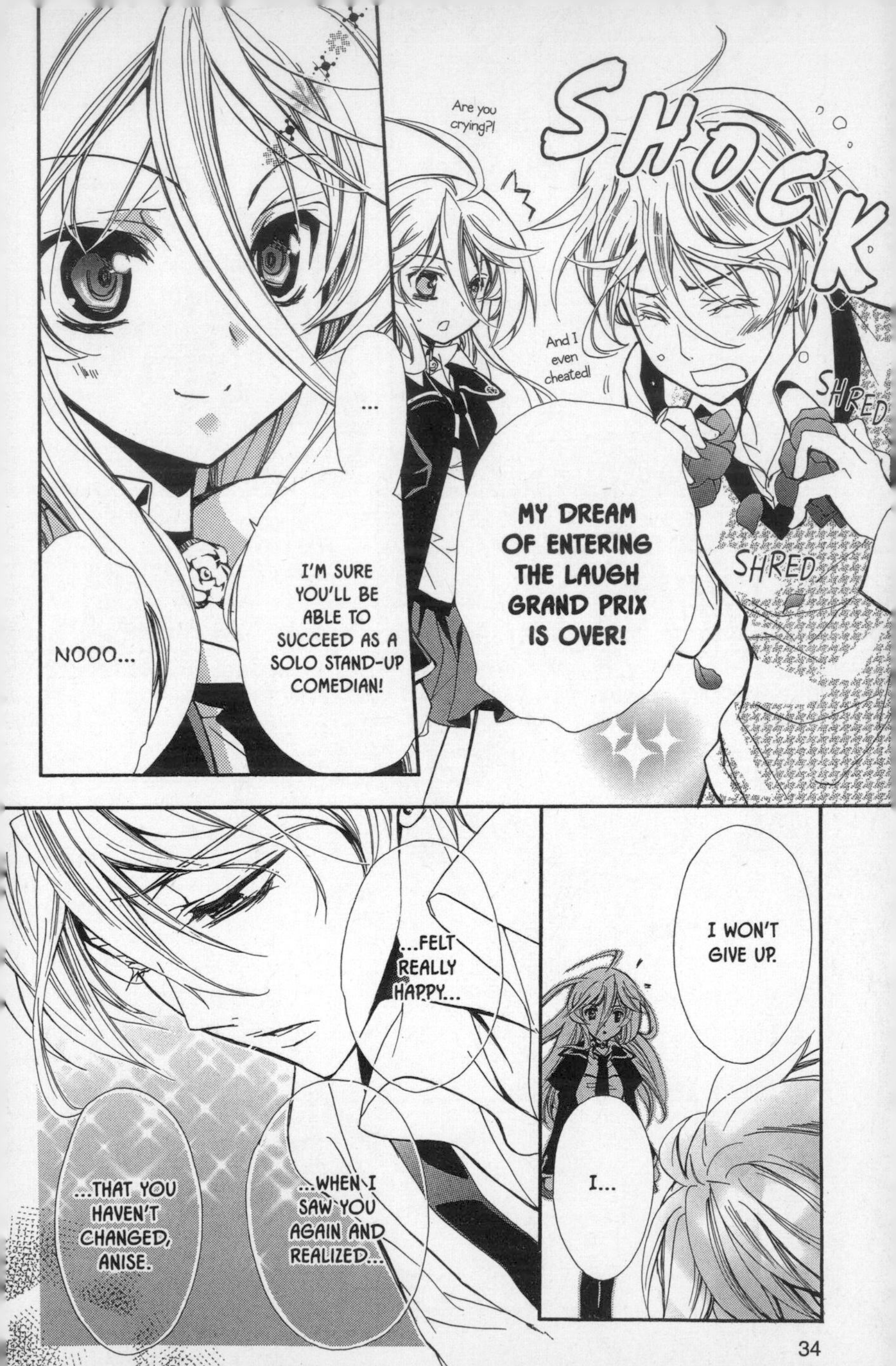
SHOCK
Are you crying?!
MY DREAM OF ENTERING THE LAUGH GRAND PRIX IS OVER!
And I even cheated!
SHRED
SHRED
...
I'M SURE YOU'LL BE ABLE TO SUCCEED AS A SOLO STAND-UP COMEDIAN!
NOOO...
I WON'T GIVE UP.
I...
...FELT REALLY HAPPY...
...WHEN I SAW YOU AGAIN AND REALIZED...
...THAT YOU HAVEN'T CHANGED, ANISE.

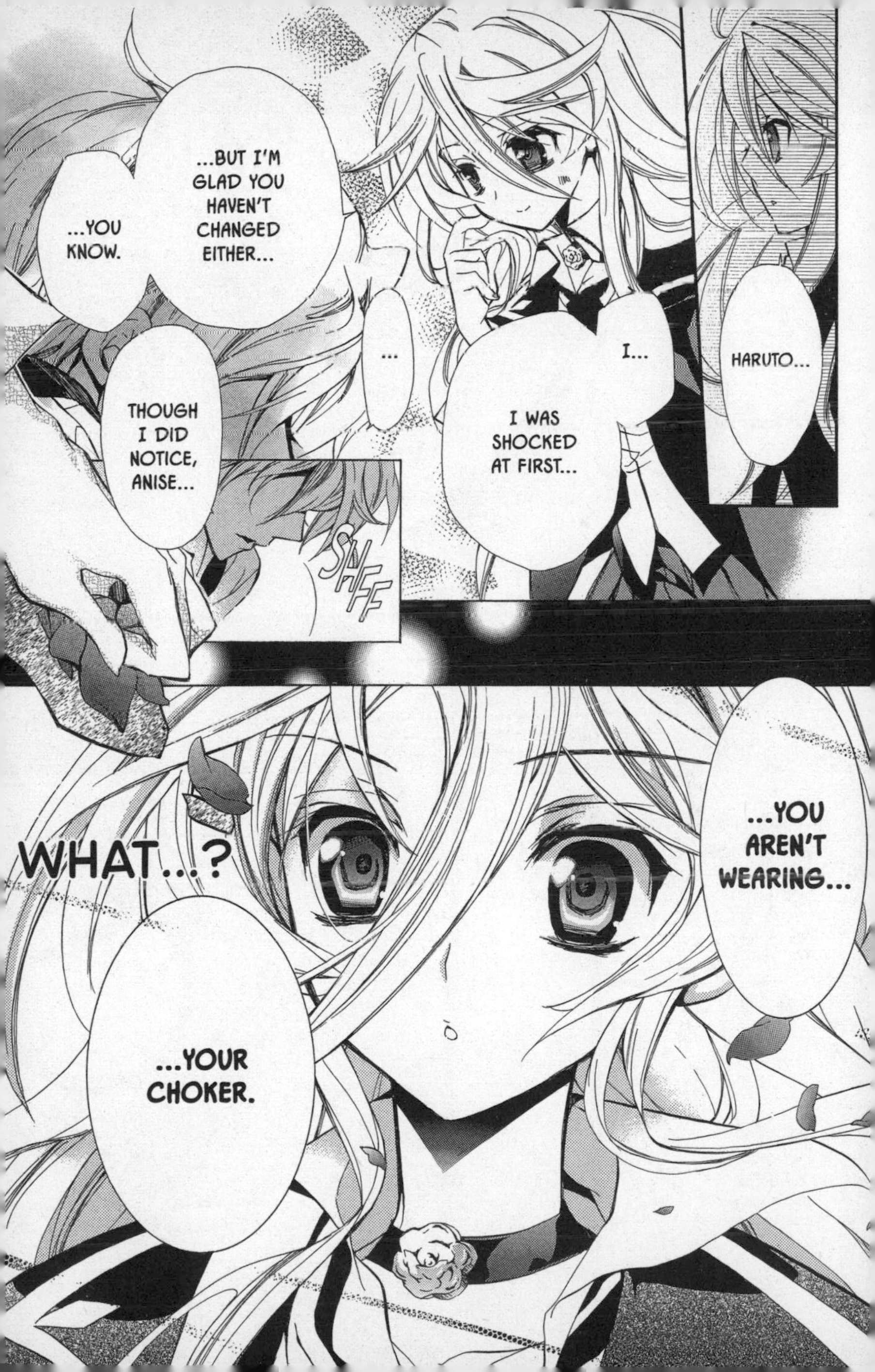
HARUTO...
I...
I WAS SHOCKED AT FIRST...
...
...BUT I'M GLAD YOU HAVEN'T CHANGED EITHER...
...YOU KNOW.
THOUGH I DID NOTICE, ANISE...
SHFF
...YOU AREN'T WEARING...
WHAT...?
...YOUR CHOKER.

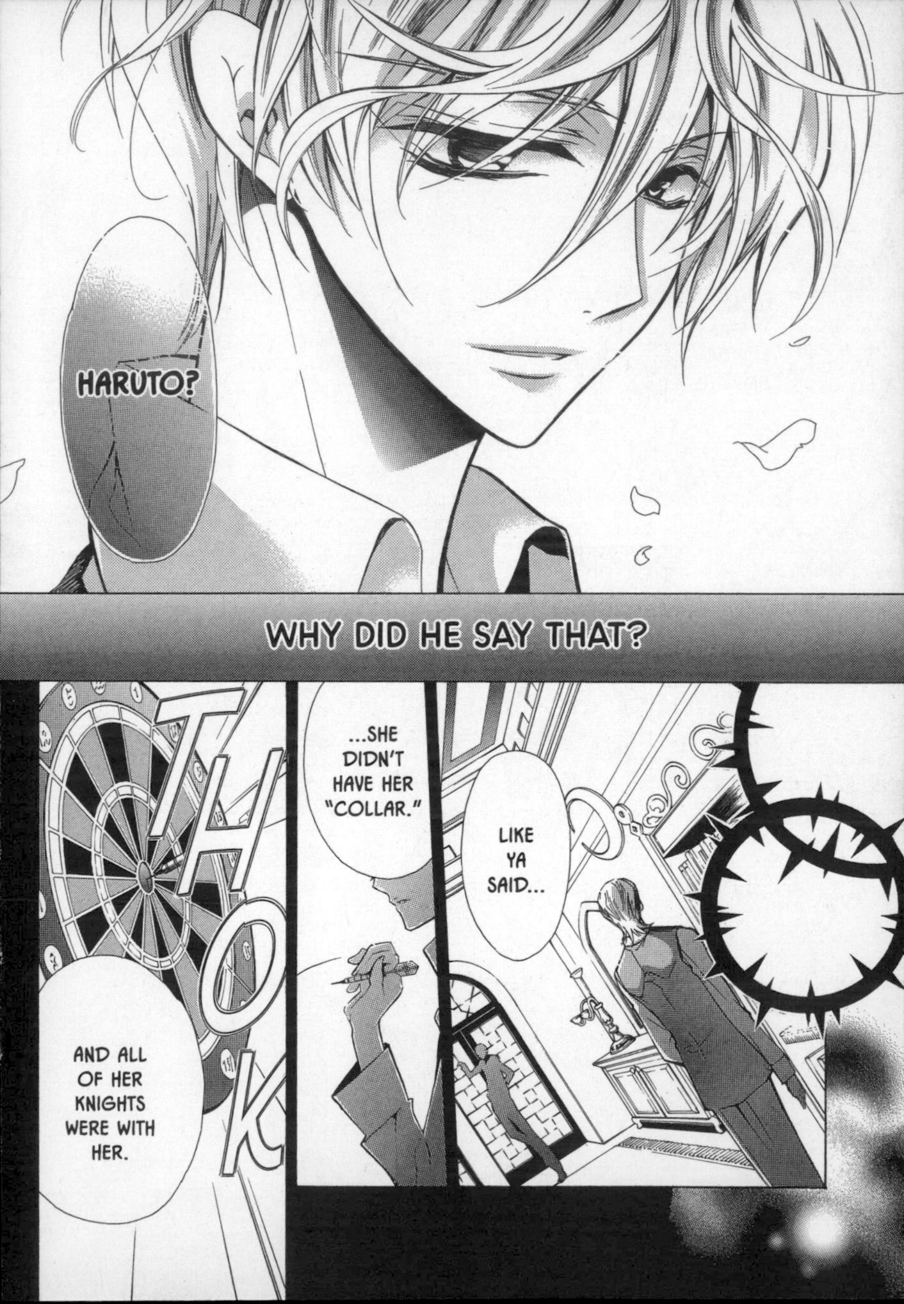
HARUTO?
WHY DID HE SAY THAT?
LIKE YA SAID...
...SHE DIDN'T HAVE HER "COLLAR."
THOK
AND ALL OF HER KNIGHTS WERE WITH HER.

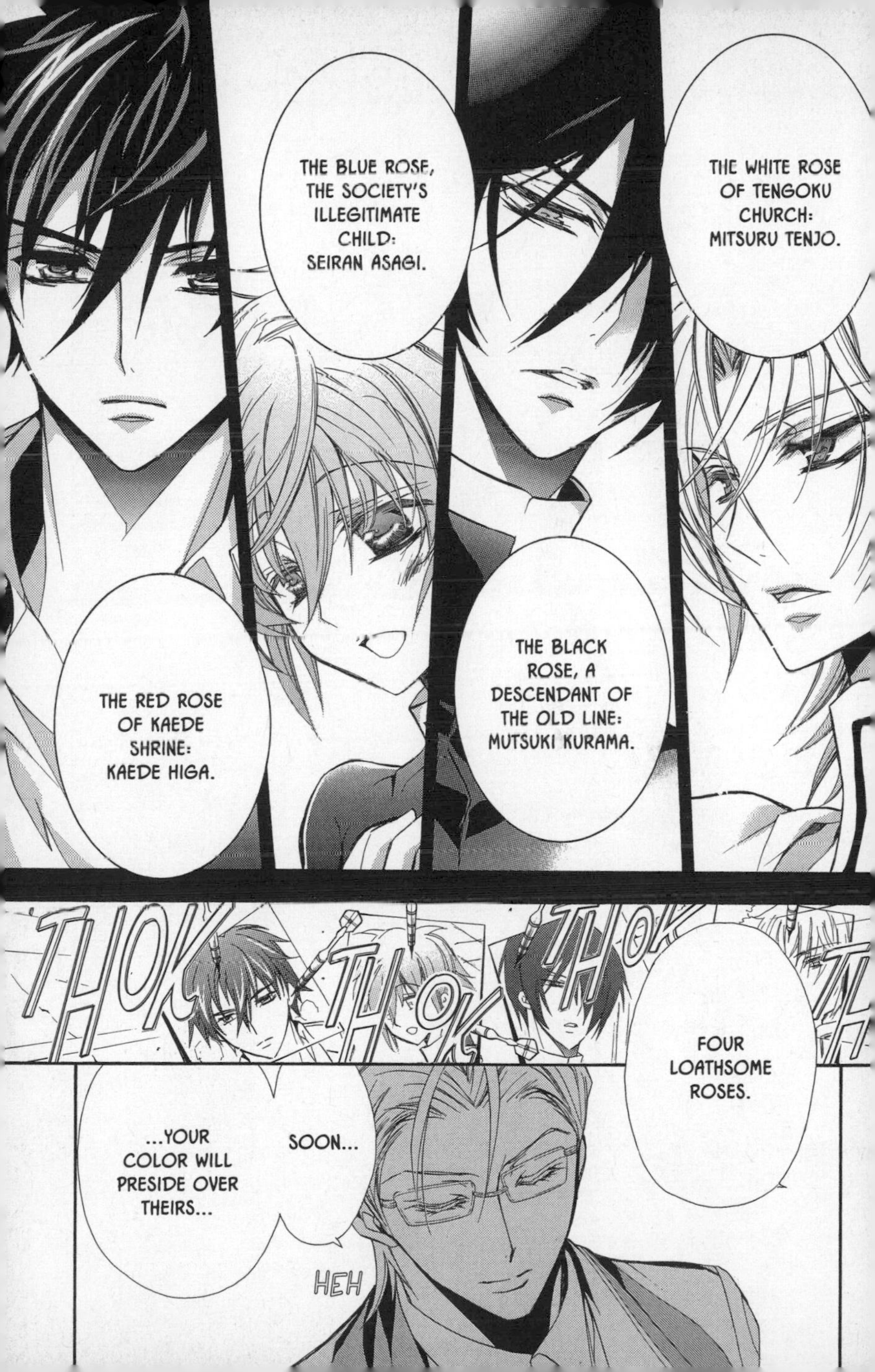
THE WHITE ROSE OF TENGOKU CHURCH: MITSURU TENJO.
THE BLACK ROSE, A DESCENDANT OF THE OLD LINE: MUTSUKI KURAMA.
THE BLUE ROSE, THE SOCIETY'S ILLEGITIMATE CHILD: SEIRAN ASAGI.
THE RED ROSE OF KAEDE SHRINE: KAEDE HIGA.
TH
THOK
THOK
THOK
FOUR LOATHSOME ROSES.
SOON...
...YOUR COLOR WILL PRESIDE OVER THEIRS...
HEH

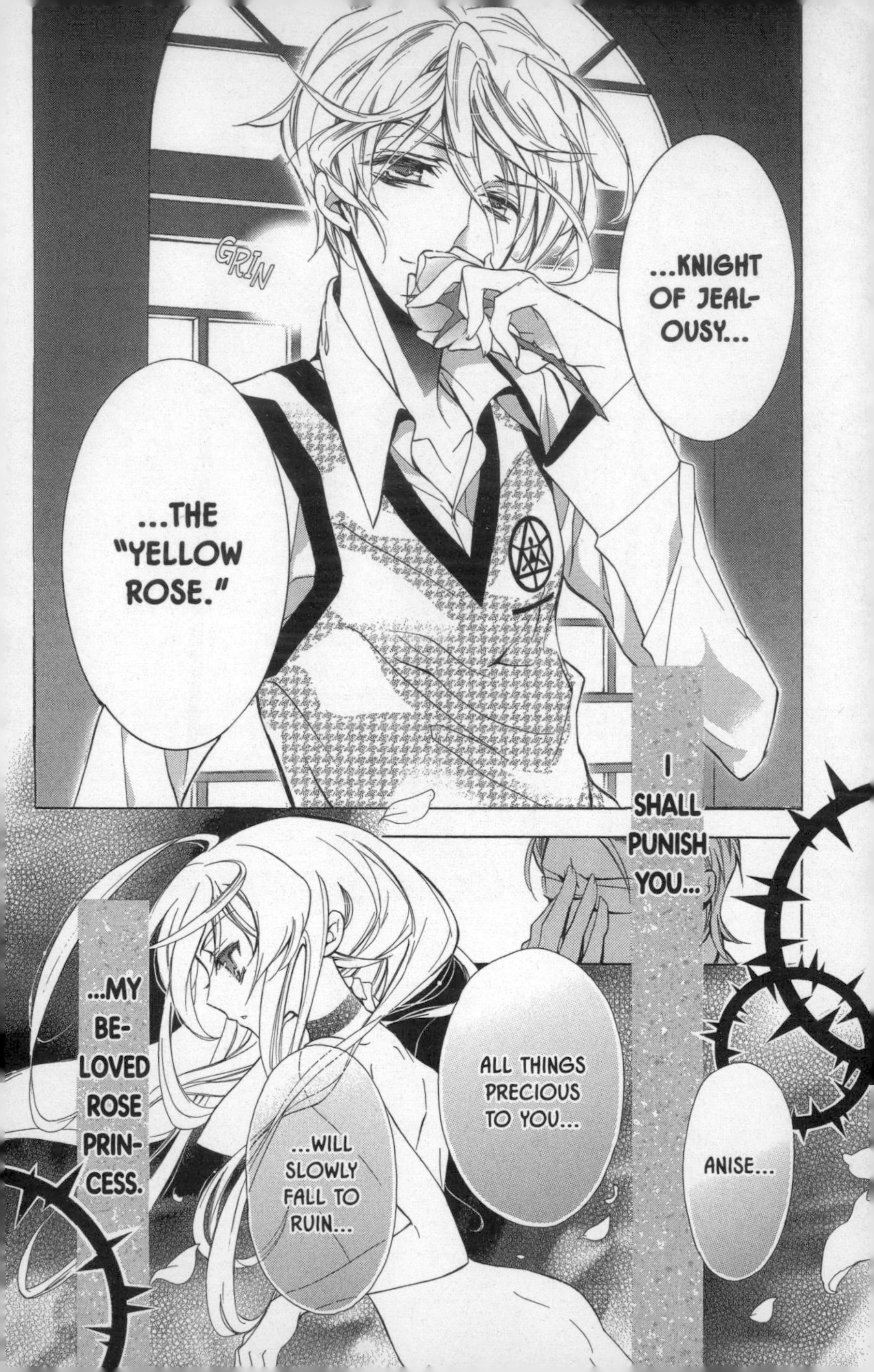
...KNIGHT OF JEAL-OUSY...
GRIN
...THE "YELLOW ROSE."
I SHALL PUNISH YOU...
ANISE...
ALL THINGS PRECIOUS TO YOU...
...WILL SLOWLY FALL TO RUIN...
...MY BE-LOVED ROSE PRIN-CESS.

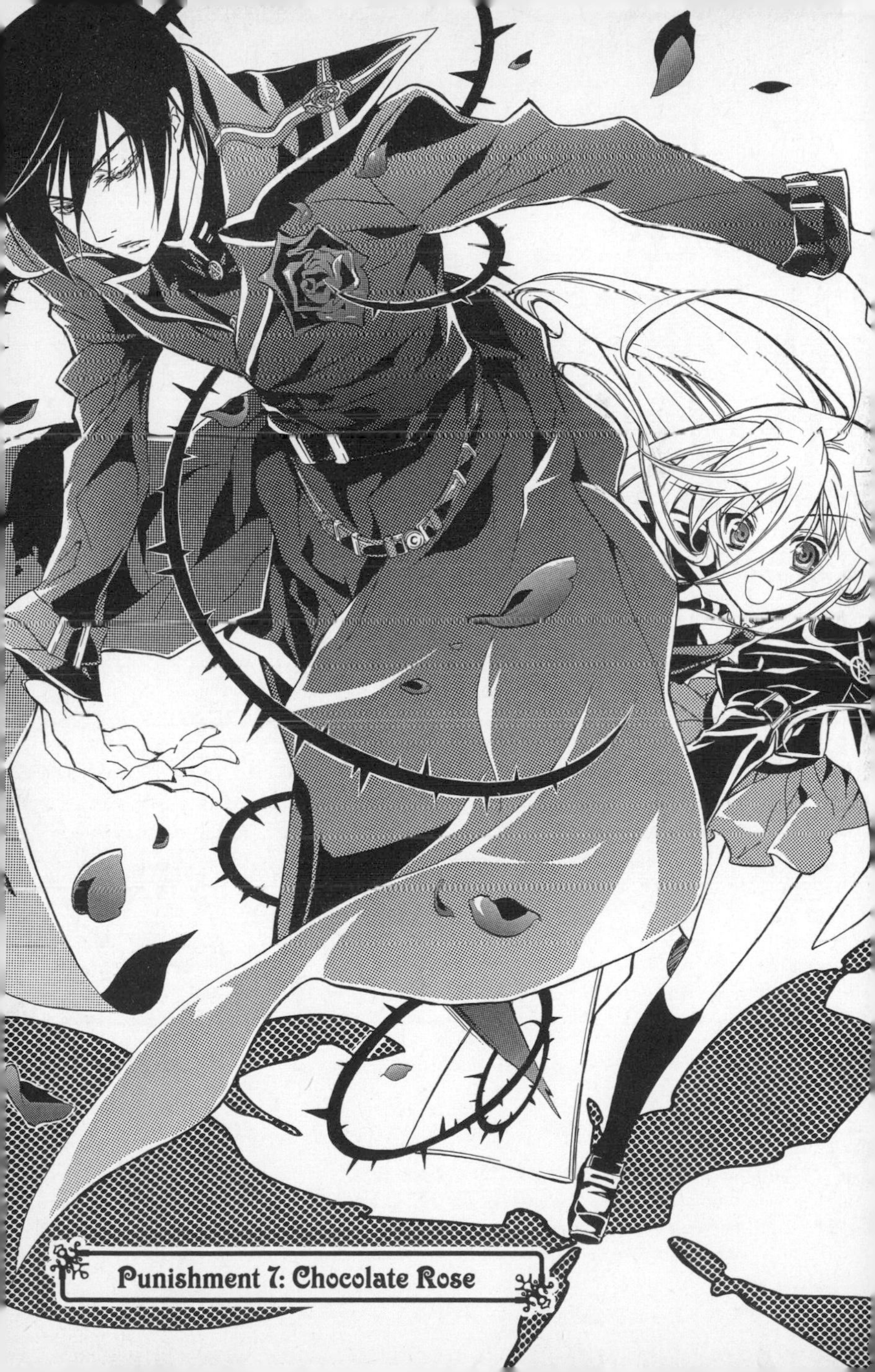

Punishment 7: Chocolate Rose

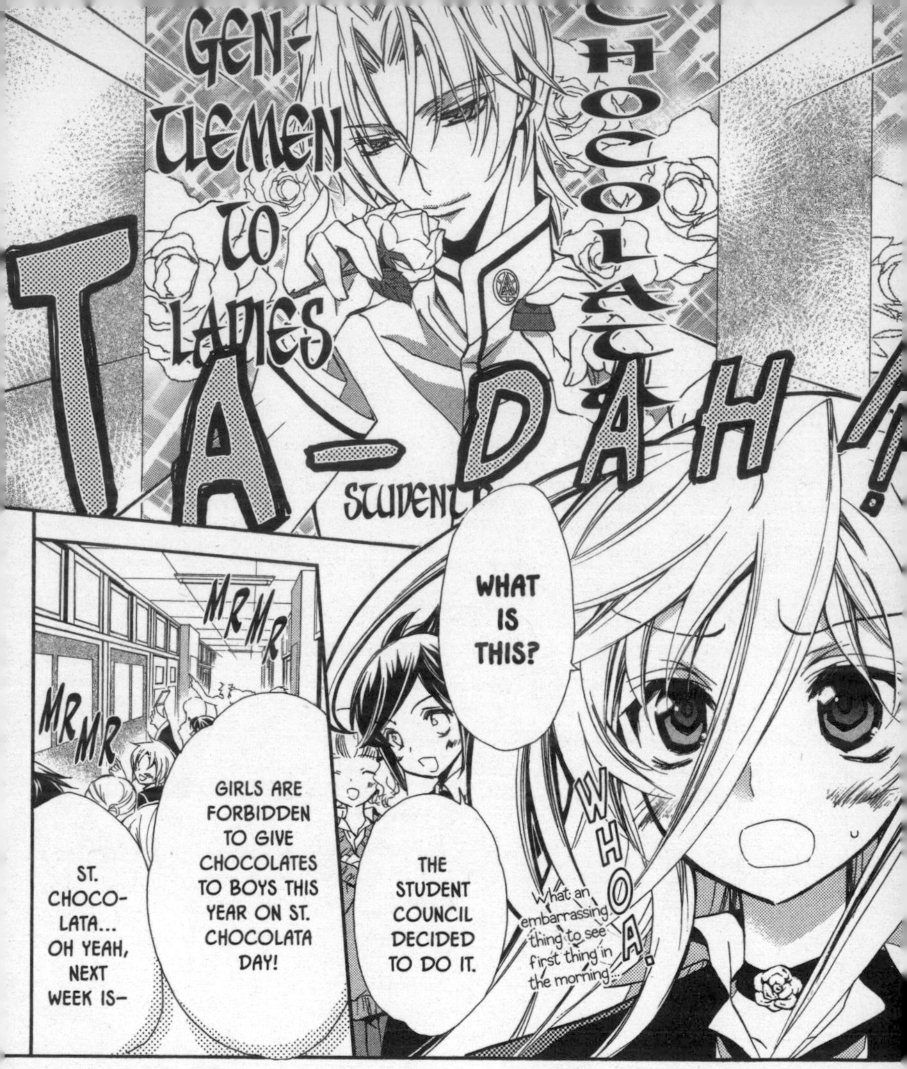
GEN-TLEMEN TO LADIES
CHOCOLATE
TA-DAH!
STUDENT
WHAT IS THIS?
WHOA.
What an embarrassing thing to see first thing in the morning...
THE STUDENT COUNCIL DECIDED TO DO IT.
GIRLS ARE FORBIDDEN TO GIVE CHOCOLATES TO BOYS THIS YEAR ON ST. CHOCOLATA DAY!
MRMR
MRMR
ST. CHOCO-LATA... OH YEAH, NEXT WEEK IS—

Itsushi Narumi

Itsushi Narumi. He teaches Classics. He perpetually suffers from bedhead. He wears glasses that are too large for his face and a baggy lab coat. The teachers tease him, but they like him too. There seems to be a secret in his past...

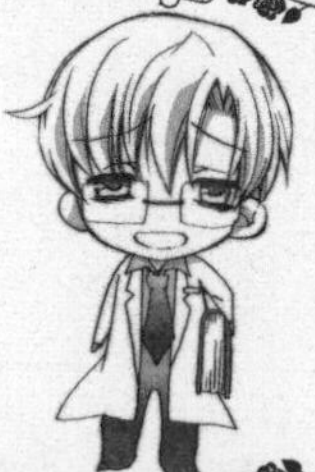

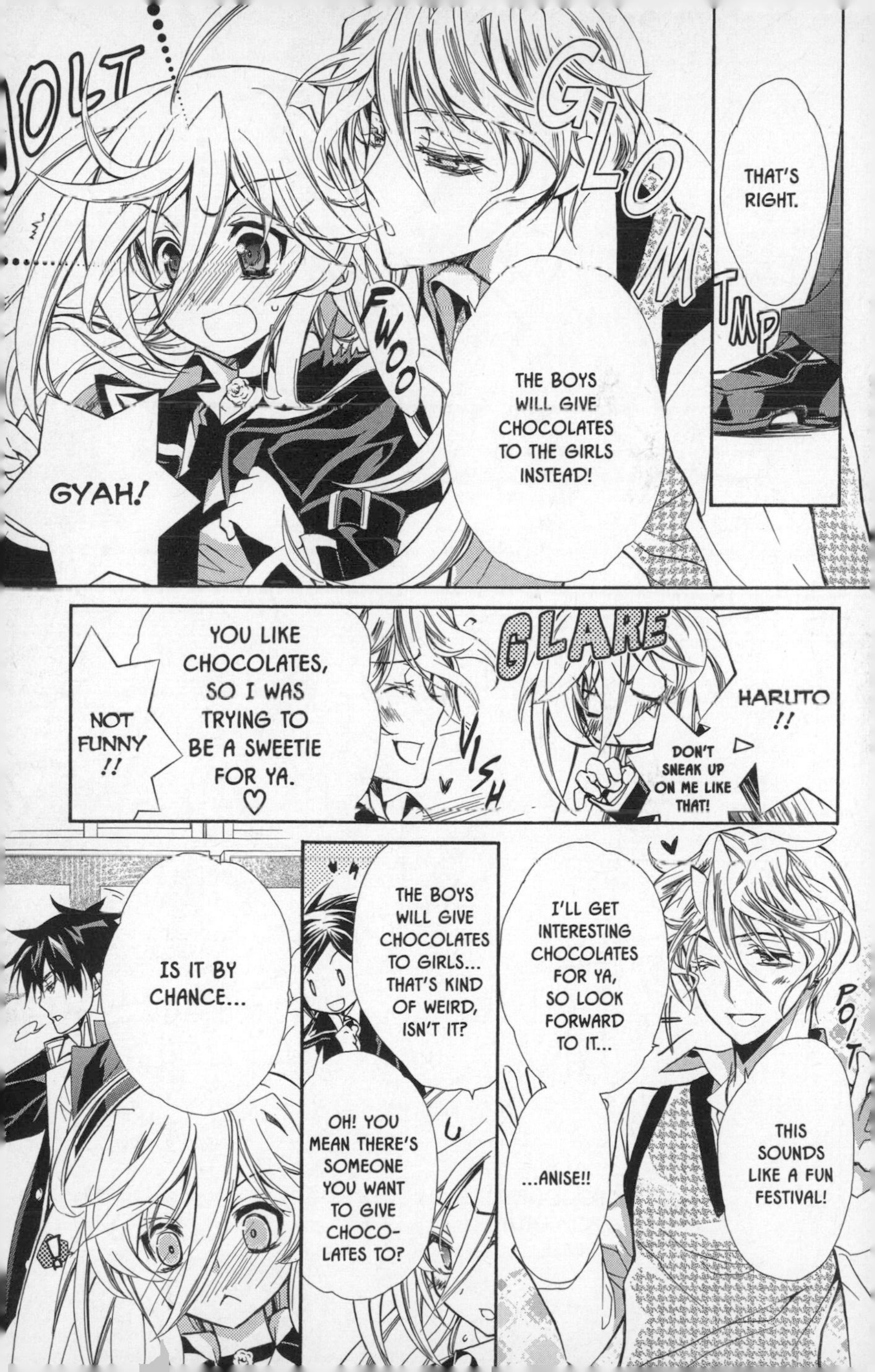
THAT'S RIGHT.
TMP
GLOM
THE BOYS WILL GIVE CHOCOLATES TO THE GIRLS INSTEAD!
FWOO
JOLT
GYAH!
HARUTO!!
DON'T SNEAK UP ON ME LIKE THAT!
GLARE
VISH
YOU LIKE CHOCOLATES, SO I WAS TRYING TO BE A SWEETIE FOR YA. ♡
NOT FUNNY!!
POIT
THIS SOUNDS LIKE A FUN FESTIVAL!
I'LL GET INTERESTING CHOCOLATES FOR YA, SO LOOK FORWARD TO IT...
...ANISE!!
THE BOYS WILL GIVE CHOCOLATES TO GIRLS... THAT'S KIND OF WEIRD, ISN'T IT?
OH! YOU MEAN THERE'S SOMEONE YOU WANT TO GIVE CHOCO-LATES TO?
IS IT BY CHANCE...

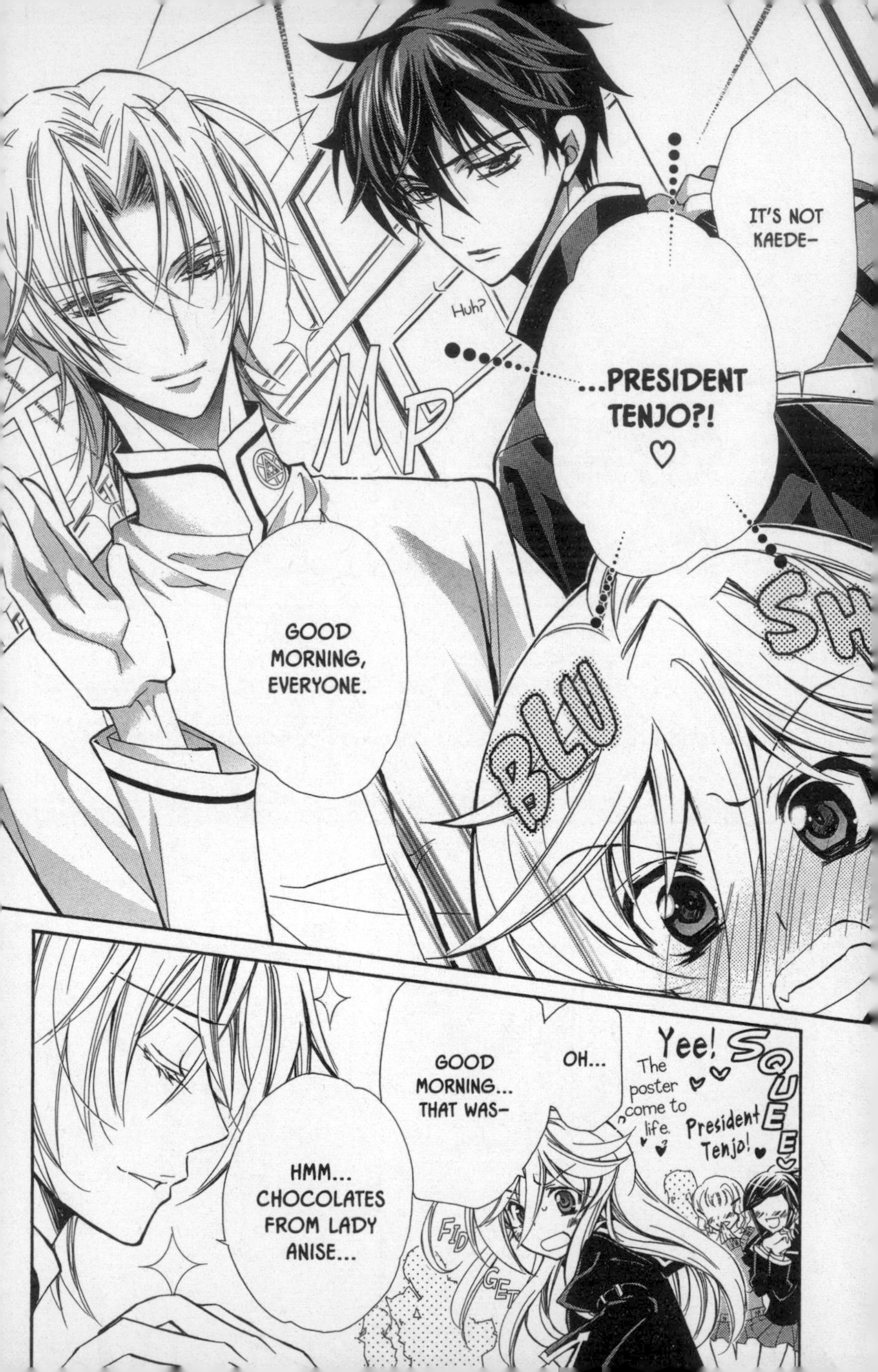
IT'S NOT KAEDE-
...PRESIDENT TENJO?! ♡
Huh?
SH
BLU
MP
GOOD MORNING, EVERYONE.
SQUEEE
Yee! ♡
President Tenjo!
The poster come to life.
OH...
GOOD MORNING... THAT WAS-
HMM... CHOCOLATES FROM LADY ANISE...
FID
GET

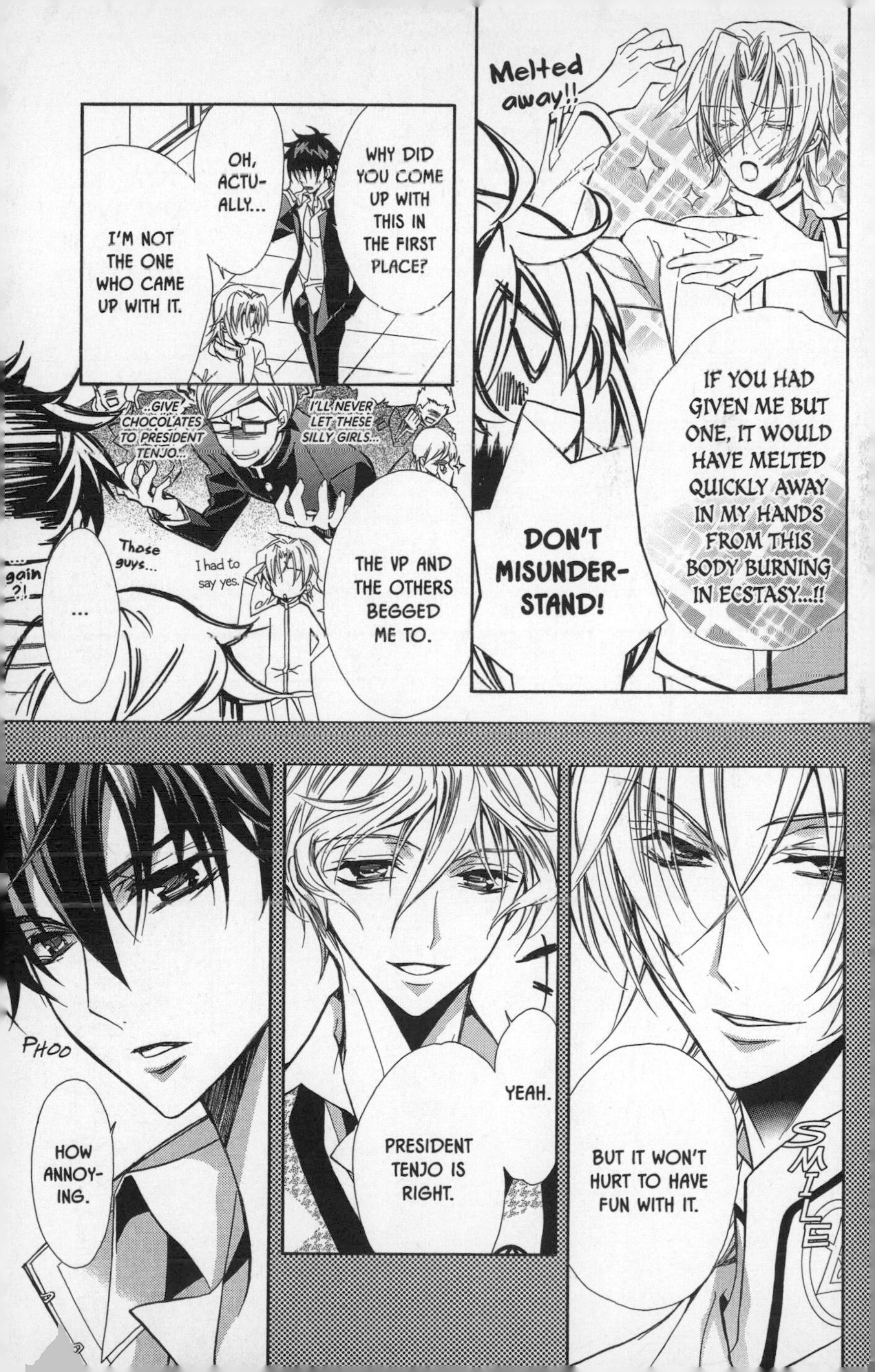
Melted away!!
IF YOU HAD GIVEN ME BUT ONE, IT WOULD HAVE MELTED QUICKLY AWAY IN MY HANDS FROM THIS BODY BURNING IN ECSTASY...!!
DON'T MISUNDERSTAND!
WHY DID YOU COME UP WITH THIS IN THE FIRST PLACE?
OH, ACTUALLY...
I'M NOT THE ONE WHO CAME UP WITH IT.
THE VP AND THE OTHERS BEGGED ME TO.
I'LL NEVER LET THESE SILLY GIRLS...
...GIVE CHOCOLATES TO PRESIDENT TENJO...
I had to say yes.
Those guys...
...gain ?!
...
SMILE
BUT IT WON'T HURT TO HAVE FUN WITH IT.
YEAH.
PRESIDENT TENJO IS RIGHT.
PHOO
HOW ANNOYING.

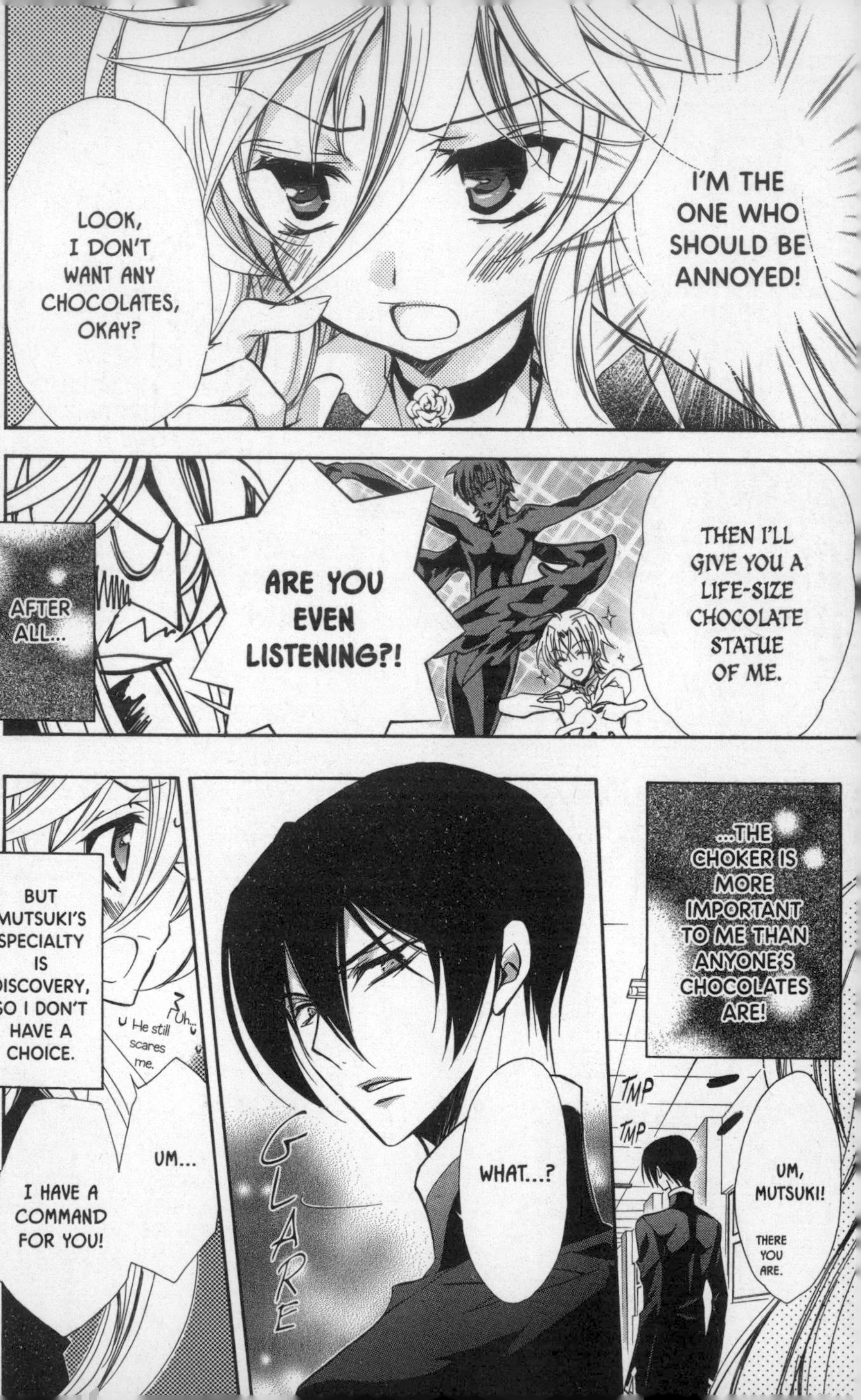
I'M THE ONE WHO SHOULD BE ANNOYED!
LOOK, I DON'T WANT ANY CHOCOLATES, OKAY?
THEN I'LL GIVE YOU A LIFE-SIZE CHOCOLATE STATUE OF ME.
ARE YOU EVEN LISTENING?!
AFTER ALL...
...THE CHOKER IS MORE IMPORTANT TO ME THAN ANYONE'S CHOCOLATES ARE!
TMP
TMP
UM, MUTSUKI!
THERE YOU ARE.
WHAT...?
GLARE
BUT MUTSUKI'S SPECIALTY IS DISCOVERY, SO I DON'T HAVE A CHOICE.
Uh...
He still scares me.
UM...
I HAVE A COMMAND FOR YOU!

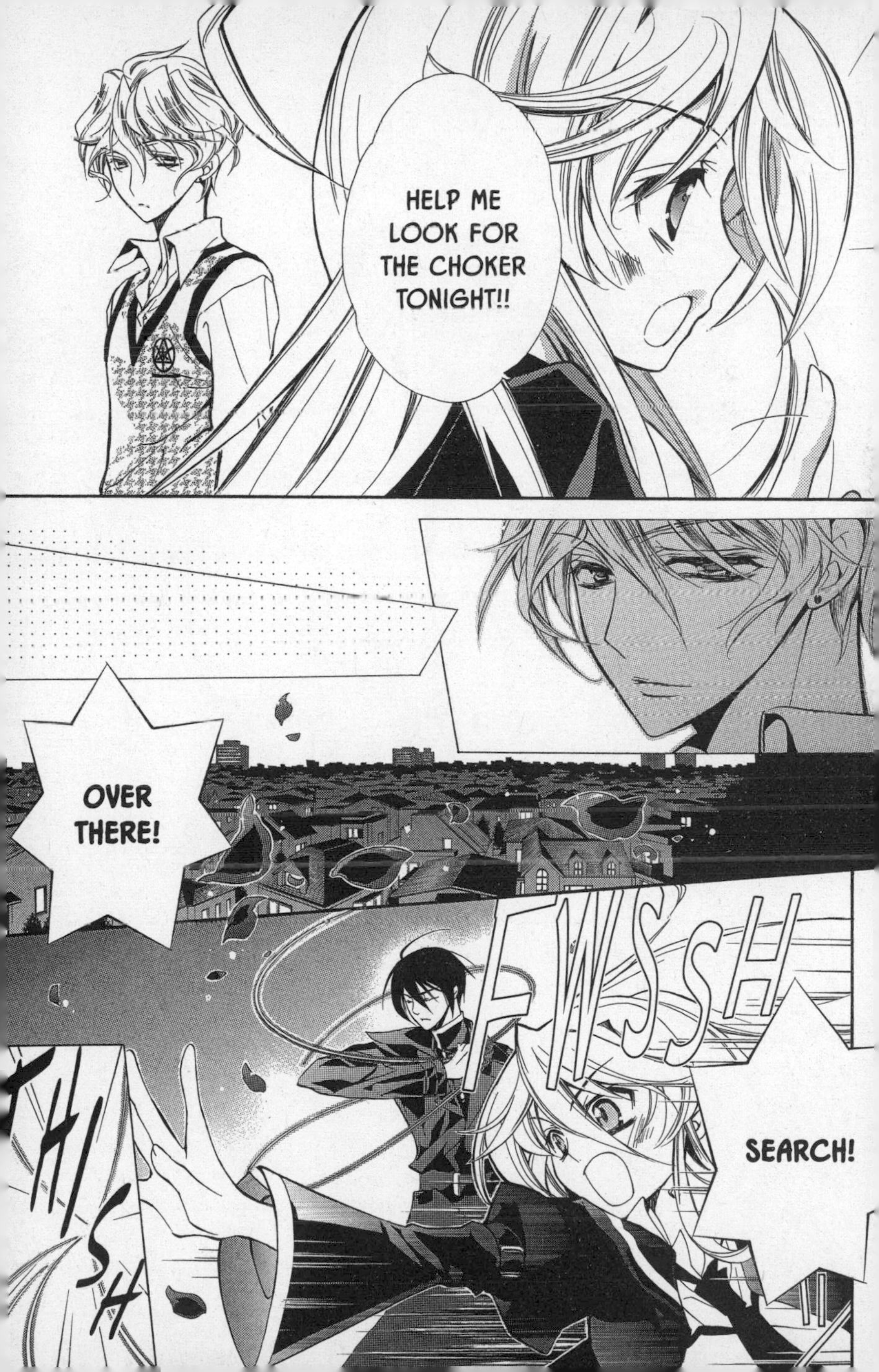
HELP ME LOOK FOR THE CHOKER TONIGHT!!
SEARCH!
FWSSH
OVER THERE!

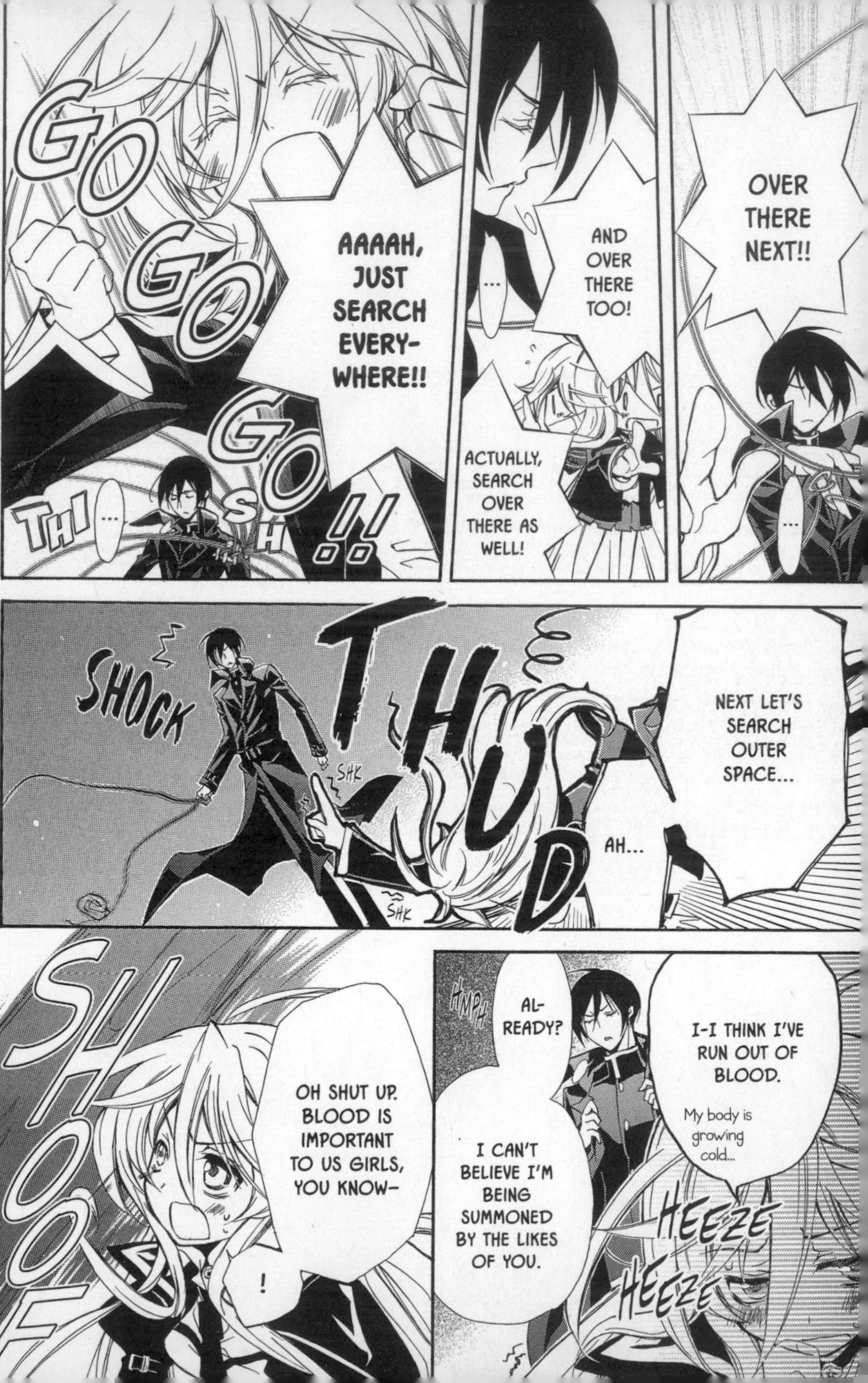
OVER THERE NEXT!!
...
AND OVER THERE TOO!
...
ACTUALLY, SEARCH OVER THERE AS WELL!
AAAAH, JUST SEARCH EVERY-WHERE!!
GO GO GO GO!!
THI...SH
...
NEXT LET'S SEARCH OUTER SPACE...
AH...
THUD
SHK
SHK
SHOCK
I-I THINK I'VE RUN OUT OF BLOOD.
My body is growing cold...
HEEZE HEEZE
AL-READY?
HMPH
I CAN'T BELIEVE I'M BEING SUMMONED BY THE LIKES OF YOU.
OH SHUT UP. BLOOD IS IMPORTANT TO US GIRLS, YOU KNOW—
!
SHOOOF

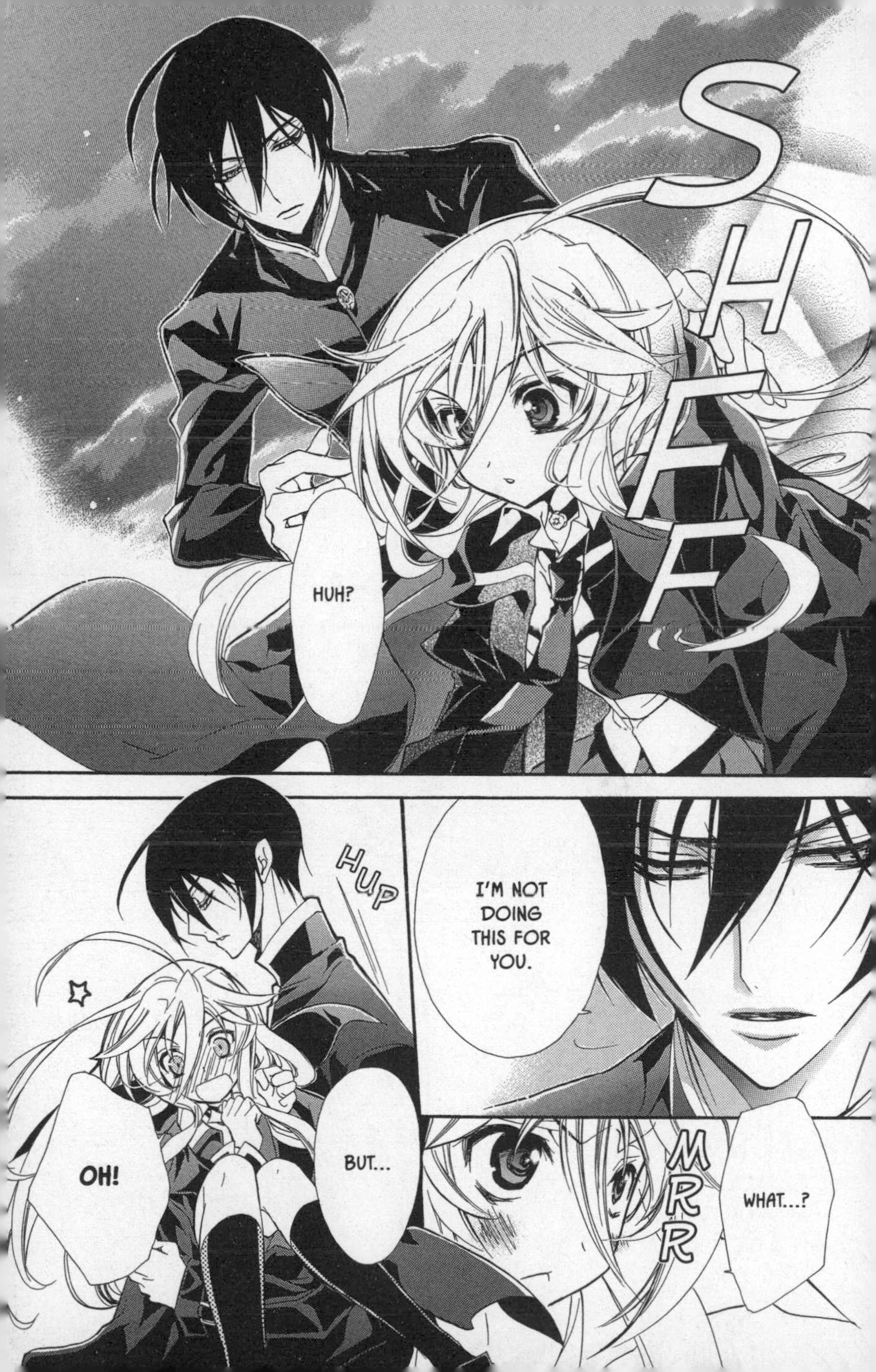
SHFFF
HUH?
I'M NOT DOING THIS FOR YOU.
MRRR
WHAT...?
HUP
BUT...
OH!

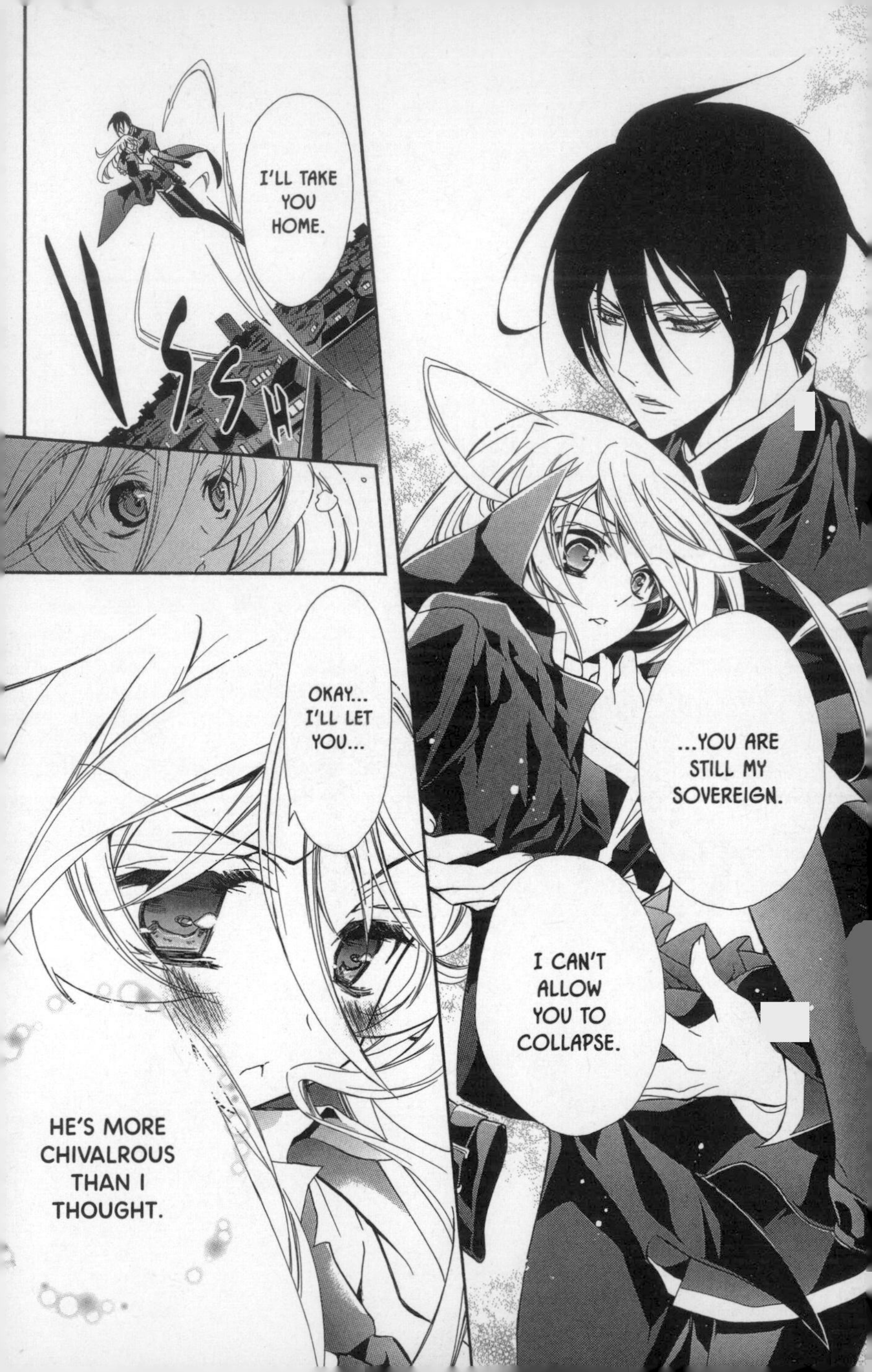
...YOU ARE STILL MY SOVEREIGN.
I CAN'T ALLOW YOU TO COLLAPSE.
I'LL TAKE YOU HOME.
VSSH
OKAY... I'LL LET YOU...
HE'S MORE CHIVALROUS THAN I THOUGHT.

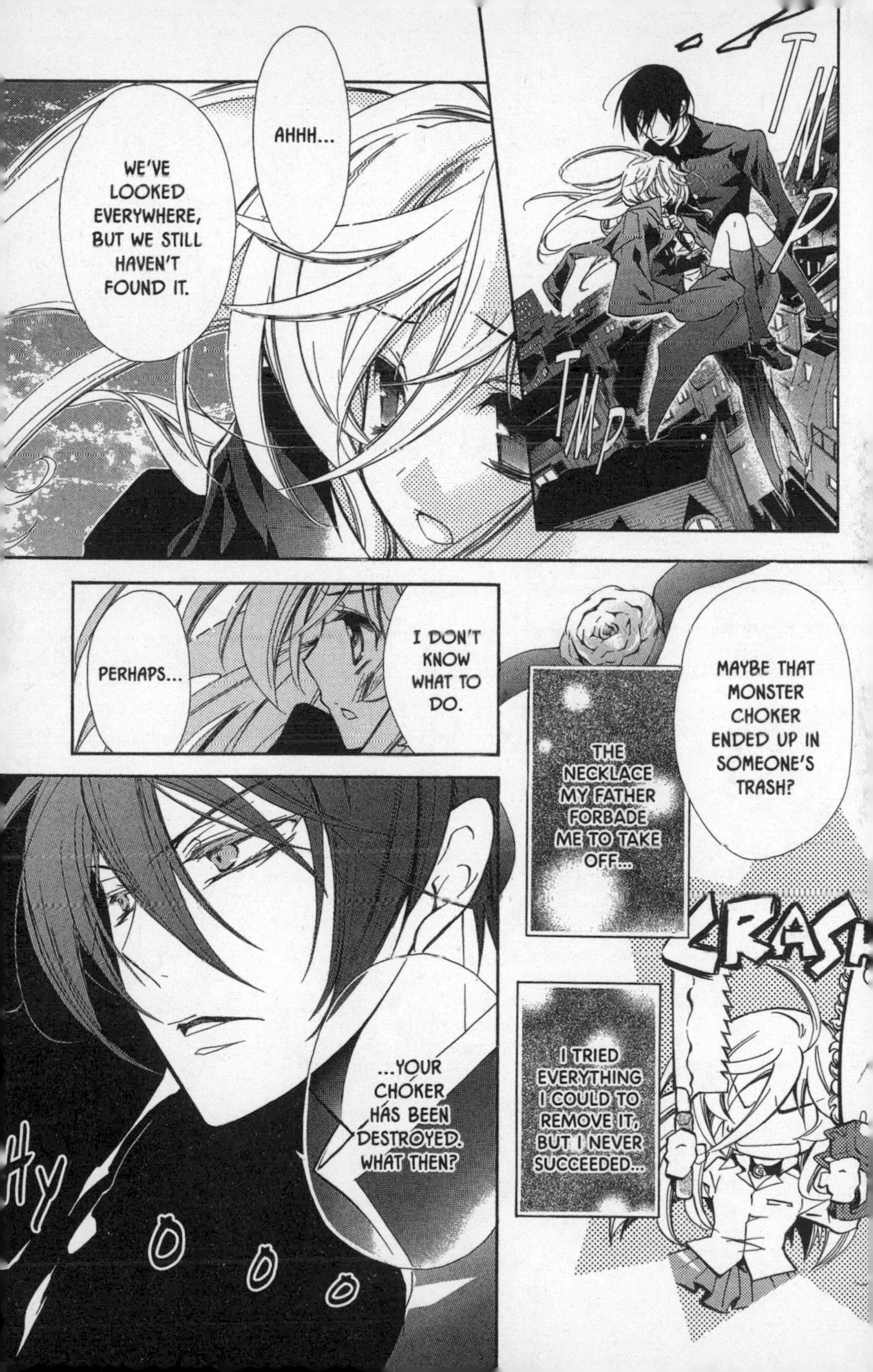
TMP
TMP
AHHH...
WE'VE LOOKED EVERYWHERE, BUT WE STILL HAVEN'T FOUND IT.
MAYBE THAT MONSTER CHOKER ENDED UP IN SOMEONE'S TRASH?
THE NECKLACE MY FATHER FORBADE ME TO TAKE OFF...
CRASH
I TRIED EVERYTHING I COULD TO REMOVE IT, BUT I NEVER SUCCEEDED...
I DON'T KNOW WHAT TO DO.
PERHAPS...
...YOUR CHOKER HAS BEEN DESTROYED. WHAT THEN?
HYOOO

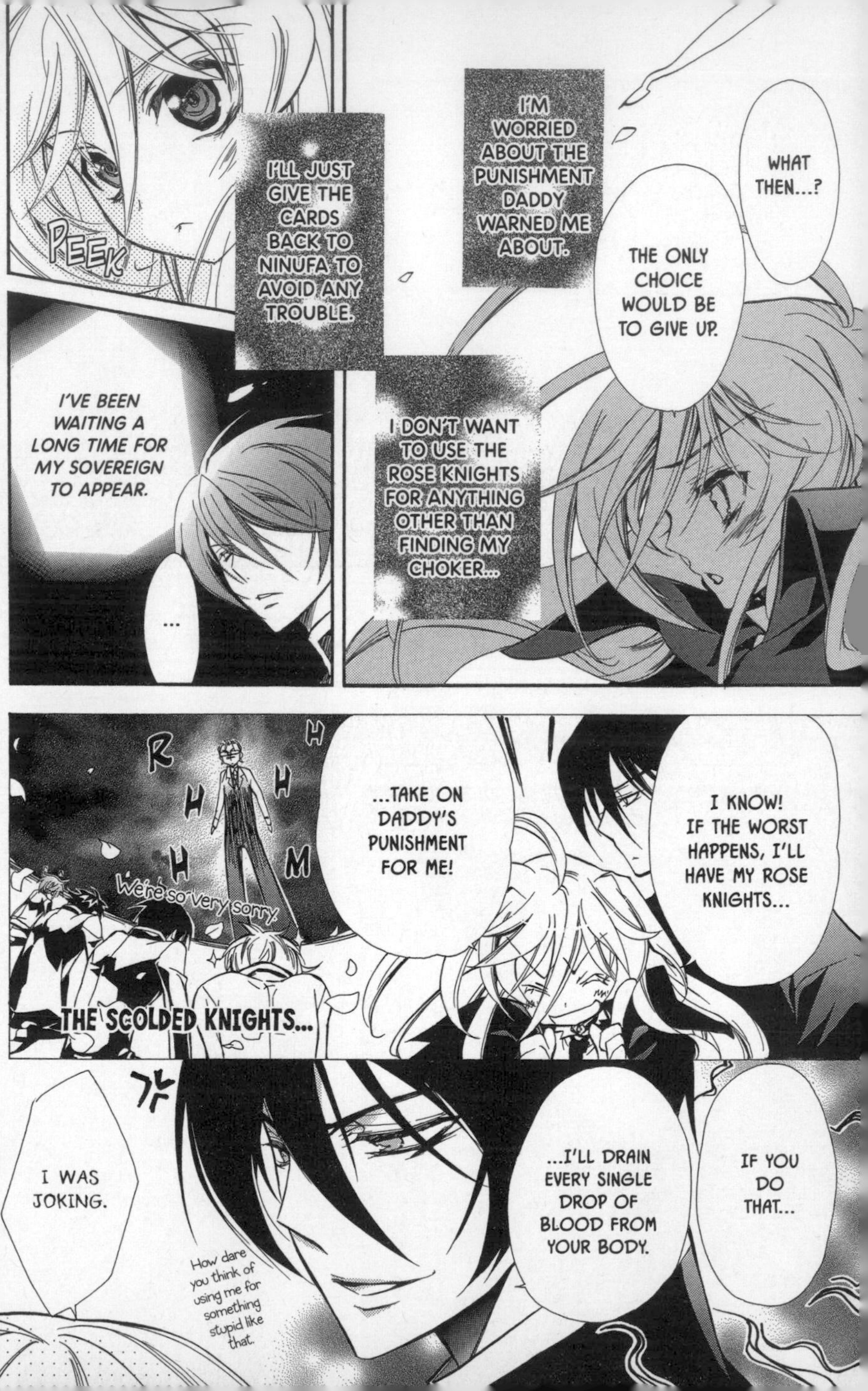
WHAT THEN...?
I'M WORRIED ABOUT THE PUNISHMENT DADDY WARNED ME ABOUT.
THE ONLY CHOICE WOULD BE TO GIVE UP.
I DON'T WANT TO USE THE ROSE KNIGHTS FOR ANYTHING OTHER THAN FINDING MY CHOKER...
I'LL JUST GIVE THE CARDS BACK TO NINUFA TO AVOID ANY TROUBLE.
PEEK
I'VE BEEN WAITING A LONG TIME FOR MY SOVEREIGN TO APPEAR.
...
I KNOW! IF THE WORST HAPPENS, I'LL HAVE MY ROSE KNIGHTS...
...TAKE ON DADDY'S PUNISHMENT FOR ME!
RHHHHMH
We're so very sorry.
THE SCOLDED KNIGHTS...
IF YOU DO THAT...
...I'LL DRAIN EVERY SINGLE DROP OF BLOOD FROM YOUR BODY.
I WAS JOKING.
How dare you think of using me for something stupid like that.

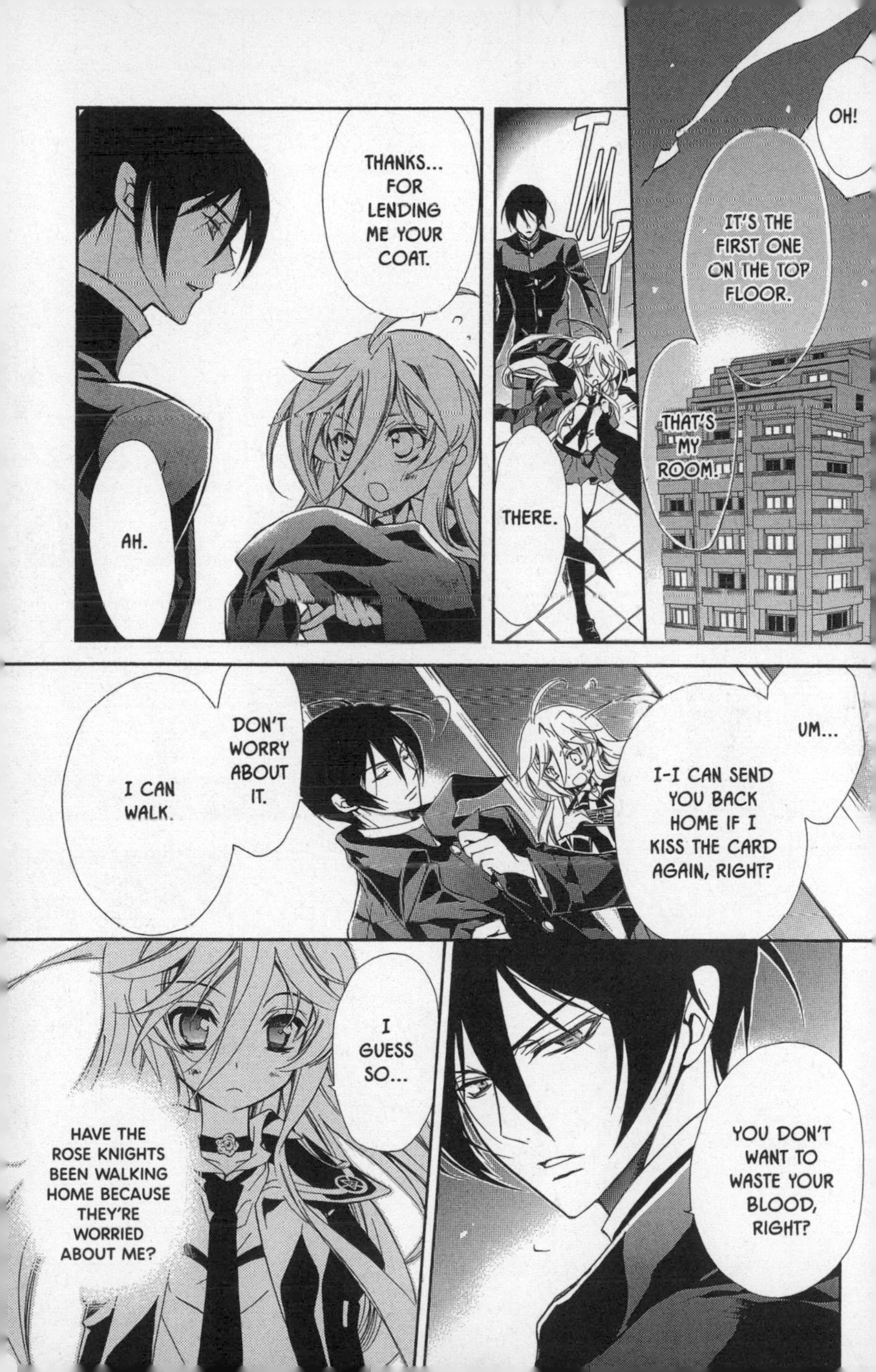
OH!
IT'S THE FIRST ONE ON THE TOP FLOOR.
THAT'S MY ROOM.
TMP
THERE.
THANKS... FOR LENDING ME YOUR COAT.
AH.
UM...
I-I CAN SEND YOU BACK HOME IF I KISS THE CARD AGAIN, RIGHT?
DON'T WORRY ABOUT IT.
I CAN WALK.
YOU DON'T WANT TO WASTE YOUR BLOOD, RIGHT?
I GUESS SO...
HAVE THE ROSE KNIGHTS BEEN WALKING HOME BECAUSE THEY'RE WORRIED ABOUT ME?

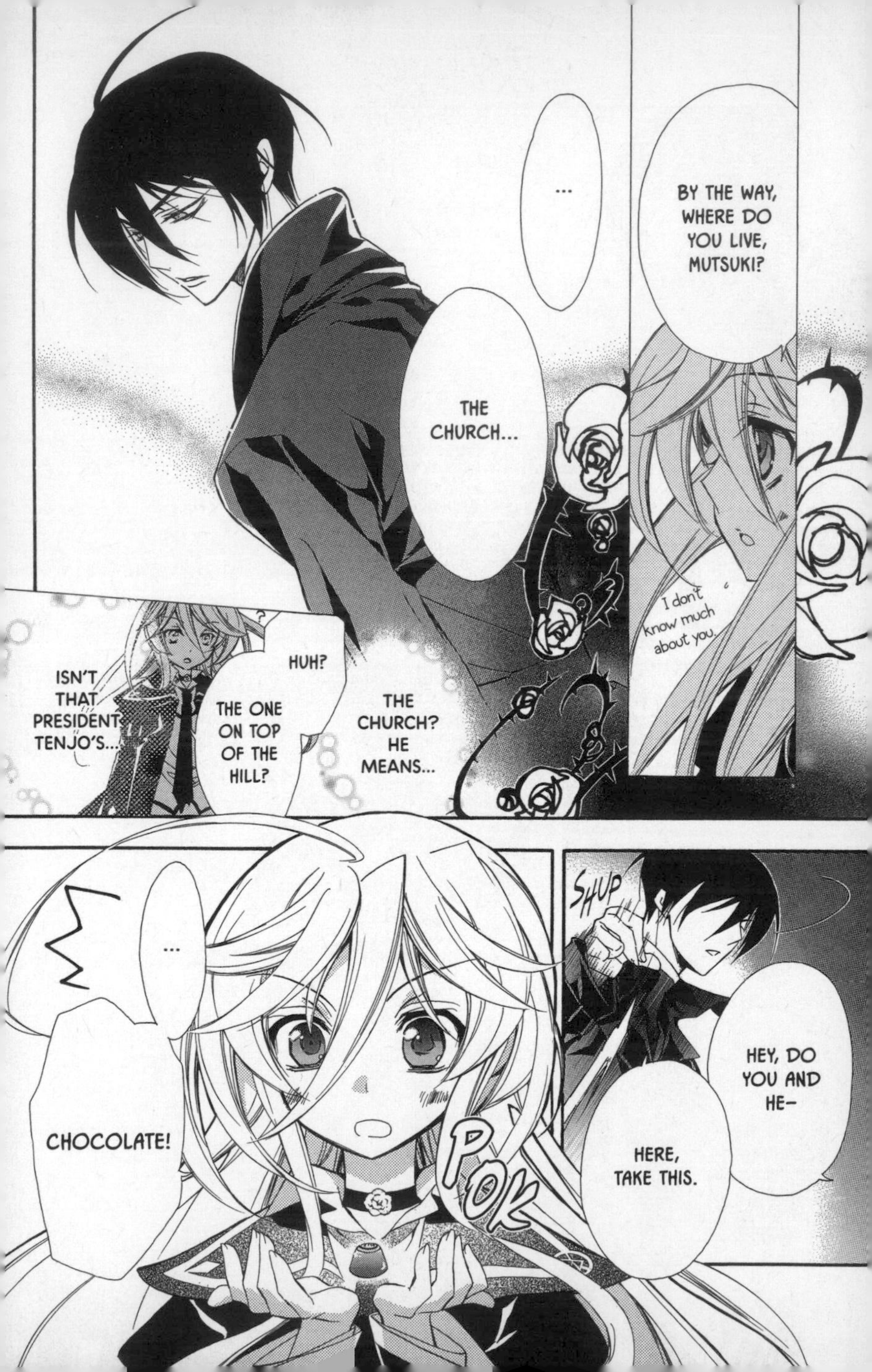
BY THE WAY, WHERE DO YOU LIVE, MUTSUKI?
I don't know much about you.
...
THE CHURCH...
THE CHURCH? HE MEANS...
HUH?
THE ONE ON TOP OF THE HILL?
ISN'T THAT PRESIDENT TENJO'S...
SHUP
HEY, DO YOU AND HE–
HERE, TAKE THIS.
POK
...
CHOCOLATE!

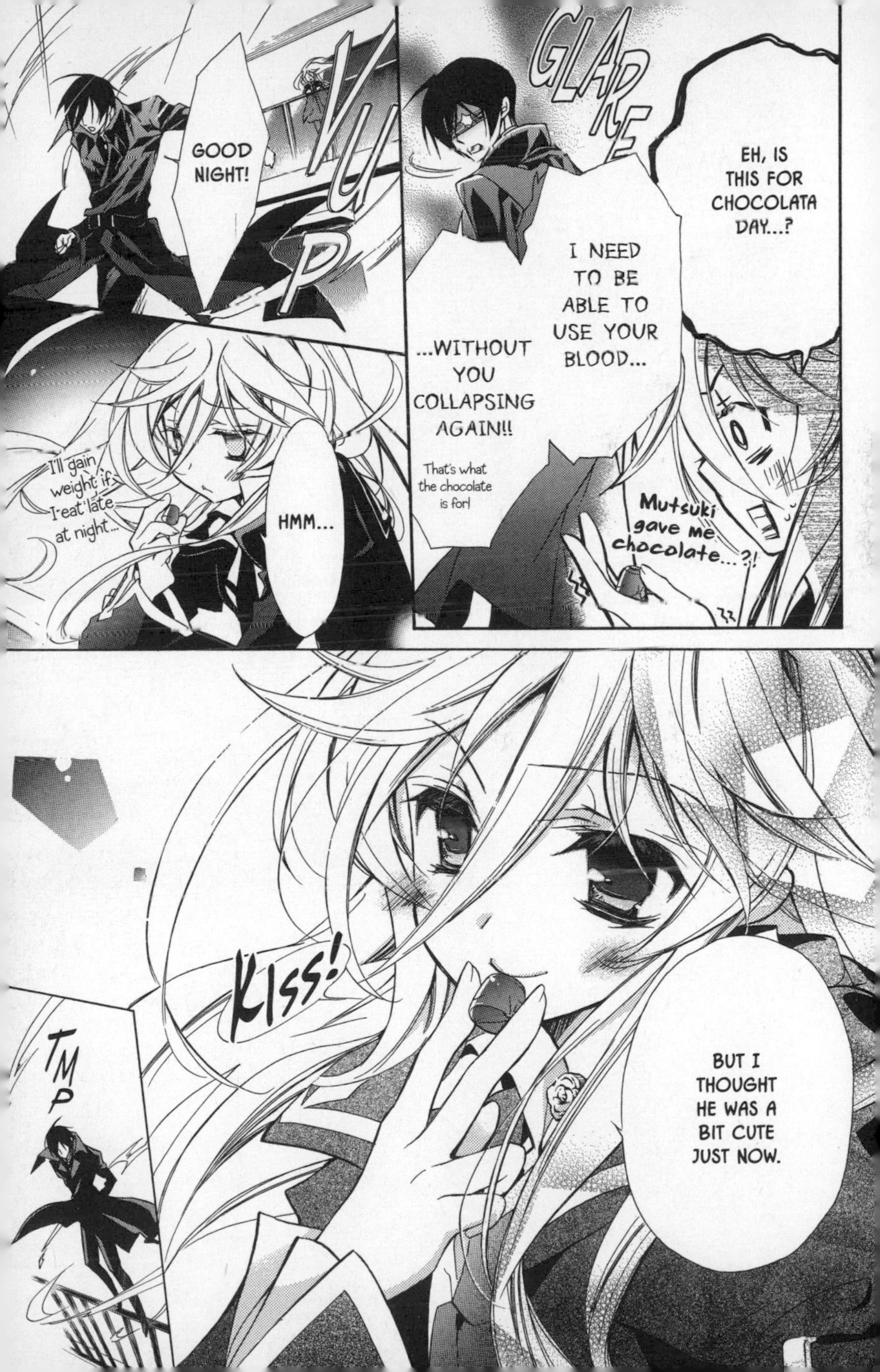
GLARE
EH, IS THIS FOR CHOCOLATA DAY...?
I NEED TO BE ABLE TO USE YOUR BLOOD...
...WITHOUT YOU COLLAPSING AGAIN!!
That's what the chocolate is for!
Mutsuki gave me chocolate...?!
GOOD NIGHT!
VUP
HMM...
I'll gain weight if I eat late at night...
BUT I THOUGHT HE WAS A BIT CUTE JUST NOW.
KISS!
TMP

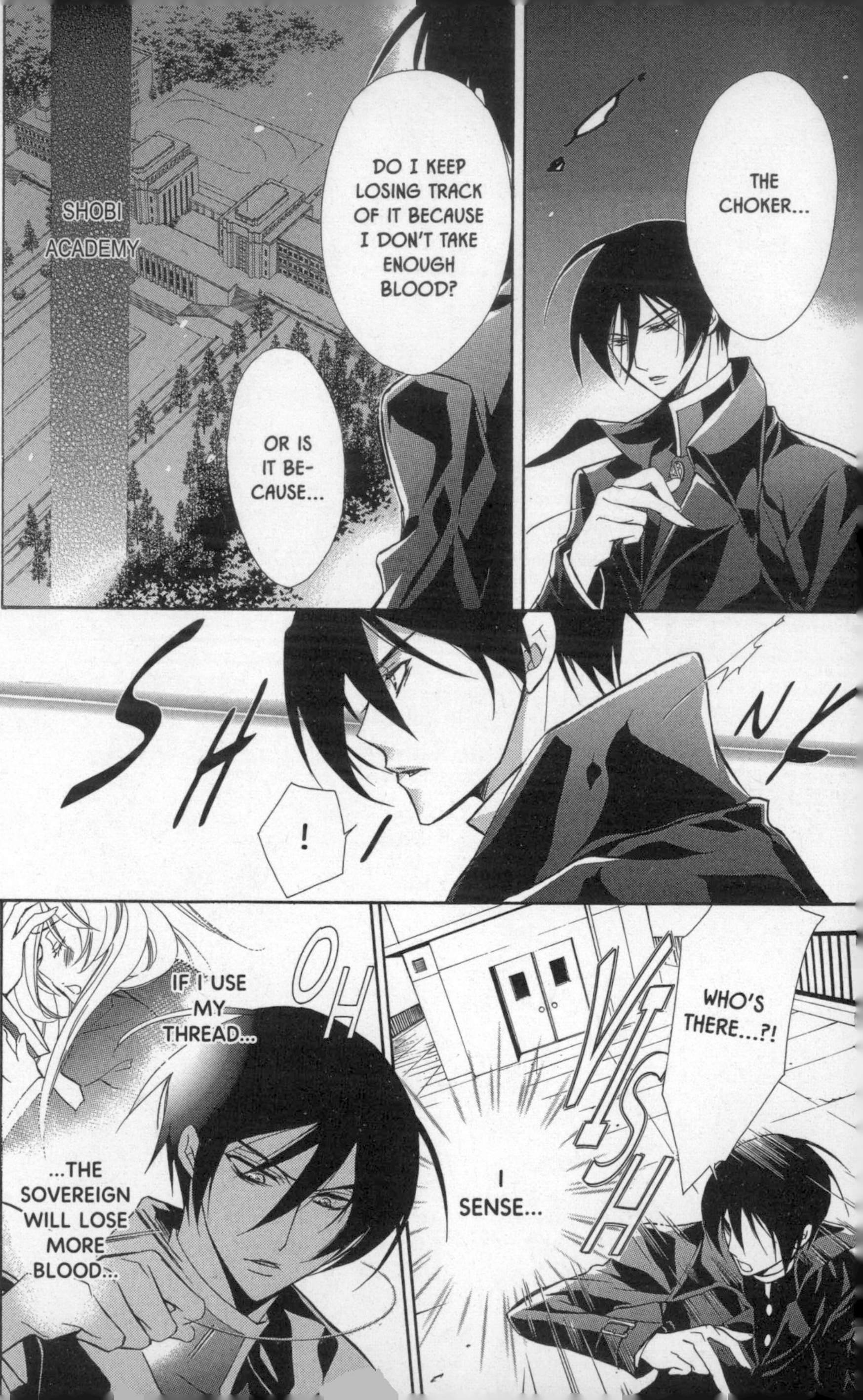
THE CHOKER...
DO I KEEP LOSING TRACK OF IT BECAUSE I DON'T TAKE ENOUGH BLOOD?
SHOBI ACADEMY
OR IS IT BE-CAUSE...
SHINK
!
WHO'S THERE...?!
IF I USE MY THREAD...
I SENSE...
...THE SOVEREIGN WILL LOSE MORE BLOOD...

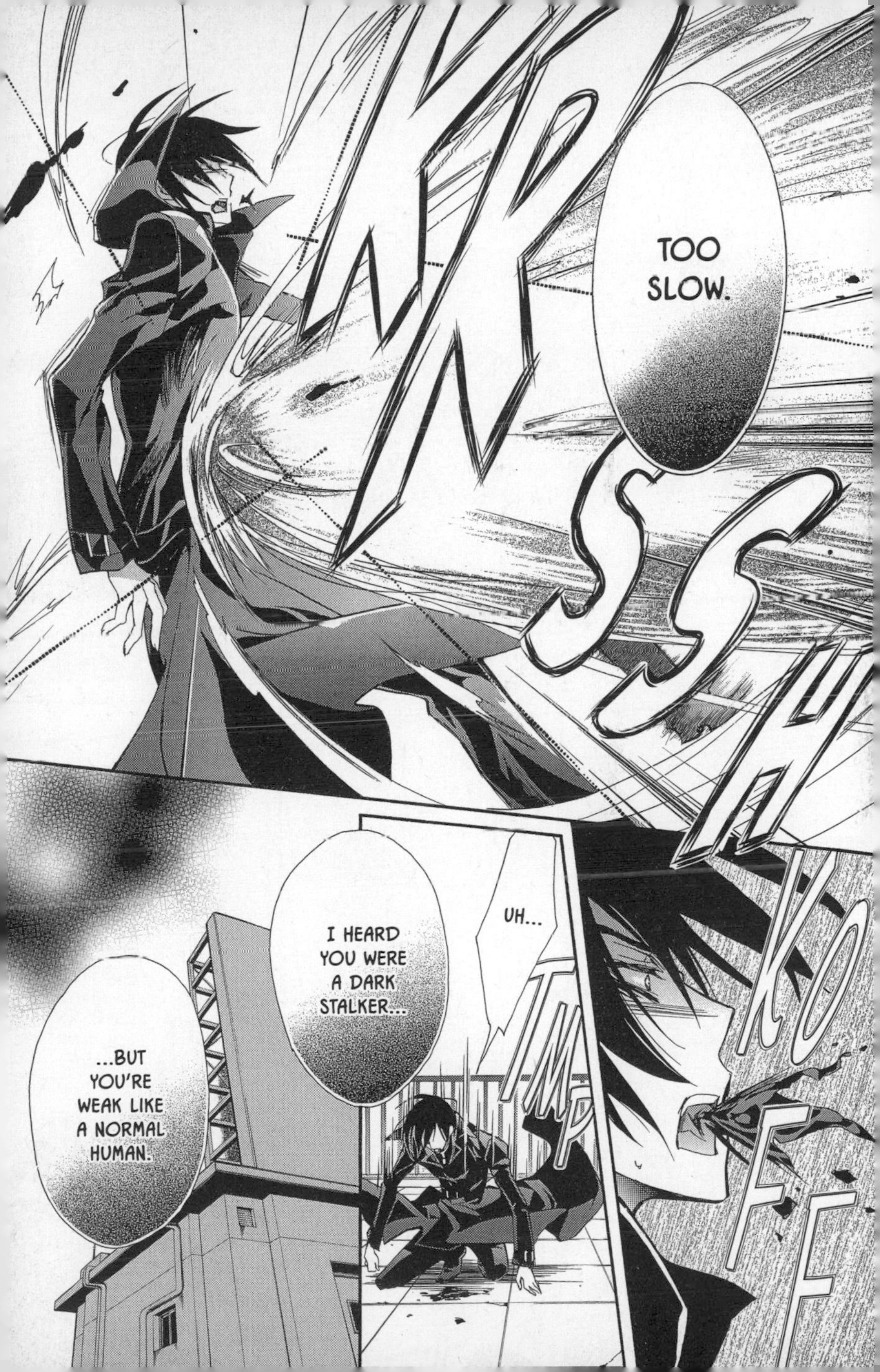

TOO SLOW.
UH...
I HEARD YOU WERE A DARK STALKER...
...BUT YOU'RE WEAK LIKE A NORMAL HUMAN.

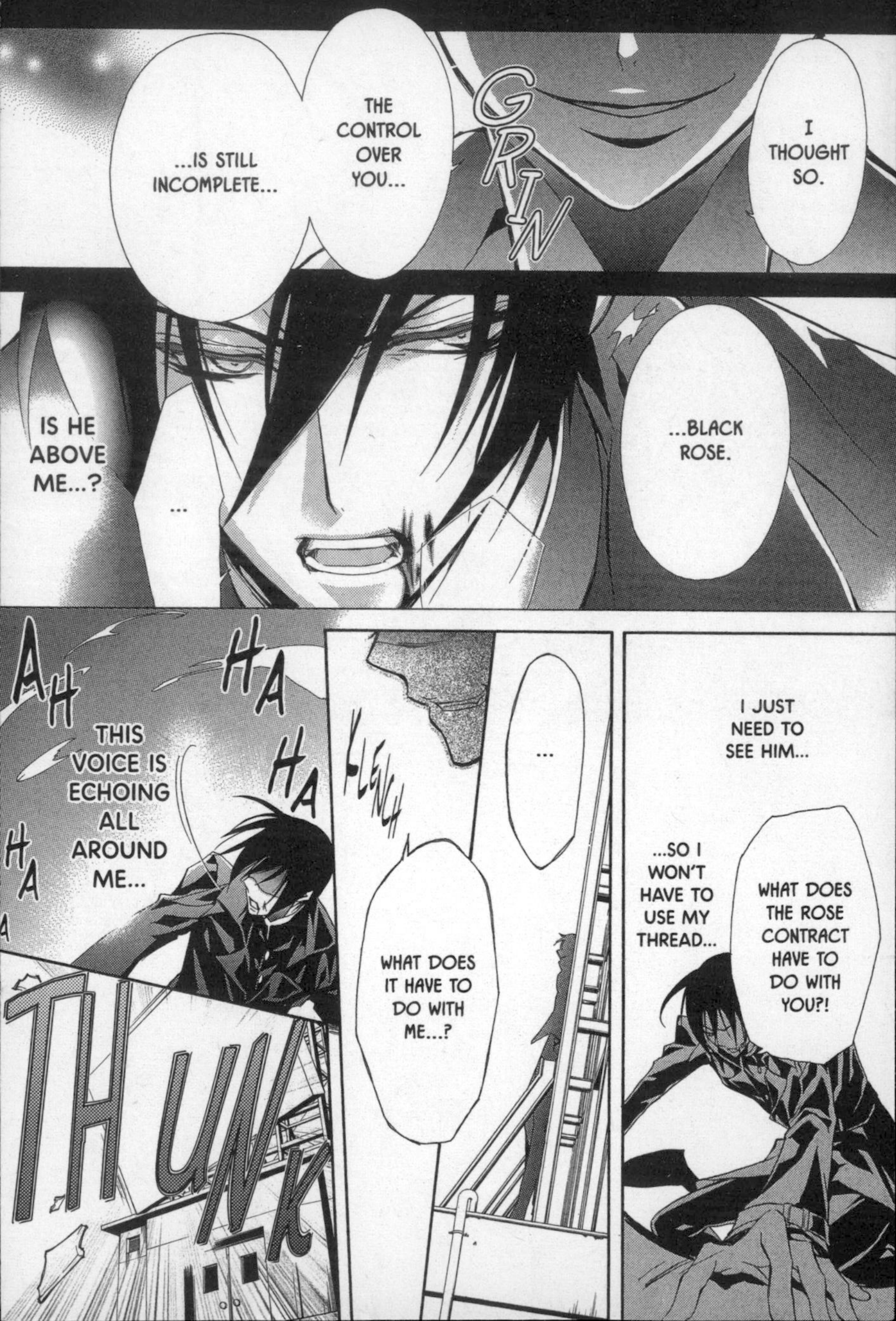
I THOUGHT SO.
GRIN
THE CONTROL OVER YOU...
...IS STILL INCOMPLETE...
...BLACK ROSE.
...
IS HE ABOVE ME...?
I JUST NEED TO SEE HIM...
WHAT DOES THE ROSE CONTRACT HAVE TO DO WITH YOU?!
...SO I WON'T HAVE TO USE MY THREAD...
...
KLENCH
WHAT DOES IT HAVE TO DO WITH ME...?
HA HA
AH
THIS VOICE IS ECHOING ALL AROUND ME...
HA HA
THUNK

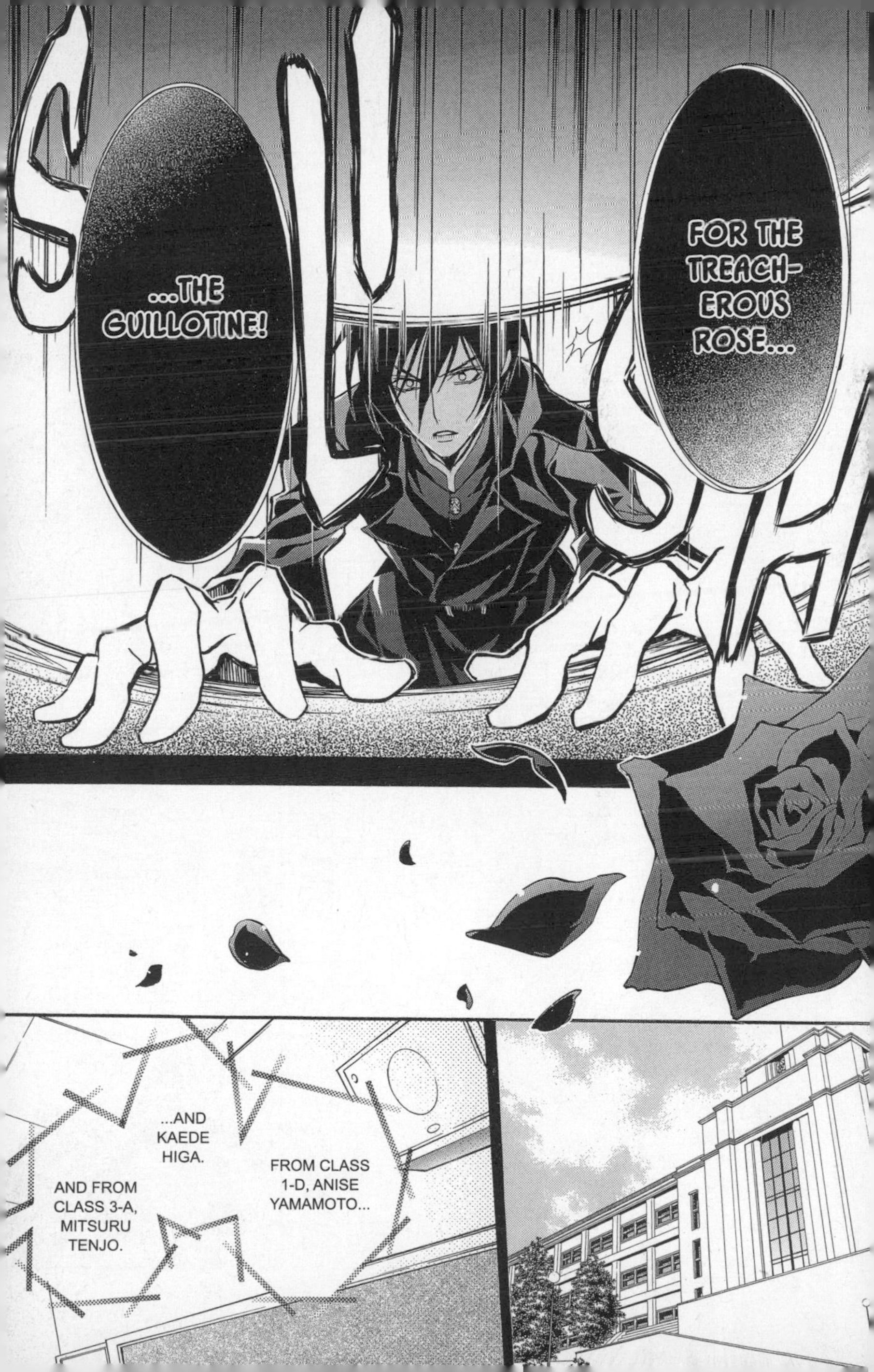
FOR THE TREACHEROUS ROSE...
...THE GUILLOTINE!
FROM CLASS 1-D, ANISE YAMAMOTO...
...AND KAEDE HIGA.
AND FROM CLASS 3-A, MITSURU TENJO.

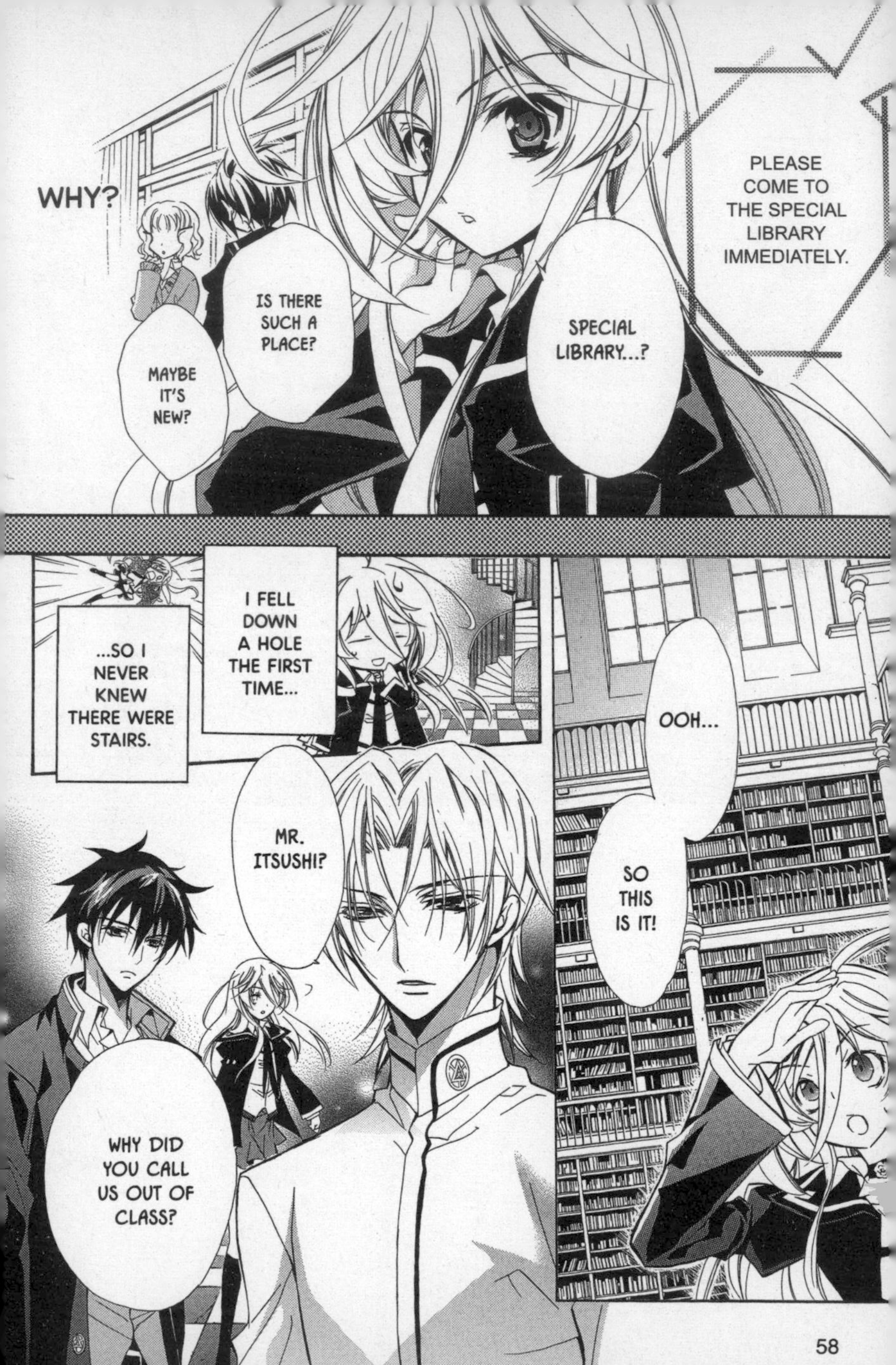
PLEASE COME TO THE SPECIAL LIBRARY IMMEDIATELY.
SPECIAL LIBRARY...?
IS THERE SUCH A PLACE?
MAYBE IT'S NEW?
WHY?
OOH...
SO THIS IS IT!
I FELL DOWN A HOLE THE FIRST TIME...
...SO I NEVER KNEW THERE WERE STAIRS.
MR. ITSUSHI?
WHY DID YOU CALL US OUT OF CLASS?

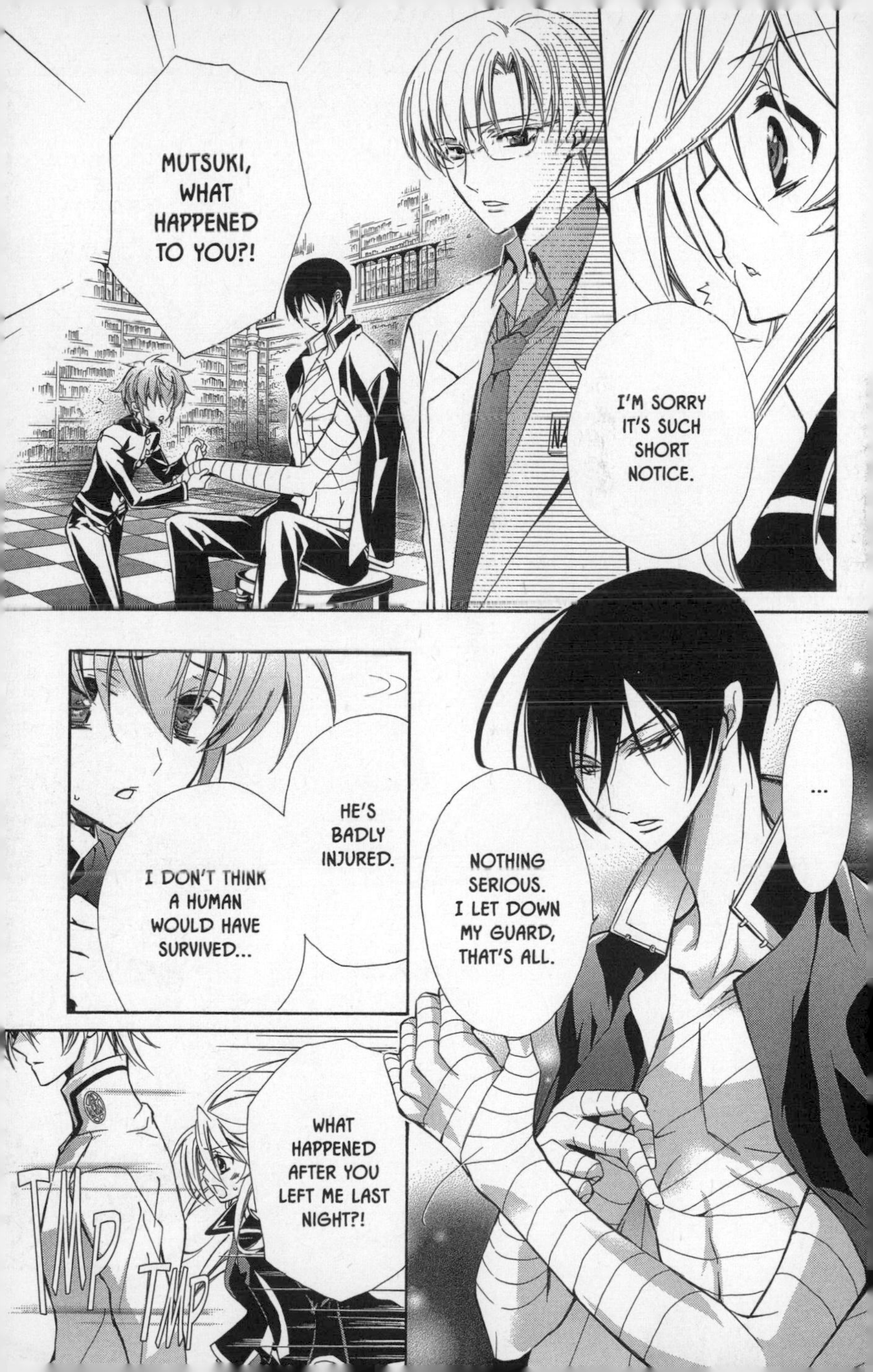
I'M SORRY IT'S SUCH SHORT NOTICE.
MUTSUKI, WHAT HAPPENED TO YOU?!
...
NOTHING SERIOUS. I LET DOWN MY GUARD, THAT'S ALL.
HE'S BADLY INJURED.
I DON'T THINK A HUMAN WOULD HAVE SURVIVED...
WHAT HAPPENED AFTER YOU LEFT ME LAST NIGHT?!
TMP TMP

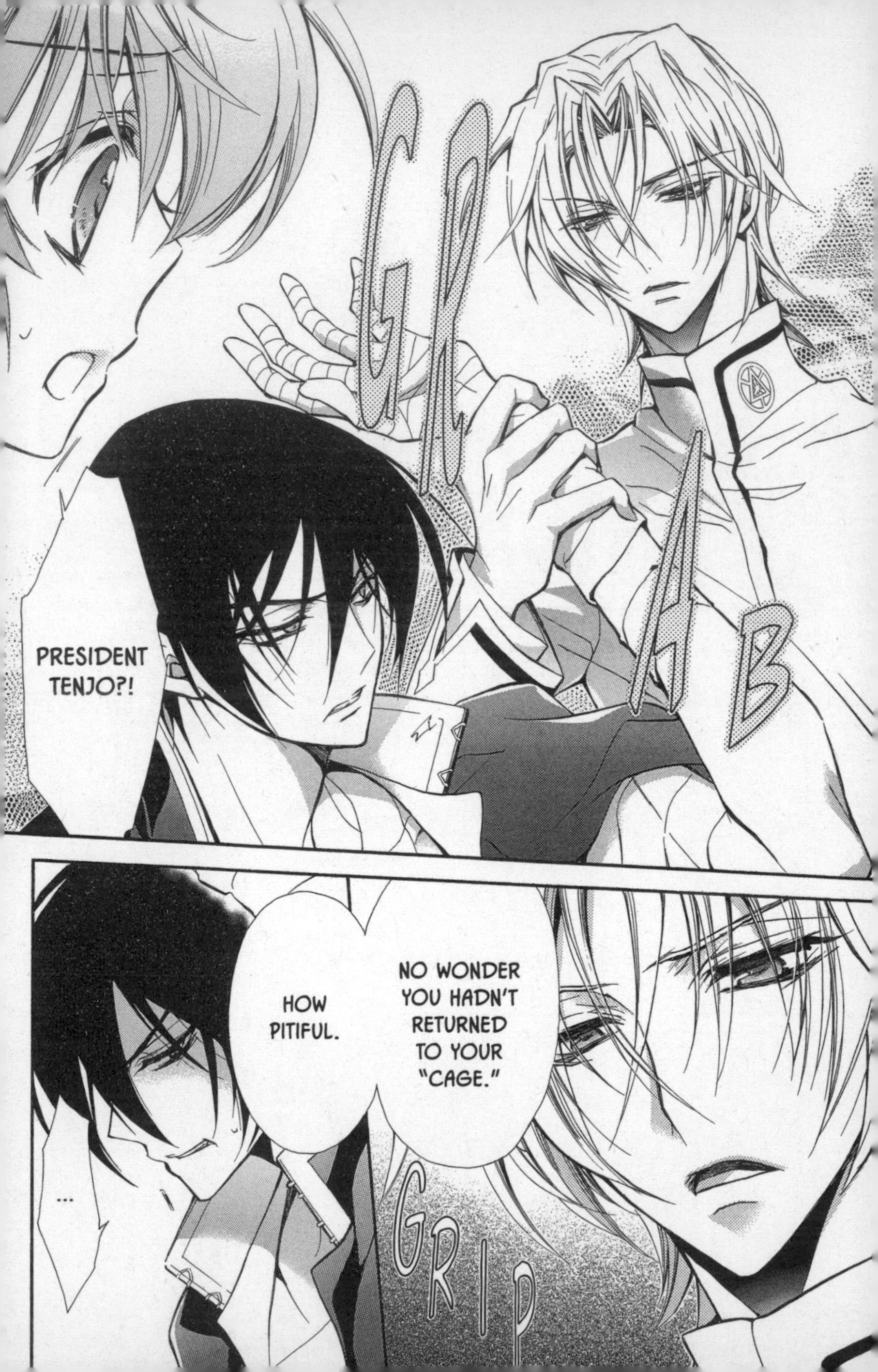
GRAB
PRESIDENT TENJO?!
NO WONDER YOU HADN'T RETURNED TO YOUR "CAGE."
HOW PITIFUL.
GRIP
...

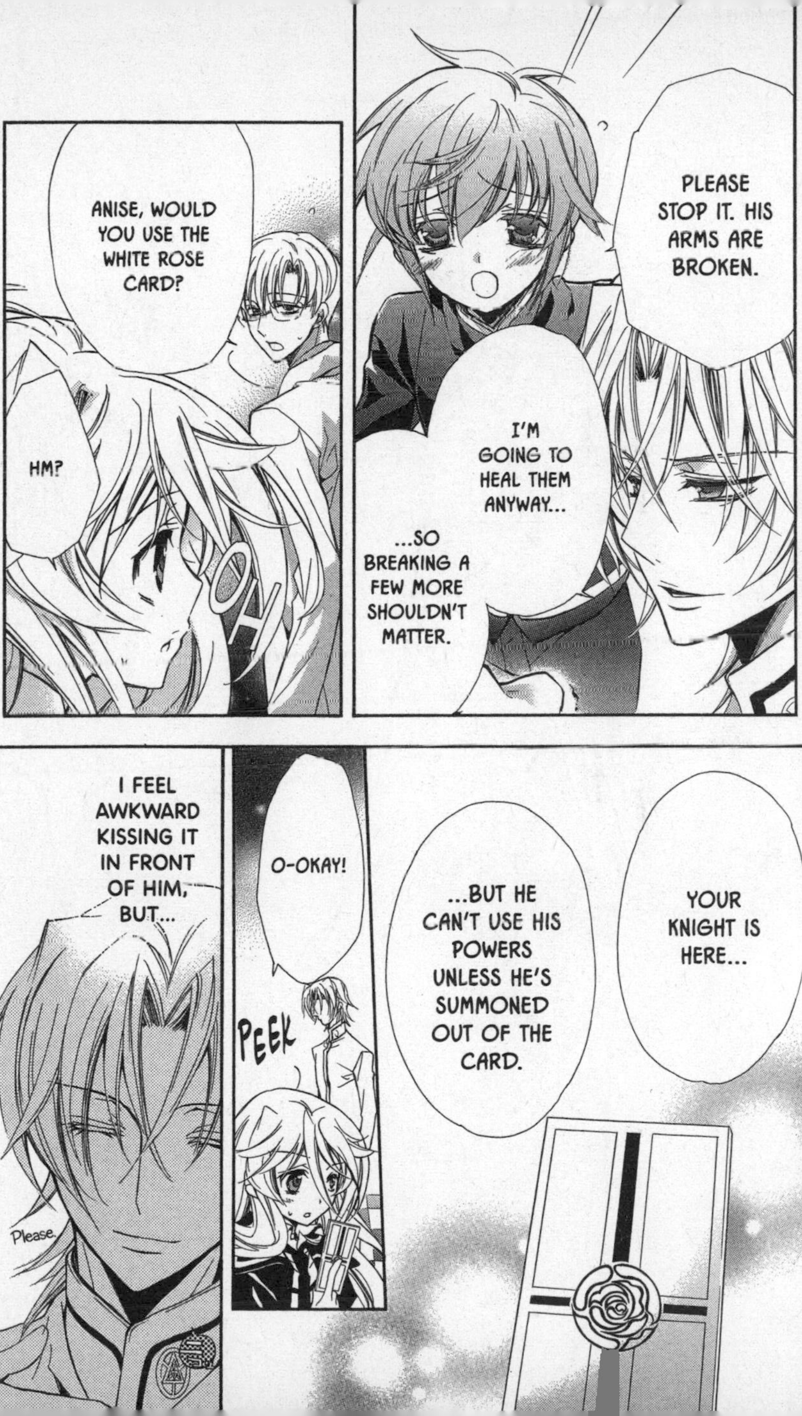
PLEASE STOP IT. HIS ARMS ARE BROKEN.
I'M GOING TO HEAL THEM ANYWAY...
...SO BREAKING A FEW MORE SHOULDN'T MATTER.
ANISE, WOULD YOU USE THE WHITE ROSE CARD?
HM?
OH
YOUR KNIGHT IS HERE...
...BUT HE CAN'T USE HIS POWERS UNLESS HE'S SUMMONED OUT OF THE CARD.
O-OKAY!
PEEK
I FEEL AWKWARD KISSING IT IN FRONT OF HIM, BUT...
Please.

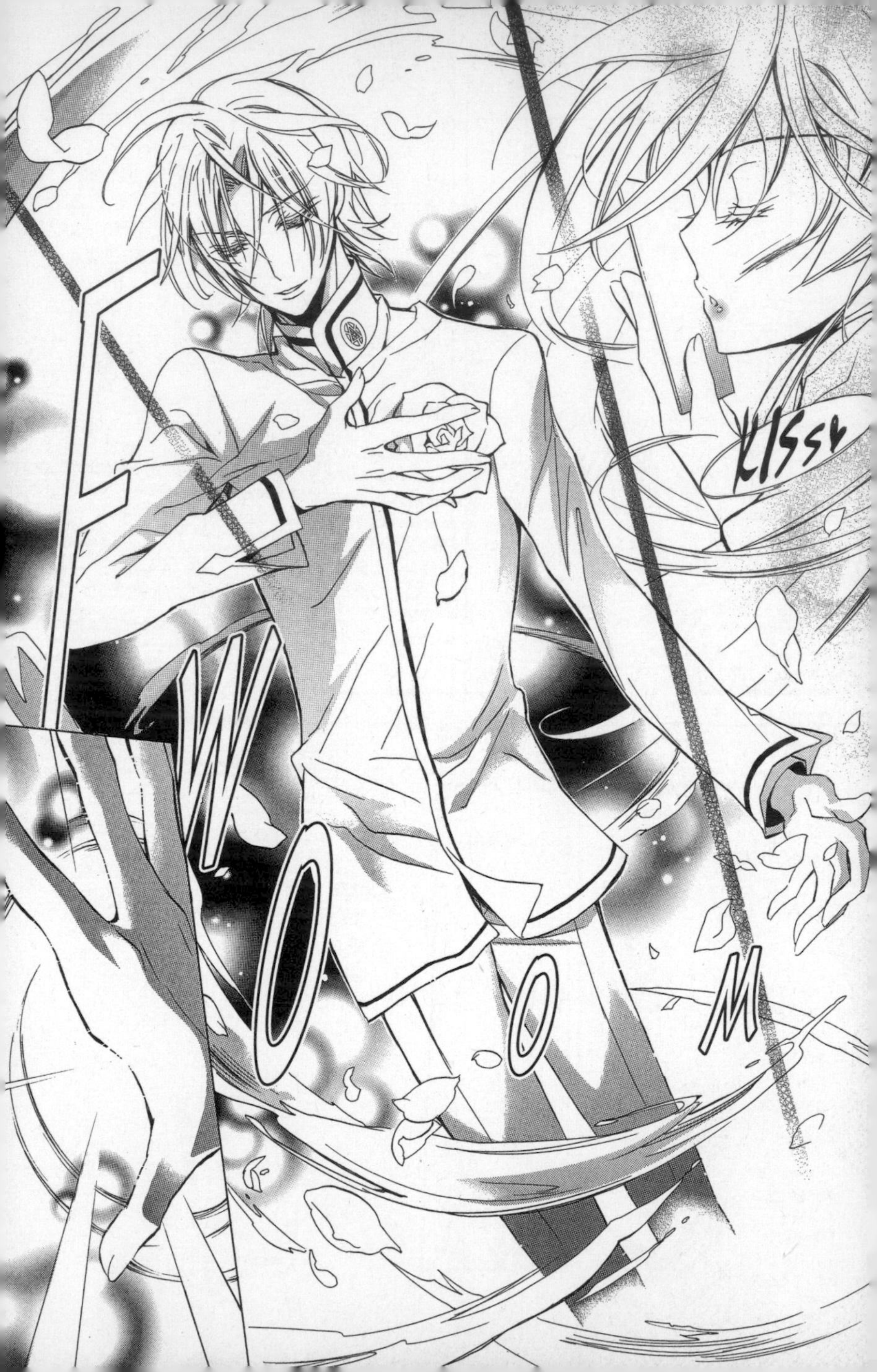
KISS♥
FWOOM

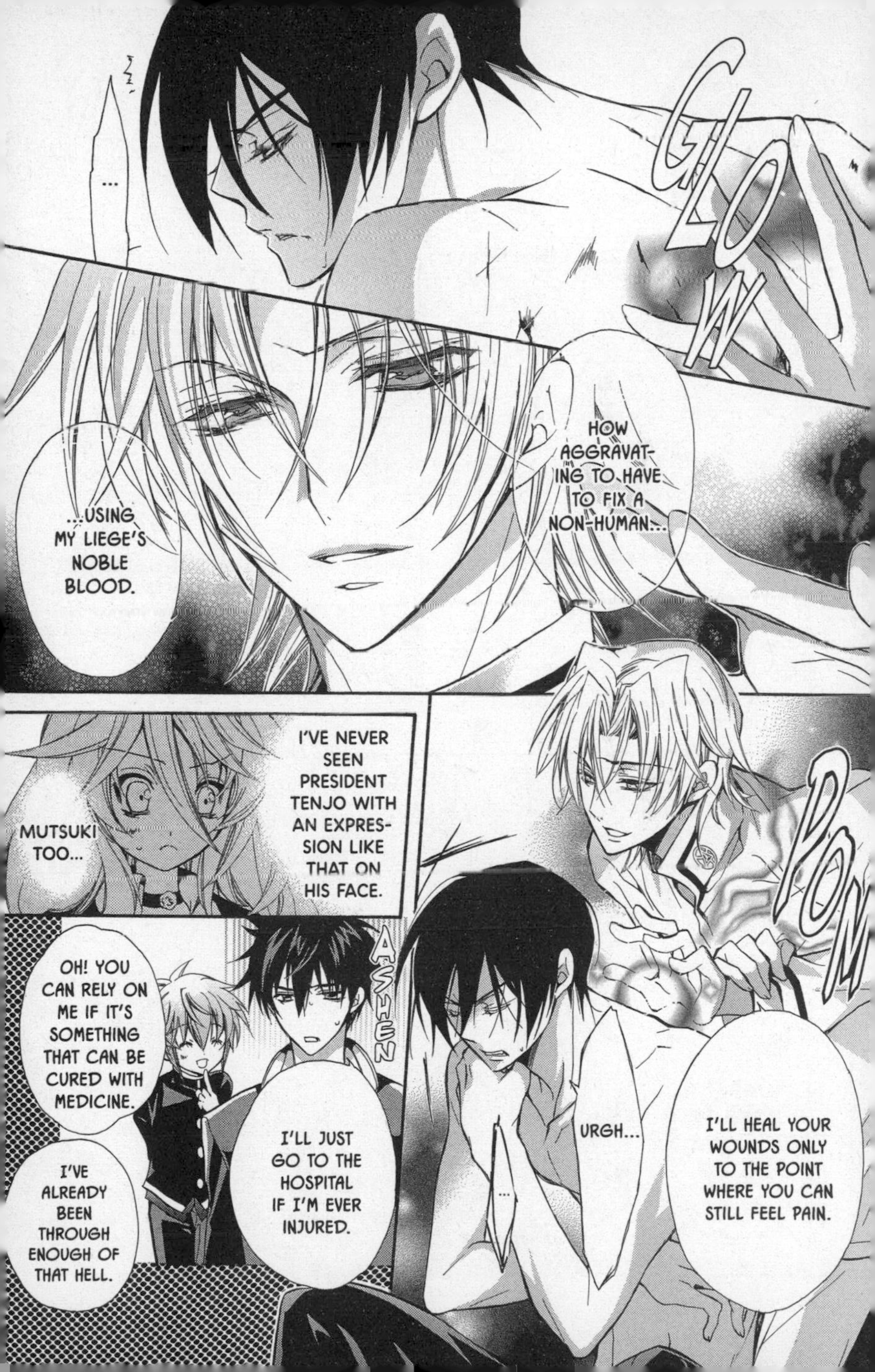
...
GLOW
HOW AGGRAVATING TO HAVE TO FIX A NON-HUMAN...
...USING MY LIEGE'S NOBLE BLOOD.
POM
I'LL HEAL YOUR WOUNDS ONLY TO THE POINT WHERE YOU CAN STILL FEEL PAIN.
URGH...
...
I'VE NEVER SEEN PRESIDENT TENJO WITH AN EXPRESSION LIKE THAT ON HIS FACE.
MUTSUKI TOO...
ASHEN
I'LL JUST GO TO THE HOSPITAL IF I'M EVER INJURED.
OH! YOU CAN RELY ON ME IF IT'S SOMETHING THAT CAN BE CURED WITH MEDICINE.
I'VE ALREADY BEEN THROUGH ENOUGH OF THAT HELL.

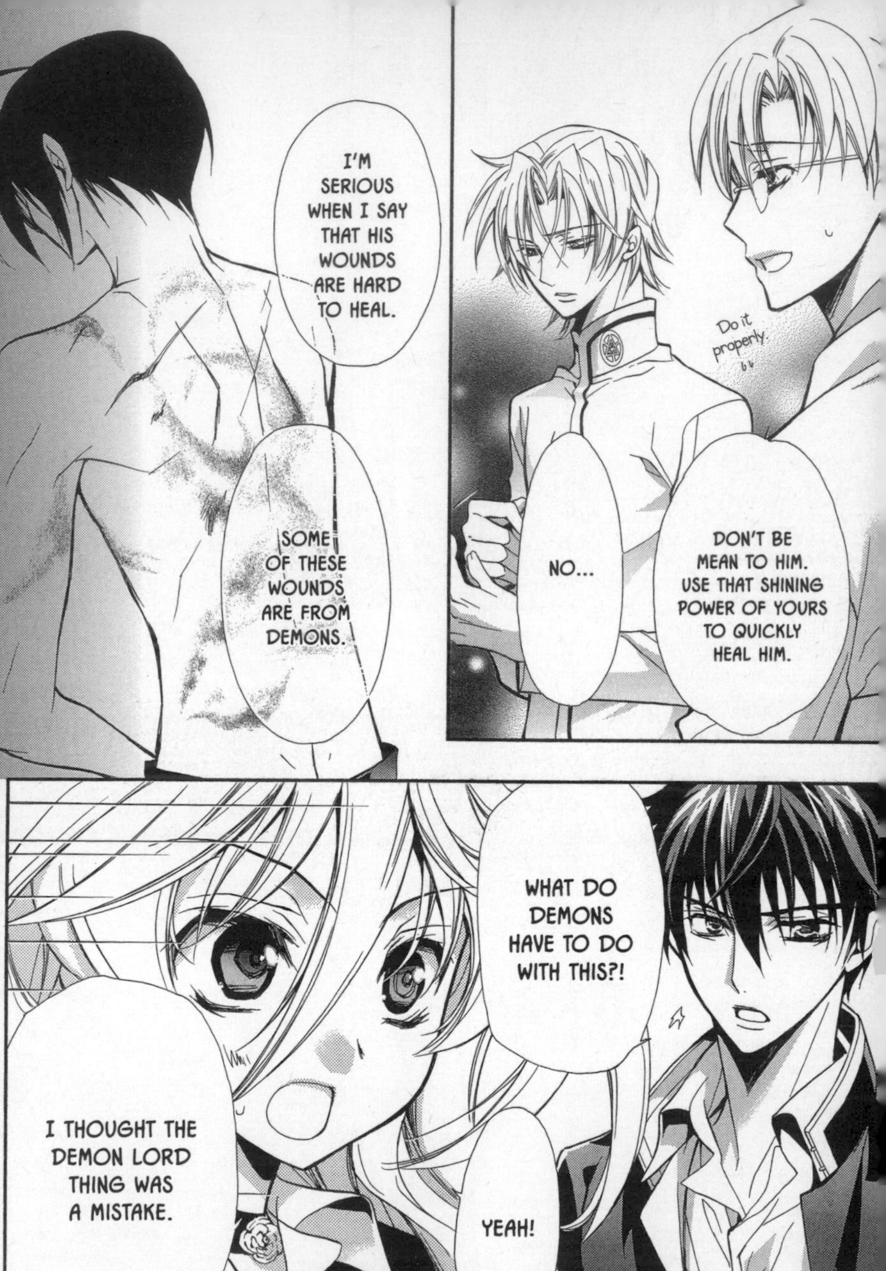
Do it properly.
DON'T BE MEAN TO HIM. USE THAT SHINING POWER OF YOURS TO QUICKLY HEAL HIM.
NO...
I'M SERIOUS WHEN I SAY THAT HIS WOUNDS ARE HARD TO HEAL.
SOME OF THESE WOUNDS ARE FROM DEMONS.
WHAT DO DEMONS HAVE TO DO WITH THIS?!
I THOUGHT THE DEMON LORD THING WAS A MISTAKE.
YEAH!

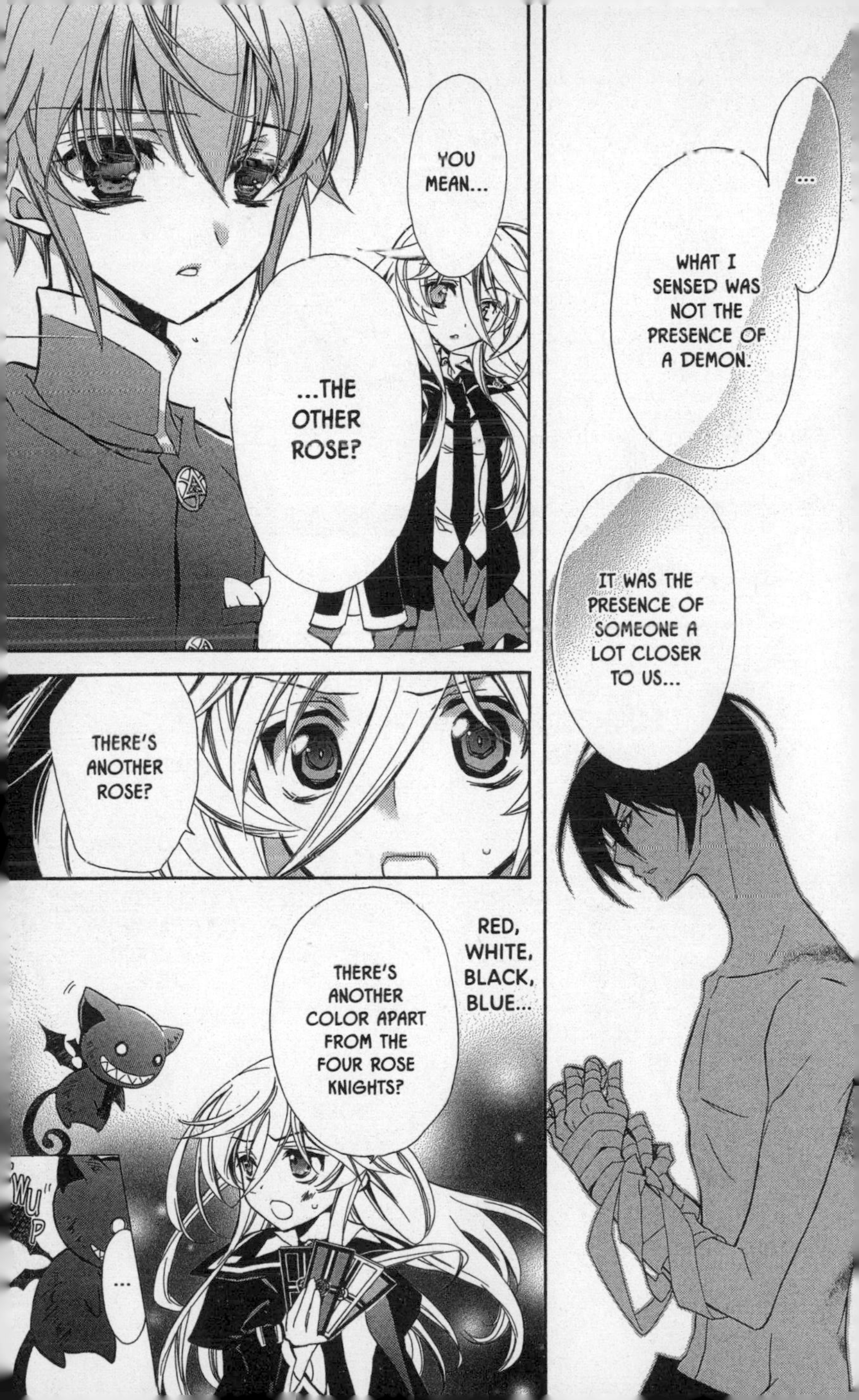
...
WHAT I SENSED WAS NOT THE PRESENCE OF A DEMON.
IT WAS THE PRESENCE OF SOMEONE A LOT CLOSER TO US...
YOU MEAN...
...THE OTHER ROSE?
THERE'S ANOTHER ROSE?
RED, WHITE, BLACK, BLUE...
THERE'S ANOTHER COLOR APART FROM THE FOUR ROSE KNIGHTS?
WUP
...

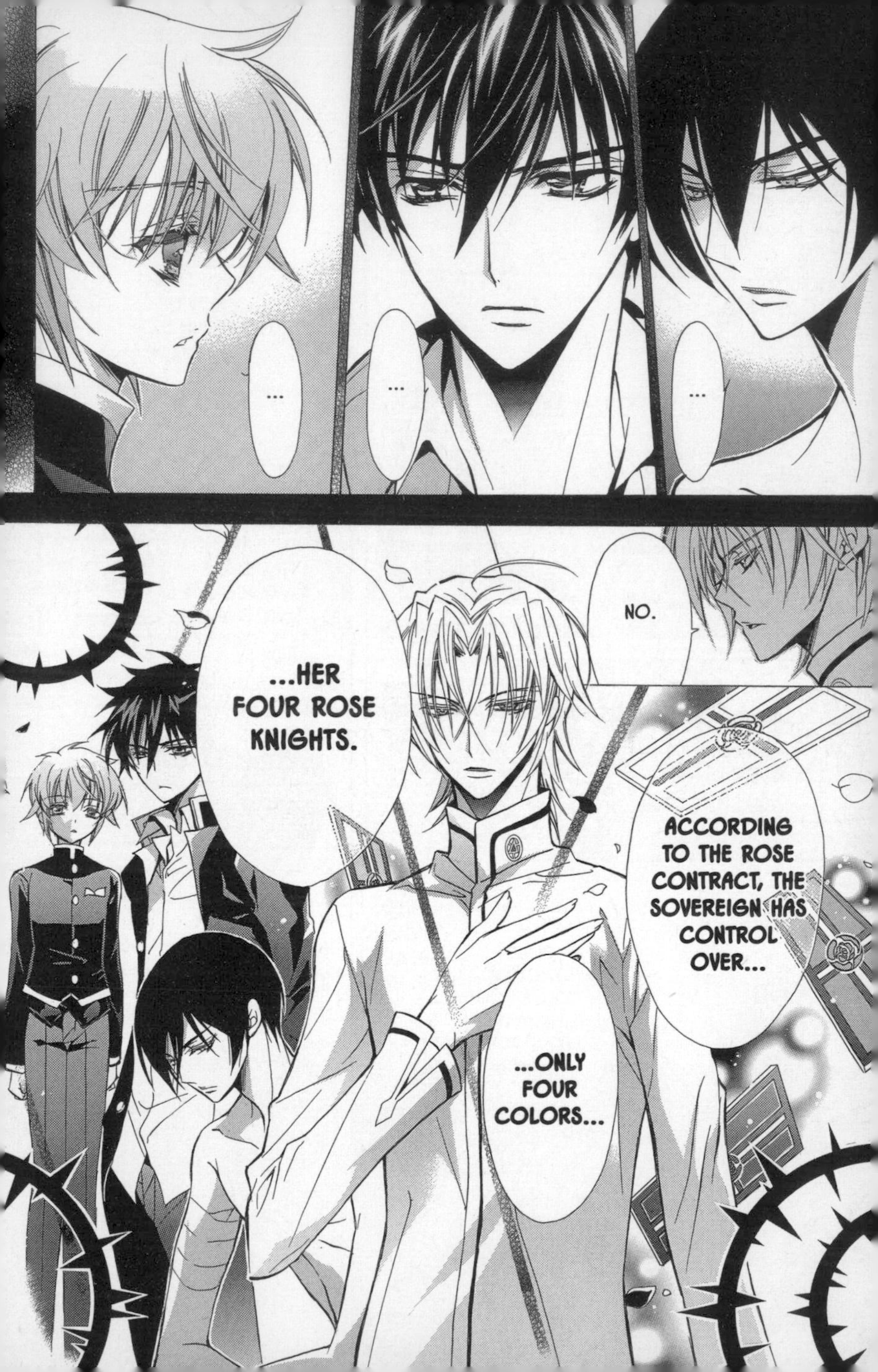
...
...
...
NO.
ACCORDING TO THE ROSE CONTRACT, THE SOVEREIGN HAS CONTROL OVER...
...ONLY FOUR COLORS...
...HER FOUR ROSE KNIGHTS.

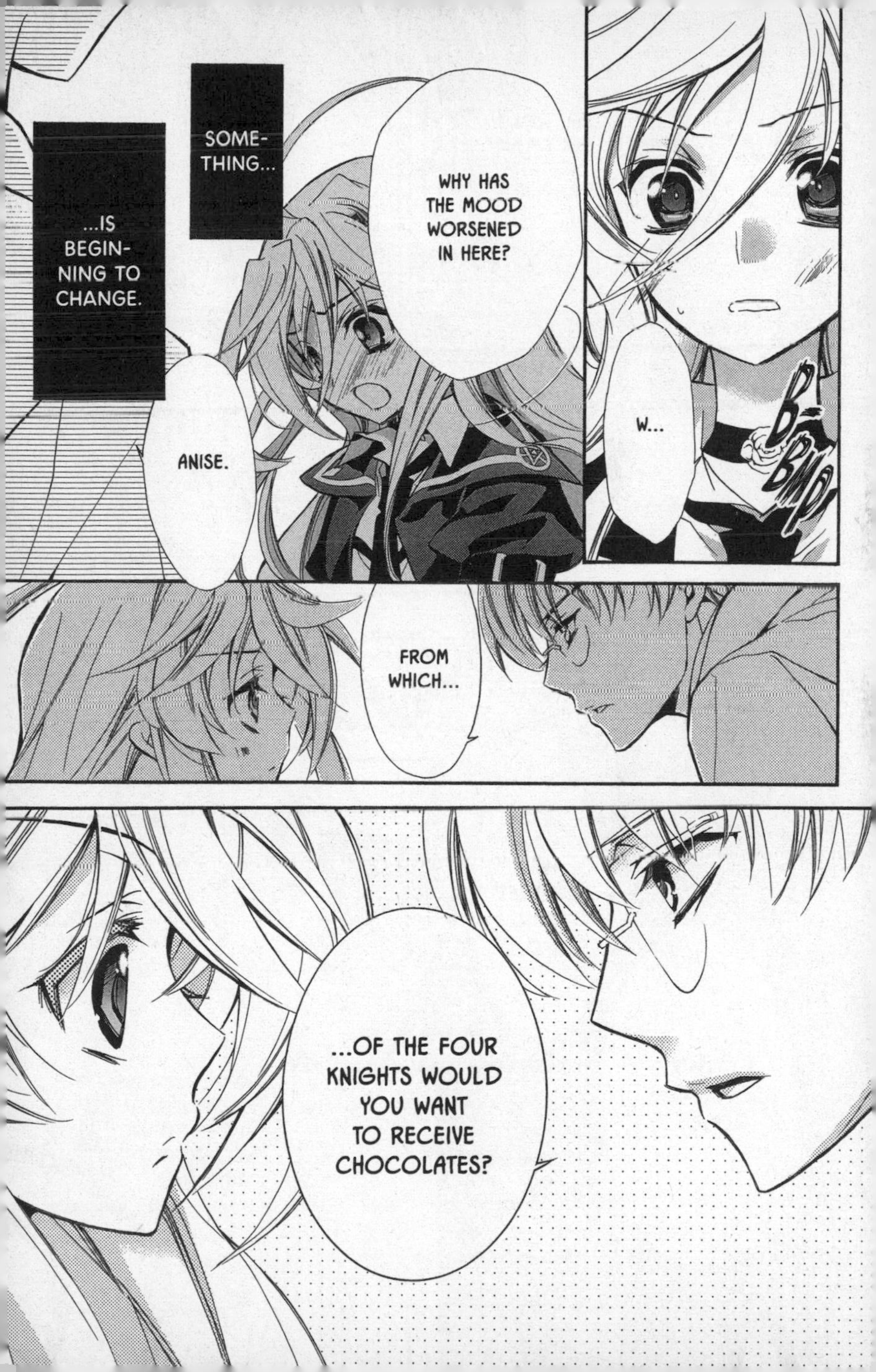
W...
B-BMP
WHY HAS THE MOOD WORSENED IN HERE?
SOME-THING...
...IS BEGIN-NING TO CHANGE.
ANISE.
FROM WHICH...
...OF THE FOUR KNIGHTS WOULD YOU WANT TO RECEIVE CHOCOLATES?

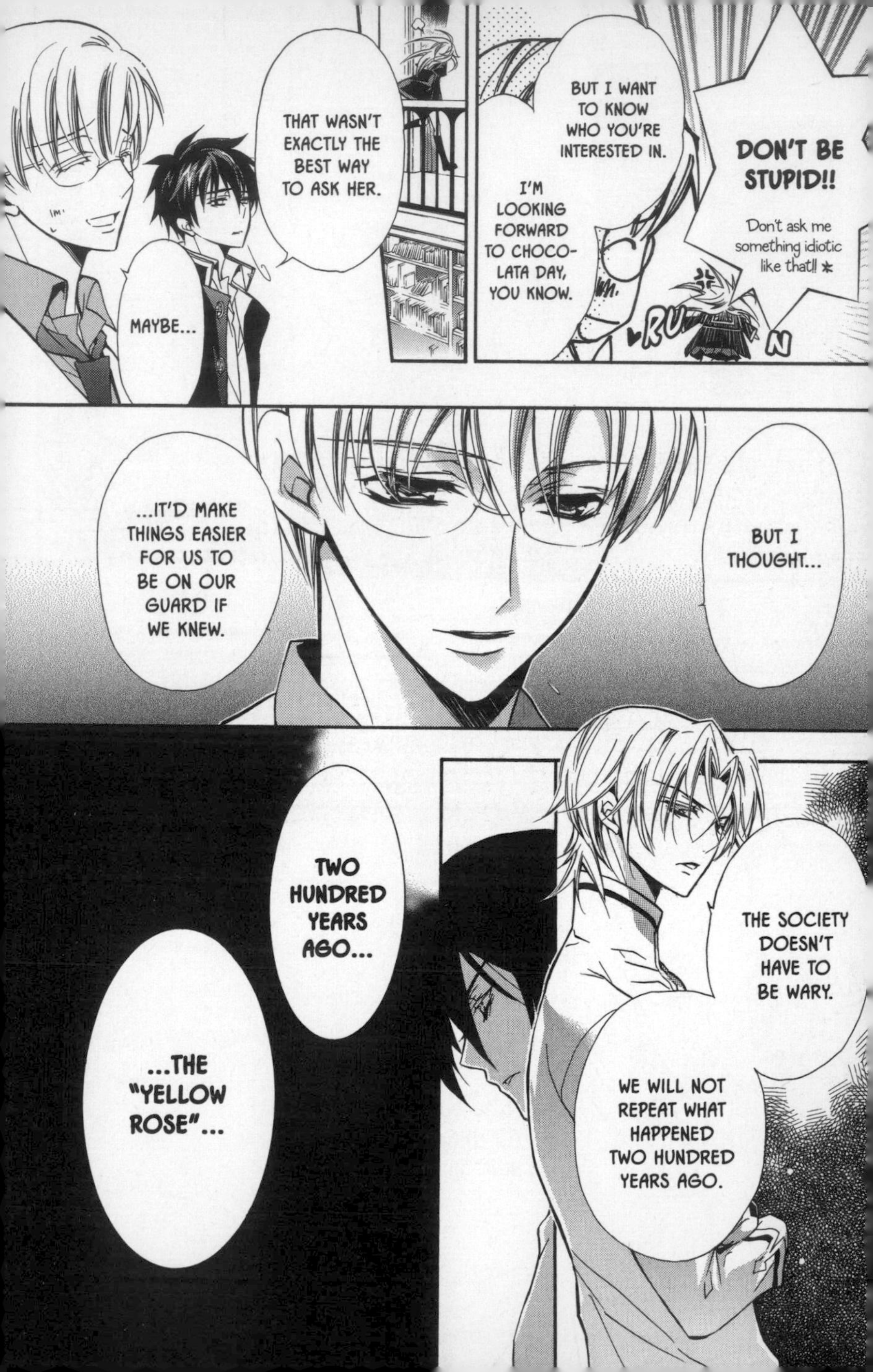
BUT I WANT TO KNOW WHO YOU'RE INTERESTED IN.
I'M LOOKING FORWARD TO CHOCO-LATA DAY, YOU KNOW.
DON'T BE STUPID!!
Don't ask me something idiotic like that!! *
RUN
THAT WASN'T EXACTLY THE BEST WAY TO ASK HER.
MAYBE...
BUT I THOUGHT...
...IT'D MAKE THINGS EASIER FOR US TO BE ON OUR GUARD IF WE KNEW.
THE SOCIETY DOESN'T HAVE TO BE WARY.
WE WILL NOT REPEAT WHAT HAPPENED TWO HUNDRED YEARS AGO.
TWO HUNDRED YEARS AGO...
...THE "YELLOW ROSE"...

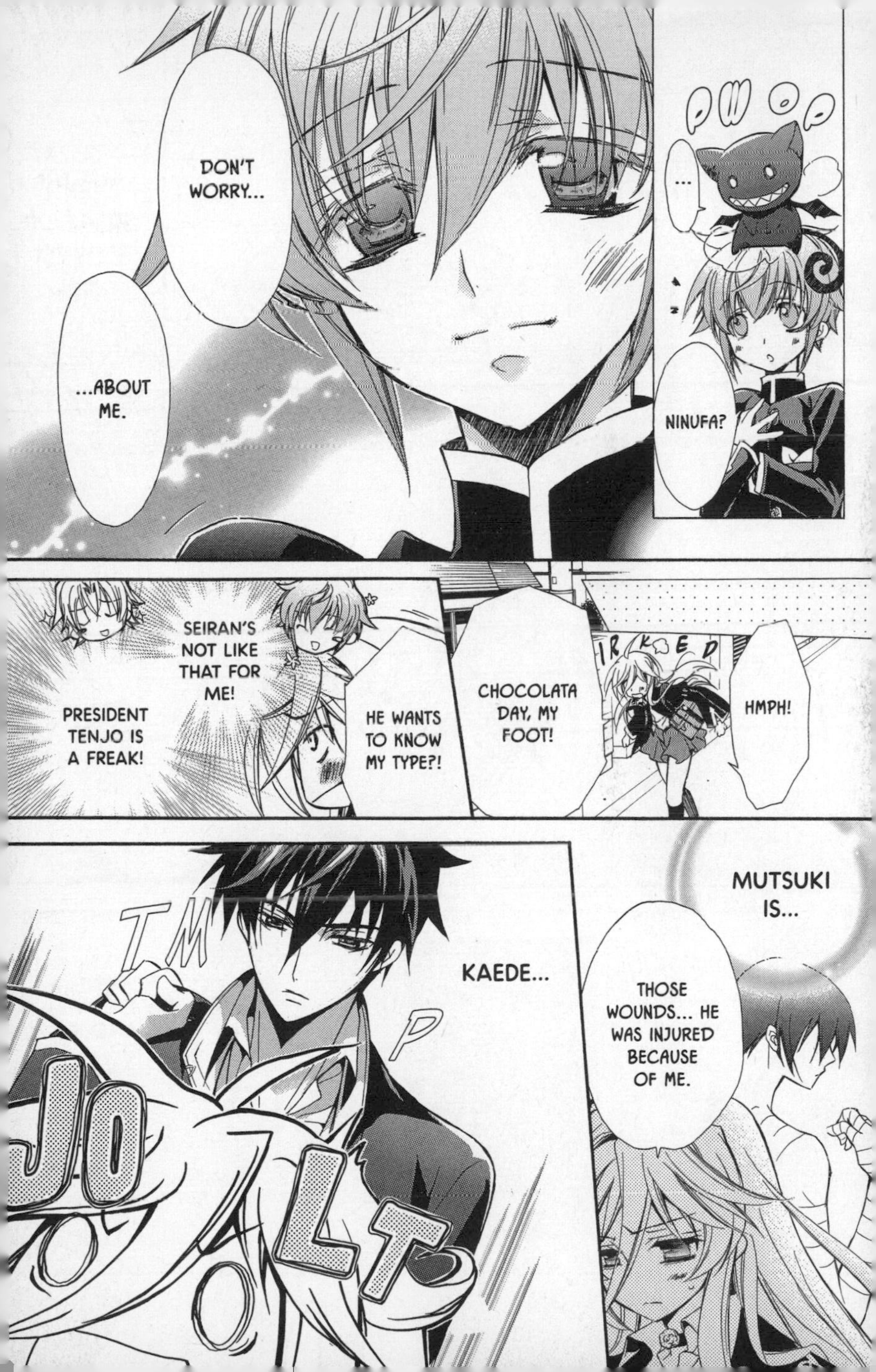
…
NINUFA?
DON'T WORRY…
…ABOUT ME.
HMPH!
IRKED
CHOCOLATA DAY, MY FOOT!
HE WANTS TO KNOW MY TYPE?!
SEIRAN'S NOT LIKE THAT FOR ME!
PRESIDENT TENJO IS A FREAK!
MUTSUKI IS…
THOSE WOUNDS… HE WAS INJURED BECAUSE OF ME.
KAEDE…
TMP
JOLT

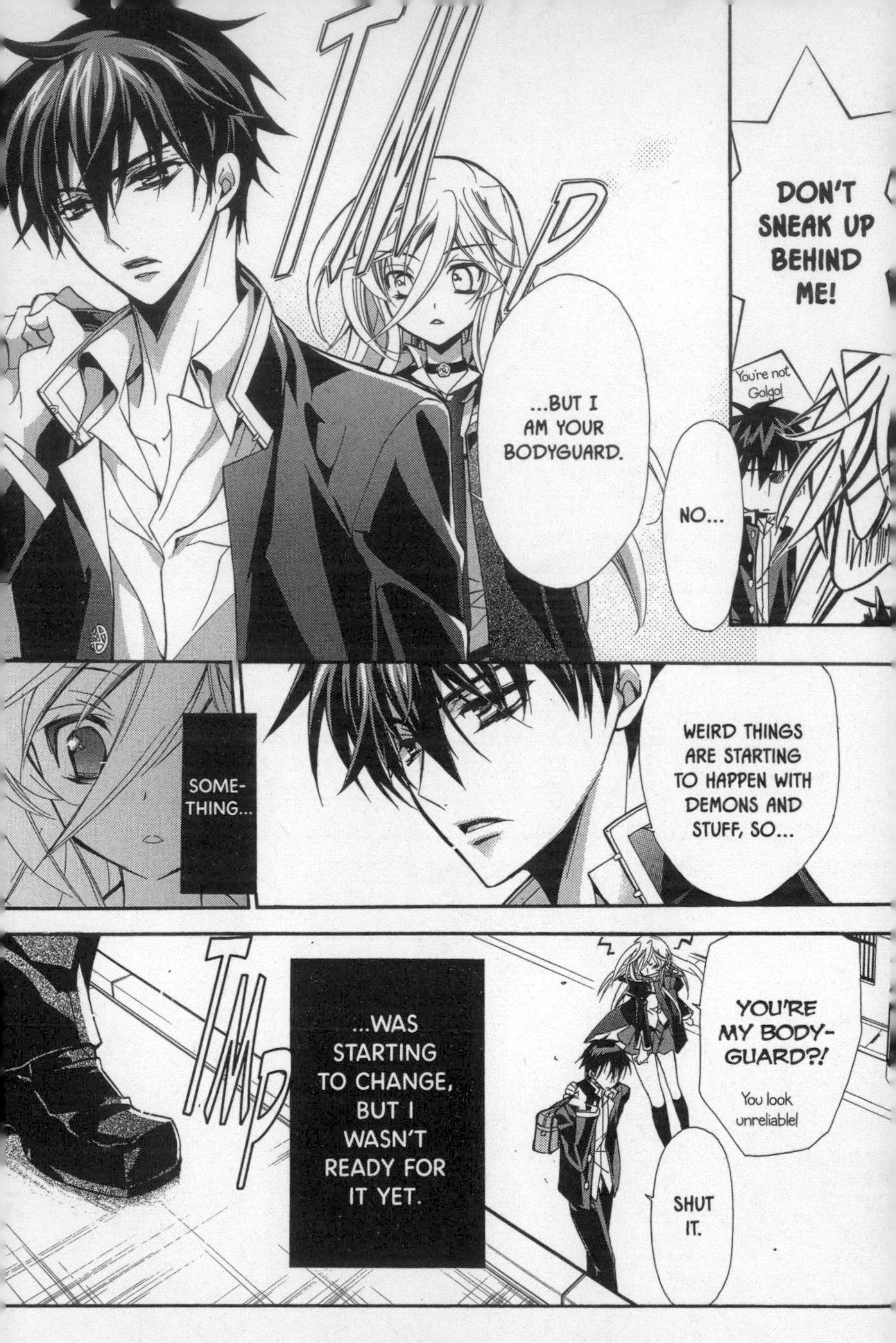
DON'T SNEAK UP BEHIND ME!
You're not Golgo!
NO...
...BUT I AM YOUR BODYGUARD.
WEIRD THINGS ARE STARTING TO HAPPEN WITH DEMONS AND STUFF, SO...
SOME-THING...
YOU'RE MY BODY-GUARD?!
You look unreliable!
SHUT IT.
...WAS STARTING TO CHANGE, BUT I WASN'T READY FOR IT YET.

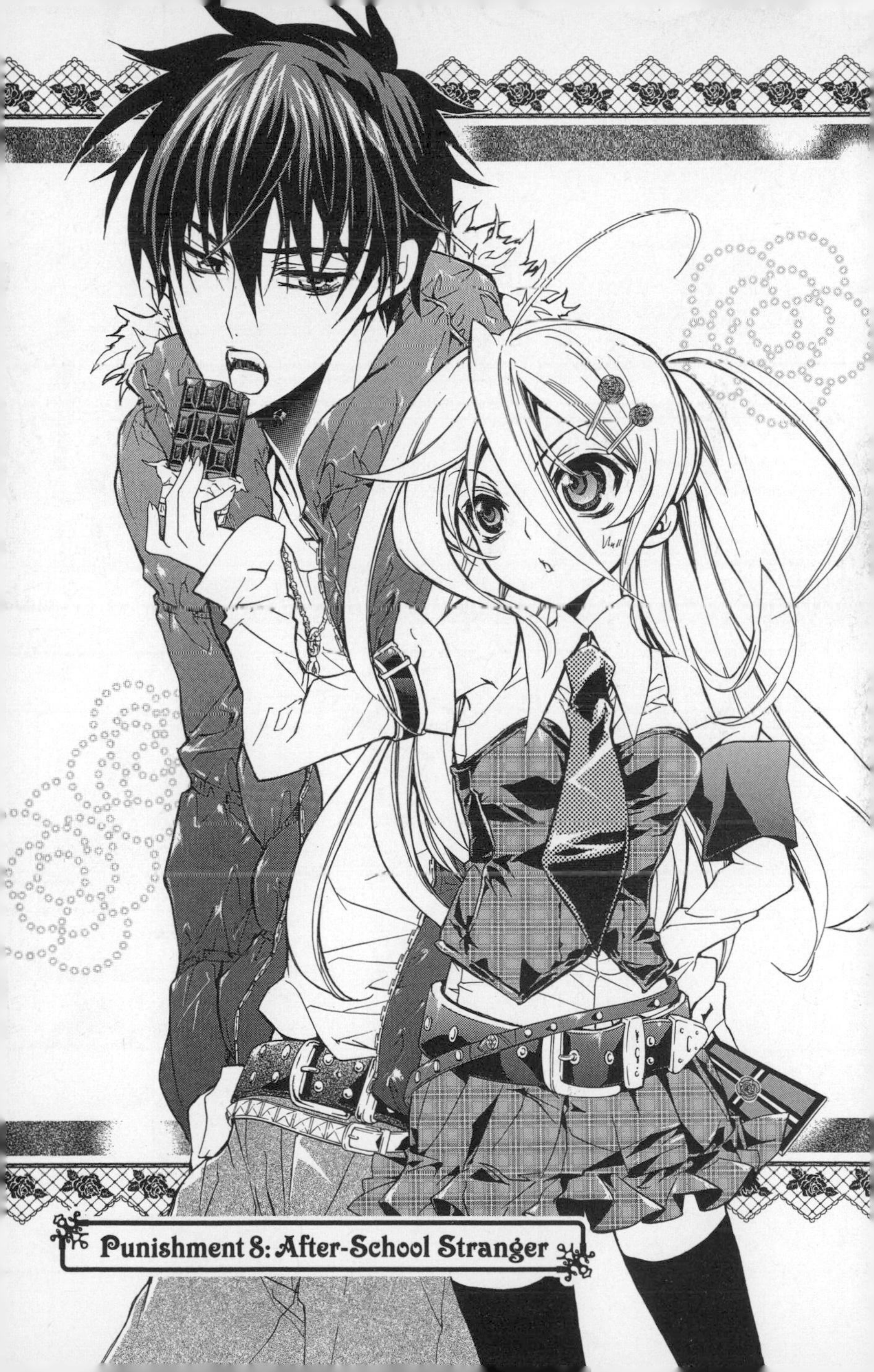

Punishment 8: After-School Stranger

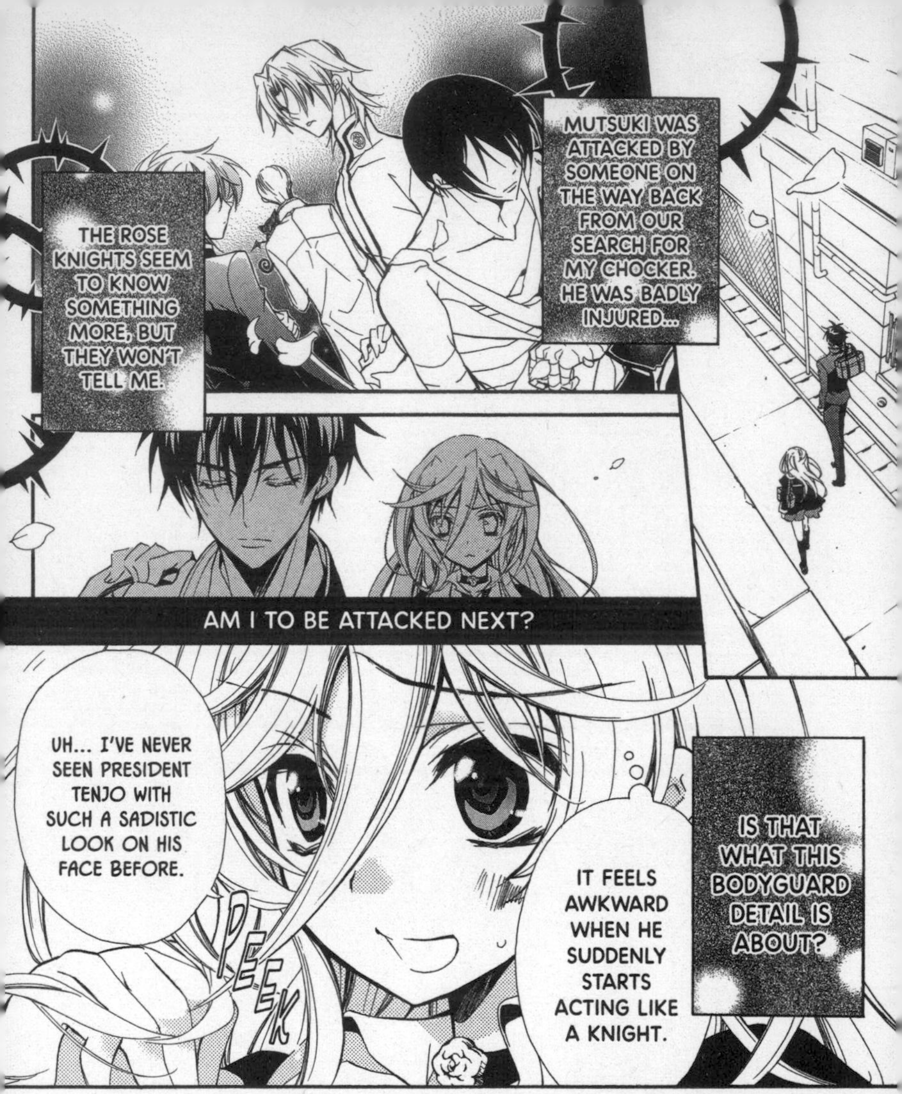
MUTSUKI WAS ATTACKED BY SOMEONE ON THE WAY BACK FROM OUR SEARCH FOR MY CHOCKER. HE WAS BADLY INJURED...
THE ROSE KNIGHTS SEEM TO KNOW SOMETHING MORE, BUT THEY WON'T TELL ME.
AM I TO BE ATTACKED NEXT?
IS THAT WHAT THIS BODYGUARD DETAIL IS ABOUT?
IT FEELS AWKWARD WHEN HE SUDDENLY STARTS ACTING LIKE A KNIGHT.
UH... I'VE NEVER SEEN PRESIDENT TENJO WITH SUCH A SADISTIC LOOK ON HIS FACE BEFORE.
PEEK

Ninufa

A baby dragon. No matter what anyone says, I say that Ninufa is a baby dragon. (The large form is its true form!!) The guardian of the cards. Ninufa loves cream puffs.

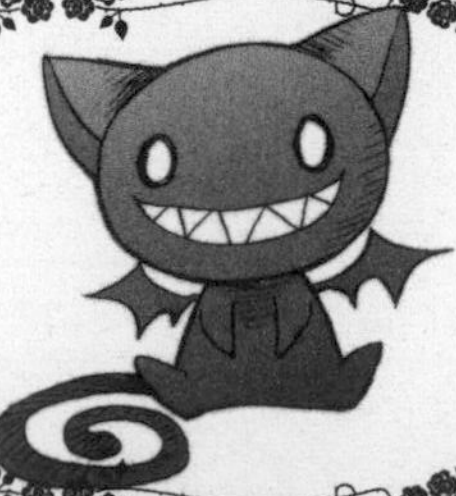

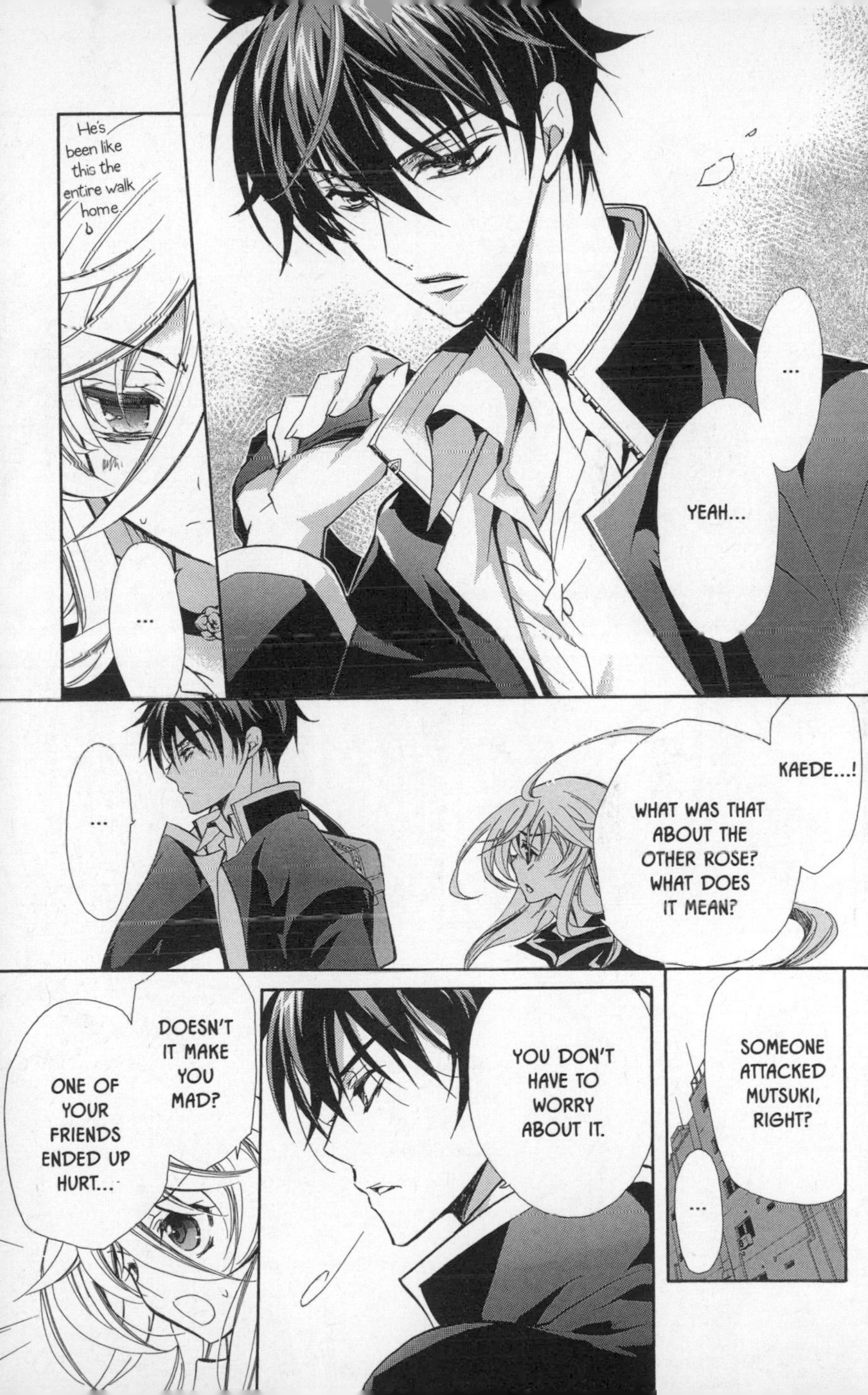
...
YEAH...
He's been like this the entire walk home.
...
KAEDE...! WHAT WAS THAT ABOUT THE OTHER ROSE? WHAT DOES IT MEAN?
...
SOMEONE ATTACKED MUTSUKI, RIGHT?
...
YOU DON'T HAVE TO WORRY ABOUT IT.
DOESN'T IT MAKE YOU MAD?
ONE OF YOUR FRIENDS ENDED UP HURT...

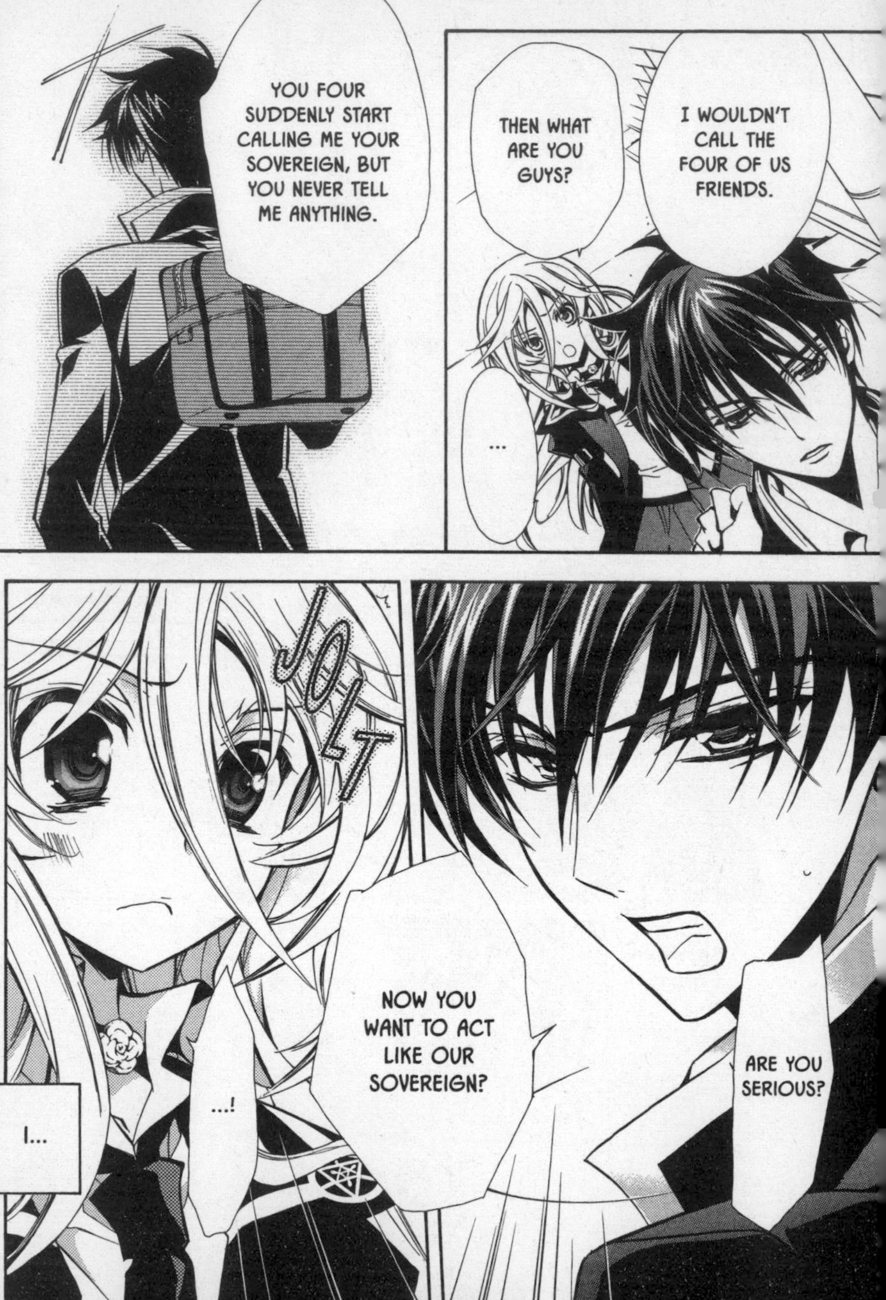
I WOULDN'T CALL THE FOUR OF US FRIENDS.
THEN WHAT ARE YOU GUYS?
...
YOU FOUR SUDDENLY START CALLING ME YOUR SOVEREIGN, BUT YOU NEVER TELL ME ANYTHING.
ARE YOU SERIOUS?
NOW YOU WANT TO ACT LIKE OUR SOVEREIGN?
JOLT
...!
I...

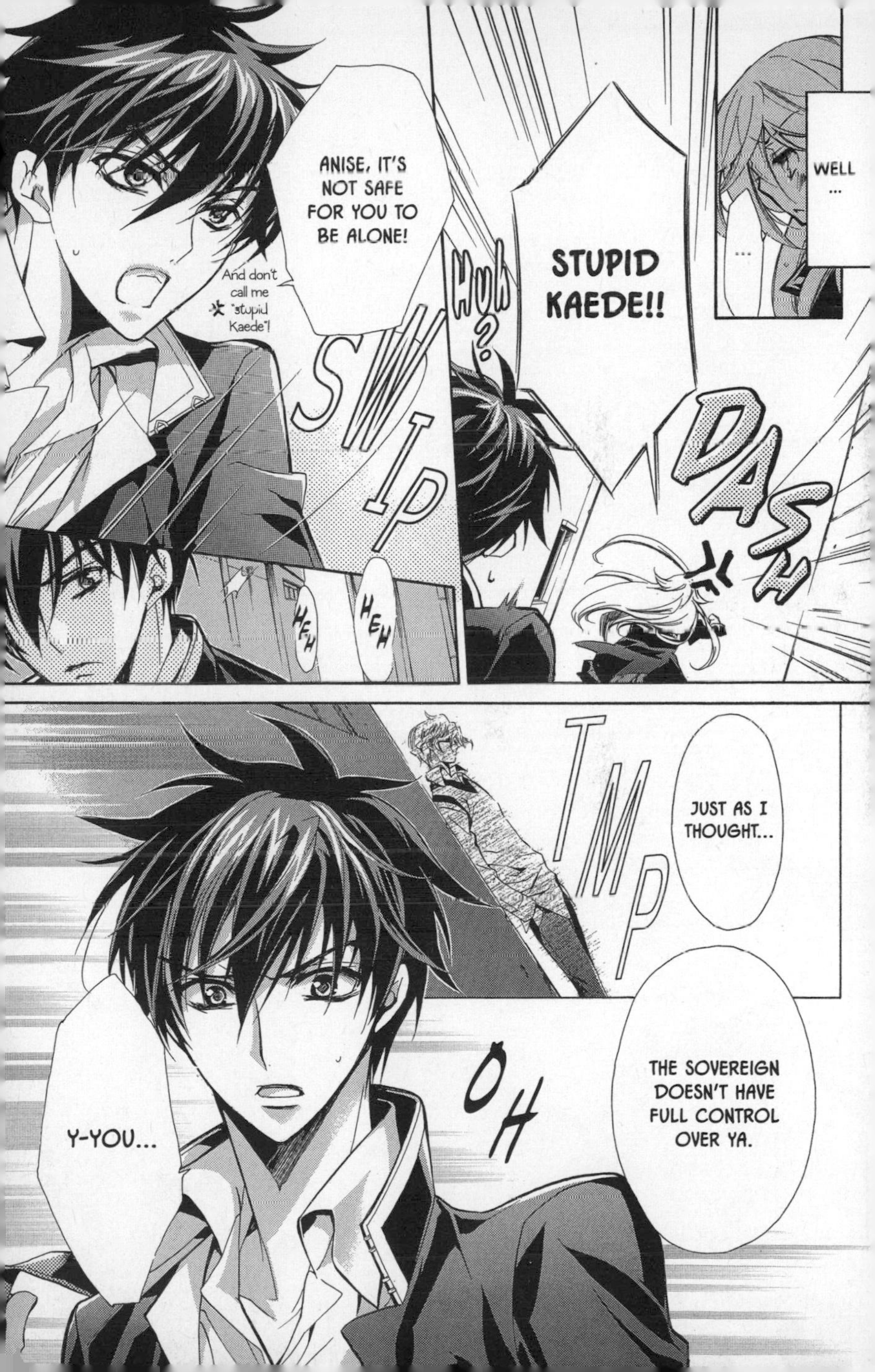
WELL ...
...
STUPID KAEDE!!
Huh?
DASH
ANISE, IT'S NOT SAFE FOR YOU TO BE ALONE!
And don't call me "stupid Kaede"!
SWIP
HEH
HEH
JUST AS I THOUGHT...
TMP
THE SOVEREIGN DOESN'T HAVE FULL CONTROL OVER YA.
OH
Y-YOU...

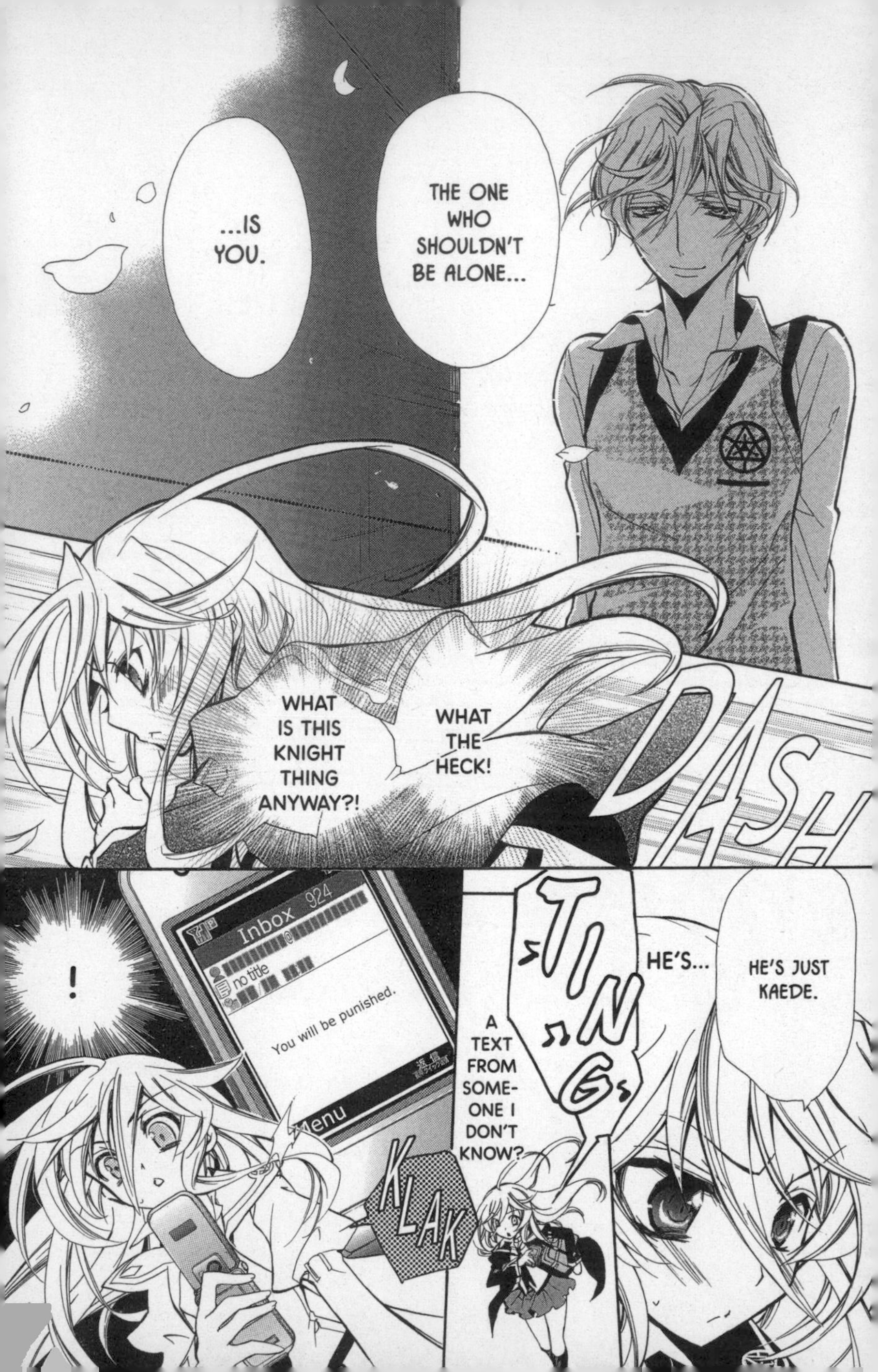
THE ONE WHO SHOULDN'T BE ALONE...
...IS YOU.
DASH
WHAT THE HECK!
WHAT IS THIS KNIGHT THING ANYWAY?!
HE'S JUST KAEDE.
HE'S...
TING
A TEXT FROM SOME-ONE I DON'T KNOW?
KLAK
Inbox 924
no title
You will be punished.
Menu
!

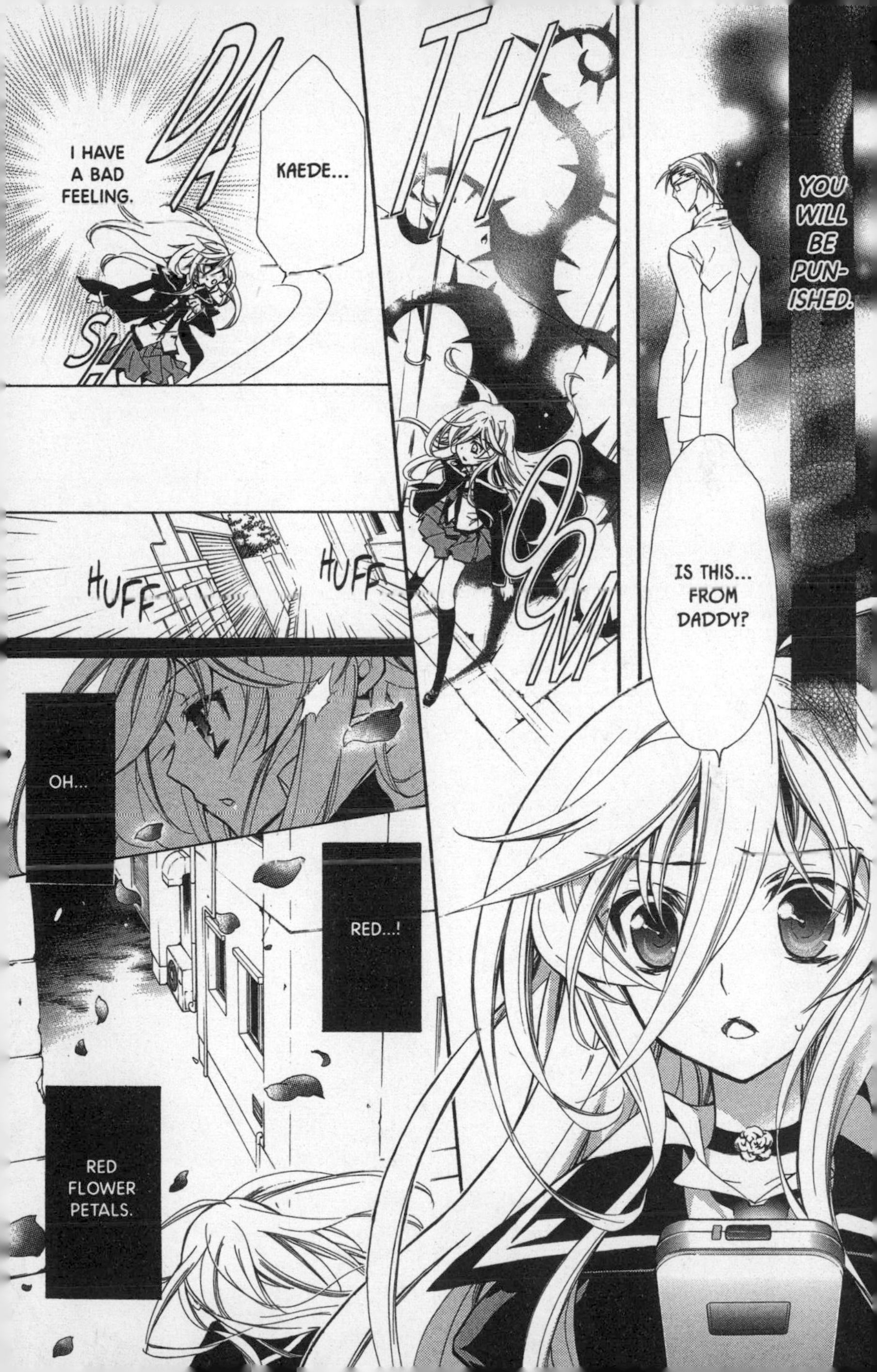
YOU WILL BE PUNISHED.
IS THIS... FROM DADDY?
TH
BOOM
KAEDE...
DA
I HAVE A BAD FEELING.
SH
HUFF
HUFF
OH...
RED...!
RED FLOWER PETALS.

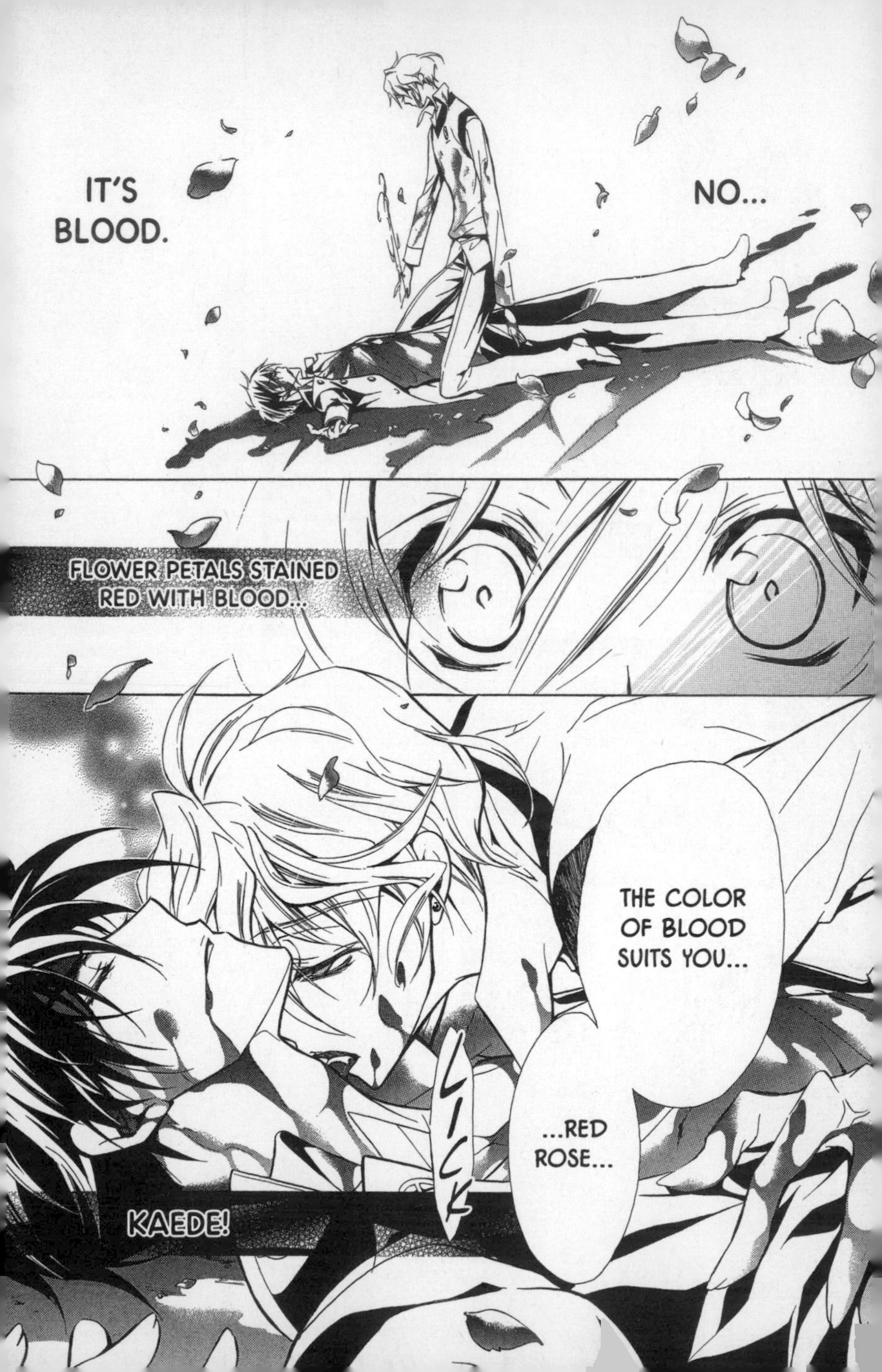
NO...
IT'S BLOOD.
FLOWER PETALS STAINED RED WITH BLOOD...
THE COLOR OF BLOOD SUITS YOU...
...RED ROSE...
LICK
KAEDE!

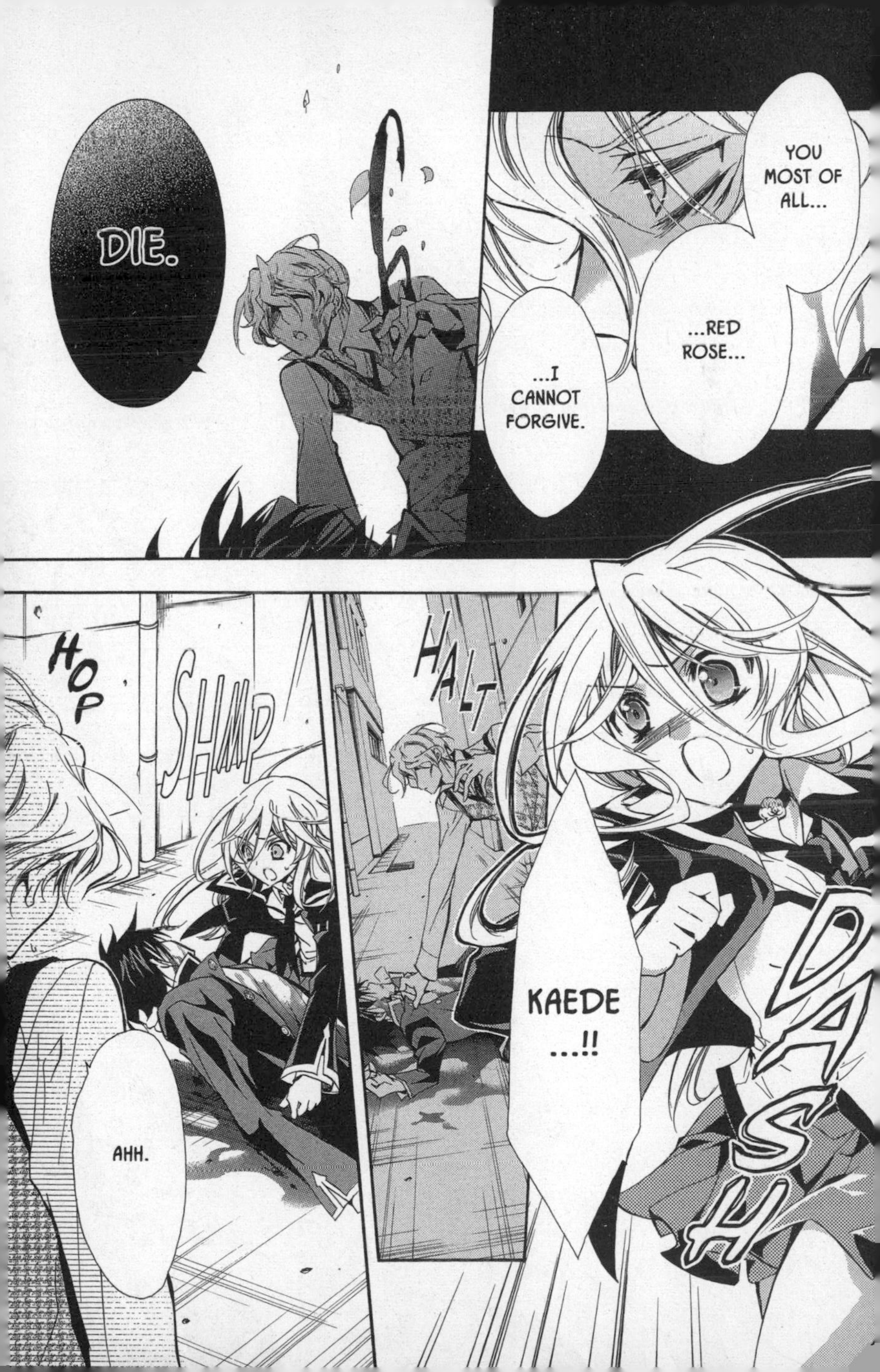
YOU MOST OF ALL...
...RED ROSE...
...I CANNOT FORGIVE.
DIE.
KAEDE ...!!
DASH
HALT
SHMP
HOP
AHH.

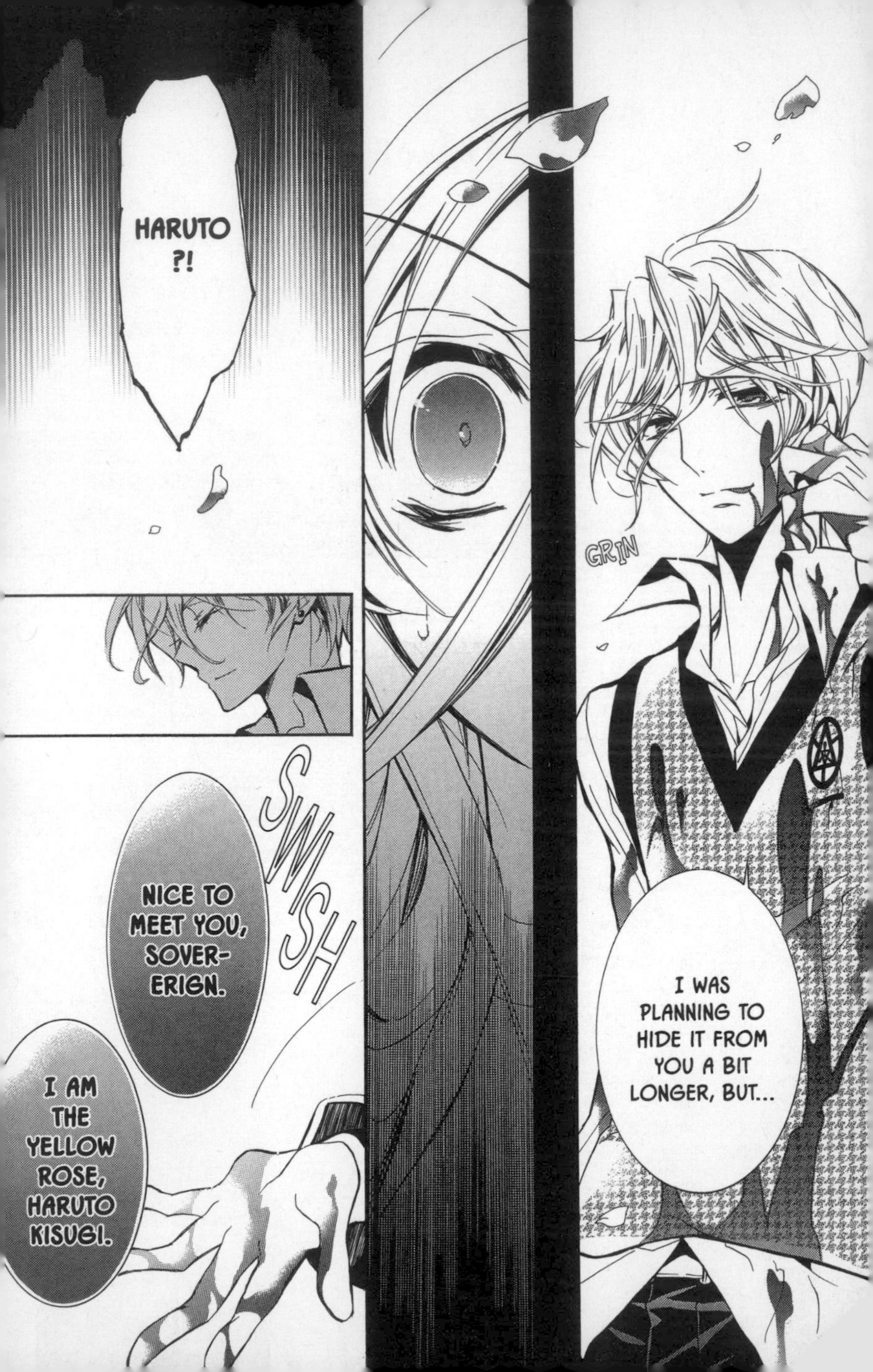
GRIN
I WAS PLANNING TO HIDE IT FROM YOU A BIT LONGER, BUT...
HARUTO ?!
SWISH
NICE TO MEET YOU, SOVER-ERIGN.
I AM THE YELLOW ROSE, HARUTO KISUGI.

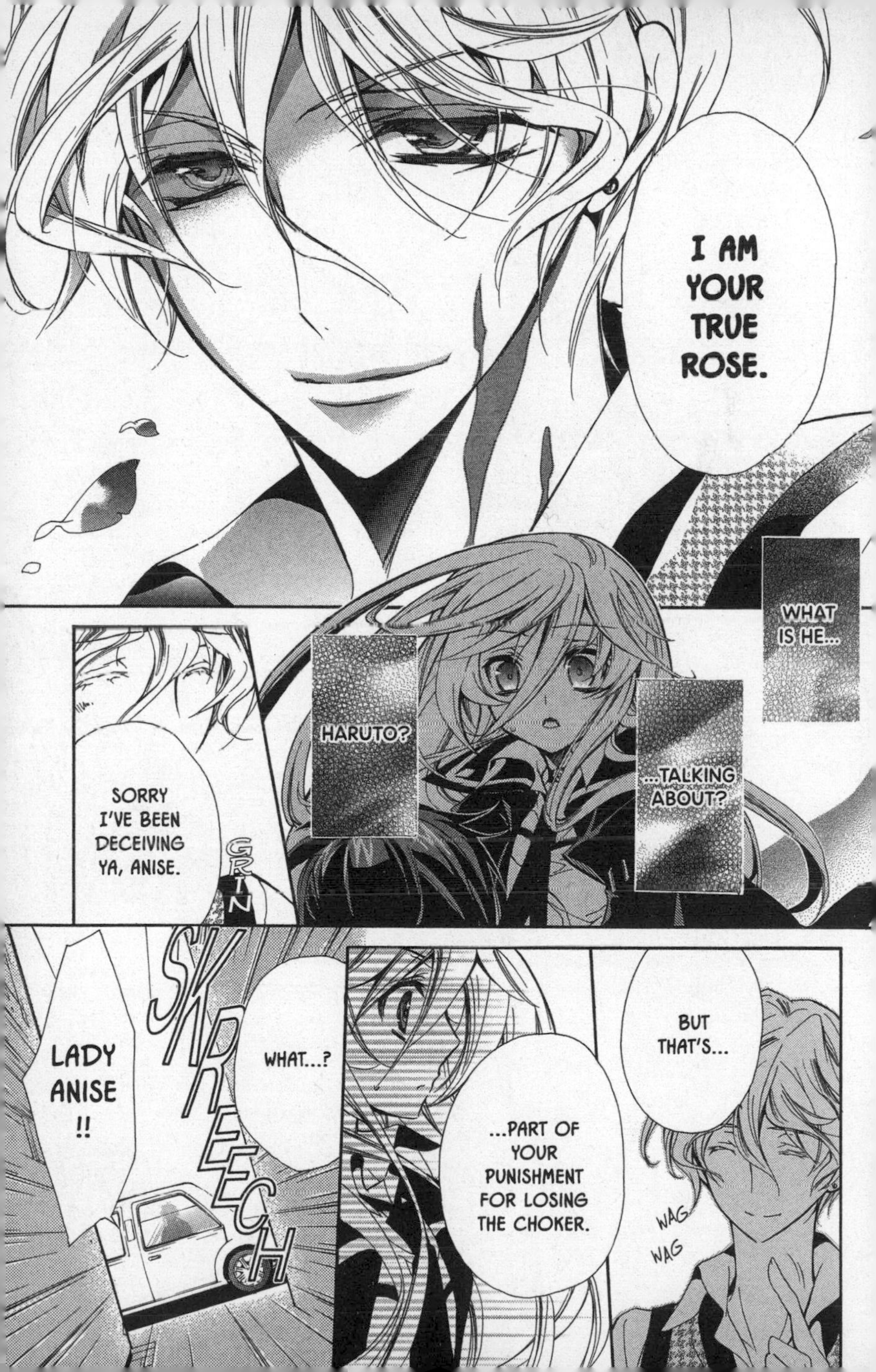
I AM YOUR TRUE ROSE.
WHAT IS HE...
...TALKING ABOUT?
HARUTO?
SORRY I'VE BEEN DECEIVING YA, ANISE.
GRIN
BUT THAT'S...
...PART OF YOUR PUNISHMENT FOR LOSING THE CHOKER.
WAG WAG
WHAT...?
SKREECH
LADY ANISE !!

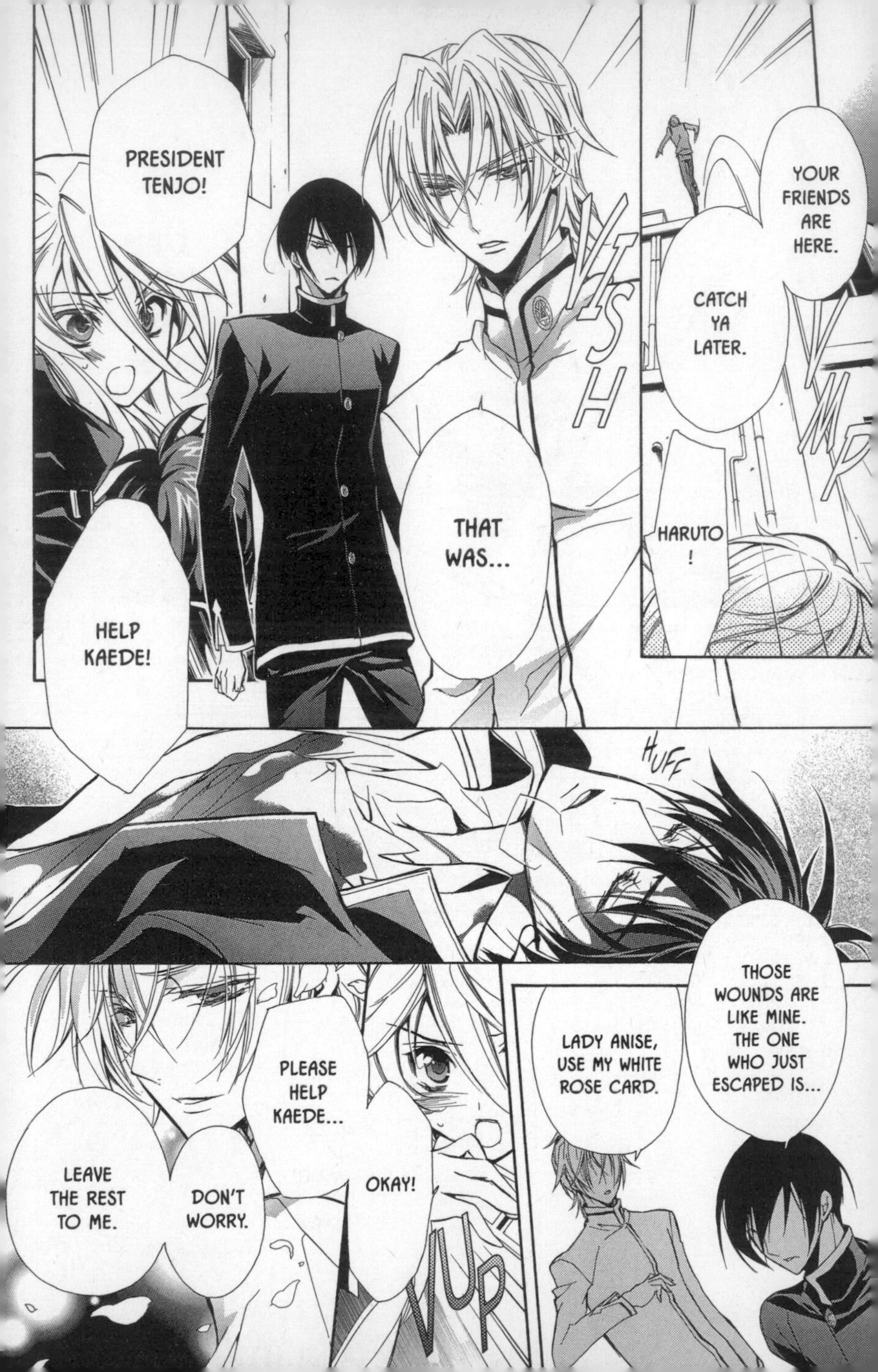
YOUR FRIENDS ARE HERE.
CATCH YA LATER.
VMP
HARUTO!
PRESIDENT TENJO!
VISH
THAT WAS...
HELP KAEDE!
HUFF
THOSE WOUNDS ARE LIKE MINE. THE ONE WHO JUST ESCAPED IS...
LADY ANISE, USE MY WHITE ROSE CARD.
PLEASE HELP KAEDE...
OKAY!
DON'T WORRY.
LEAVE THE REST TO ME.
VUP

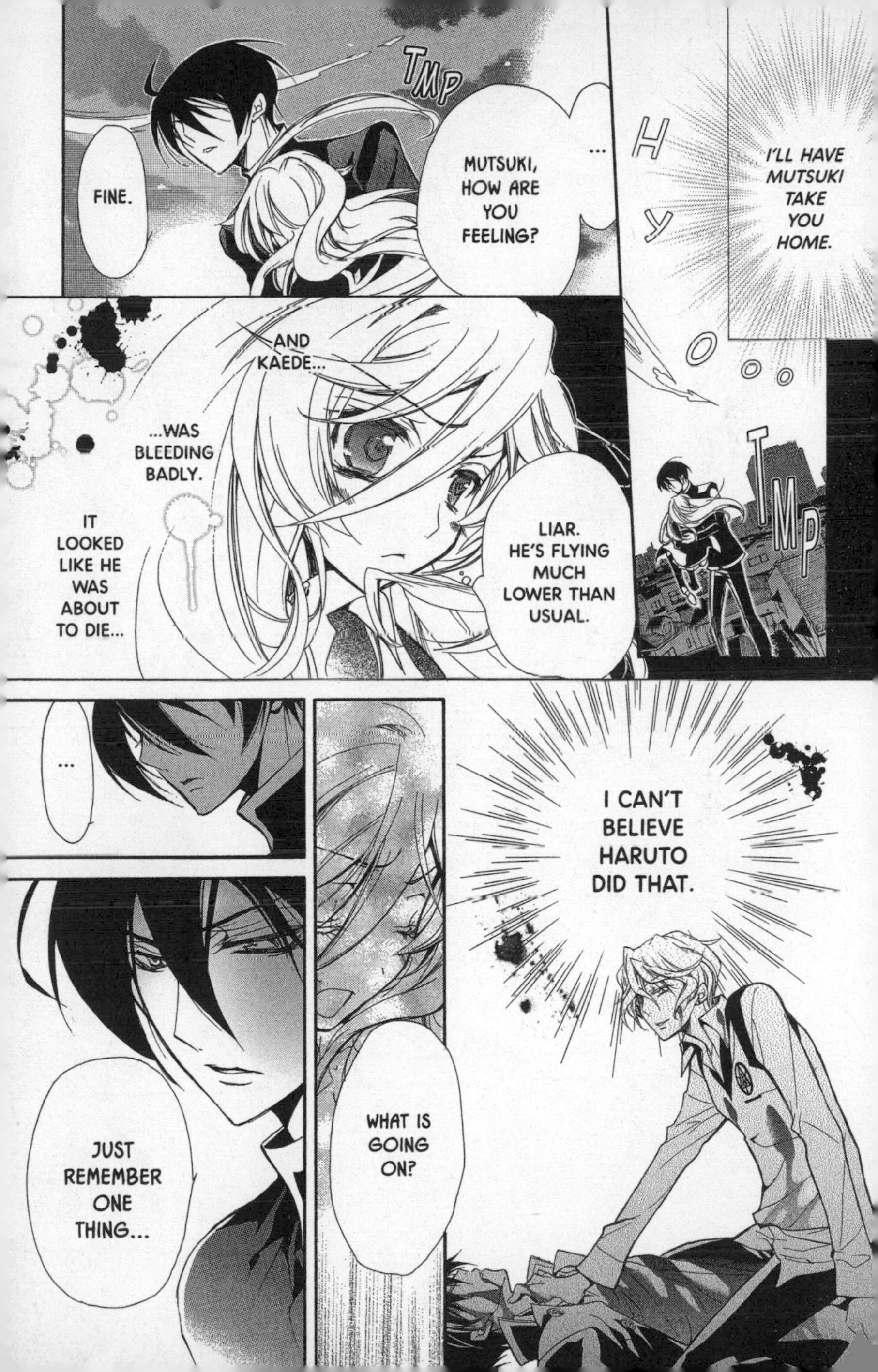
I'LL HAVE MUTSUKI TAKE YOU HOME.
HYOOOO
...
MUTSUKI, HOW ARE YOU FEELING?
TMP
FINE.
TMP
LIAR. HE'S FLYING MUCH LOWER THAN USUAL.
AND KAEDE...
...WAS BLEEDING BADLY.
IT LOOKED LIKE HE WAS ABOUT TO DIE...
I CAN'T BELIEVE HARUTO DID THAT.
WHAT IS GOING ON?
...
JUST REMEMBER ONE THING...

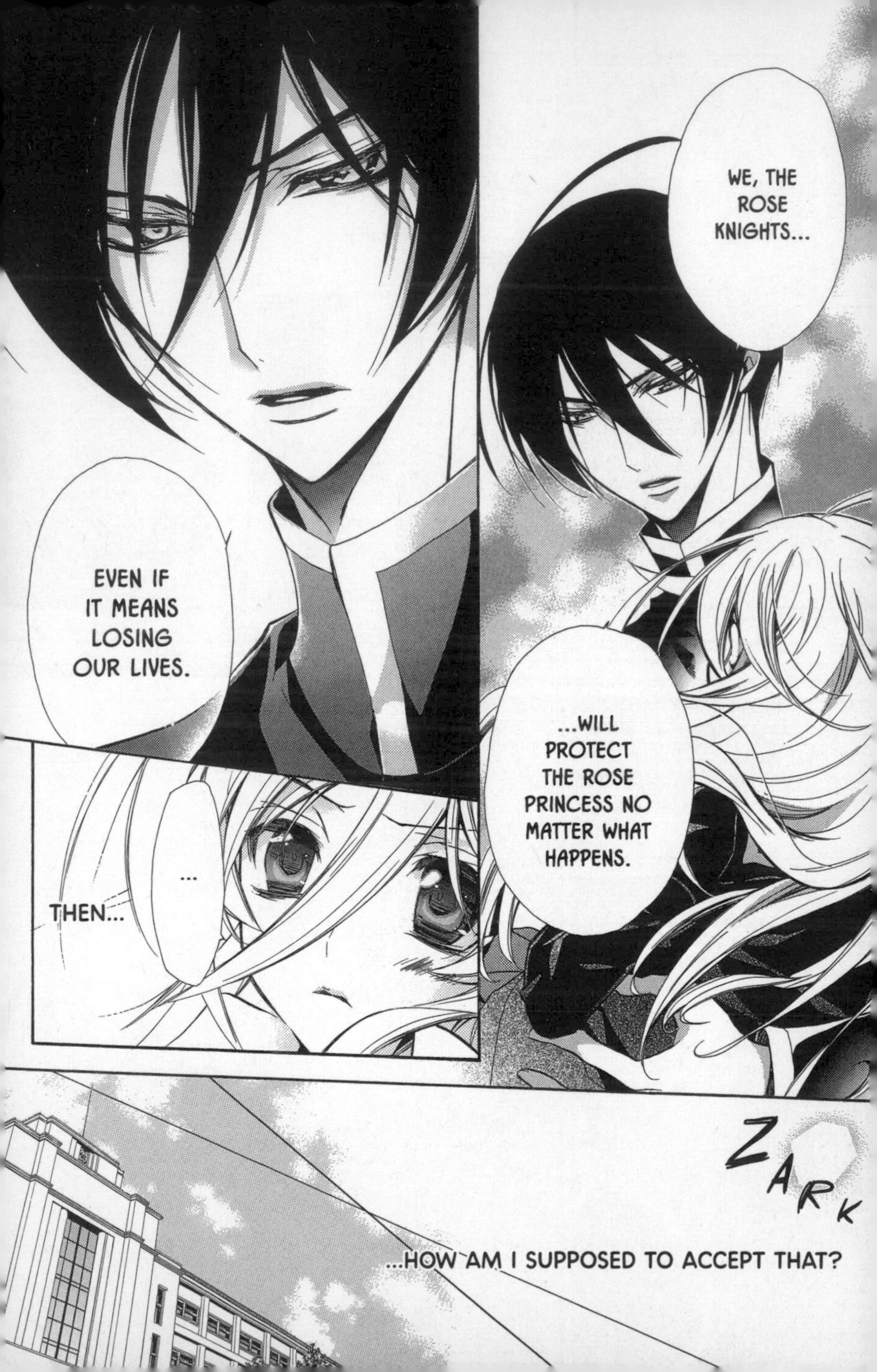
WE, THE ROSE KNIGHTS...
...WILL PROTECT THE ROSE PRINCESS NO MATTER WHAT HAPPENS.
EVEN IF IT MEANS LOSING OUR LIVES.
...
THEN...
ZARK
...HOW AM I SUPPOSED TO ACCEPT THAT?

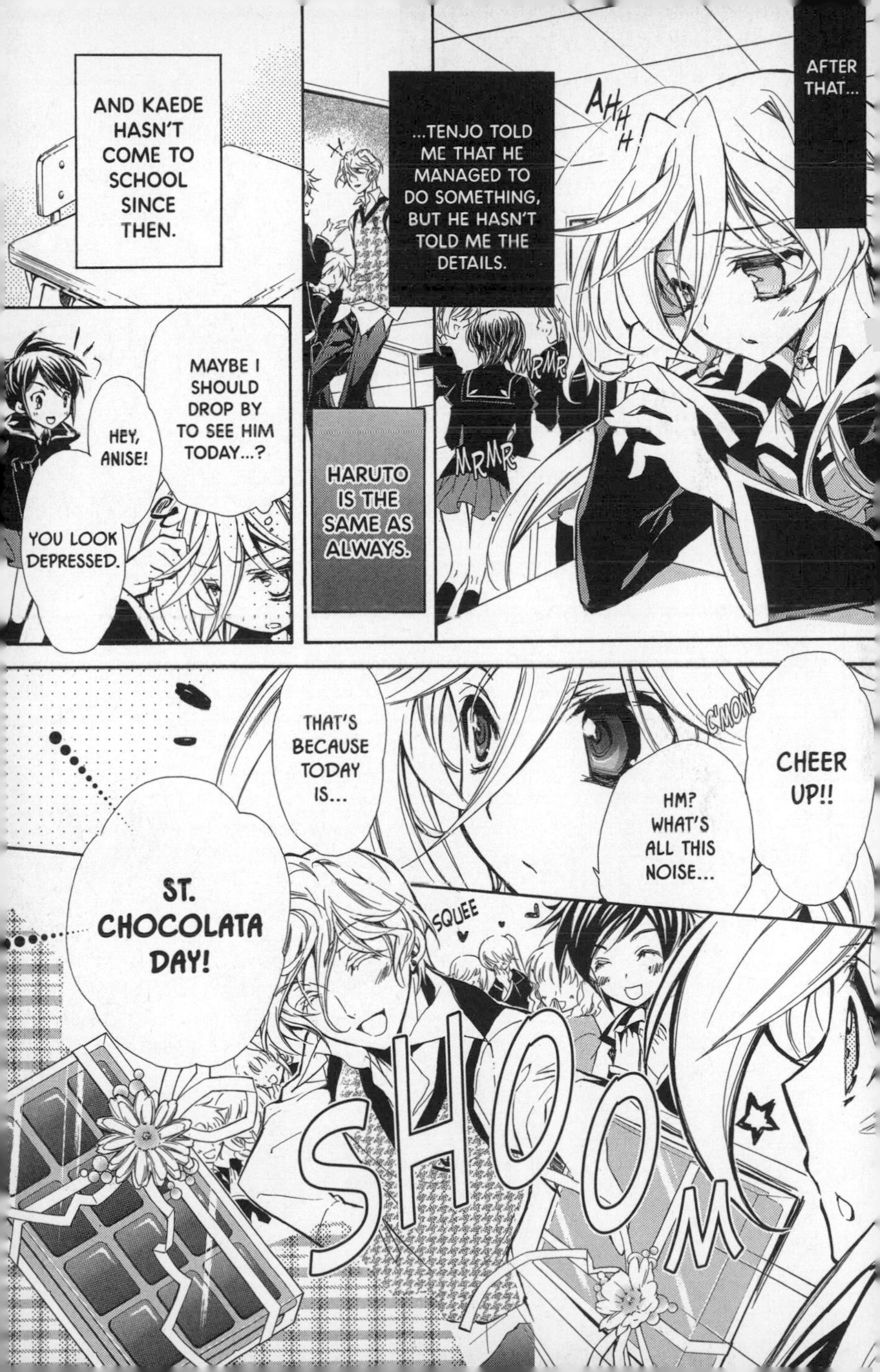
AFTER THAT...
AHHH
...TENJO TOLD ME THAT HE MANAGED TO DO SOMETHING, BUT HE HASN'T TOLD ME THE DETAILS.
AND KAEDE HASN'T COME TO SCHOOL SINCE THEN.
MRMR
MRMR
HARUTO IS THE SAME AS ALWAYS.
MAYBE I SHOULD DROP BY TO SEE HIM TODAY...?
HEY, ANISE!
YOU LOOK DEPRESSED.
C'MON!
CHEER UP!!
HM? WHAT'S ALL THIS NOISE...
THAT'S BECAUSE TODAY IS...
ST. CHOCOLATA DAY!
SQUEE
SHOOOM

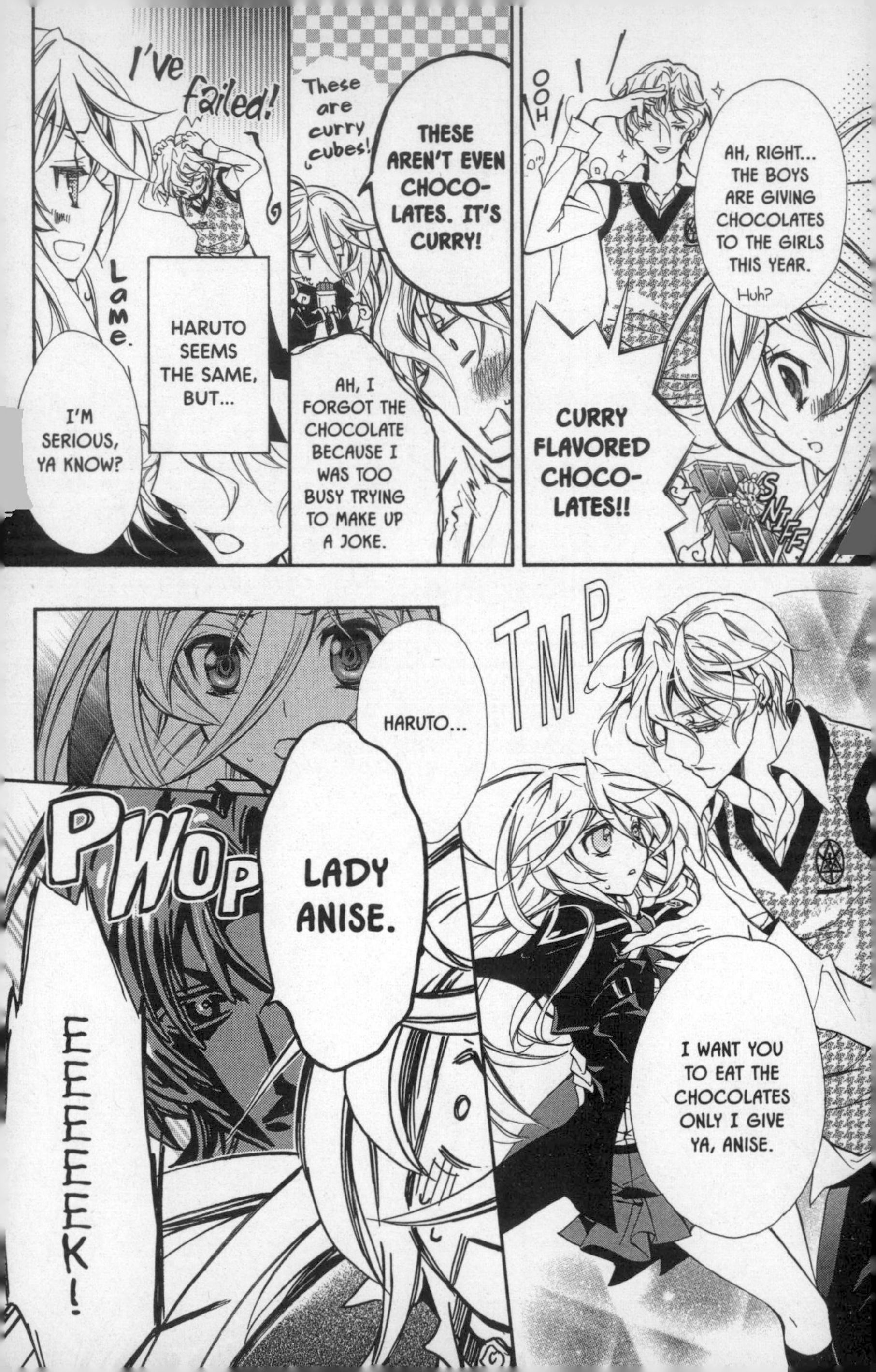
OOH
AH, RIGHT... THE BOYS ARE GIVING CHOCOLATES TO THE GIRLS THIS YEAR.
Huh?
CURRY FLAVORED CHOCOLATES!!
SNIFF
These are curry cubes!
THESE AREN'T EVEN CHOCOLATES. IT'S CURRY!
AH, I FORGOT THE CHOCOLATE BECAUSE I WAS TOO BUSY TRYING TO MAKE UP A JOKE.
I've failed!
HARUTO SEEMS THE SAME, BUT...
Lame.
I'M SERIOUS, YA KNOW?
TMP
I WANT YOU TO EAT THE CHOCOLATES ONLY I GIVE YA, ANISE.
HARUTO...
PWOP
LADY ANISE.
EEEEEEK!

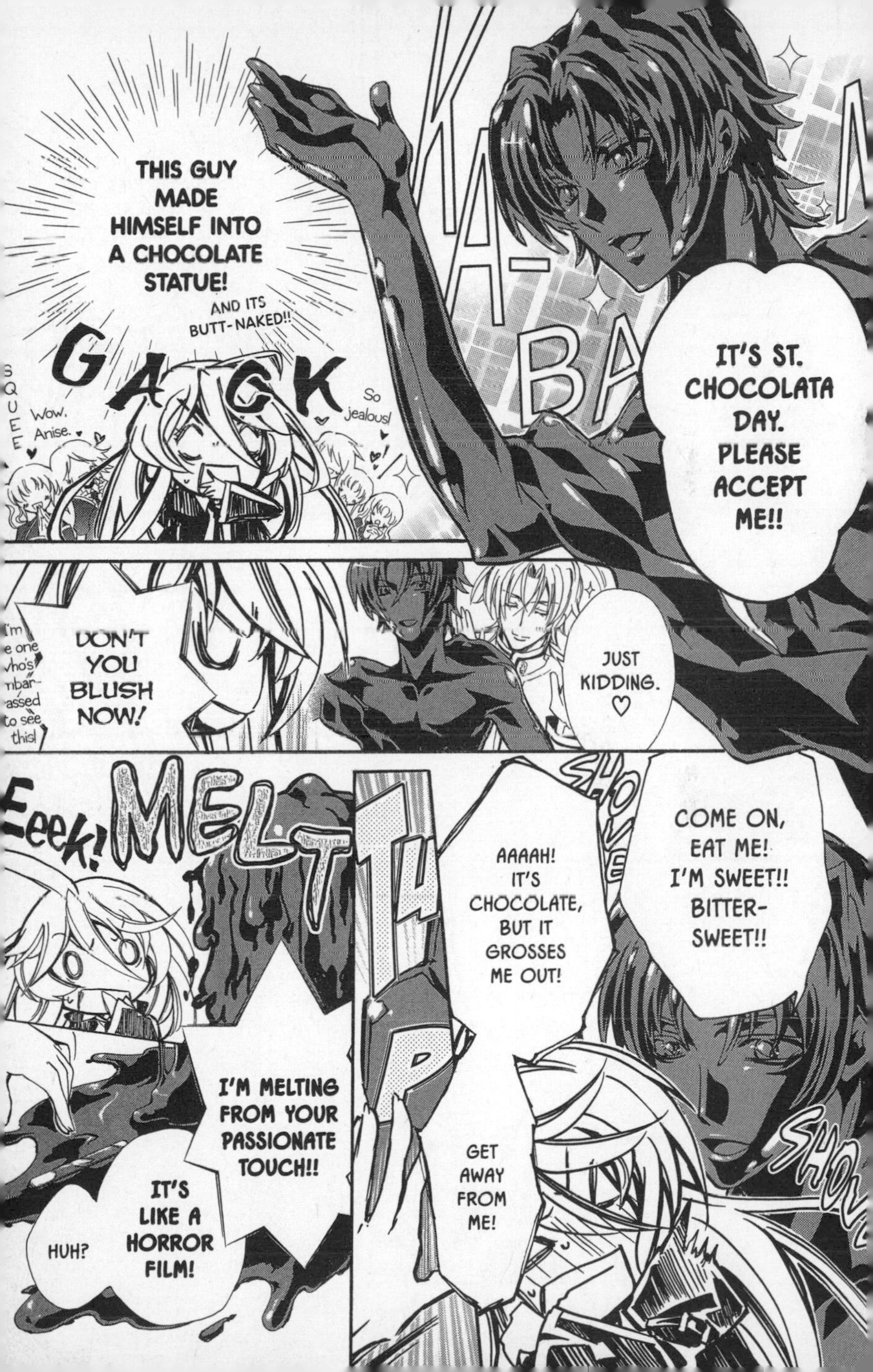
KA-BAM
IT'S ST. CHOCOLATA DAY. PLEASE ACCEPT ME!!
THIS GUY MADE HIMSELF INTO A CHOCOLATE STATUE!
AND ITS BUTT-NAKED!!
GACK
So jealous!
Wow, Anise.
SQUEE
JUST KIDDING.
DON'T YOU BLUSH NOW!
I'm e one who's mbar- rassed to see this!
SHOVE
COME ON, EAT ME! I'M SWEET!! BITTER-SWEET!!
AAAAH! IT'S CHOCOLATE, BUT IT GROSSES ME OUT!
SHOVE
GET AWAY FROM ME!
THWP
MELT
Eeek!
I'M MELTING FROM YOUR PASSIONATE TOUCH!!
IT'S LIKE A HORROR FILM!
HUH?

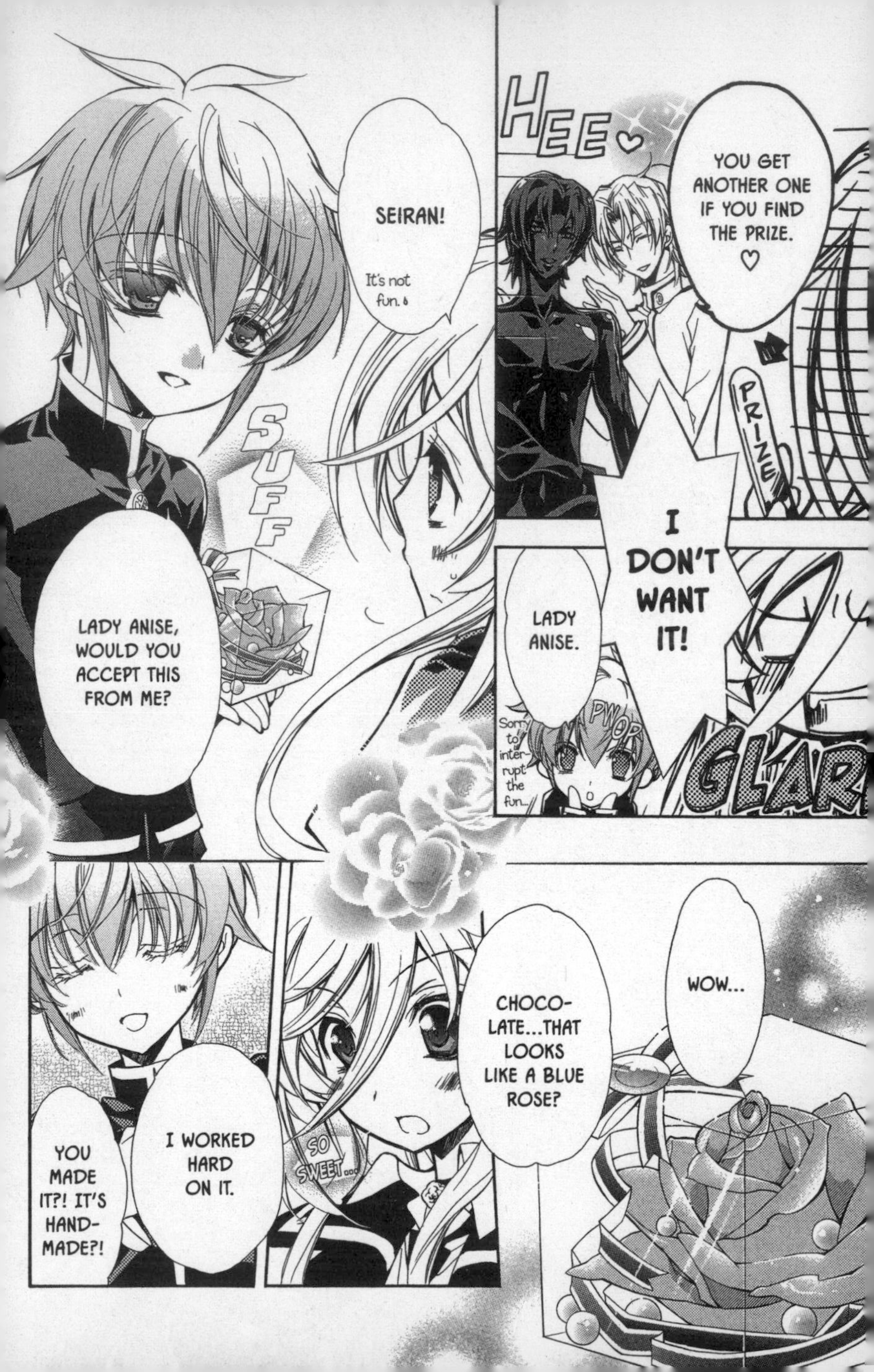
HEE ♡
YOU GET ANOTHER ONE IF YOU FIND THE PRIZE. ♡
PRIZE
I DON'T WANT IT!
GLAR
LADY ANISE.
PWOP
Sorry to interrupt the fun...
SEIRAN!
It's not fun.
SUFF
LADY ANISE, WOULD YOU ACCEPT THIS FROM ME?
WOW...
CHOCOLATE...THAT LOOKS LIKE A BLUE ROSE?
SO SWEET...
I WORKED HARD ON IT.
YOU MADE IT?! IT'S HANDMADE?!

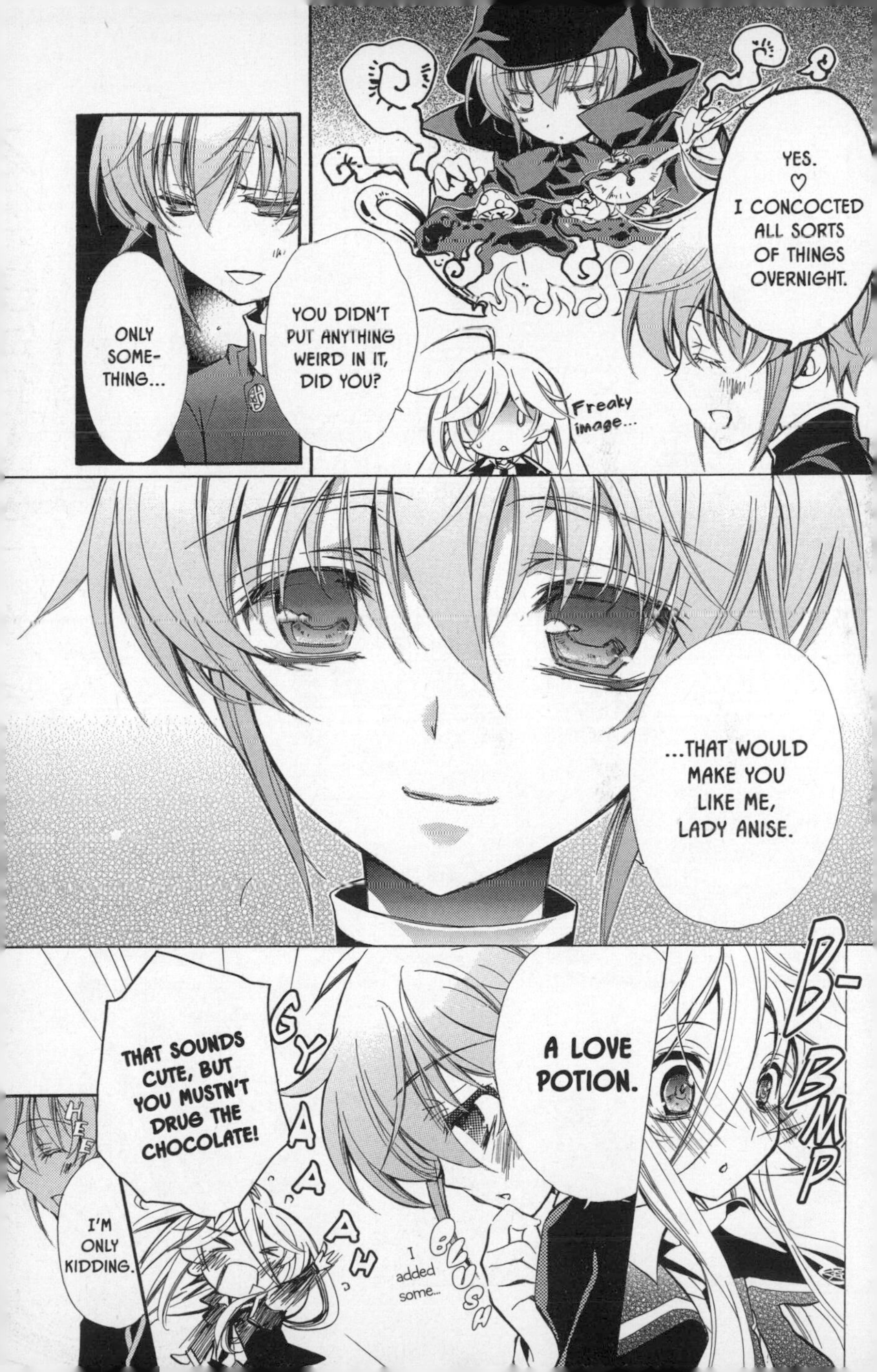
YES. ♥ I CONCOCTED ALL SORTS OF THINGS OVERNIGHT.
YOU DIDN'T PUT ANYTHING WEIRD IN IT, DID YOU?
Freaky image...
ONLY SOME-THING...
...THAT WOULD MAKE YOU LIKE ME, LADY ANISE.
B-BMP
A LOVE POTION.
I added some...
GYAAAH
THAT SOUNDS CUTE, BUT YOU MUSTN'T DRUG THE CHOCOLATE!
HEE
I'M ONLY KIDDING.

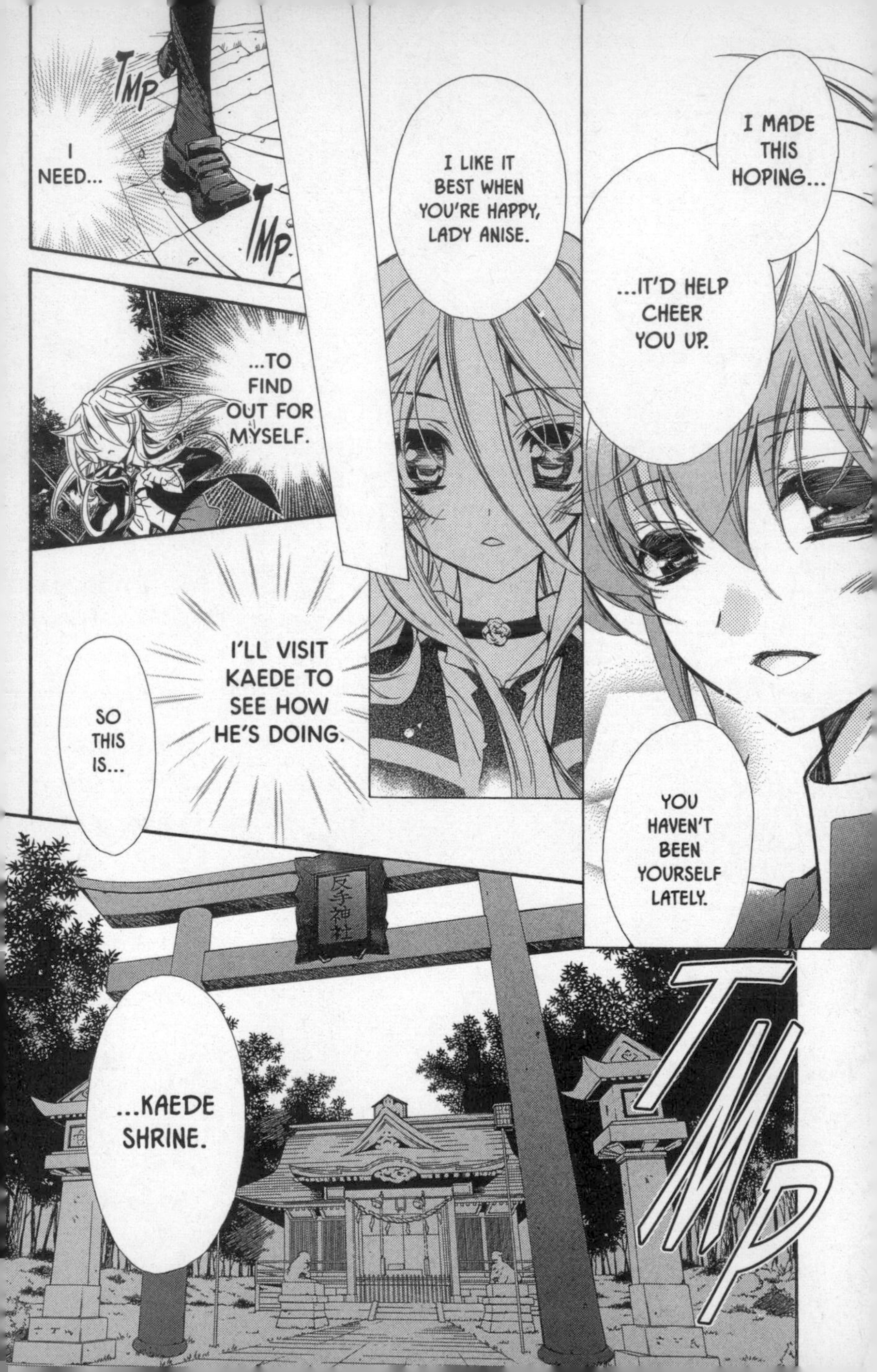
I MADE THIS HOPING...
...IT'D HELP CHEER YOU UP.
YOU HAVEN'T BEEN YOURSELF LATELY.
I LIKE IT BEST WHEN YOU'RE HAPPY, LADY ANISE.
TMP
I NEED...
TMP
...TO FIND OUT FOR MYSELF.
I'LL VISIT KAEDE TO SEE HOW HE'S DOING.
SO THIS IS...
TMP
...KAEDE SHRINE.

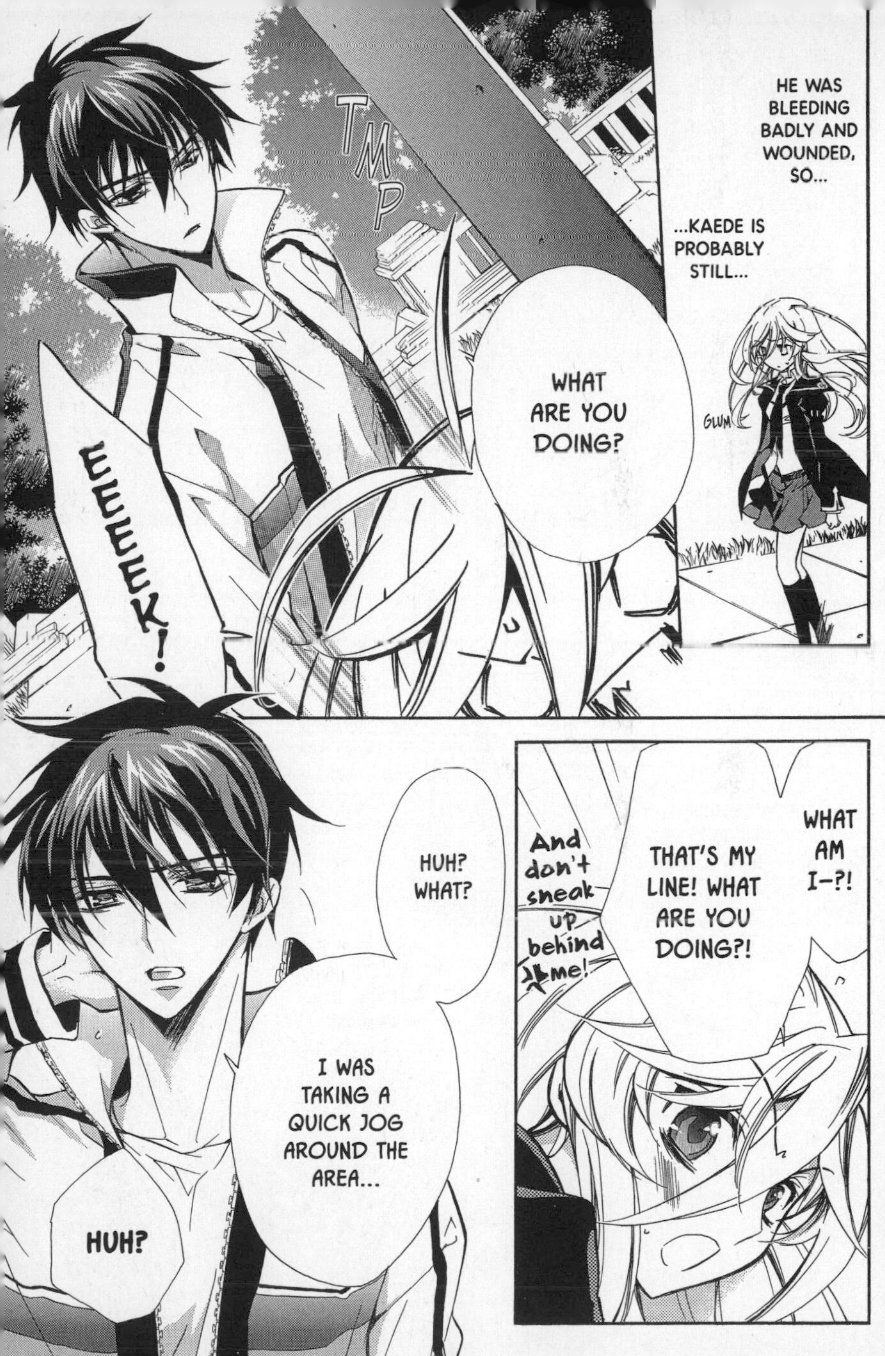
HE WAS BLEEDING BADLY AND WOUNDED, SO...
...KAEDE IS PROBABLY STILL...
GLUM
TMP
WHAT ARE YOU DOING?
EEEEEK!
WHAT AM I—?!
THAT'S MY LINE! WHAT ARE YOU DOING?!
And don't sneak up behind me!
HUH? WHAT?
I WAS TAKING A QUICK JOG AROUND THE AREA...
HUH?

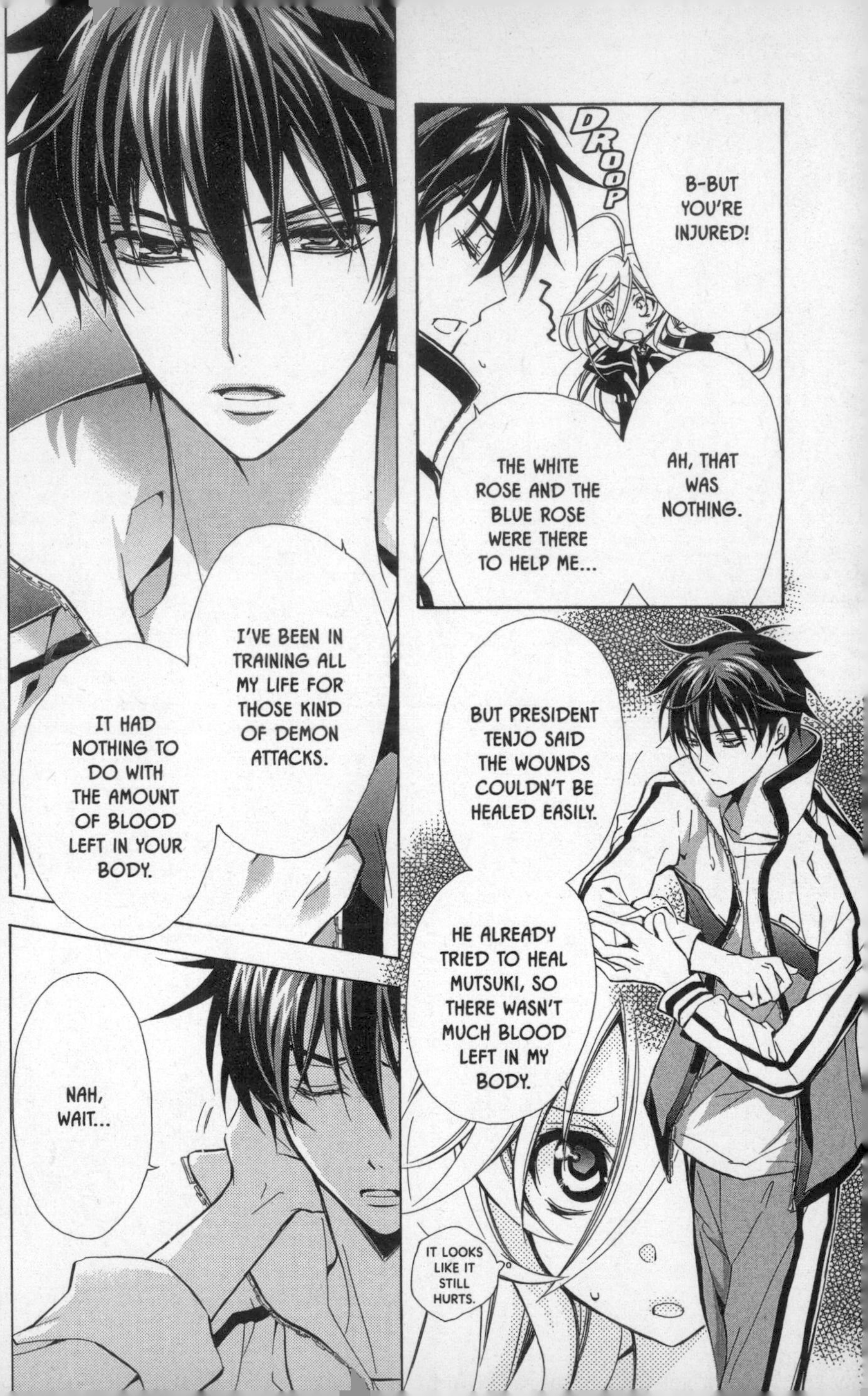
DROOP
B-BUT YOU'RE INJURED!
AH, THAT WAS NOTHING.
THE WHITE ROSE AND THE BLUE ROSE WERE THERE TO HELP ME...
BUT PRESIDENT TENJO SAID THE WOUNDS COULDN'T BE HEALED EASILY.
HE ALREADY TRIED TO HEAL MUTSUKI, SO THERE WASN'T MUCH BLOOD LEFT IN MY BODY.
IT LOOKS LIKE IT STILL HURTS.
I'VE BEEN IN TRAINING ALL MY LIFE FOR THOSE KIND OF DEMON ATTACKS.
IT HAD NOTHING TO DO WITH THE AMOUNT OF BLOOD LEFT IN YOUR BODY.
NAH, WAIT...

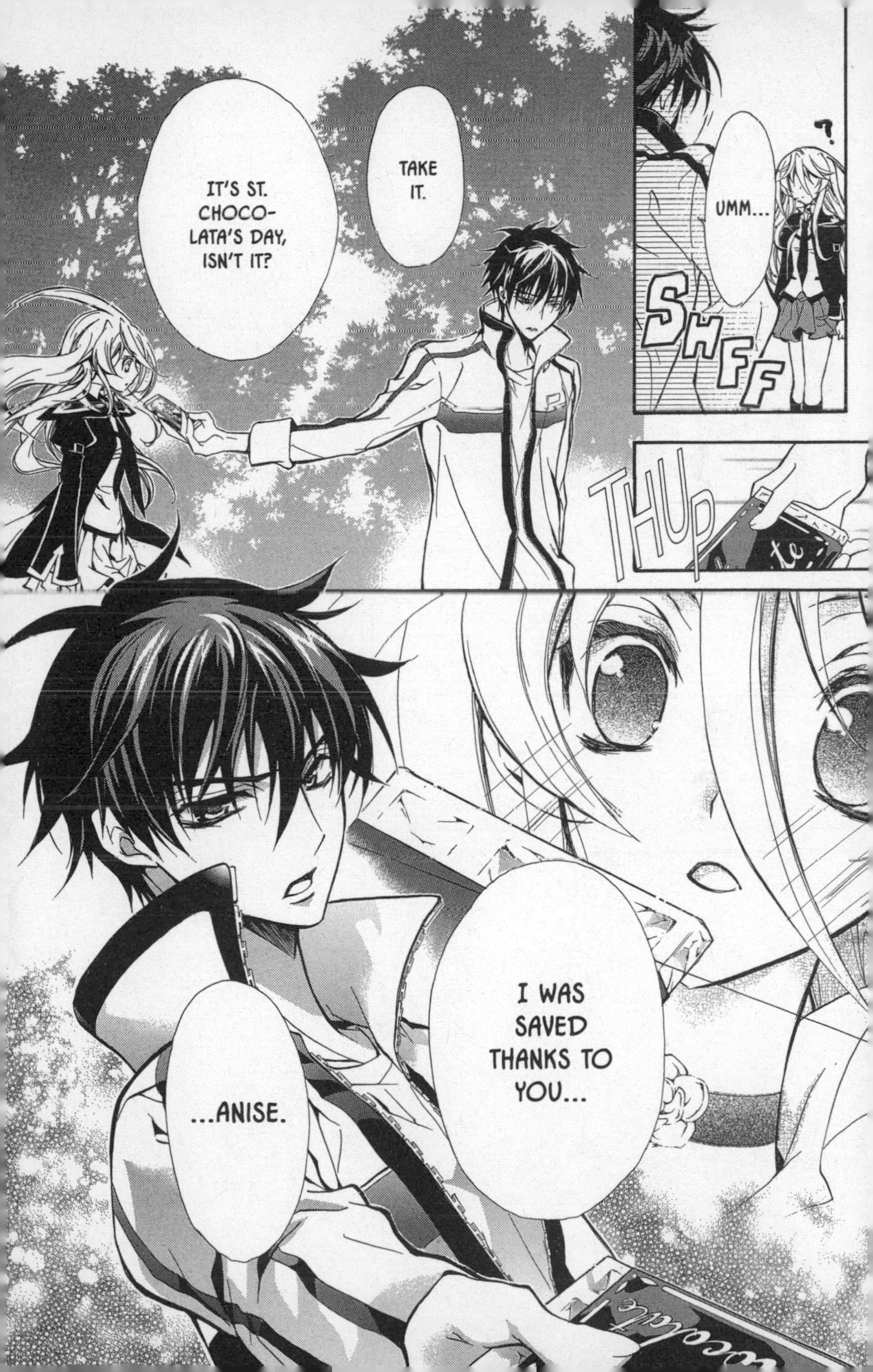
?
UMM...
SHFF
THUP
TAKE IT.
IT'S ST. CHOCOLATA'S DAY, ISN'T IT?
I WAS SAVED THANKS TO YOU...
...ANISE.

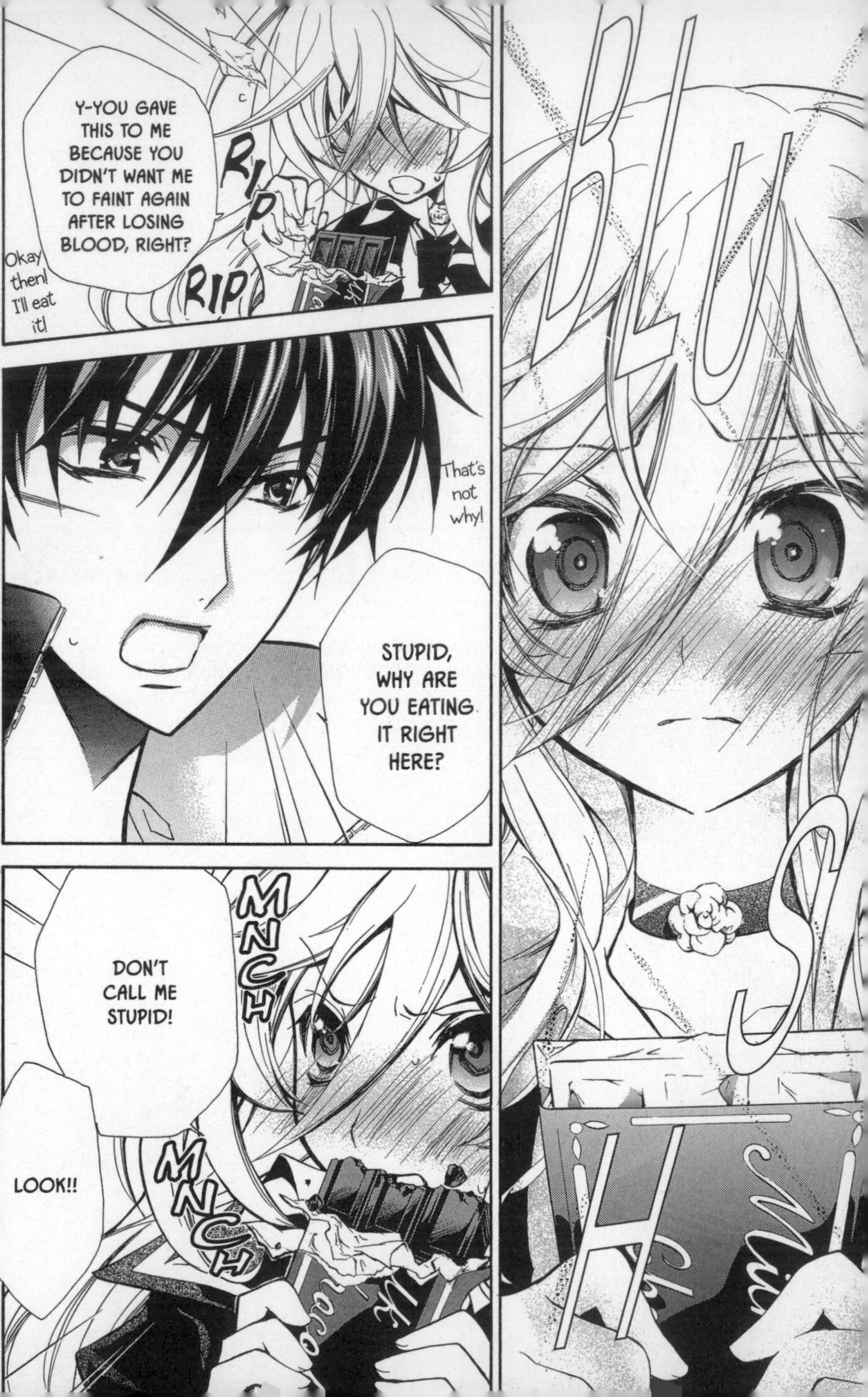
BLUSH
RIP
Y-YOU GAVE THIS TO ME BECAUSE YOU DIDN'T WANT ME TO FAINT AGAIN AFTER LOSING BLOOD, RIGHT?
RIP
Okay then! I'll eat it!
That's not why!
STUPID, WHY ARE YOU EATING IT RIGHT HERE?
MNCH
DON'T CALL ME STUPID!
MNCH
LOOK!!

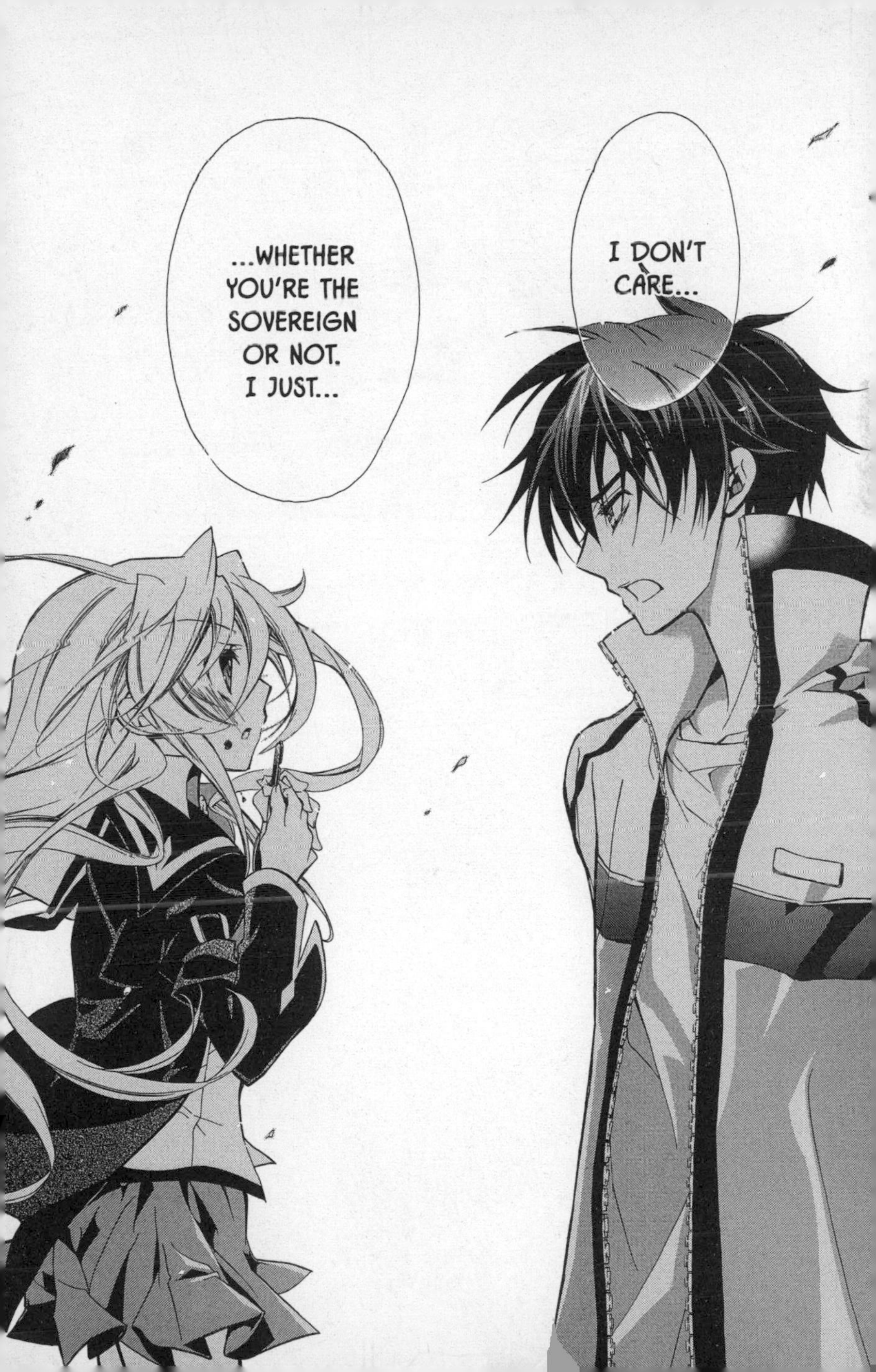
I DON'T CARE...
...WHETHER YOU'RE THE SOVEREIGN OR NOT. I JUST...

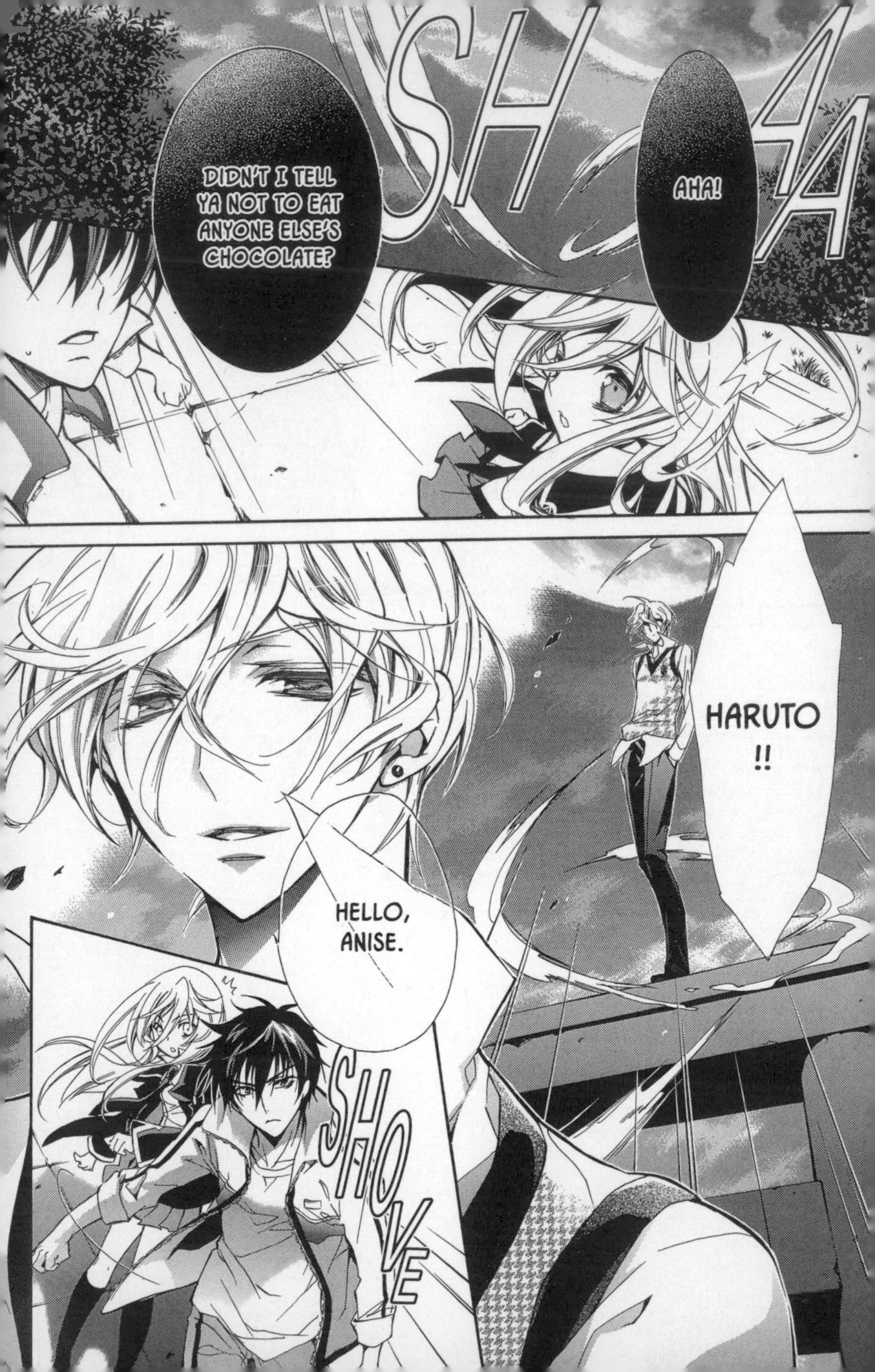
SHA
AHA!
DIDN'T I TELL YA NOT TO EAT ANYONE ELSE'S CHOCOLATE?
HARUTO !!
HELLO, ANISE.
SHOVE

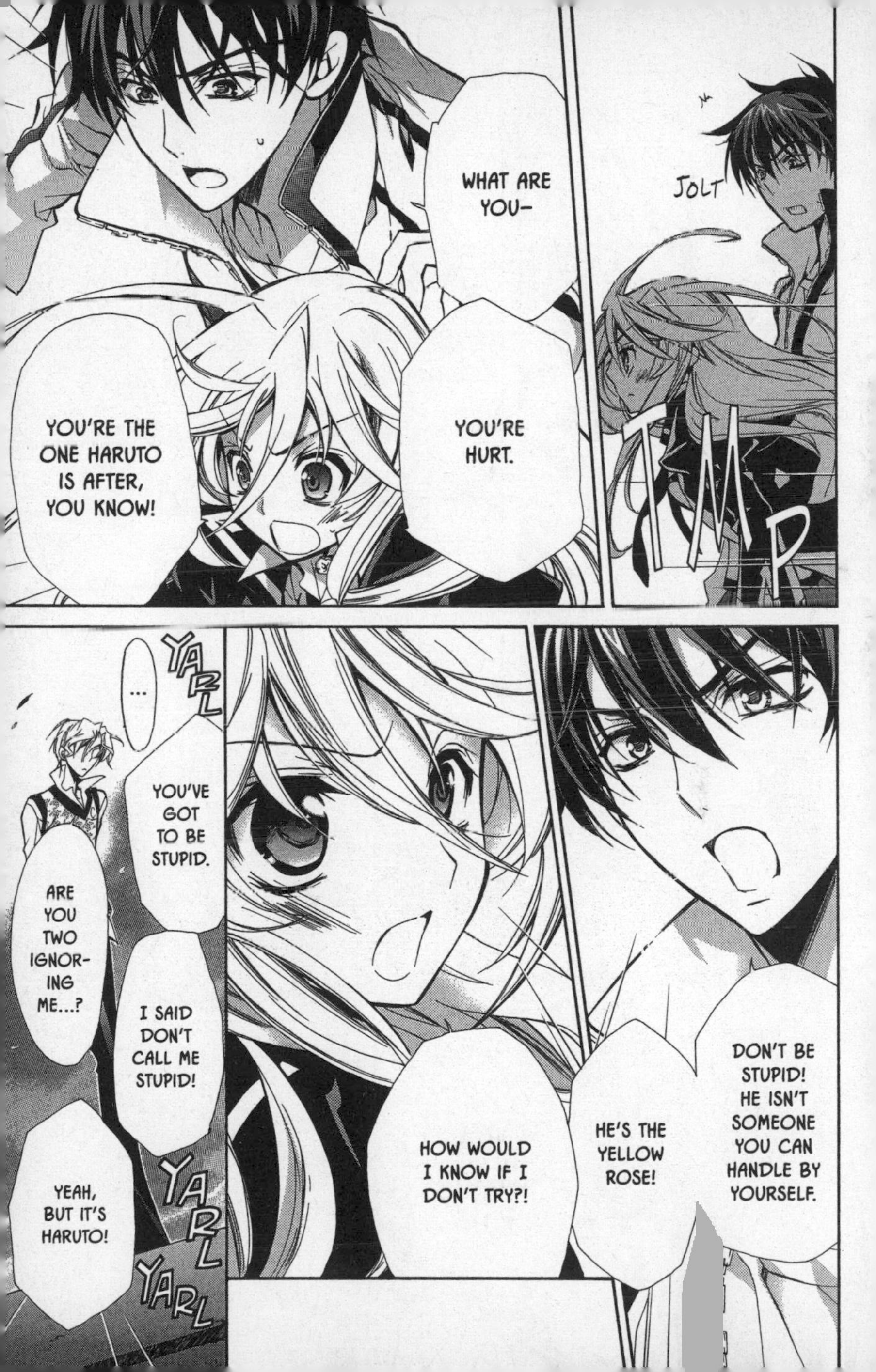
JOLT
TMP
WHAT ARE YOU-
YOU'RE HURT.
YOU'RE THE ONE HARUTO IS AFTER, YOU KNOW!
DON'T BE STUPID! HE ISN'T SOMEONE YOU CAN HANDLE BY YOURSELF.
HE'S THE YELLOW ROSE!
HOW WOULD I KNOW IF I DON'T TRY?!
YOU'VE GOT TO BE STUPID.
I SAID DON'T CALL ME STUPID!
YEAH, BUT IT'S HARUTO!
YARL
YARL
YARL
...
ARE YOU TWO IGNOR-ING ME...?

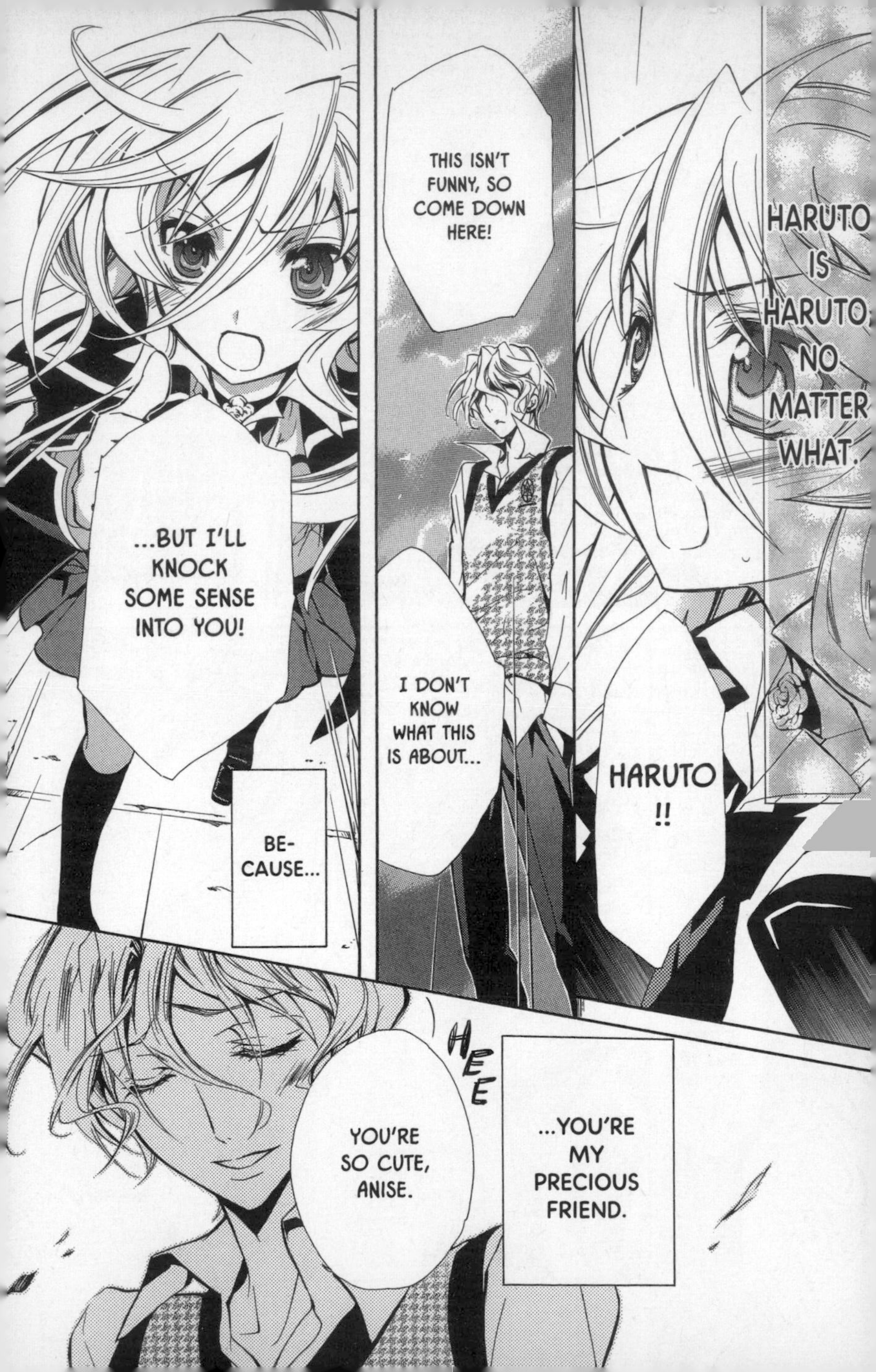
HARUTO IS HARUTO, NO MATTER WHAT.
HARUTO !!
THIS ISN'T FUNNY, SO COME DOWN HERE!
I DON'T KNOW WHAT THIS IS ABOUT...
...BUT I'LL KNOCK SOME SENSE INTO YOU!
BE-CAUSE...
...YOU'RE MY PRECIOUS FRIEND.
HEE
YOU'RE SO CUTE, ANISE.

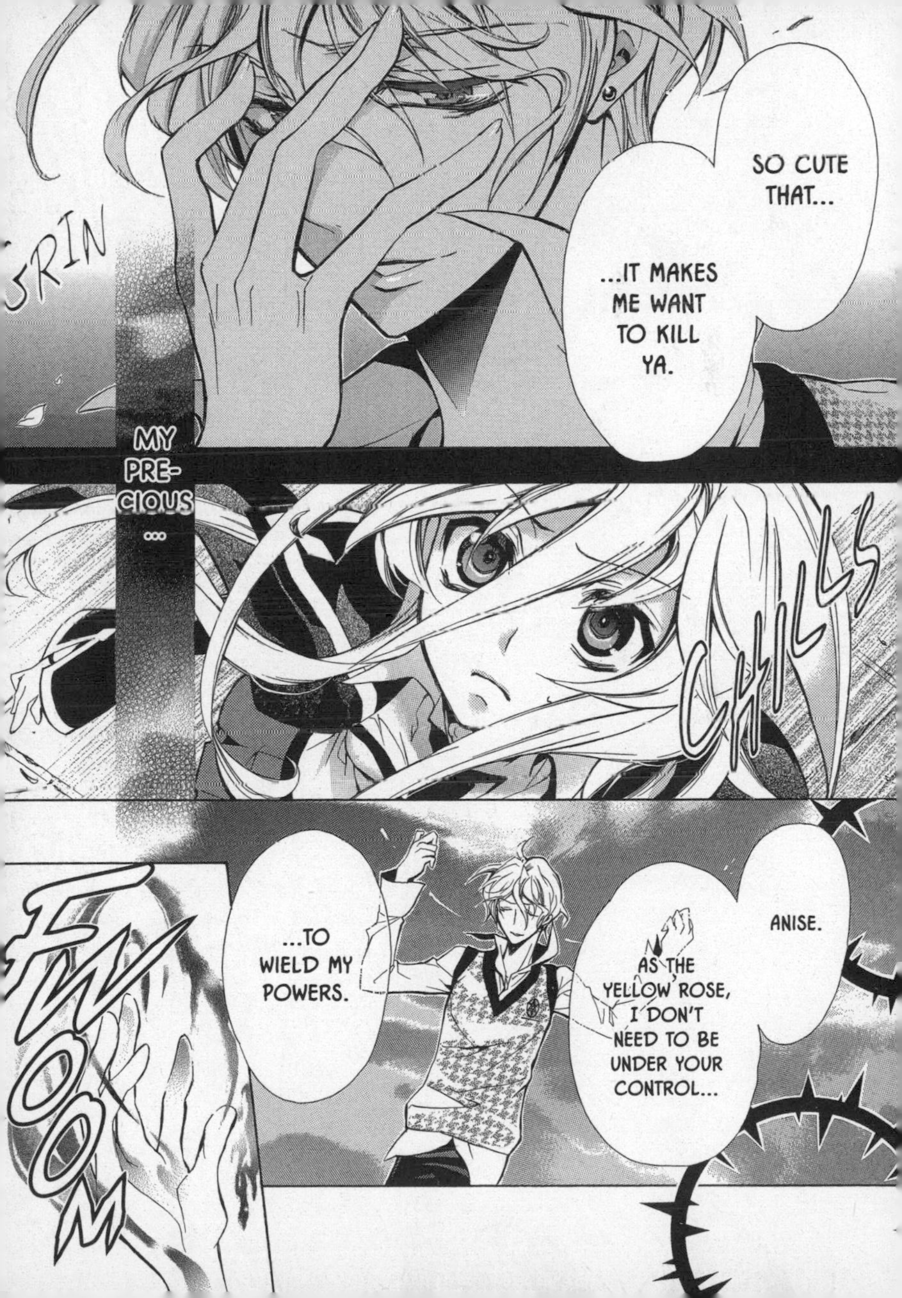
SO CUTE THAT...
...IT MAKES ME WANT TO KILL YA.
GRIN
MY PRE-CIOUS...
CHILLS
ANISE.
AS THE YELLOW ROSE, I DON'T NEED TO BE UNDER YOUR CONTROL...
...TO WIELD MY POWERS.
FWOOOM

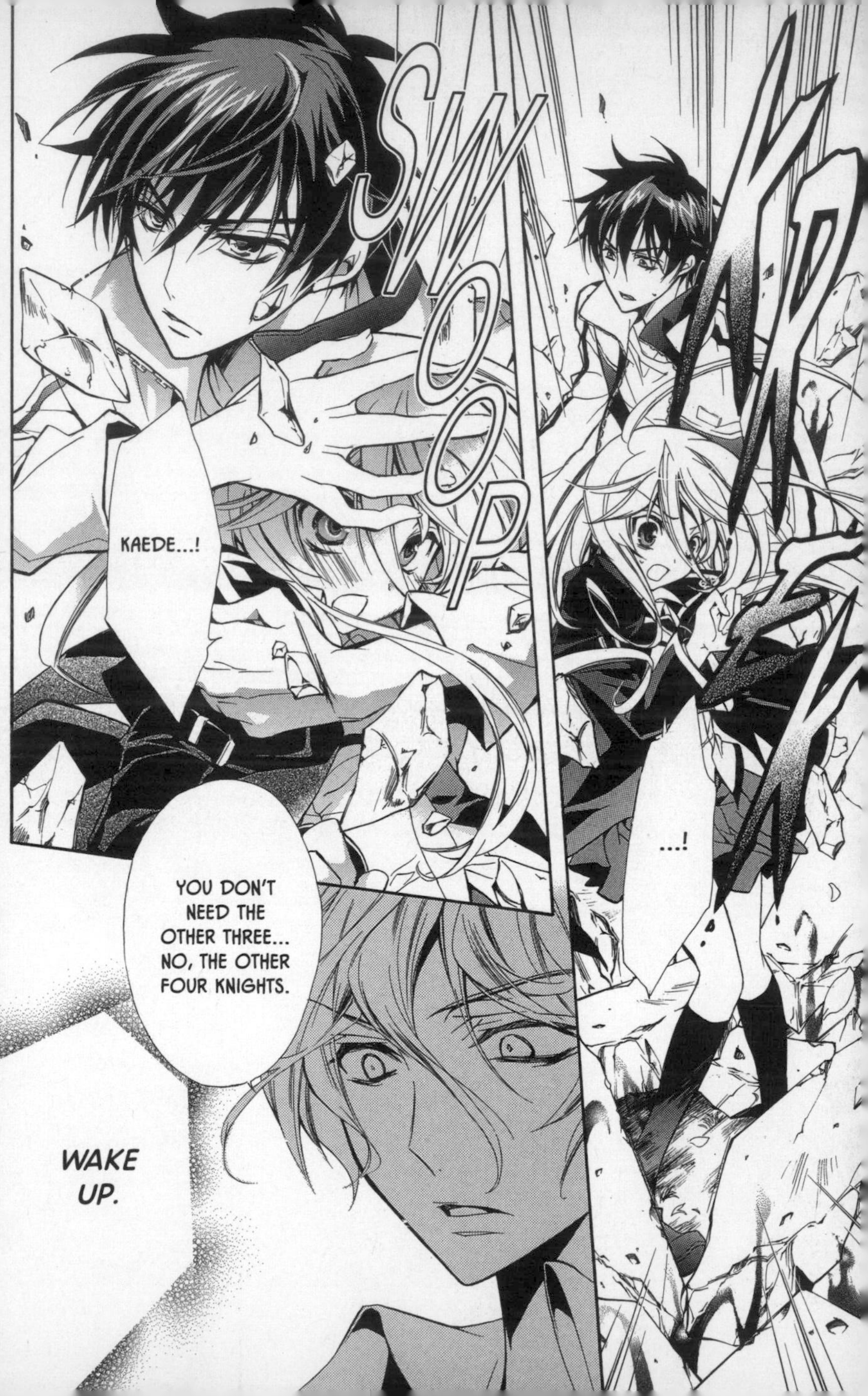
...!
SWOOP
KAEDE...!
YOU DON'T NEED THE OTHER THREE... NO, THE OTHER FOUR KNIGHTS.
WAKE UP.

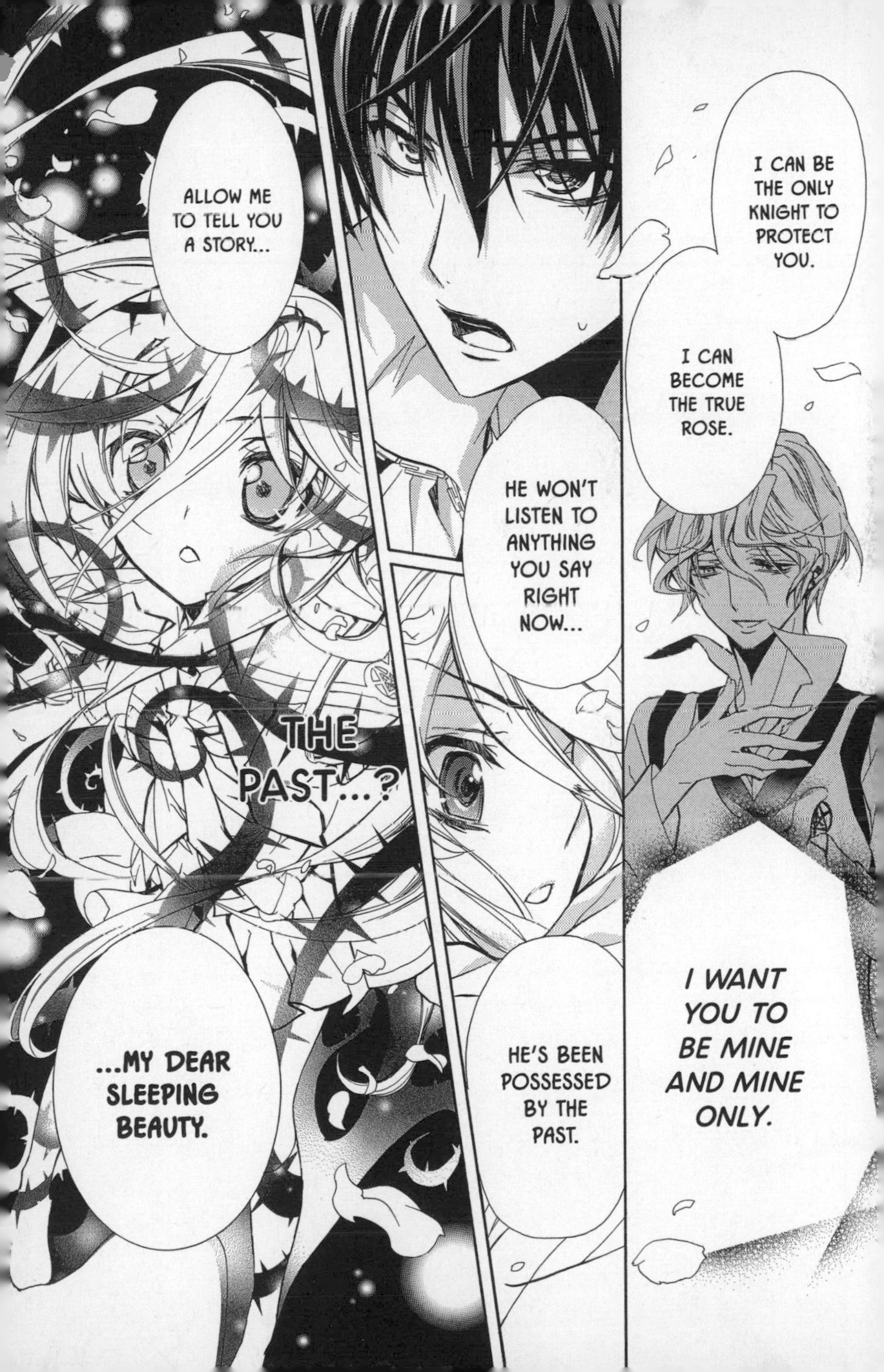
I CAN BE THE ONLY KNIGHT TO PROTECT YOU.
I CAN BECOME THE TRUE ROSE.
I WANT YOU TO BE MINE AND MINE ONLY.
HE WON'T LISTEN TO ANYTHING YOU SAY RIGHT NOW...
HE'S BEEN POSSESSED BY THE PAST.
THE PAST...?
ALLOW ME TO TELL YOU A STORY...
...MY DEAR SLEEPING BEAUTY.

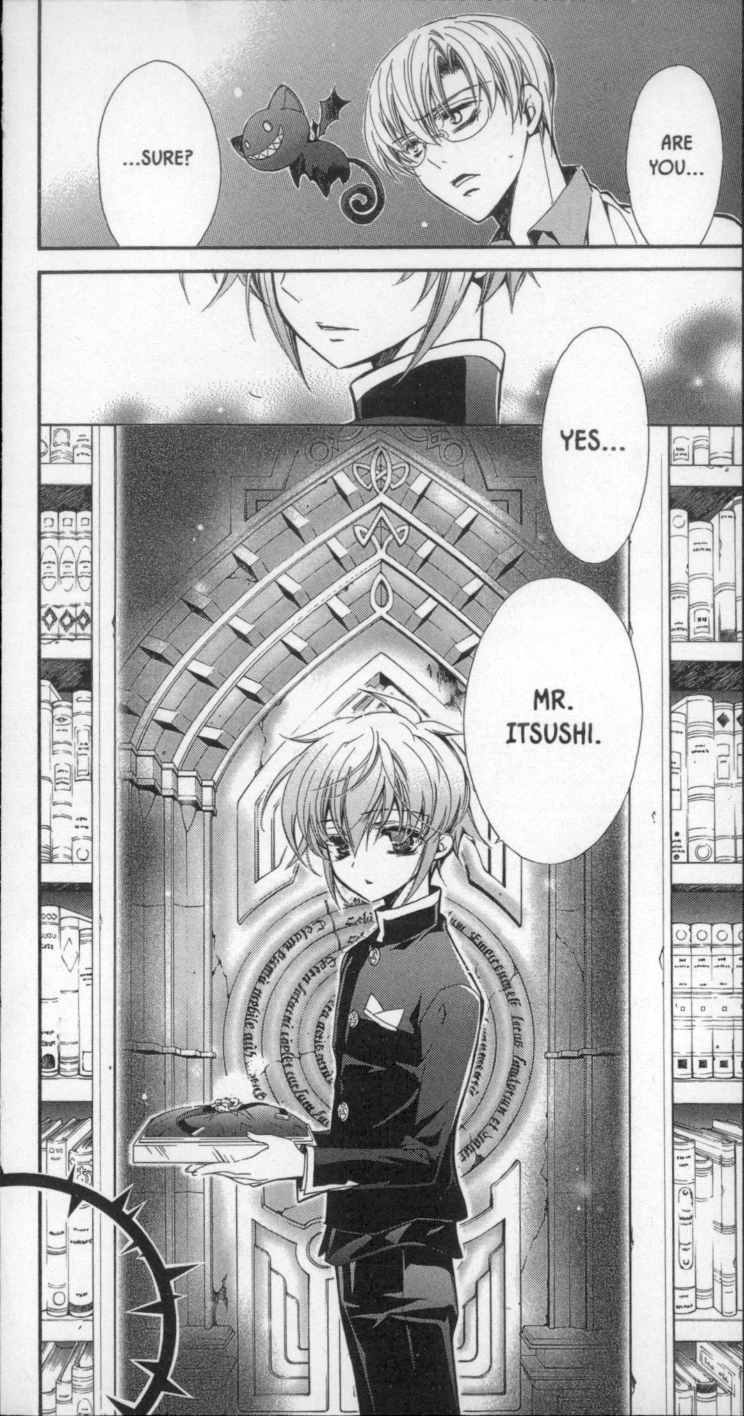
ARE YOU...
...SURE?
YES...
MR. ITSUSHI.

A LONG TIME AGO, THE ROSE KNIGHTS SINNED ...

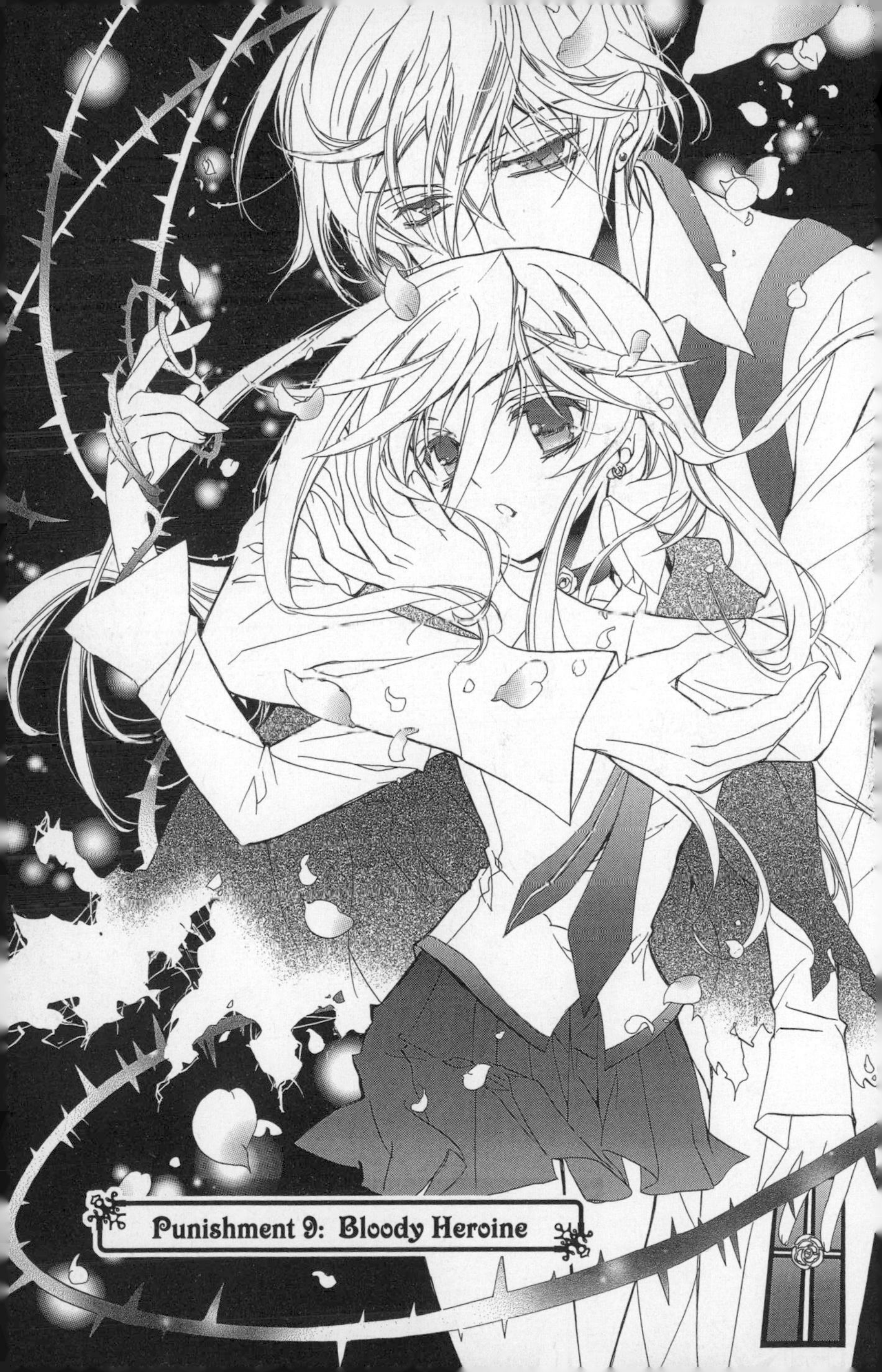
Punishment 9: Bloody Heroine

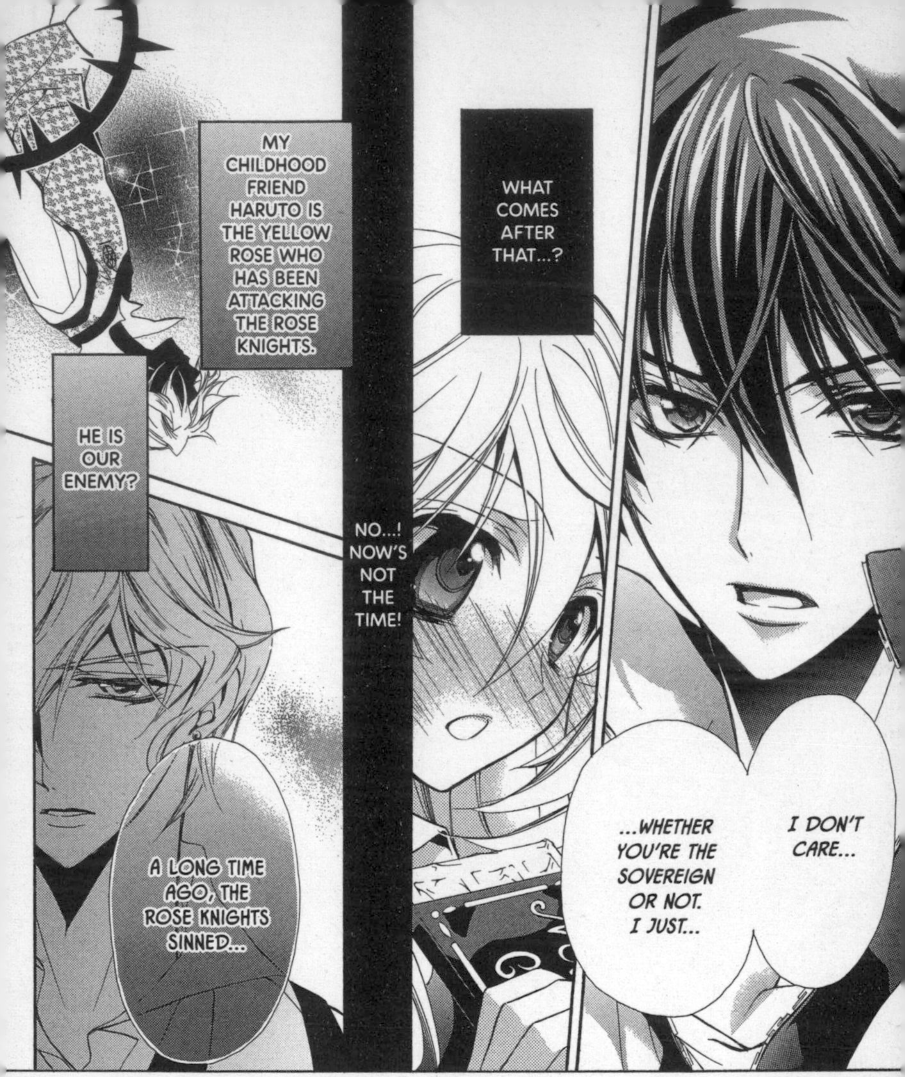
WHAT COMES AFTER THAT...?
I DON'T CARE...
...WHETHER YOU'RE THE SOVEREIGN OR NOT. I JUST...
NO...! NOW'S NOT THE TIME!
MY CHILDHOOD FRIEND HARUTO IS THE YELLOW ROSE WHO HAS BEEN ATTACKING THE ROSE KNIGHTS.
HE IS OUR ENEMY?
A LONG TIME AGO, THE ROSE KNIGHTS SINNED...

Haruto Kisugi

The Octopus Dumpling Prince. I apologize for my limited knowledge of the Osaka dialect. He's "黄薔薇" (Yellow Rose) but I tried to make him seem grander by presenting him as "黄金薔薇" (Golden Rose), so maybe some thought he was the "Gold Rose." It's hard to ignore a jealous boy. But they can be very annoying at times too.

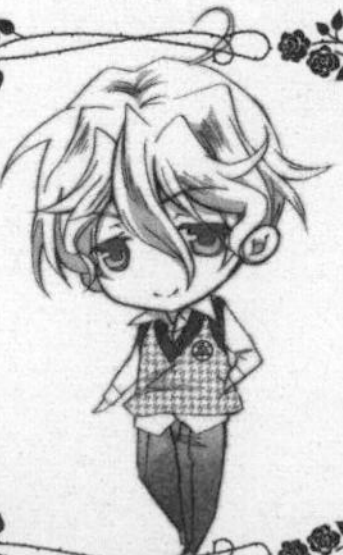

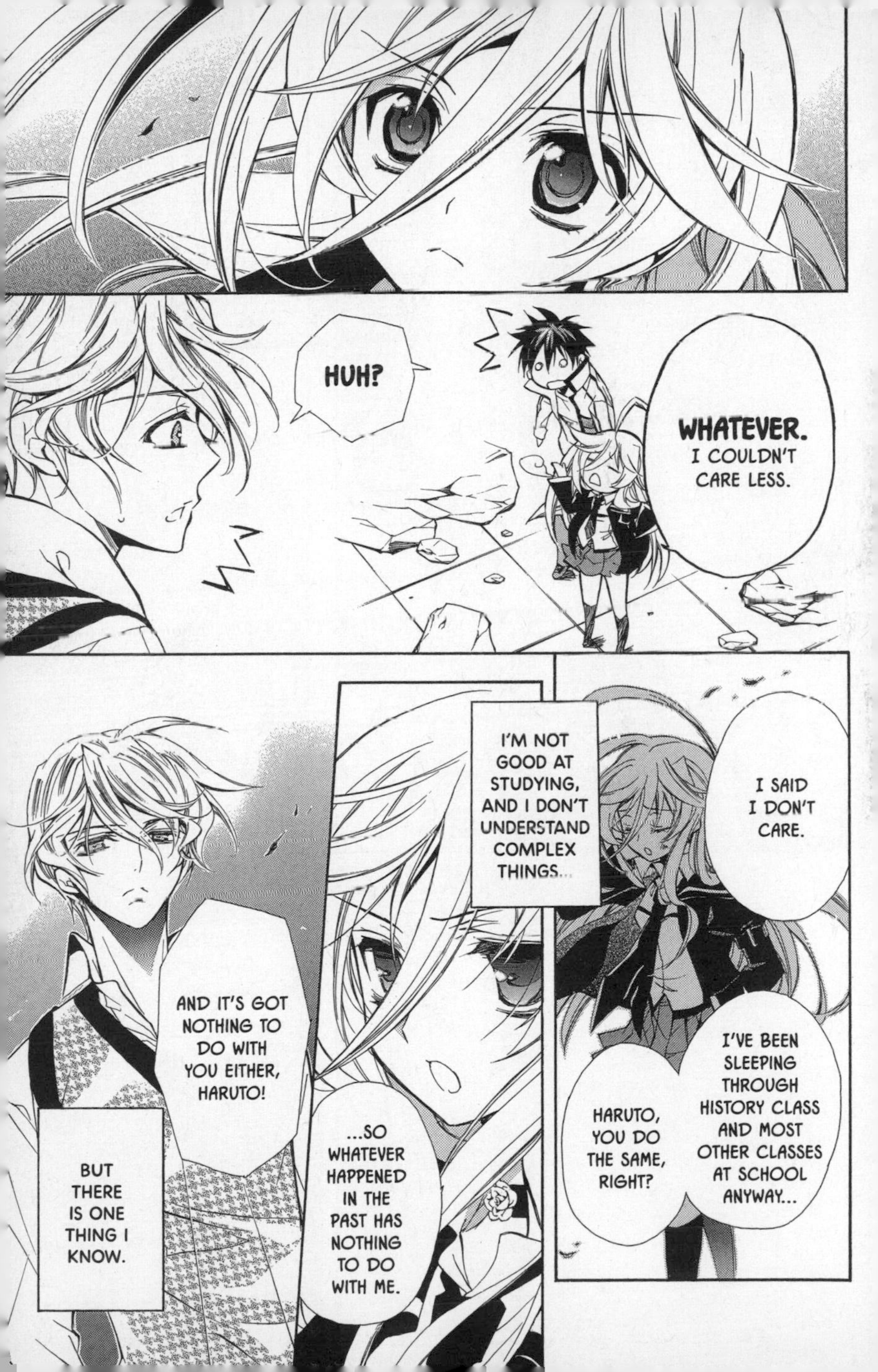
WHATEVER. I COULDN'T CARE LESS.
HUH?
I SAID I DON'T CARE.
I'M NOT GOOD AT STUDYING, AND I DON'T UNDERSTAND COMPLEX THINGS...
I'VE BEEN SLEEPING THROUGH HISTORY CLASS AND MOST OTHER CLASSES AT SCHOOL ANYWAY...
HARUTO, YOU DO THE SAME, RIGHT?
...SO WHATEVER HAPPENED IN THE PAST HAS NOTHING TO DO WITH ME.
AND IT'S GOT NOTHING TO DO WITH YOU EITHER, HARUTO!
BUT THERE IS ONE THING I KNOW.

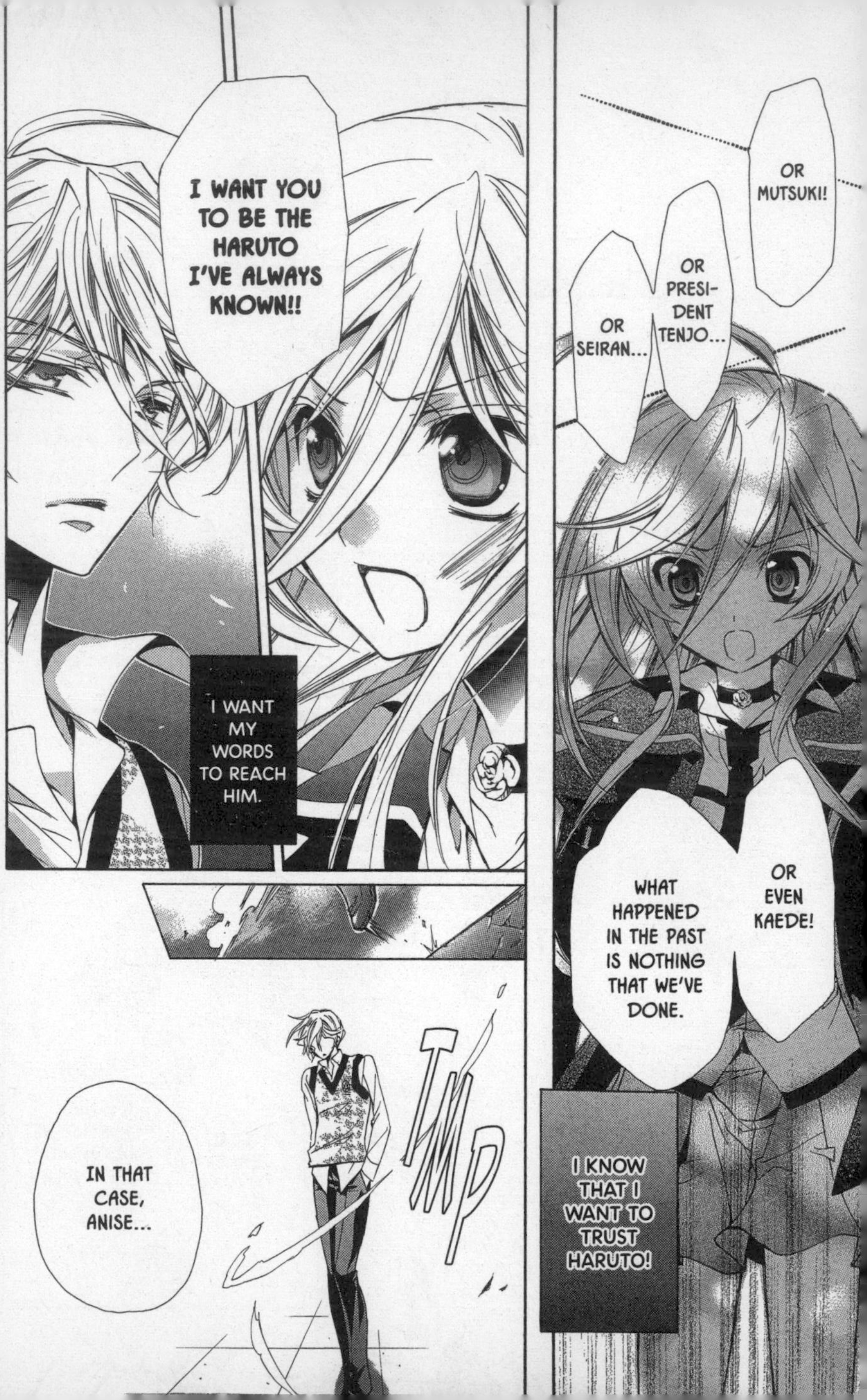
OR MUTSUKI!
OR PRESIDENT TENJO...
OR SEIRAN...
OR EVEN KAEDE!
WHAT HAPPENED IN THE PAST IS NOTHING THAT WE'VE DONE.
I KNOW THAT I WANT TO TRUST HARUTO!
I WANT YOU TO BE THE HARUTO I'VE ALWAYS KNOWN!!
I WANT MY WORDS TO REACH HIM.
TMP
IN THAT CASE, ANISE...

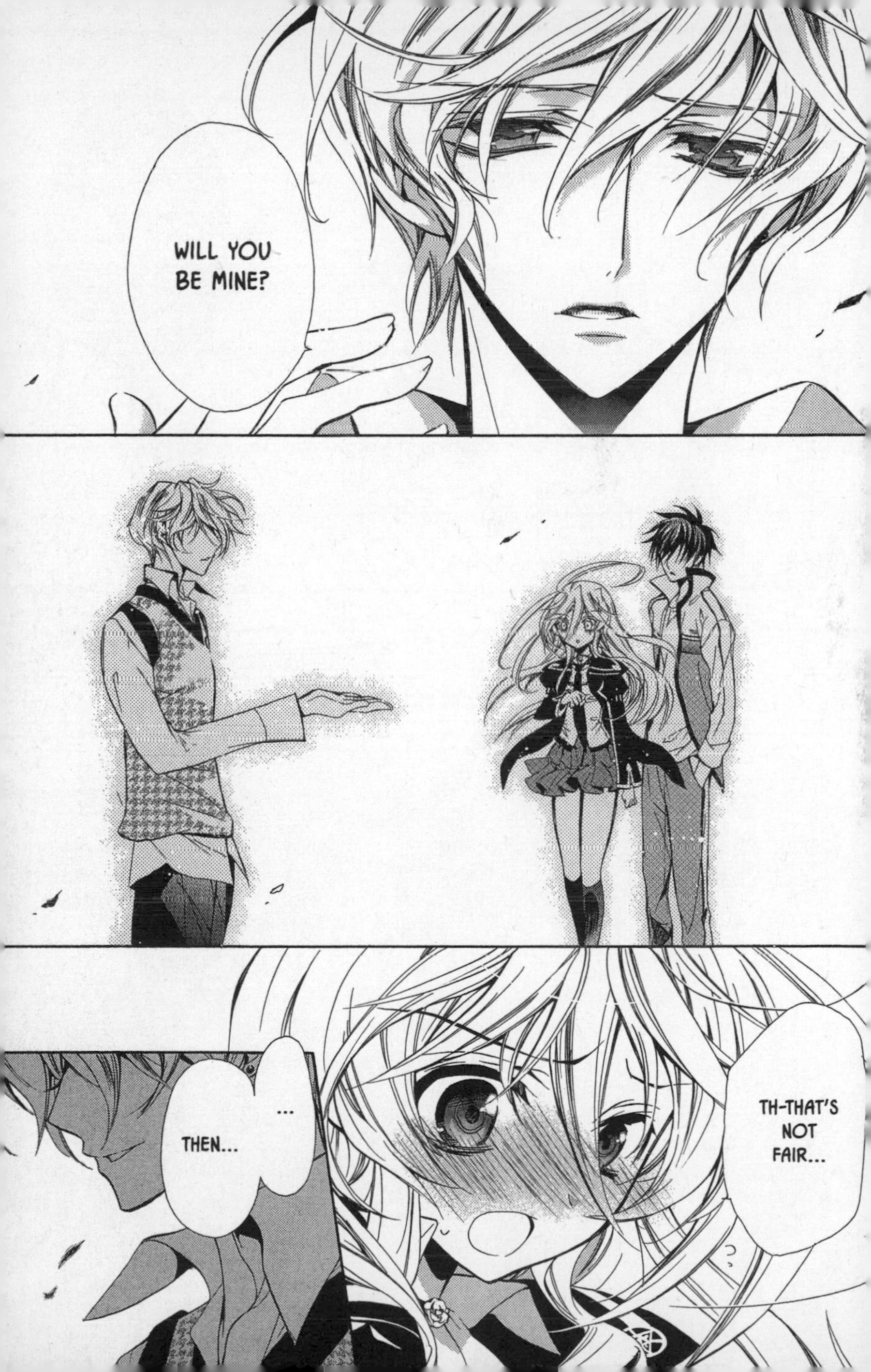
WILL YOU BE MINE?
TH-THAT'S NOT FAIR...
... THEN...

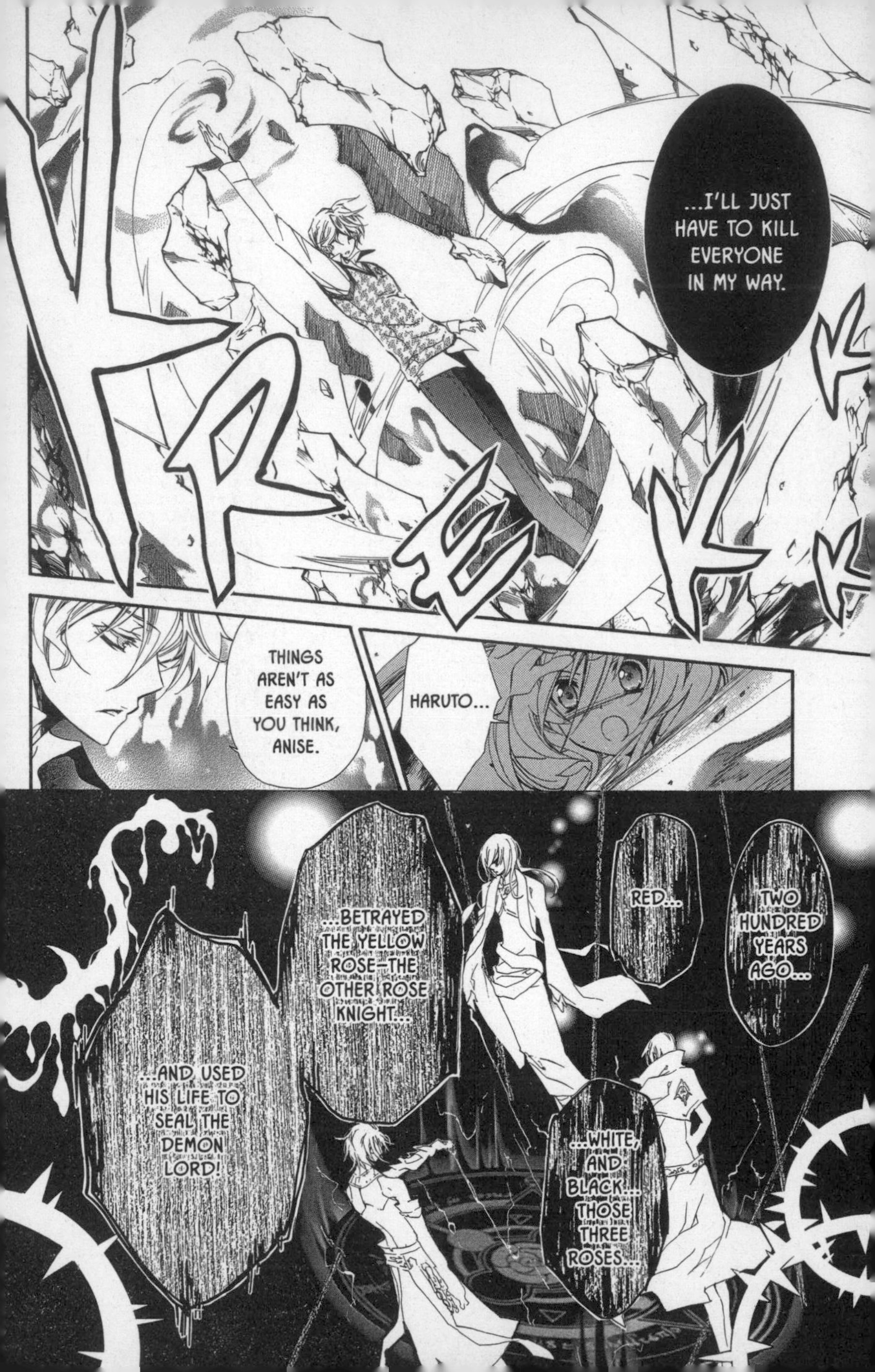
...I'LL JUST HAVE TO KILL EVERYONE IN MY WAY.
HARUTO...
THINGS AREN'T AS EASY AS YOU THINK, ANISE.
TWO HUNDRED YEARS AGO...
RED...
...WHITE, AND BLACK... THOSE THREE ROSES...
...BETRAYED THE YELLOW ROSE—THE OTHER ROSE KNIGHT...
...AND USED HIS LIFE TO SEAL THE DEMON LORD!

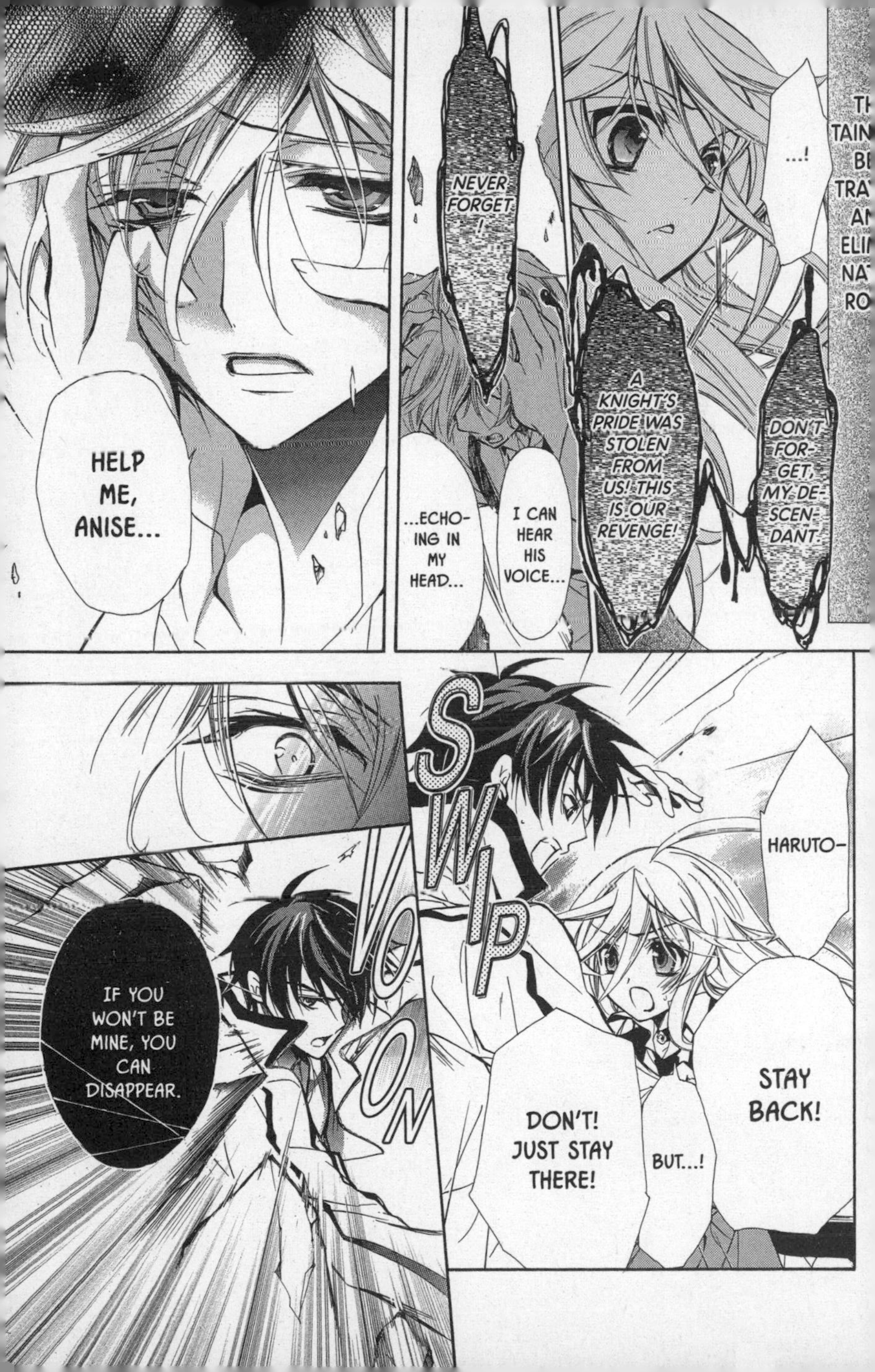
...!
DON'T FOR-GET, MY DE-SCEN-DANT.
A KNIGHT'S PRIDE WAS STOLEN FROM US! THIS IS OUR REVENGE!
NEVER FORGET!
I CAN HEAR HIS VOICE...
...ECHO-ING IN MY HEAD...
HELP ME, ANISE...
HARUTO-
SWIP
STAY BACK!
BUT...!
DON'T! JUST STAY THERE!
VOOON
IF YOU WON'T BE MINE, YOU CAN DISAPPEAR.

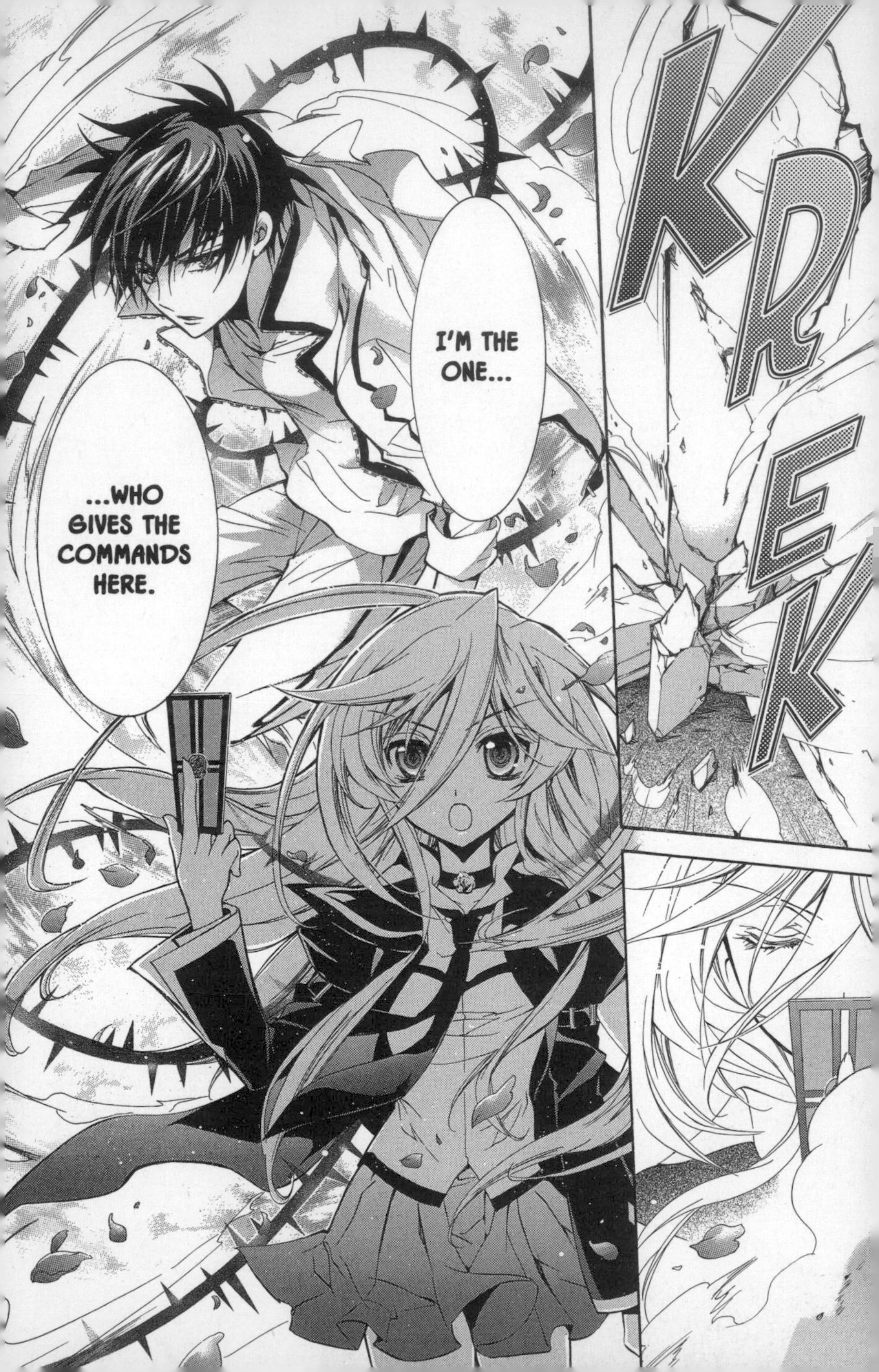
KREK
I'M THE ONE...
...WHO GIVES THE COMMANDS HERE.

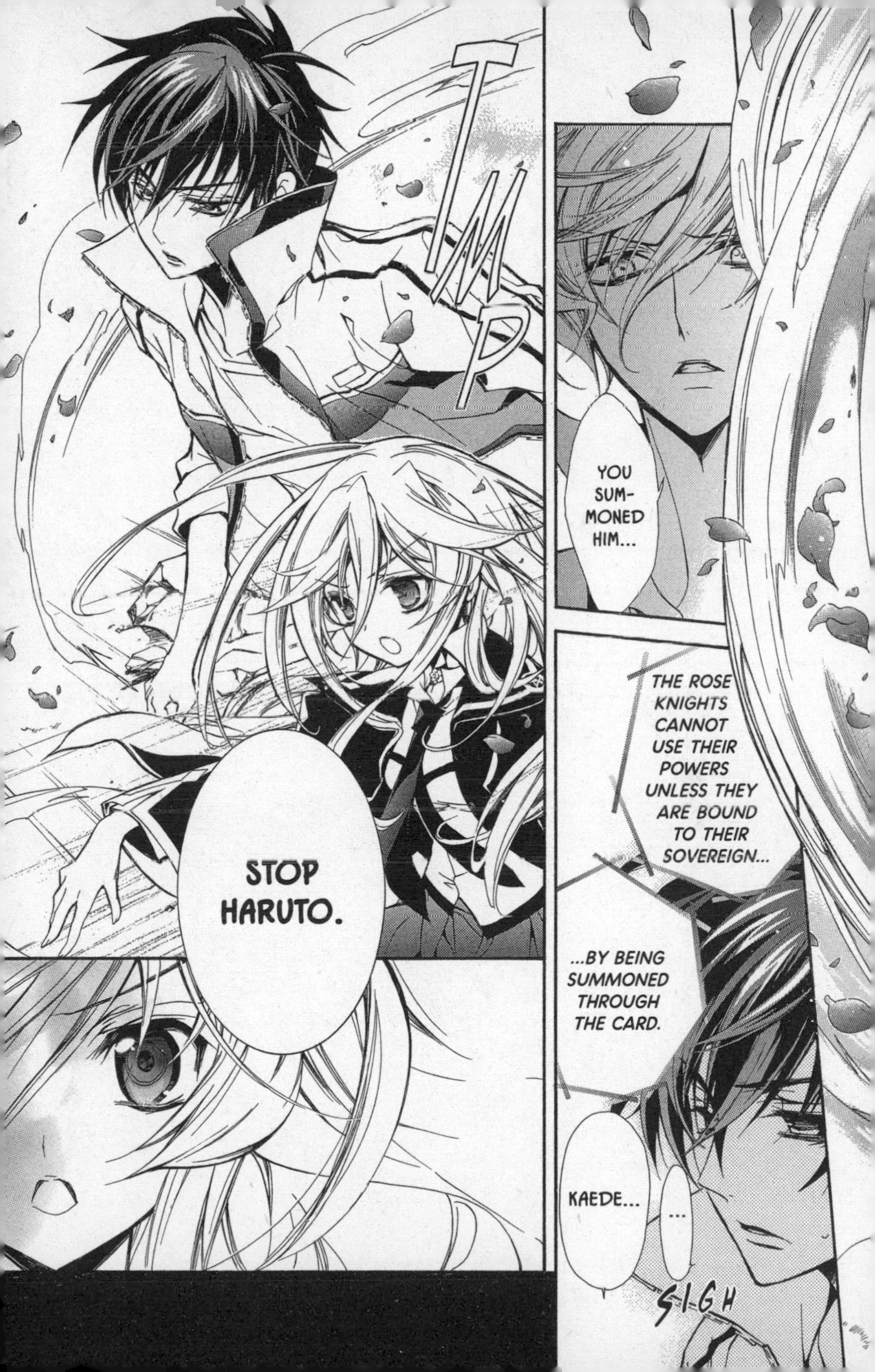
YOU SUMMONED HIM...
THE ROSE KNIGHTS CANNOT USE THEIR POWERS UNLESS THEY ARE BOUND TO THEIR SOVEREIGN...
...BY BEING SUMMONED THROUGH THE CARD.
KAEDE...
...
SIGH
TMP
STOP HARUTO.

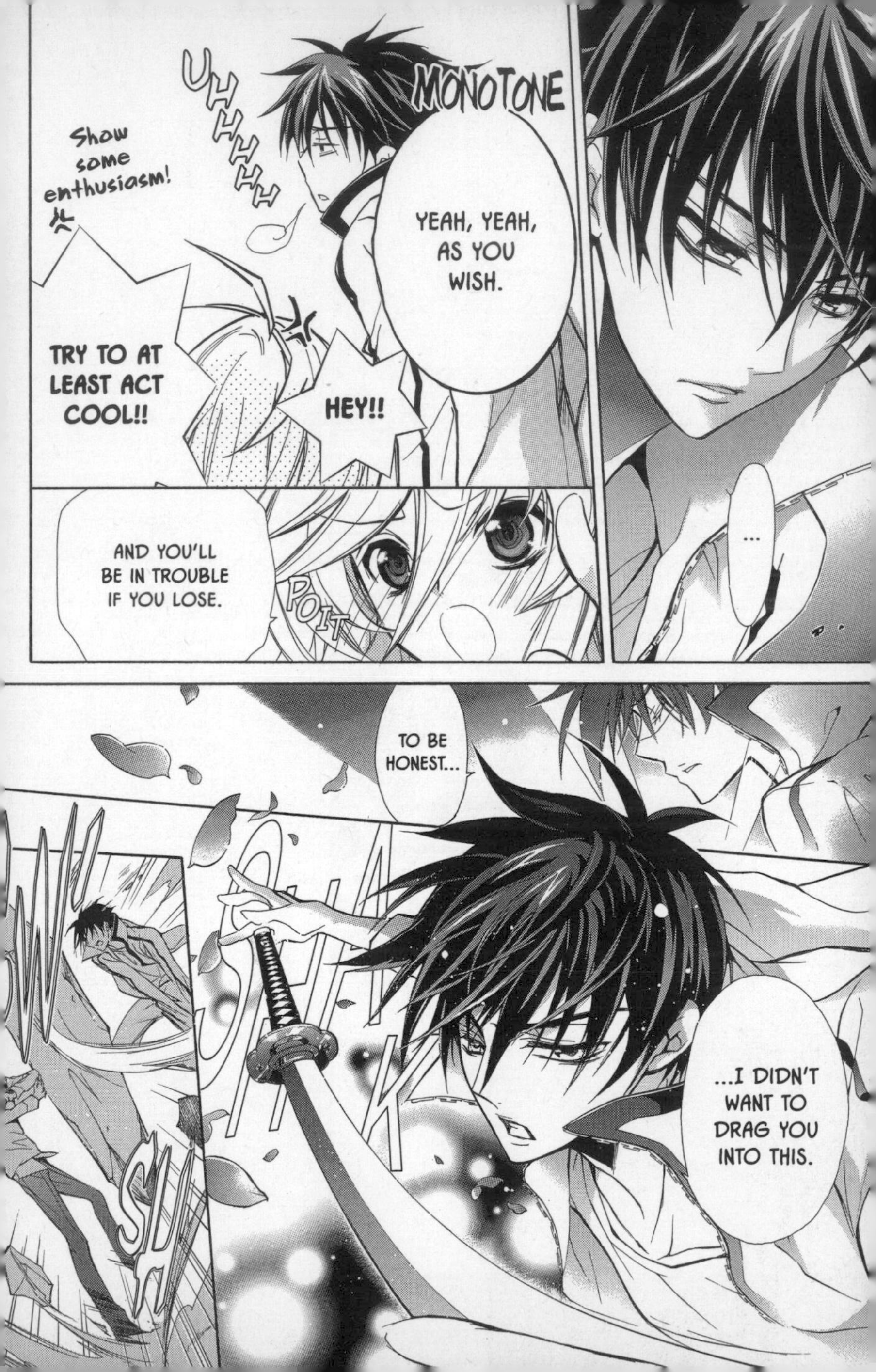
...
MONOTONE
YEAH, YEAH, AS YOU WISH.
UHHHHH
Show some enthusiasm!
HEY!!
TRY TO AT LEAST ACT COOL!!
POIT
AND YOU'LL BE IN TROUBLE IF YOU LOSE.
TO BE HONEST...
...I DIDN'T WANT TO DRAG YOU INTO THIS.

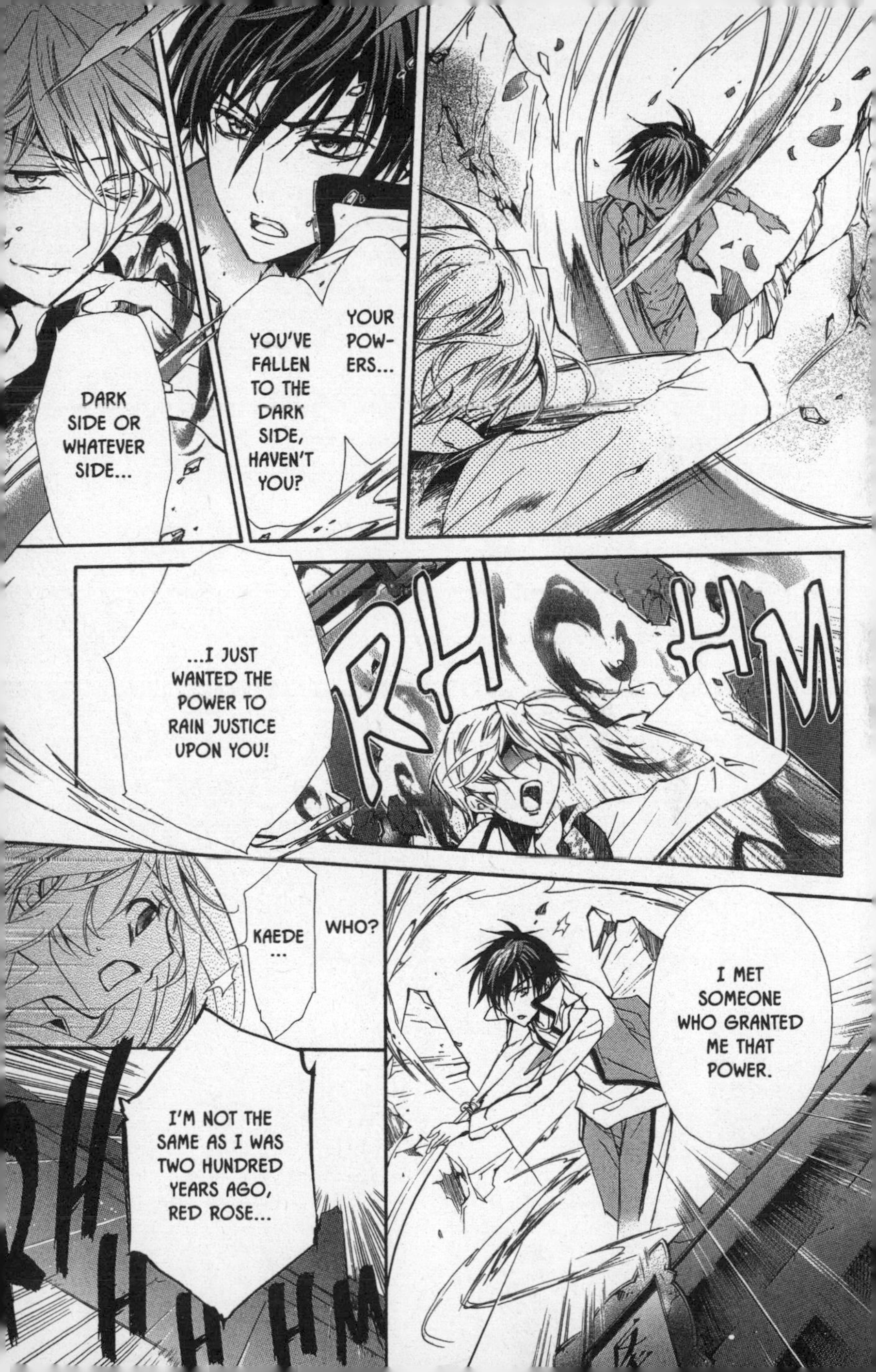
YOUR POWERS...
YOU'VE FALLEN TO THE DARK SIDE, HAVEN'T YOU?
DARK SIDE OR WHATEVER SIDE...
RHHM
...I JUST WANTED THE POWER TO RAIN JUSTICE UPON YOU!
I MET SOMEONE WHO GRANTED ME THAT POWER.
WHO?
KAEDE...
I'M NOT THE SAME AS I WAS TWO HUNDRED YEARS AGO, RED ROSE...
RHHHM

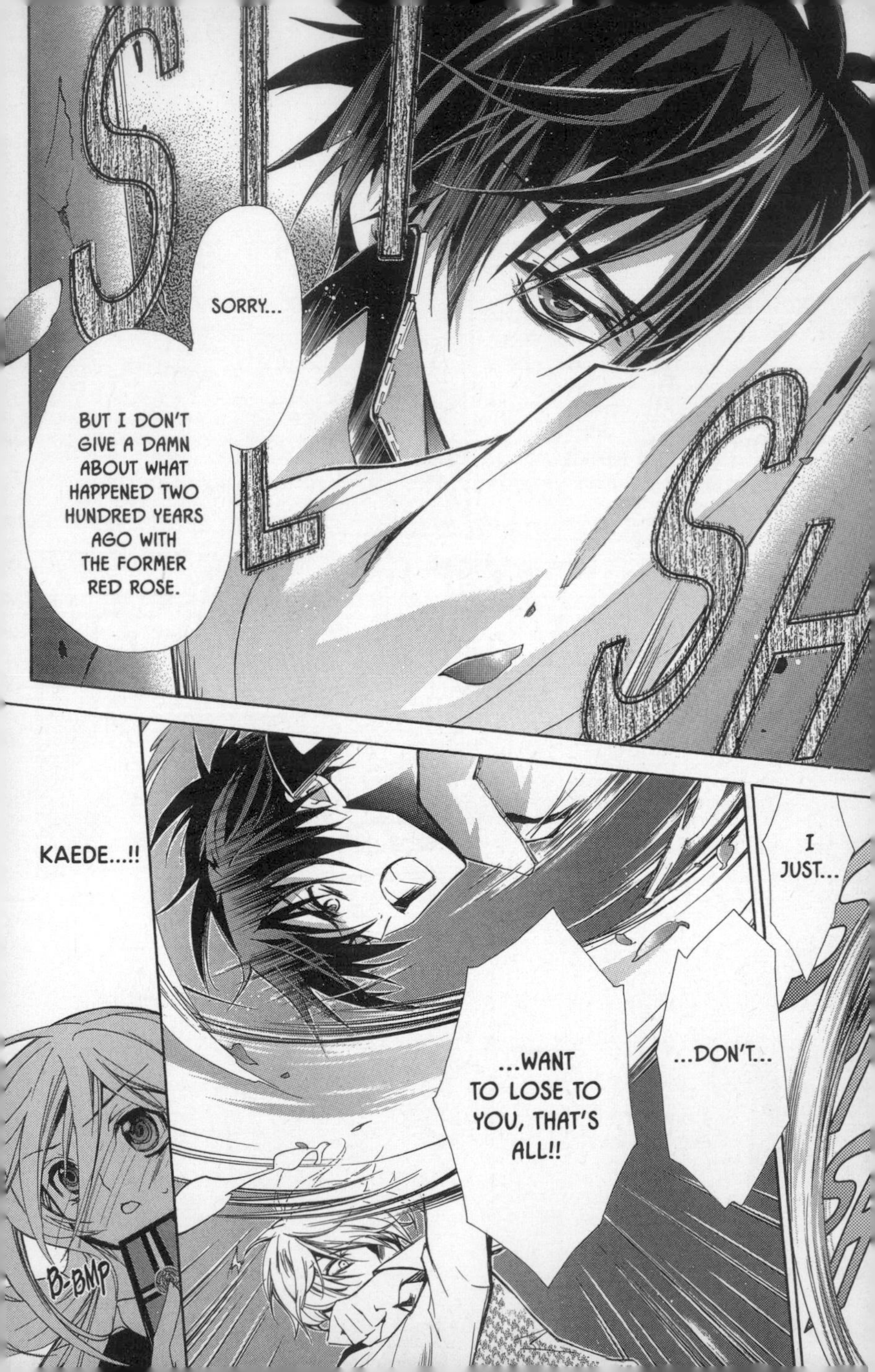
SORRY...
BUT I DON'T GIVE A DAMN ABOUT WHAT HAPPENED TWO HUNDRED YEARS AGO WITH THE FORMER RED ROSE.
I JUST...
...DON'T...
...WANT TO LOSE TO YOU, THAT'S ALL!!
KAEDE...!!
B-BMP

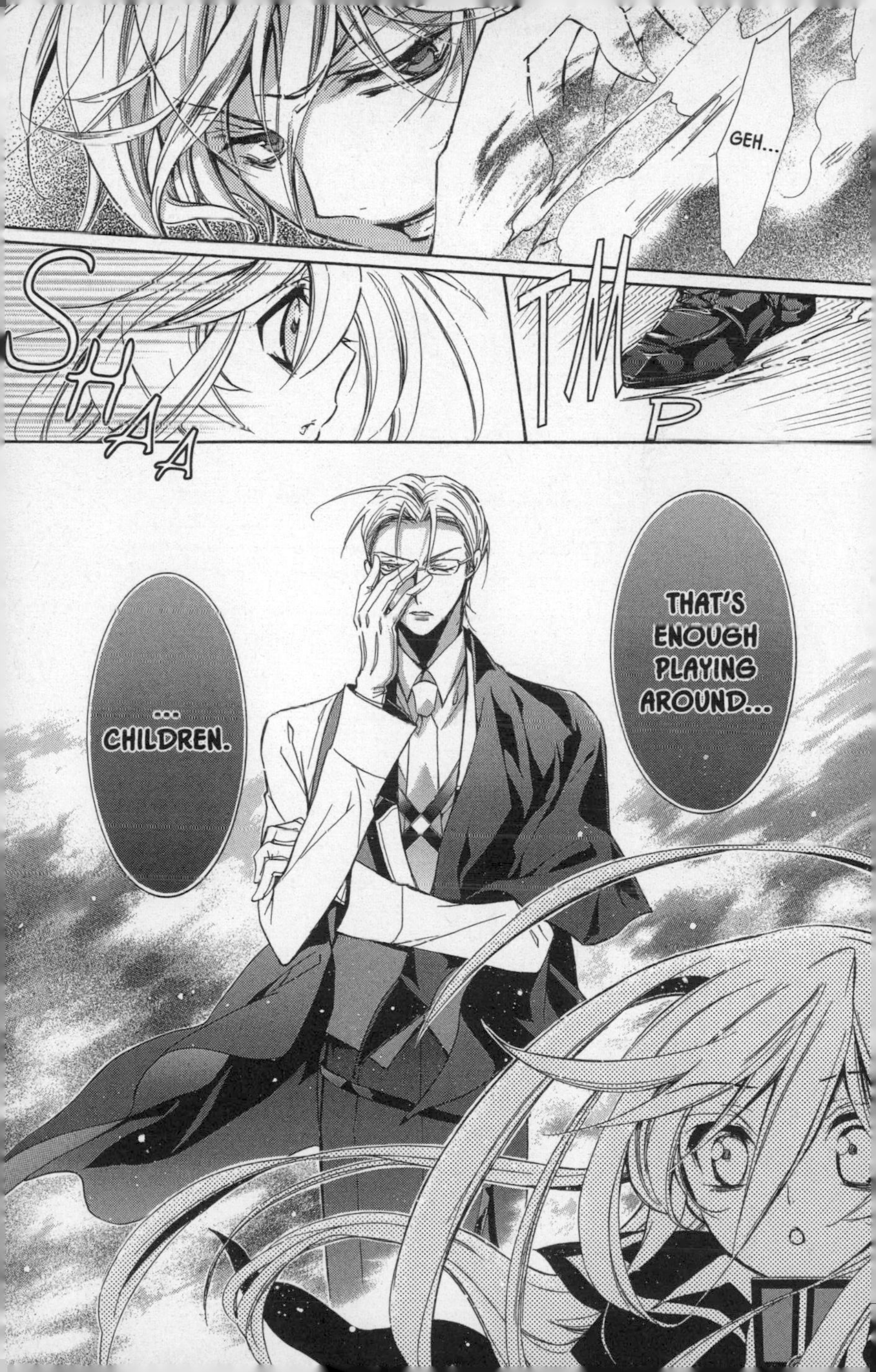
GEH...
TMP
SHAAA
THAT'S ENOUGH PLAYING AROUND...
...CHILDREN.

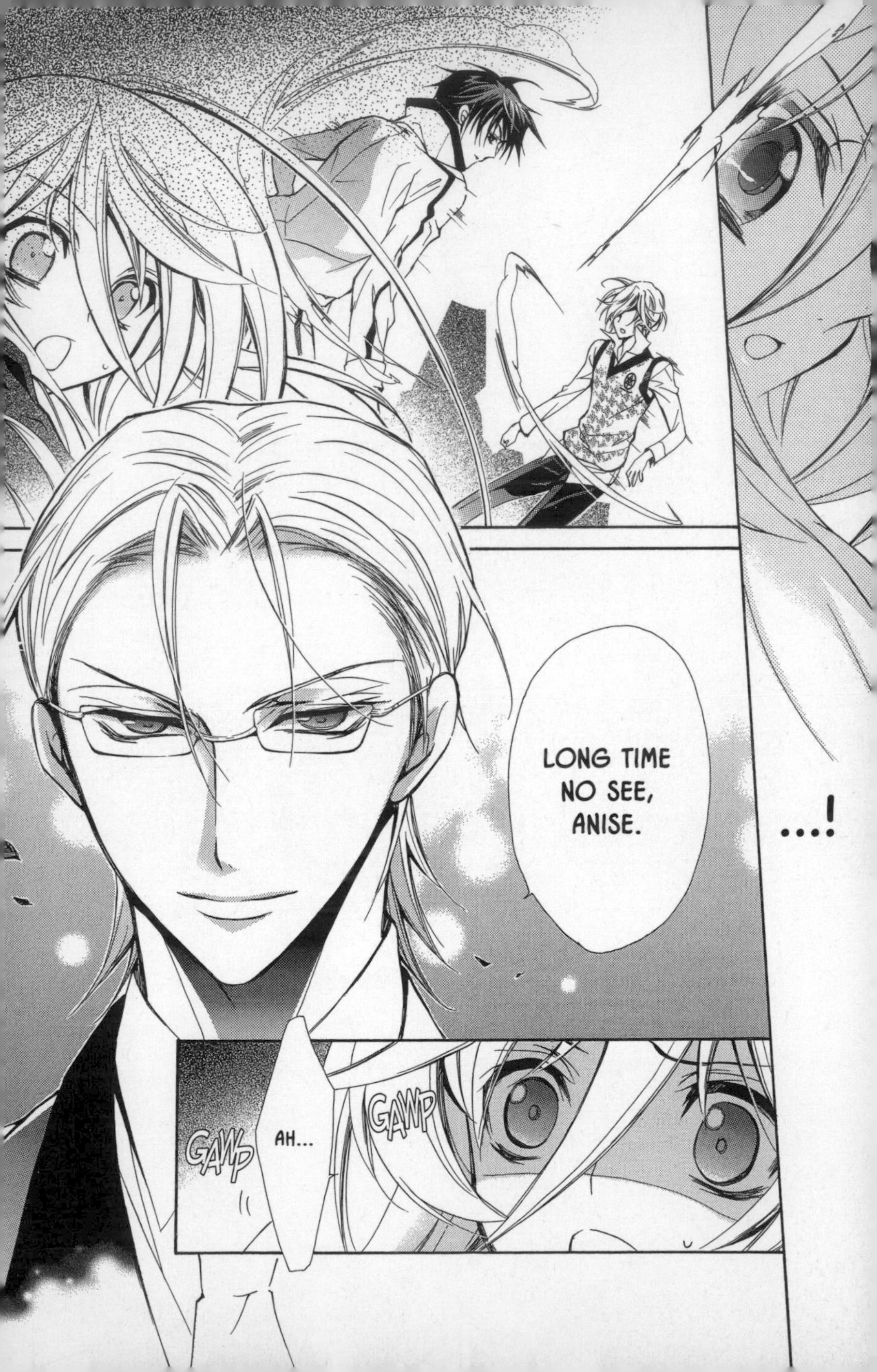
...!
LONG TIME NO SEE, ANISE.
GAWP
AH...
GAWP

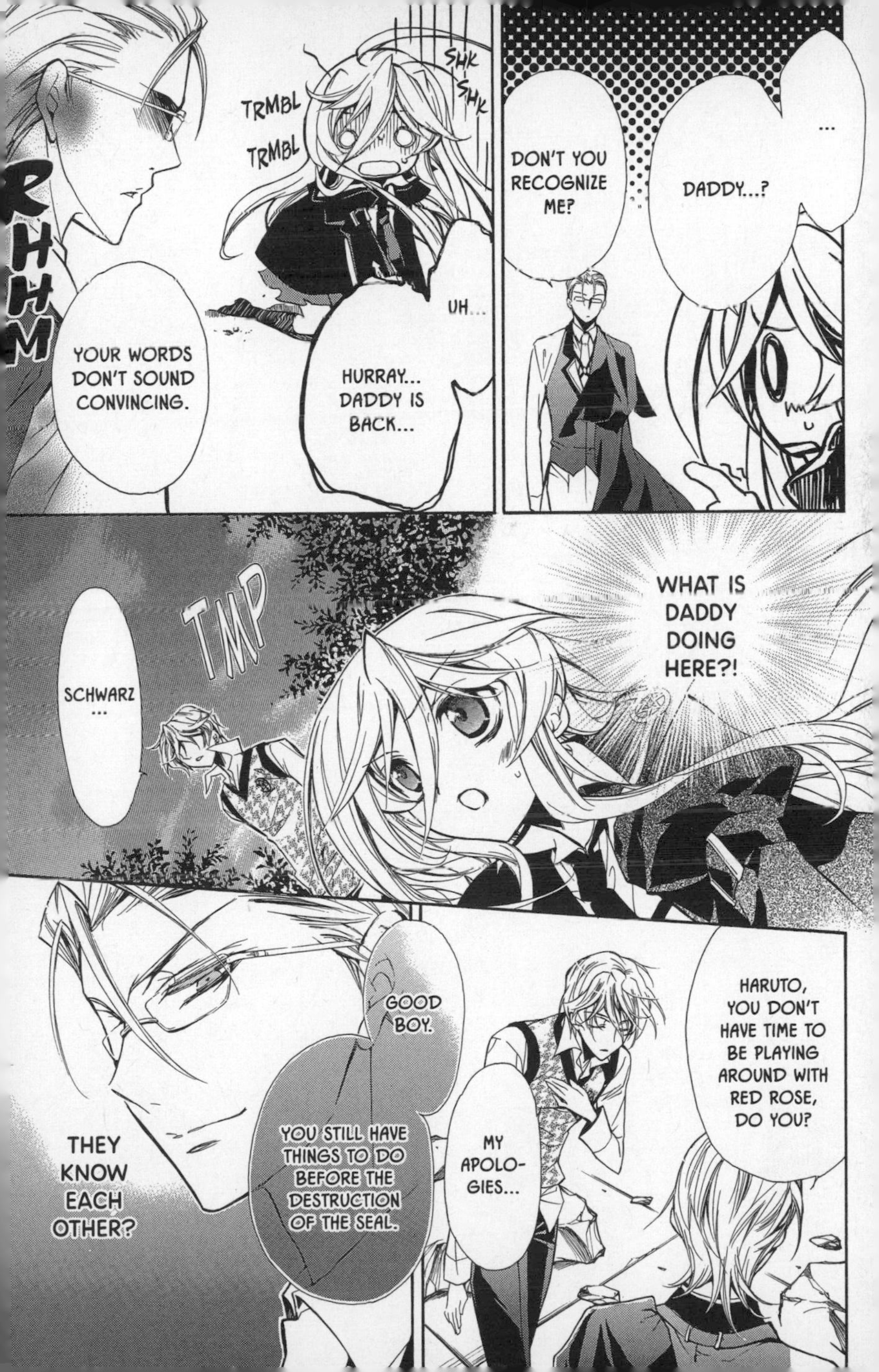
...
DADDY...?
DON'T YOU RECOGNIZE ME?
SHK SHK
TRMBL TRMBL
UH...
HURRAY... DADDY IS BACK...
RHHM
YOUR WORDS DON'T SOUND CONVINCING.
WHAT IS DADDY DOING HERE?!
TMP
SCHWARZ...
HARUTO, YOU DON'T HAVE TIME TO BE PLAYING AROUND WITH RED ROSE, DO YOU?
MY APOLOGIES...
GOOD BOY.
YOU STILL HAVE THINGS TO DO BEFORE THE DESTRUCTION OF THE SEAL.
THEY KNOW EACH OTHER?

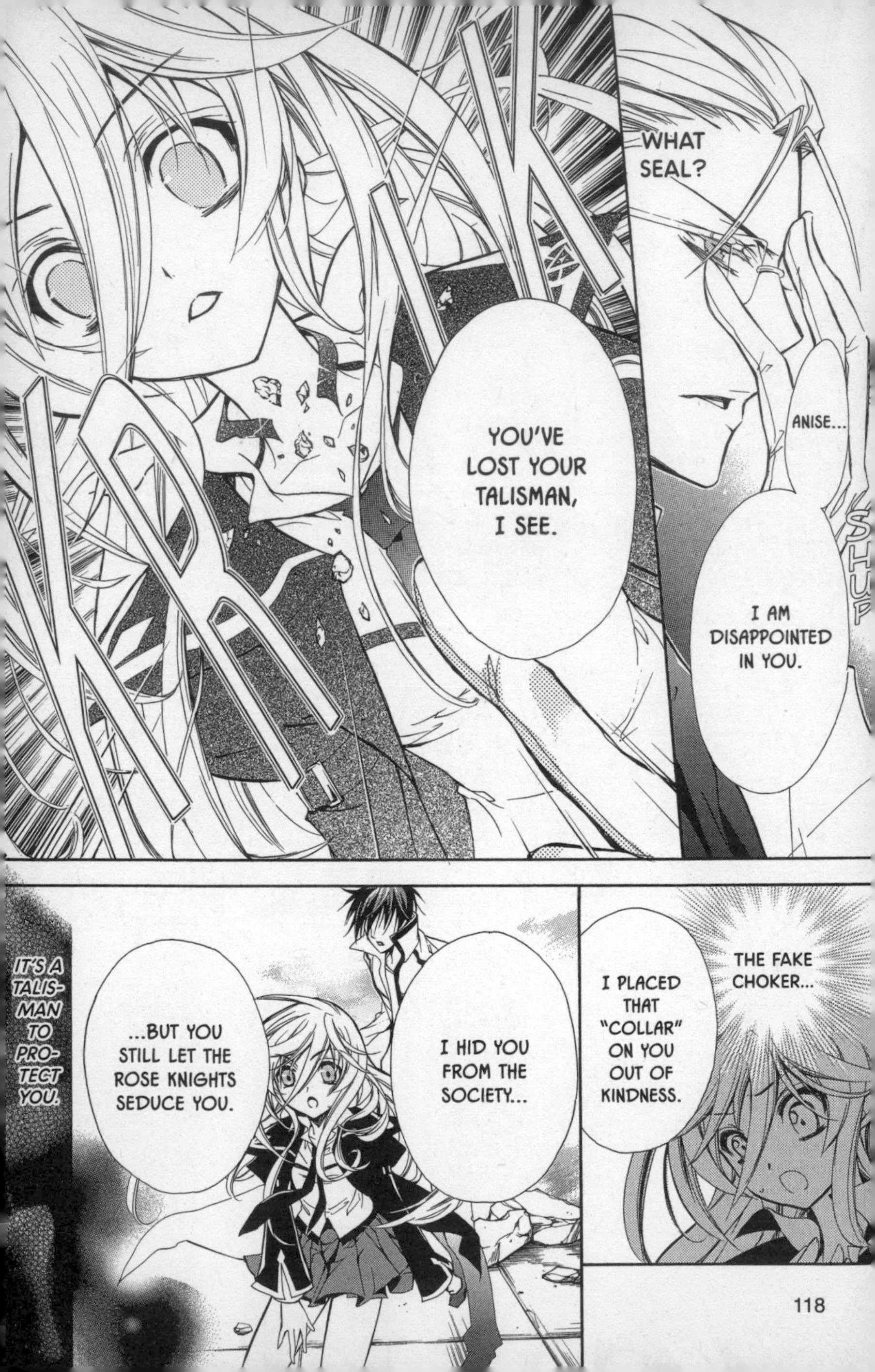
WHAT SEAL?
ANISE...
SHUP
I AM DISAPPOINTED IN YOU.
YOU'VE LOST YOUR TALISMAN, I SEE.
THE FAKE CHOKER...
I PLACED THAT "COLLAR" ON YOU OUT OF KINDNESS.
I HID YOU FROM THE SOCIETY...
...BUT YOU STILL LET THE ROSE KNIGHTS SEDUCE YOU.
IT'S A TALISMAN TO PROTECT YOU.

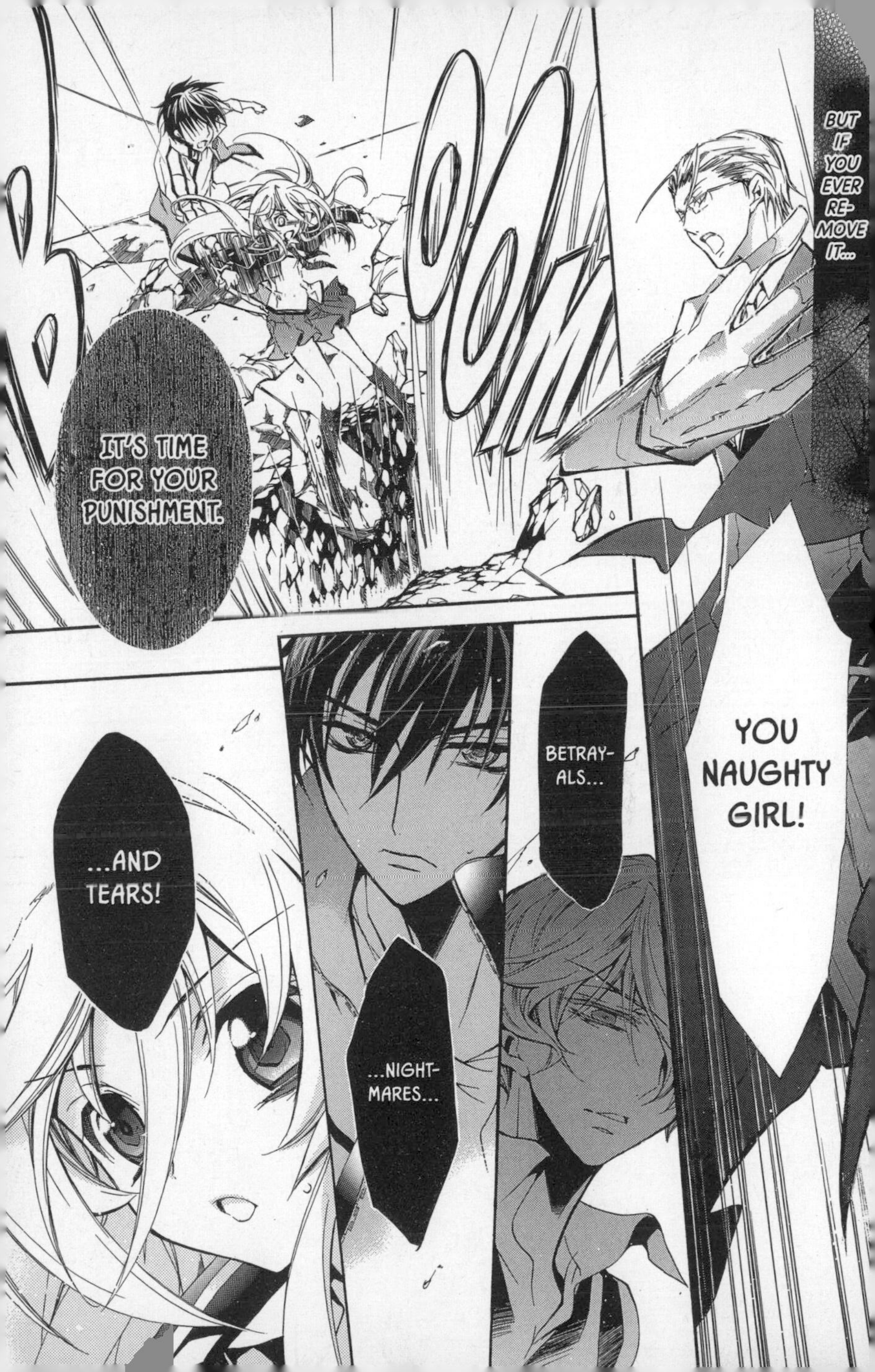
BUT IF YOU EVER RE-MOVE IT...
IT'S TIME FOR YOUR PUNISHMENT.
YOU NAUGHTY GIRL!
BETRAY-ALS...
...NIGHT-MARES...
...AND TEARS!

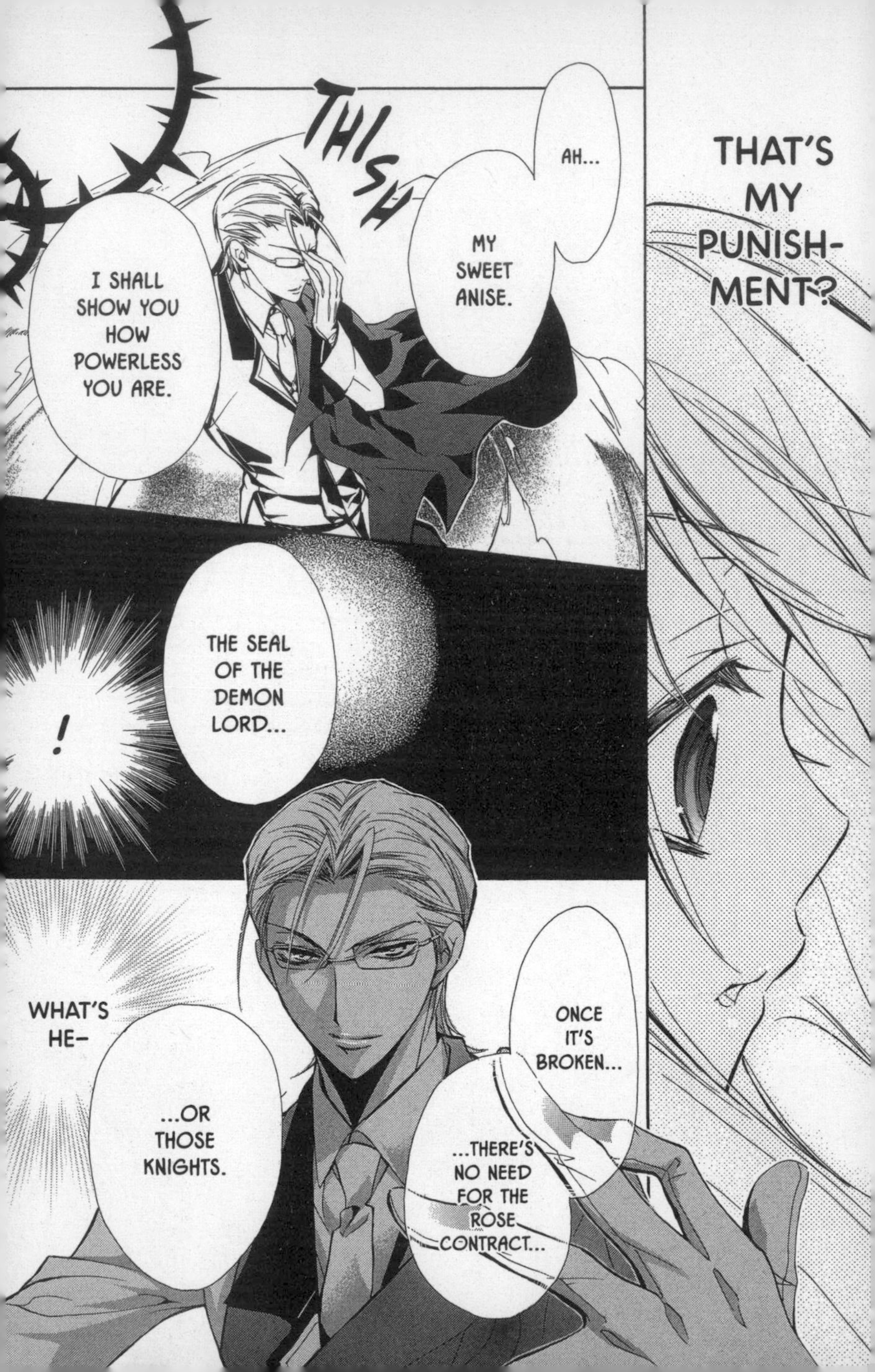
THAT'S MY PUNISHMENT?
AH...
THISH
MY SWEET ANISE.
I SHALL SHOW YOU HOW POWERLESS YOU ARE.
THE SEAL OF THE DEMON LORD...
!
ONCE IT'S BROKEN...
...THERE'S NO NEED FOR THE ROSE CONTRACT...
...OR THOSE KNIGHTS.
WHAT'S HE–

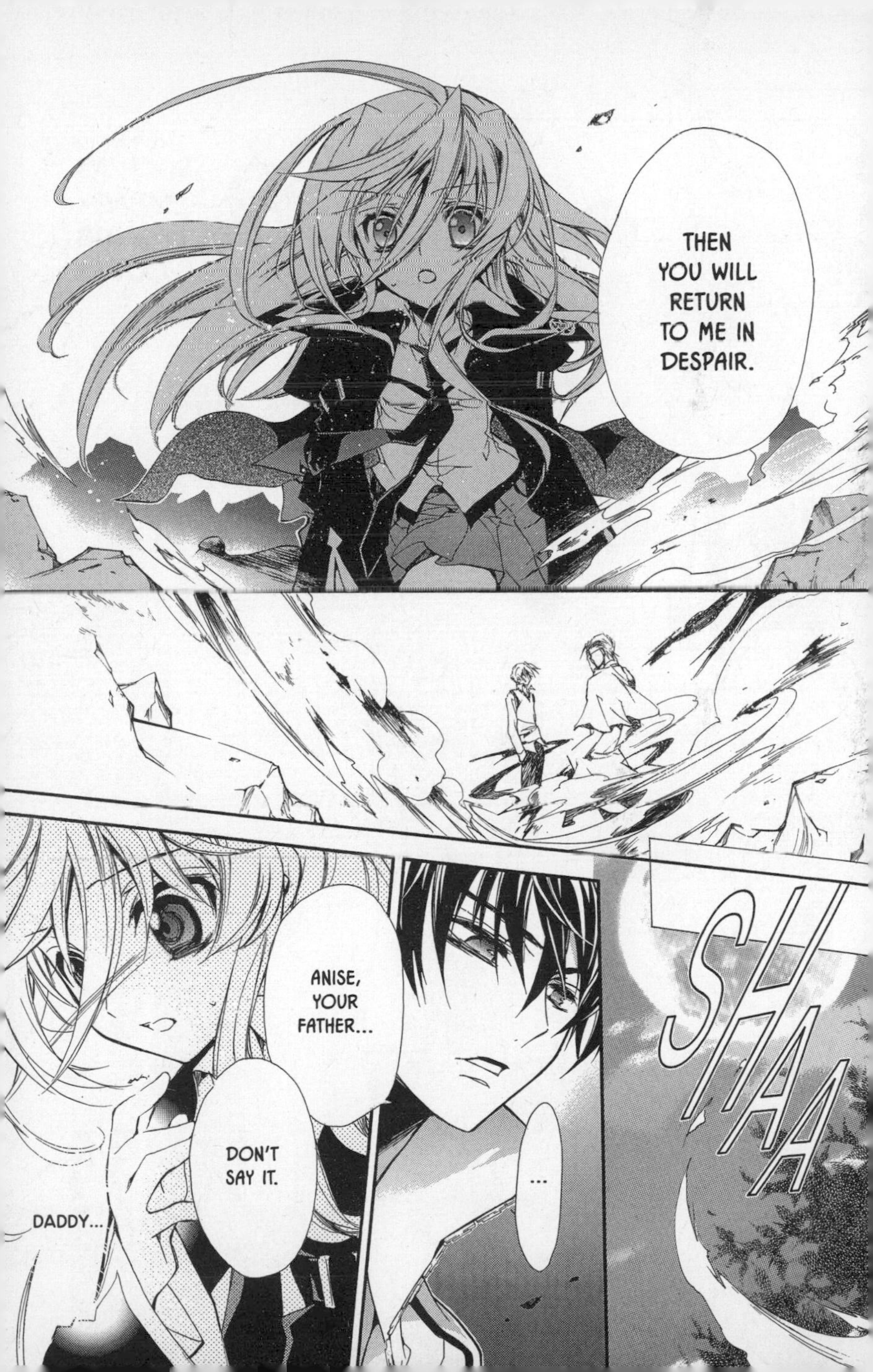
THEN YOU WILL RETURN TO ME IN DESPAIR.
SHAA
ANISE, YOUR FATHER...
...
DON'T SAY IT.
DADDY...

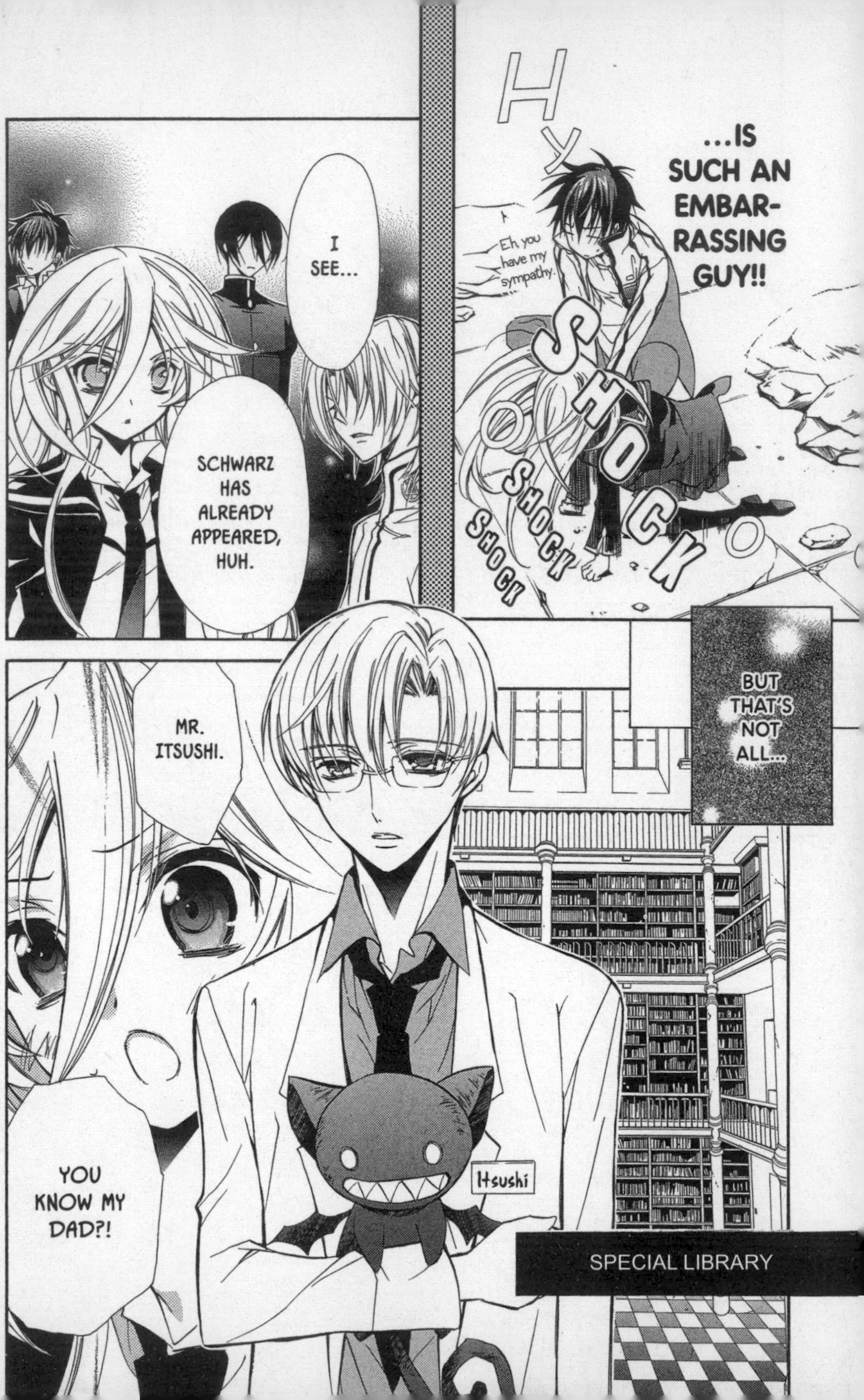
...IS SUCH AN EMBAR-RASSING GUY!!
Eh, you have my sympathy.
SHOCK
SHOCK
SHOCK
I SEE...
SCHWARZ HAS ALREADY APPEARED, HUH.
BUT THAT'S NOT ALL...
MR. ITSUSHI.
SPECIAL LIBRARY
Itsushi
YOU KNOW MY DAD?!

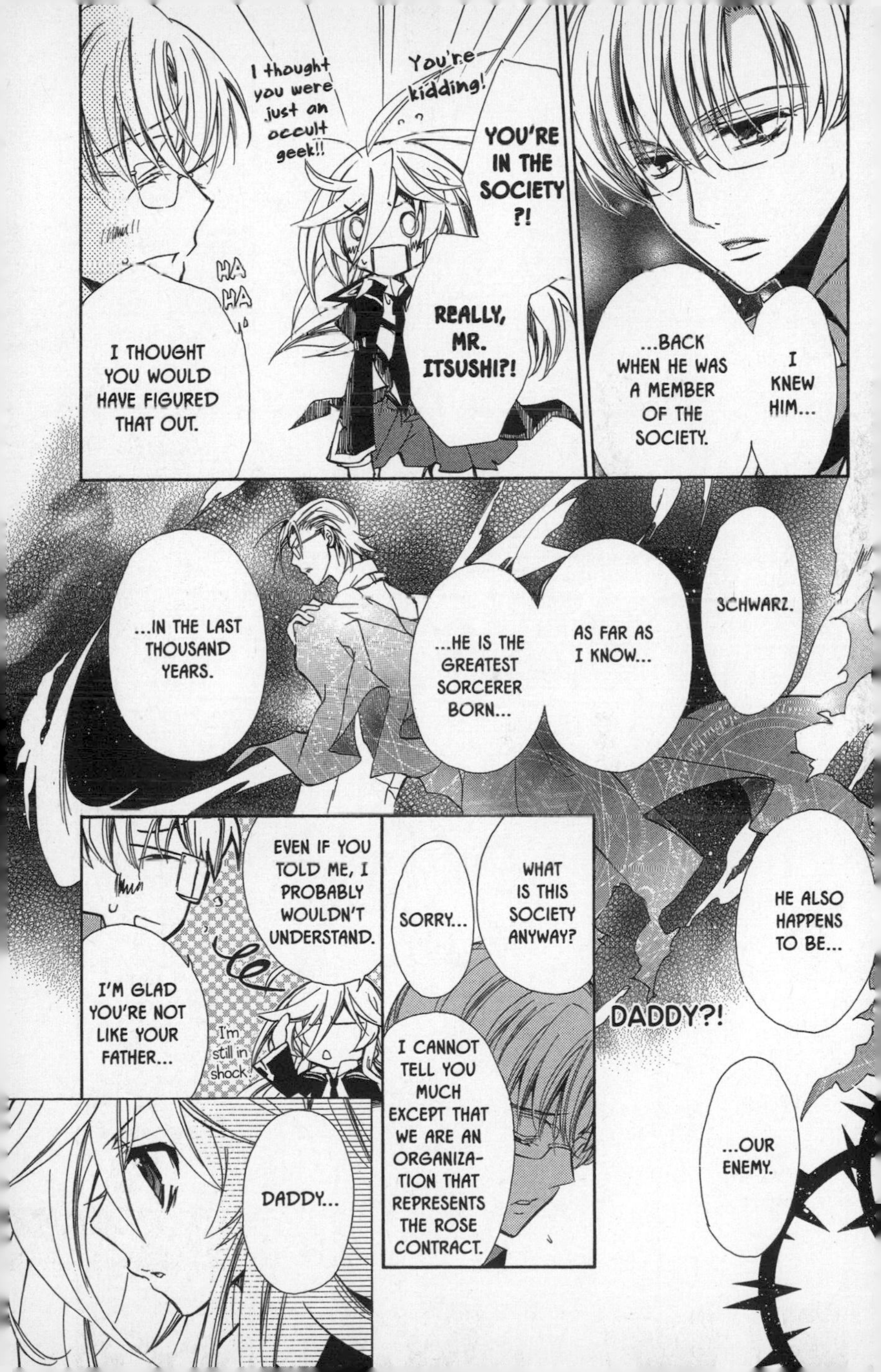
I KNEW HIM...
...BACK WHEN HE WAS A MEMBER OF THE SOCIETY.
YOU'RE IN THE SOCIETY?!
You're kidding!
REALLY, MR. ITSUSHI?!
I thought you were just an occult geek!!
HA HA
I THOUGHT YOU WOULD HAVE FIGURED THAT OUT.
SCHWARZ.
AS FAR AS I KNOW...
...HE IS THE GREATEST SORCERER BORN...
...IN THE LAST THOUSAND YEARS.
HE ALSO HAPPENS TO BE...
...OUR ENEMY.
DADDY?!
WHAT IS THIS SOCIETY ANYWAY?
SORRY...
I CANNOT TELL YOU MUCH EXCEPT THAT WE ARE AN ORGANIZA-TION THAT REPRESENTS THE ROSE CONTRACT.
EVEN IF YOU TOLD ME, I PROBABLY WOULDN'T UNDERSTAND.
I'M GLAD YOU'RE NOT LIKE YOUR FATHER...
I'm still in shock
DADDY...

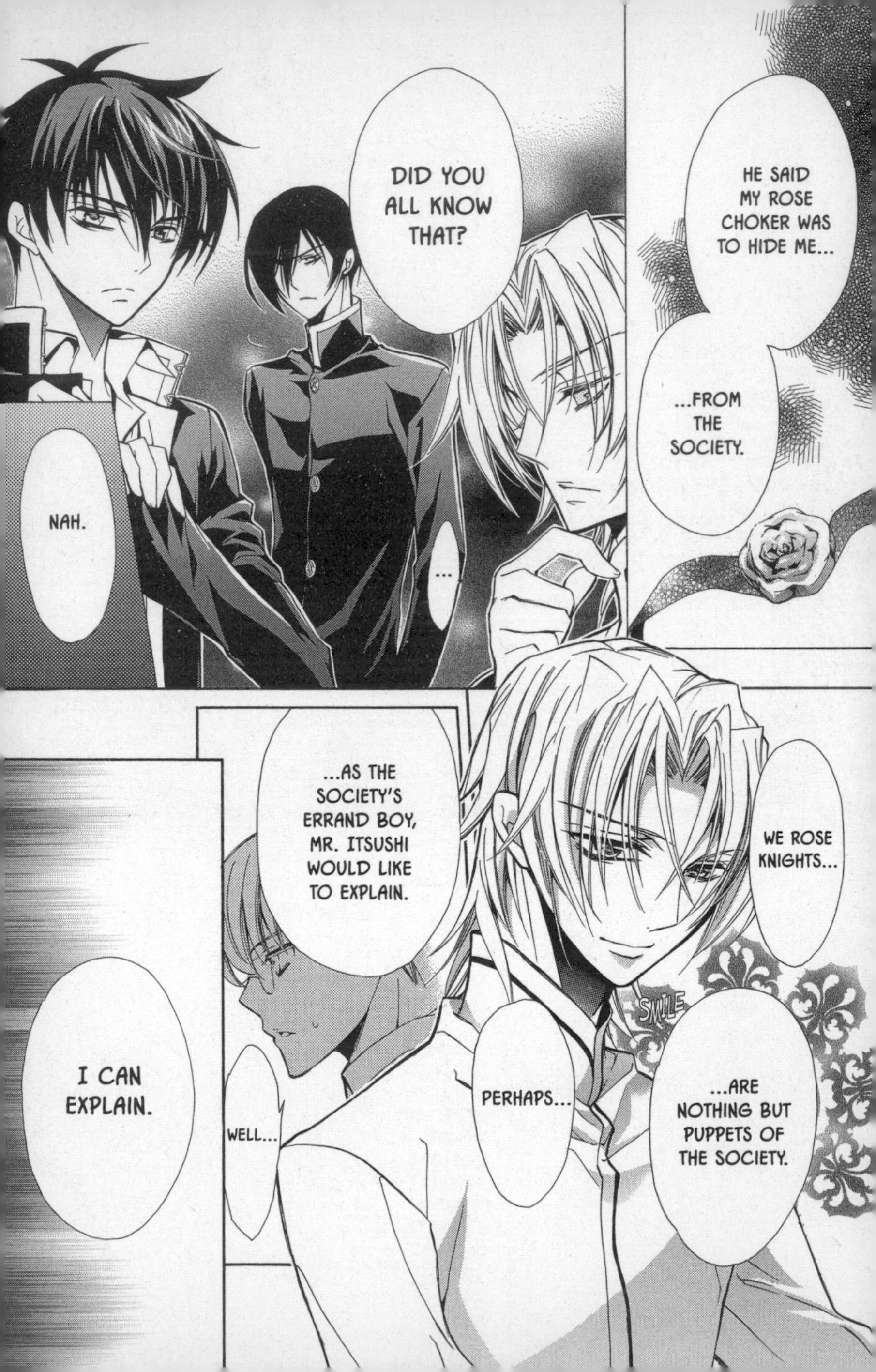
HE SAID MY ROSE CHOKER WAS TO HIDE ME...
...FROM THE SOCIETY.
DID YOU ALL KNOW THAT?
...
NAH.
WE ROSE KNIGHTS...
...ARE NOTHING BUT PUPPETS OF THE SOCIETY.
SMILE
PERHAPS...
...AS THE SOCIETY'S ERRAND BOY, MR. ITSUSHI WOULD LIKE TO EXPLAIN.
WELL...
I CAN EXPLAIN.

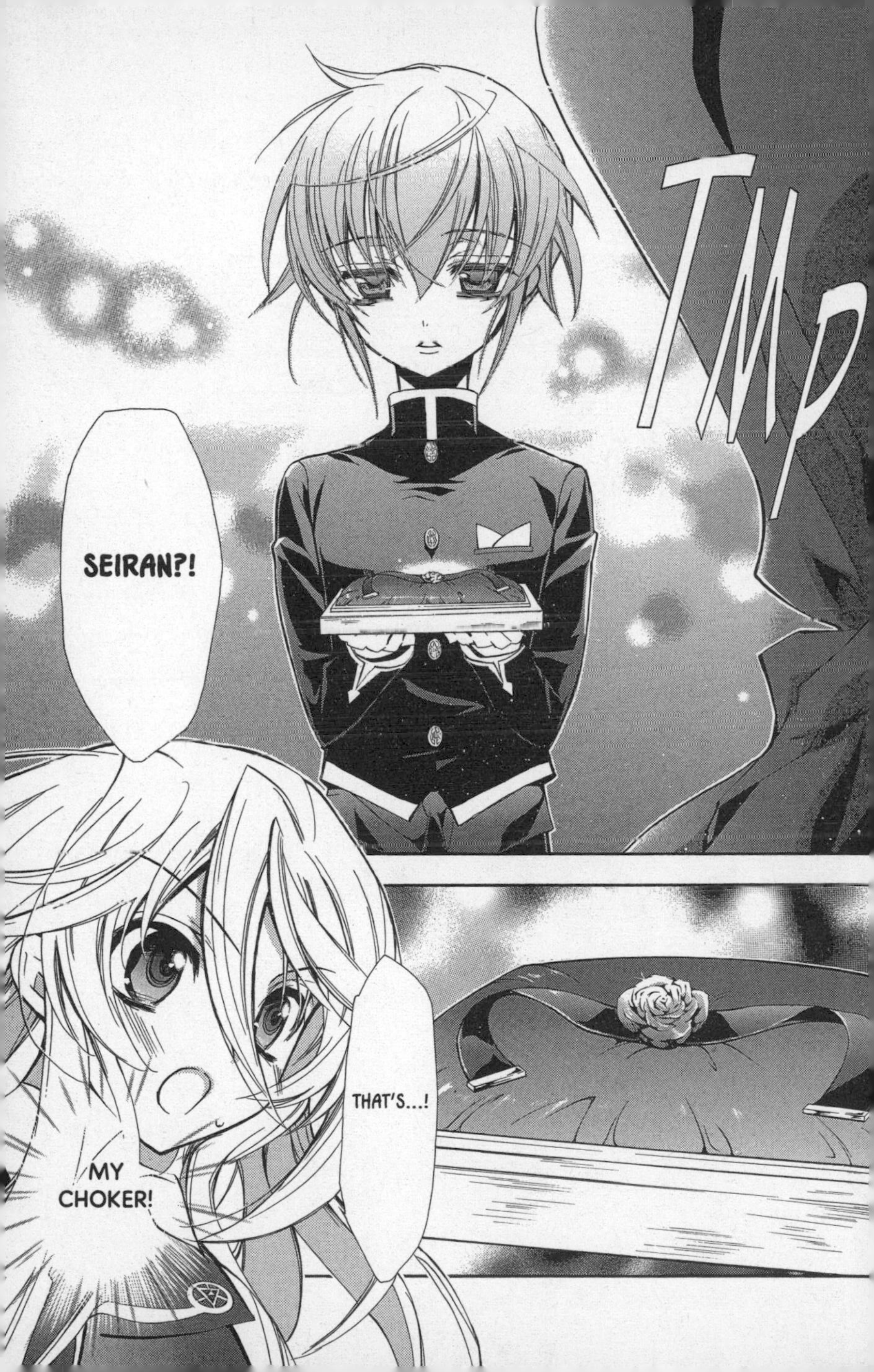
TMP
SEIRAN?!
THAT'S...!
MY CHOKER!

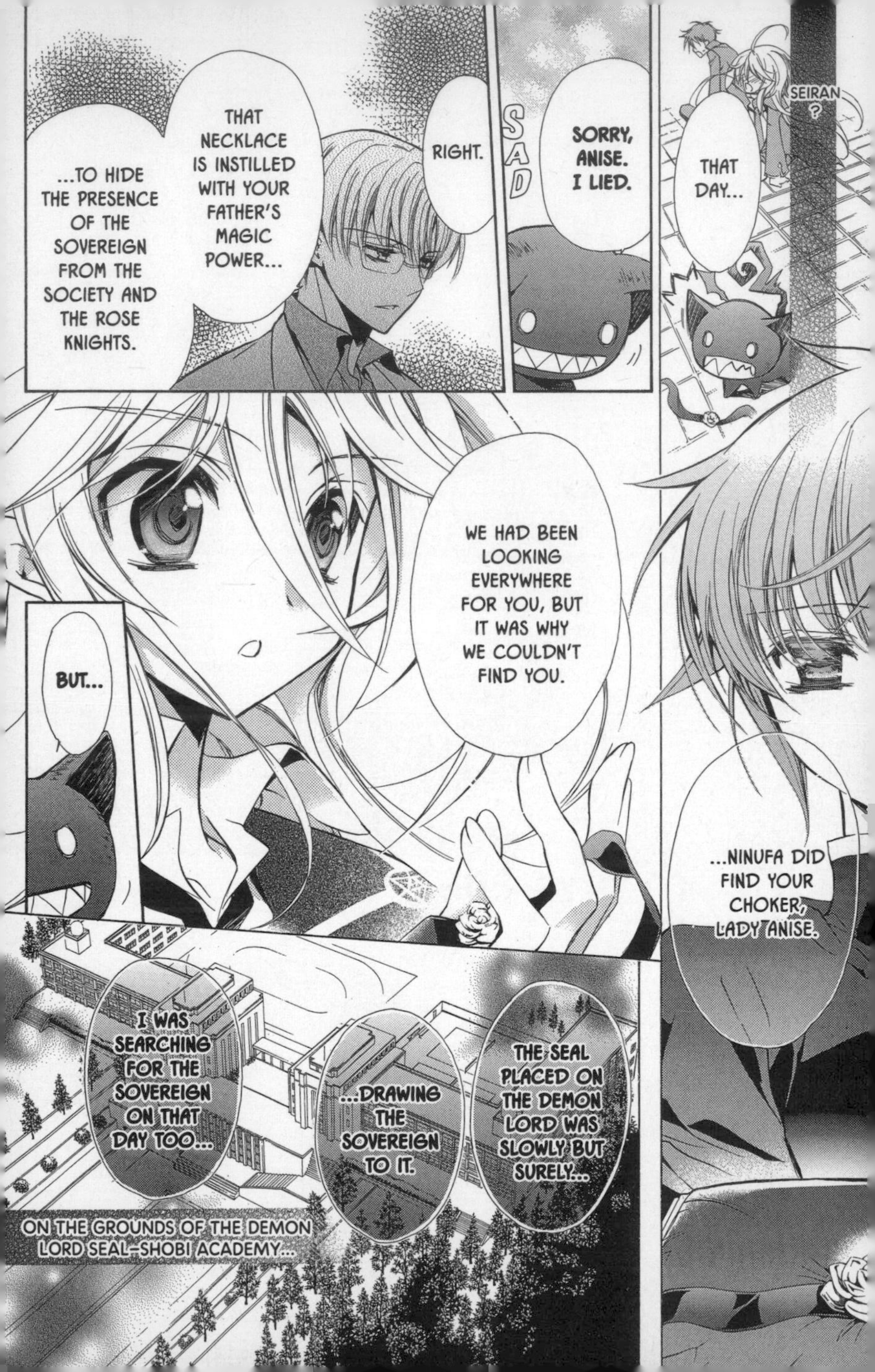
SEIRAN?
THAT DAY...
SAD
SORRY, ANISE. I LIED.
RIGHT.
THAT NECKLACE IS INSTILLED WITH YOUR FATHER'S MAGIC POWER...
...TO HIDE THE PRESENCE OF THE SOVEREIGN FROM THE SOCIETY AND THE ROSE KNIGHTS.
...NINUFA DID FIND YOUR CHOKER, LADY ANISE.
WE HAD BEEN LOOKING EVERYWHERE FOR YOU, BUT IT WAS WHY WE COULDN'T FIND YOU.
BUT...
THE SEAL PLACED ON THE DEMON LORD WAS SLOWLY BUT SURELY...
...DRAWING THE SOVEREIGN TO IT.
I WAS SEARCHING FOR THE SOVEREIGN ON THAT DAY TOO...
ON THE GROUNDS OF THE DEMON LORD SEAL-SHOBI ACADEMY...

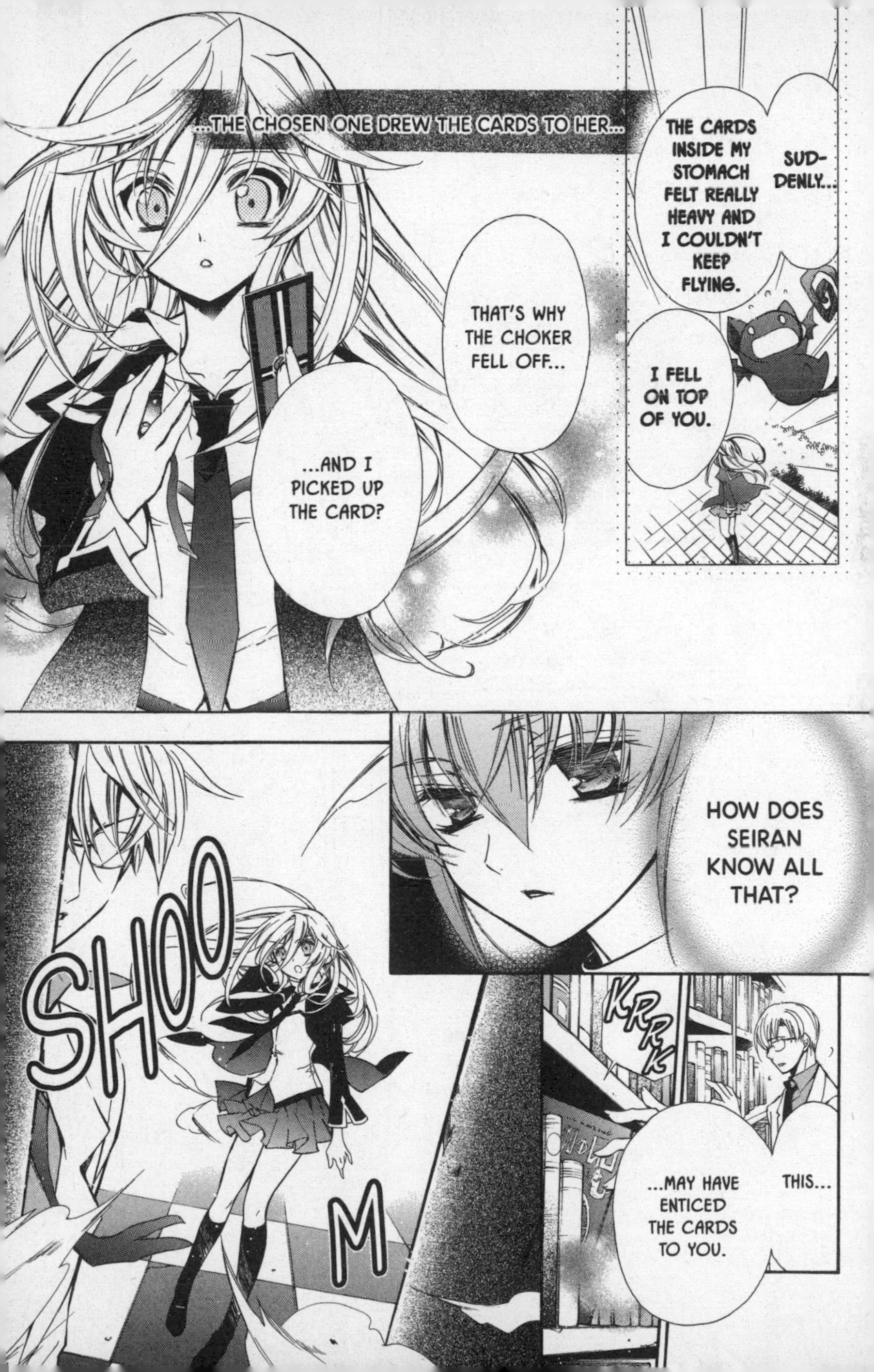
SUD-DENLY...
THE CARDS INSIDE MY STOMACH FELT REALLY HEAVY AND I COULDN'T KEEP FLYING.
I FELL ON TOP OF YOU.
...THE CHOSEN ONE DREW THE CARDS TO HER...
THAT'S WHY THE CHOKER FELL OFF...
...AND I PICKED UP THE CARD?
HOW DOES SEIRAN KNOW ALL THAT?
KRRK
THIS...
...MAY HAVE ENTICED THE CARDS TO YOU.
SHOOM

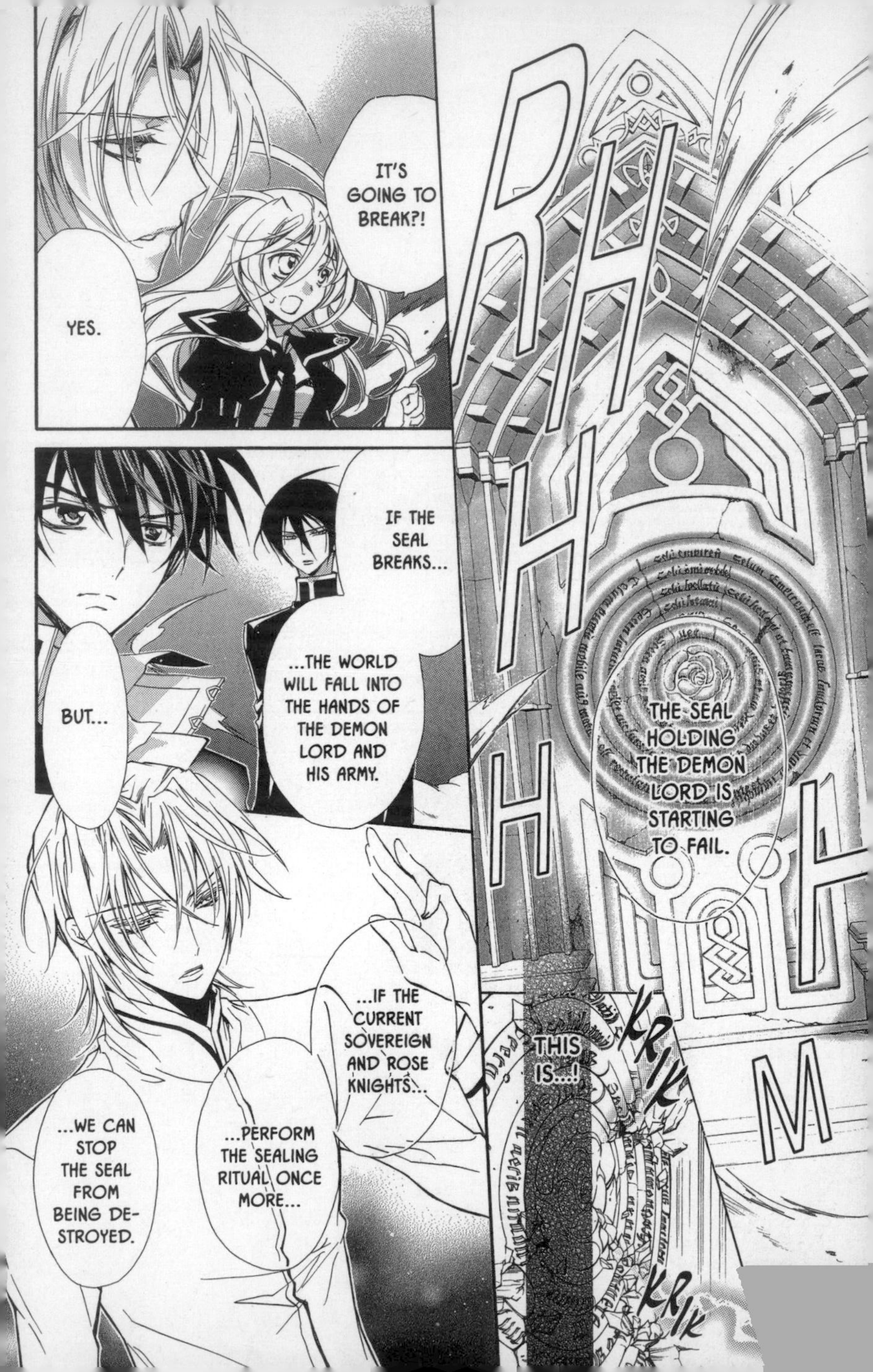
RHHHHM
THE SEAL HOLDING THE DEMON LORD IS STARTING TO FAIL.
THIS IS...!
KRIK
KRIK
IT'S GOING TO BREAK?!
YES.
IF THE SEAL BREAKS...
...THE WORLD WILL FALL INTO THE HANDS OF THE DEMON LORD AND HIS ARMY.
BUT...
...IF THE CURRENT SOVEREIGN AND ROSE KNIGHTS...
...PERFORM THE SEALING RITUAL ONCE MORE...
...WE CAN STOP THE SEAL FROM BEING DE-STROYED.

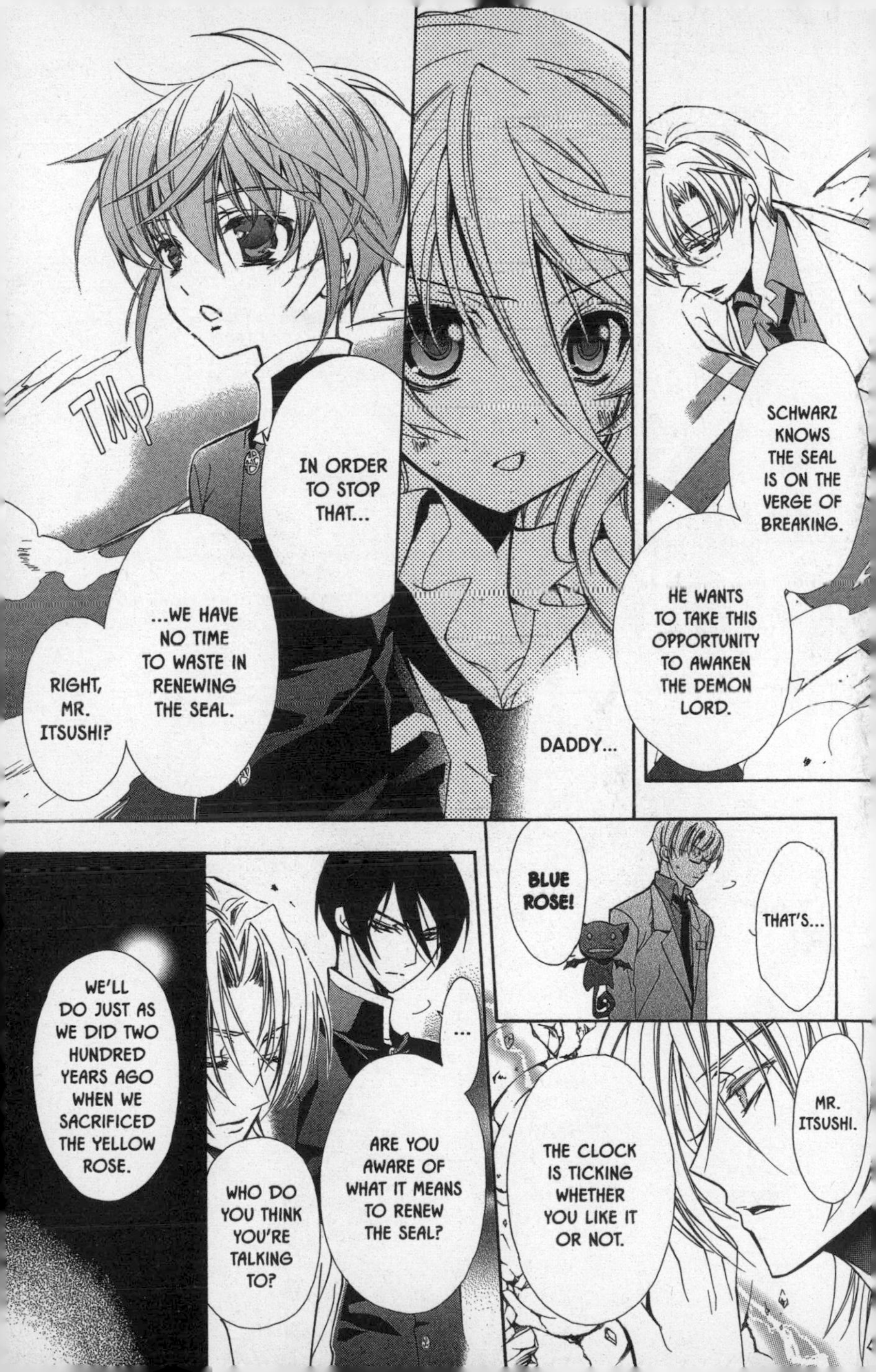
SCHWARZ KNOWS THE SEAL IS ON THE VERGE OF BREAKING.
HE WANTS TO TAKE THIS OPPORTUNITY TO AWAKEN THE DEMON LORD.
DADDY...
IN ORDER TO STOP THAT...
TMP
...WE HAVE NO TIME TO WASTE IN RENEWING THE SEAL.
RIGHT, MR. ITSUSHI?
THAT'S...
BLUE ROSE!
MR. ITSUSHI.
THE CLOCK IS TICKING WHETHER YOU LIKE IT OR NOT.
...
ARE YOU AWARE OF WHAT IT MEANS TO RENEW THE SEAL?
WHO DO YOU THINK YOU'RE TALKING TO?
WE'LL DO JUST AS WE DID TWO HUNDRED YEARS AGO WHEN WE SACRIFICED THE YELLOW ROSE.

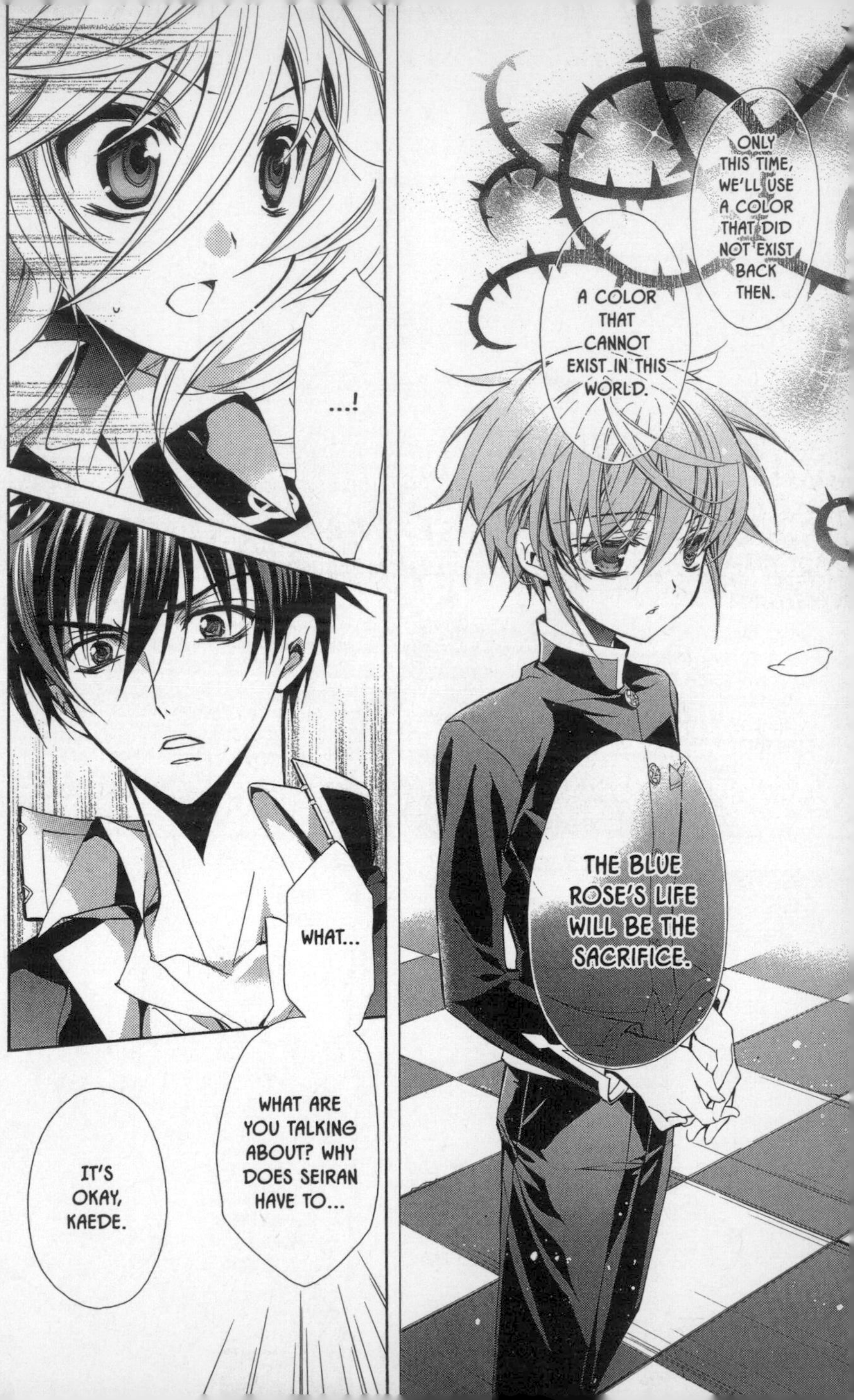
ONLY THIS TIME, WE'LL USE A COLOR THAT DID NOT EXIST BACK THEN.
A COLOR THAT CANNOT EXIST IN THIS WORLD.
THE BLUE ROSE'S LIFE WILL BE THE SACRIFICE.
...!
WHAT...
WHAT ARE YOU TALKING ABOUT? WHY DOES SEIRAN HAVE TO...
IT'S OKAY, KAEDE.

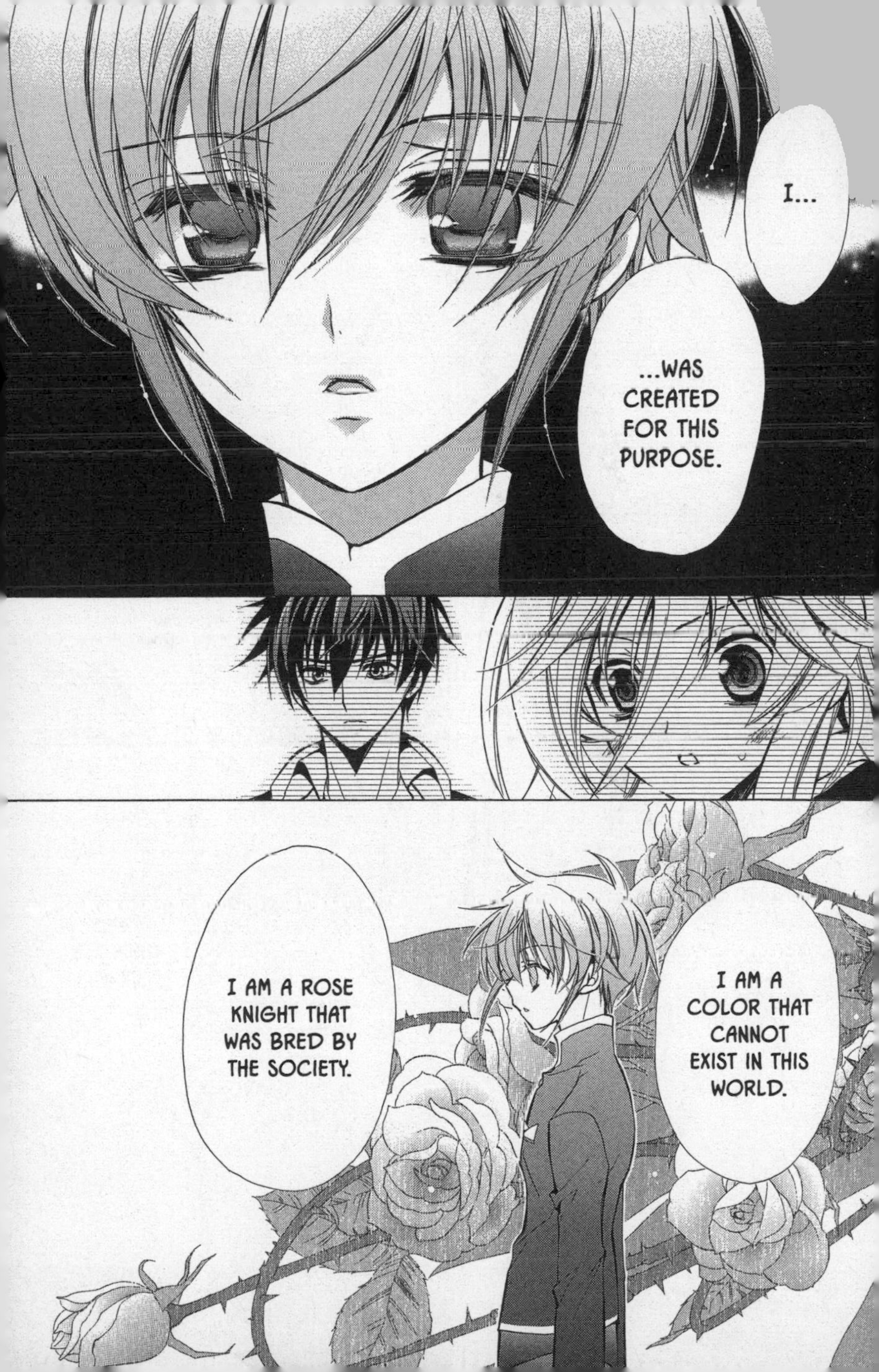
I...
...WAS CREATED FOR THIS PURPOSE.
I AM A COLOR THAT CANNOT EXIST IN THIS WORLD.
I AM A ROSE KNIGHT THAT WAS BRED BY THE SOCIETY.

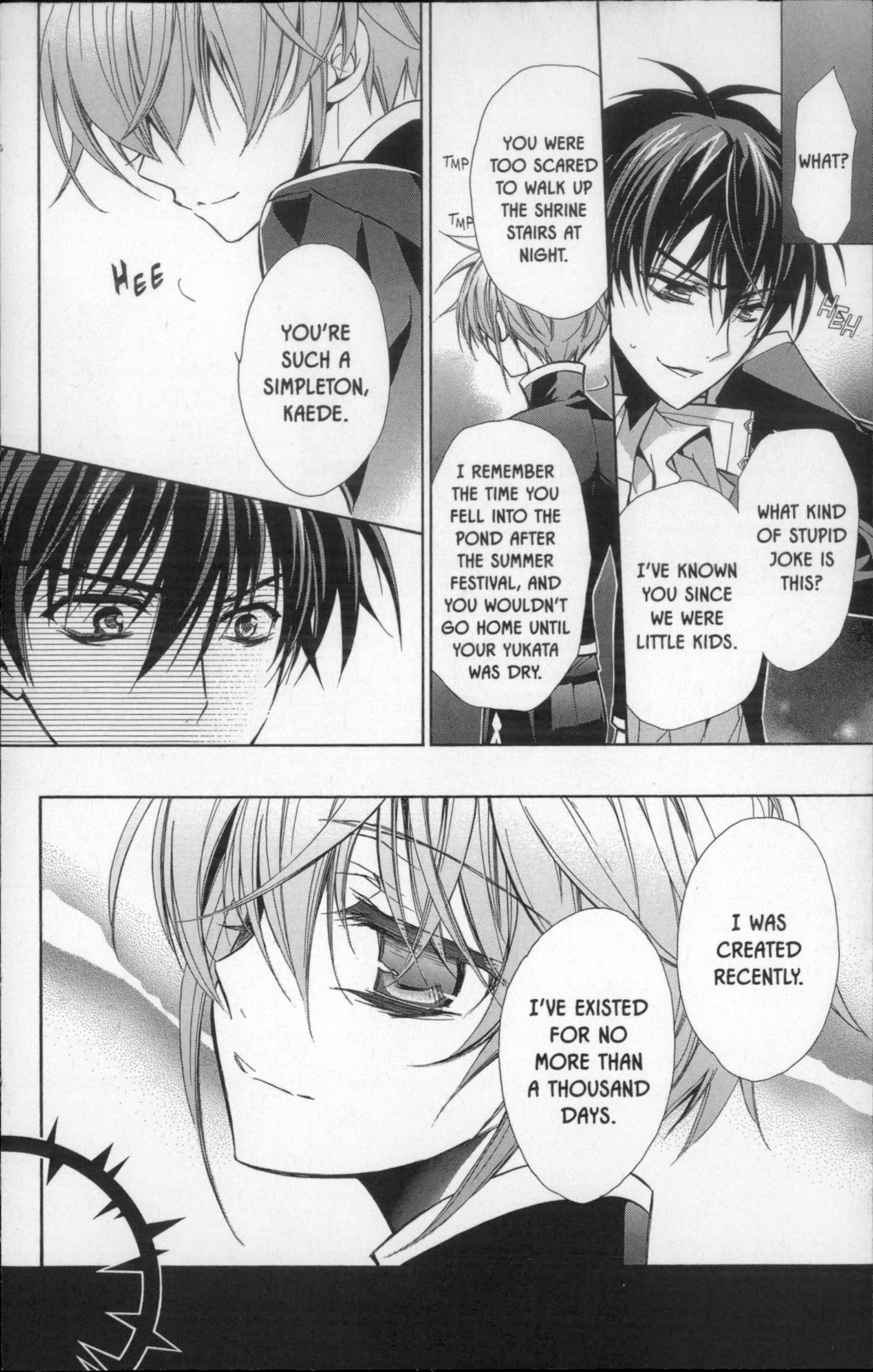
WHAT?
WHAT KIND OF STUPID JOKE IS THIS?
I'VE KNOWN YOU SINCE WE WERE LITTLE KIDS.
I REMEMBER THE TIME YOU FELL INTO THE POND AFTER THE SUMMER FESTIVAL, AND YOU WOULDN'T GO HOME UNTIL YOUR YUKATA WAS DRY.
TMP
TMP
YOU WERE TOO SCARED TO WALK UP THE SHRINE STAIRS AT NIGHT.
HEH
HEE
YOU'RE SUCH A SIMPLETON, KAEDE.
I WAS CREATED RECENTLY.
I'VE EXISTED FOR NO MORE THAN A THOUSAND DAYS.

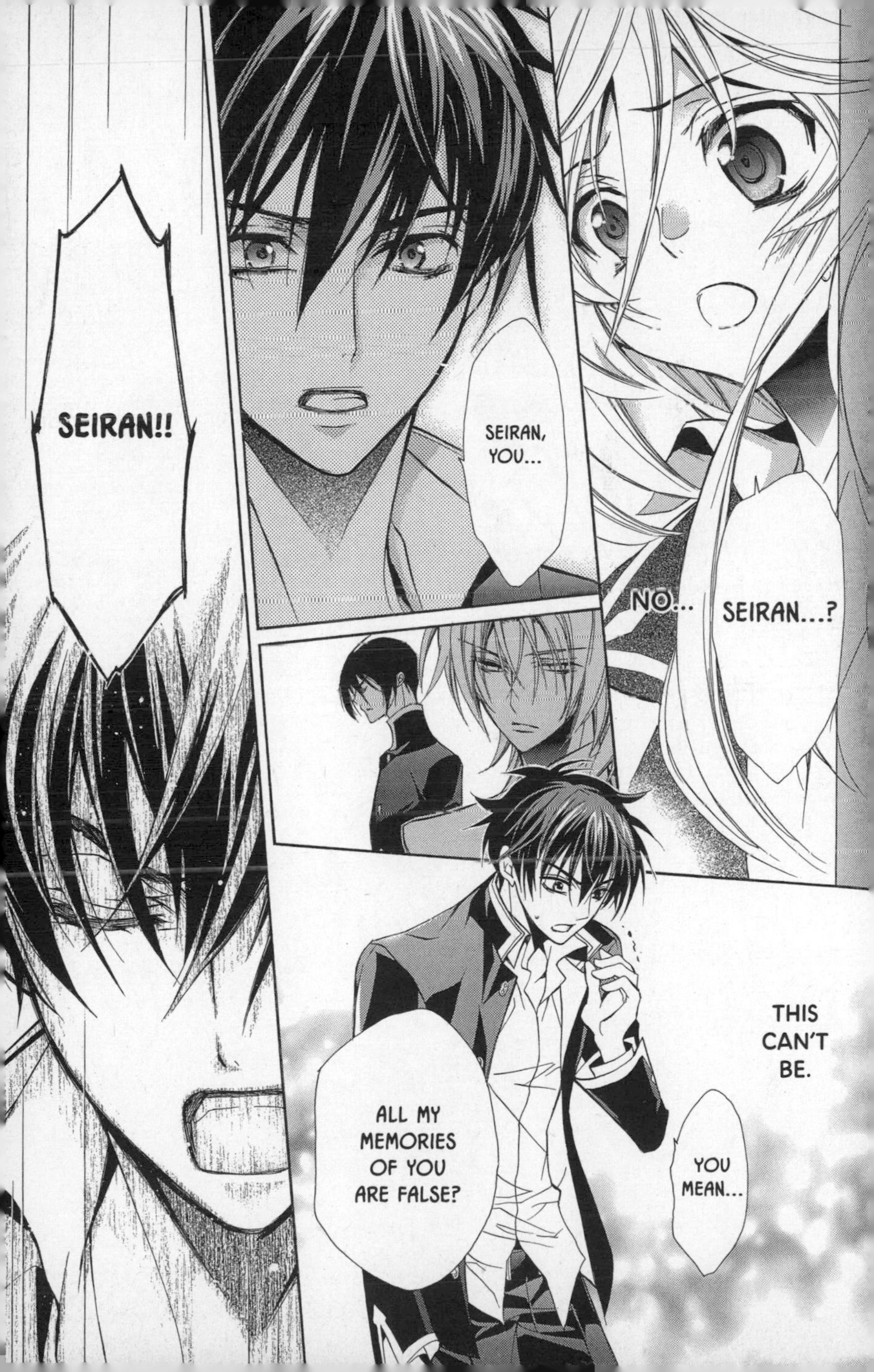
NO...
SEIRAN...?
SEIRAN, YOU...
THIS CAN'T BE.
YOU MEAN...
ALL MY MEMORIES OF YOU ARE FALSE?
SEIRAN!!

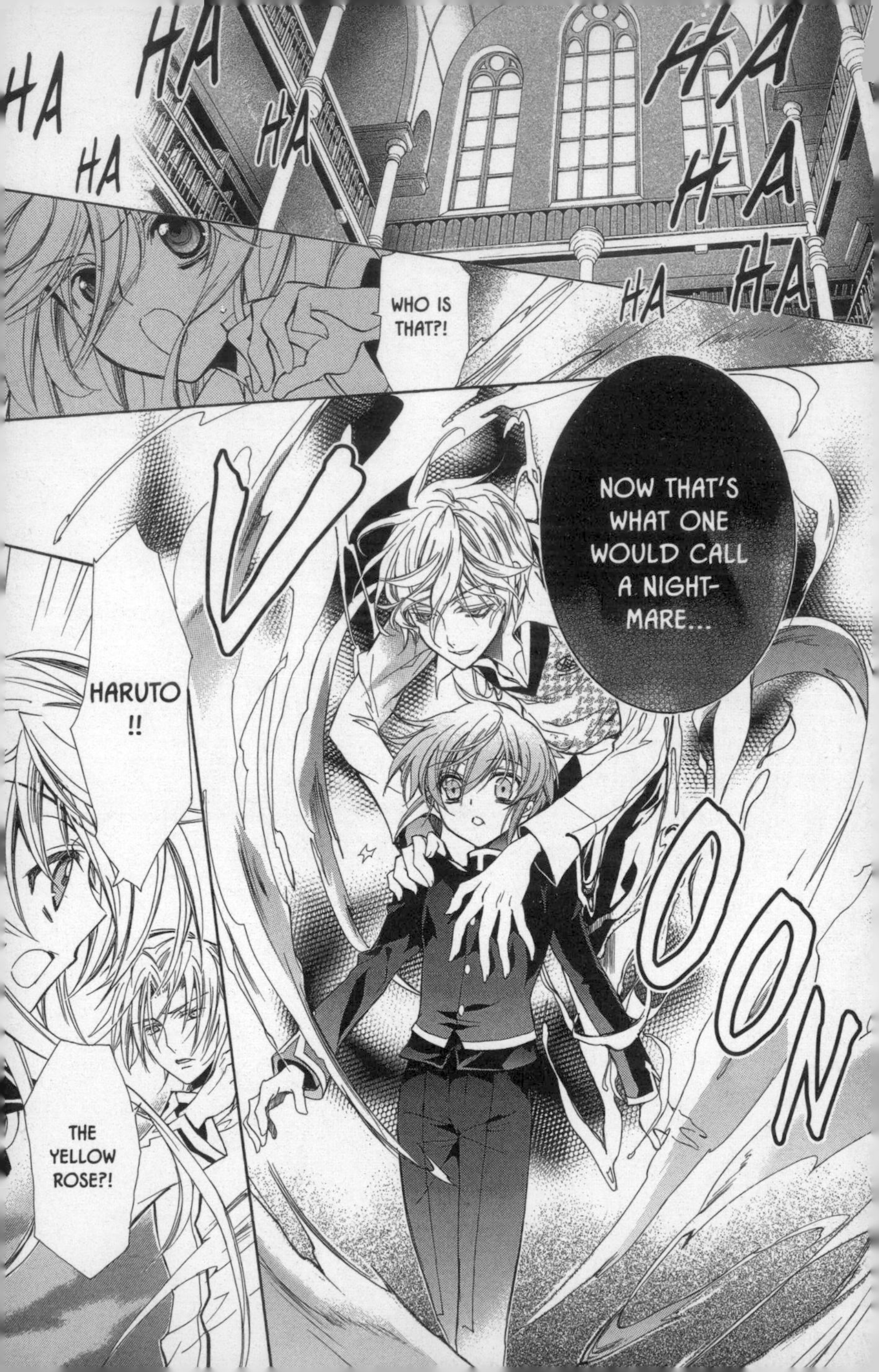
HA HA HA HA HA HA HA HA HA
WHO IS THAT?!
NOW THAT'S WHAT ONE WOULD CALL A NIGHT-MARE...
VOOOON
HARUTO !!
THE YELLOW ROSE?!

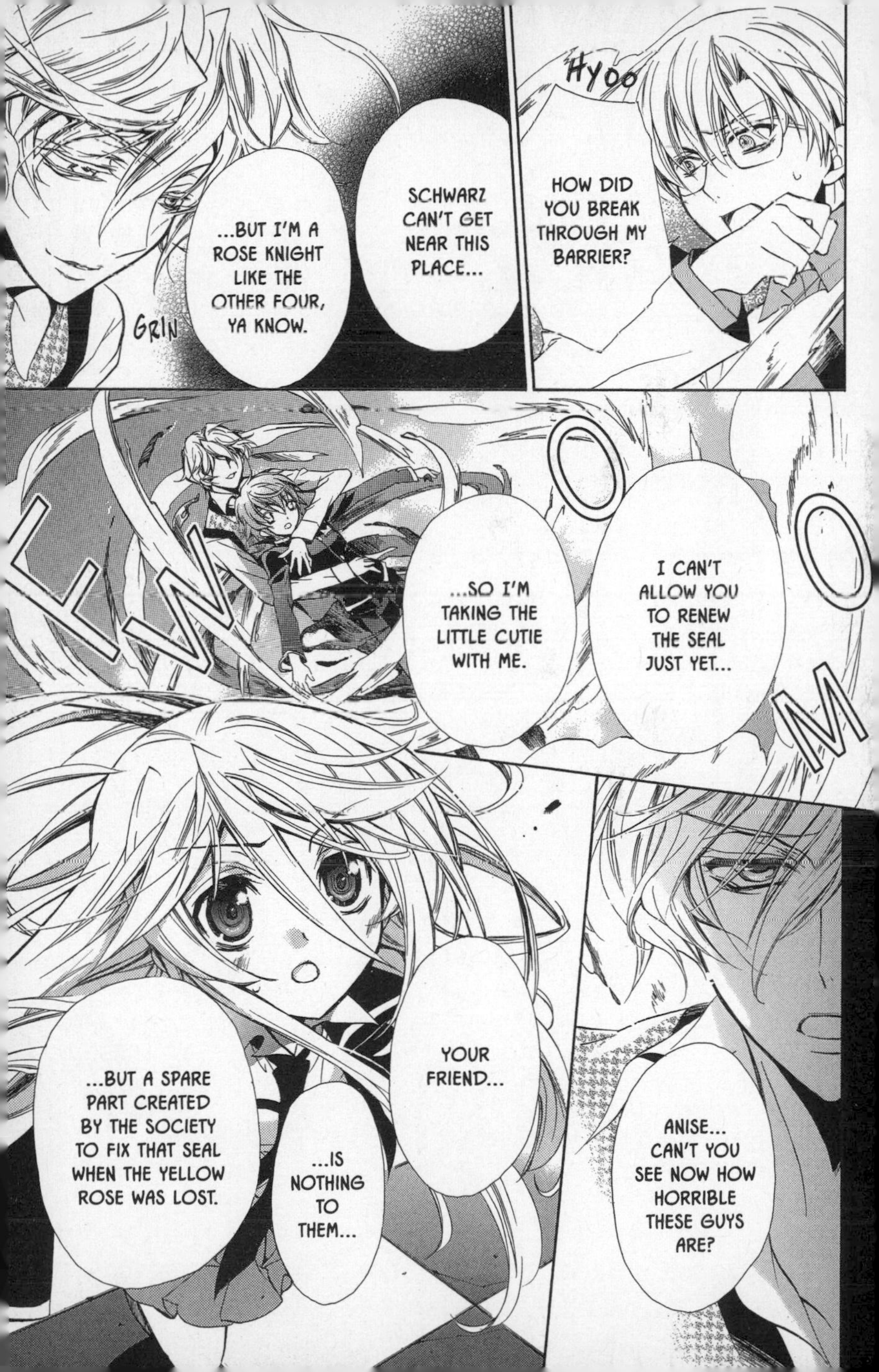
HYOO
HOW DID YOU BREAK THROUGH MY BARRIER?
SCHWARZ CAN'T GET NEAR THIS PLACE...
...BUT I'M A ROSE KNIGHT LIKE THE OTHER FOUR, YA KNOW.
GRIN
I CAN'T ALLOW YOU TO RENEW THE SEAL JUST YET...
...SO I'M TAKING THE LITTLE CUTIE WITH ME.
ANISE... CAN'T YOU SEE NOW HOW HORRIBLE THESE GUYS ARE?
YOUR FRIEND...
...IS NOTHING TO THEM...
...BUT A SPARE PART CREATED BY THE SOCIETY TO FIX THAT SEAL WHEN THE YELLOW ROSE WAS LOST.

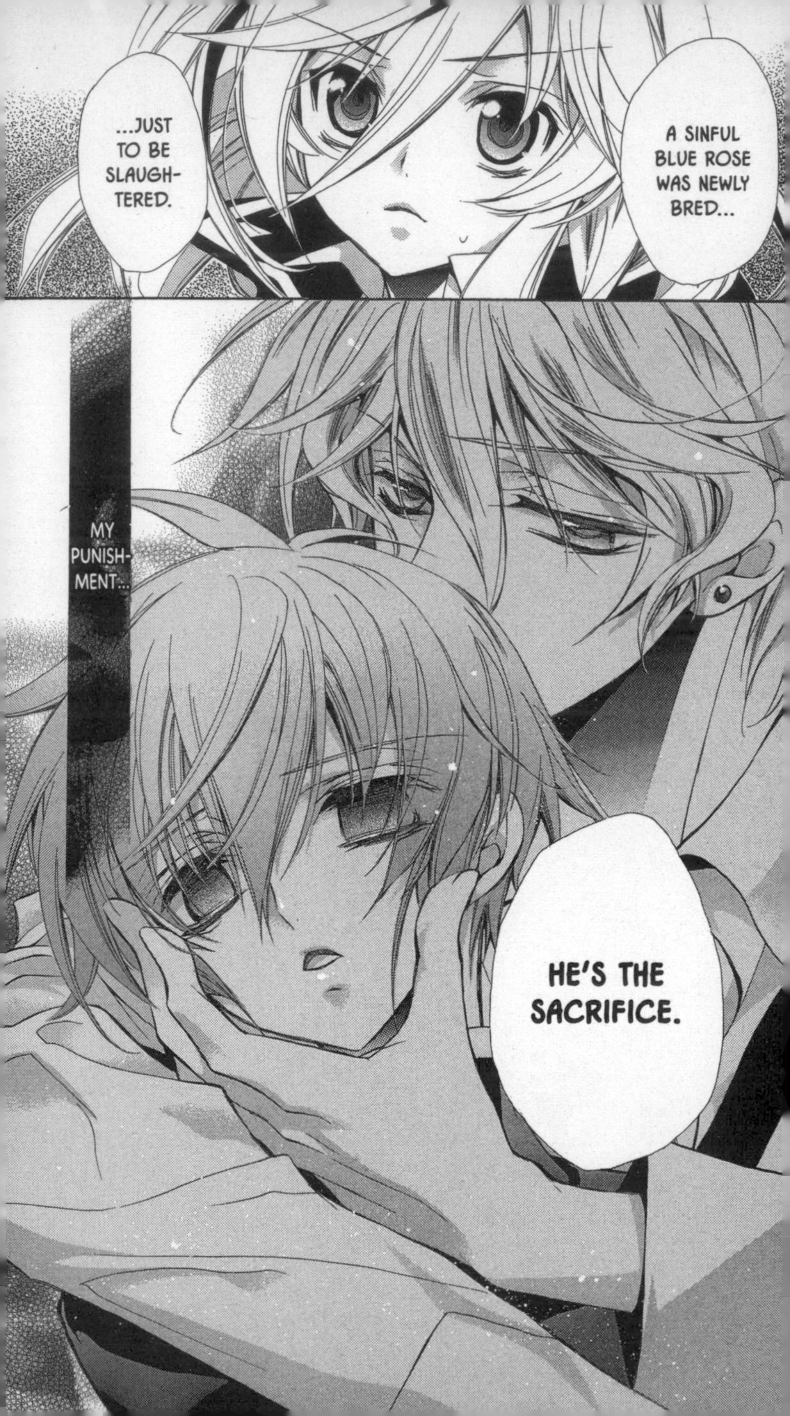
A SINFUL BLUE ROSE WAS NEWLY BRED...
...JUST TO BE SLAUGHTERED.
MY PUNISHMENT...
HE'S THE SACRIFICE.

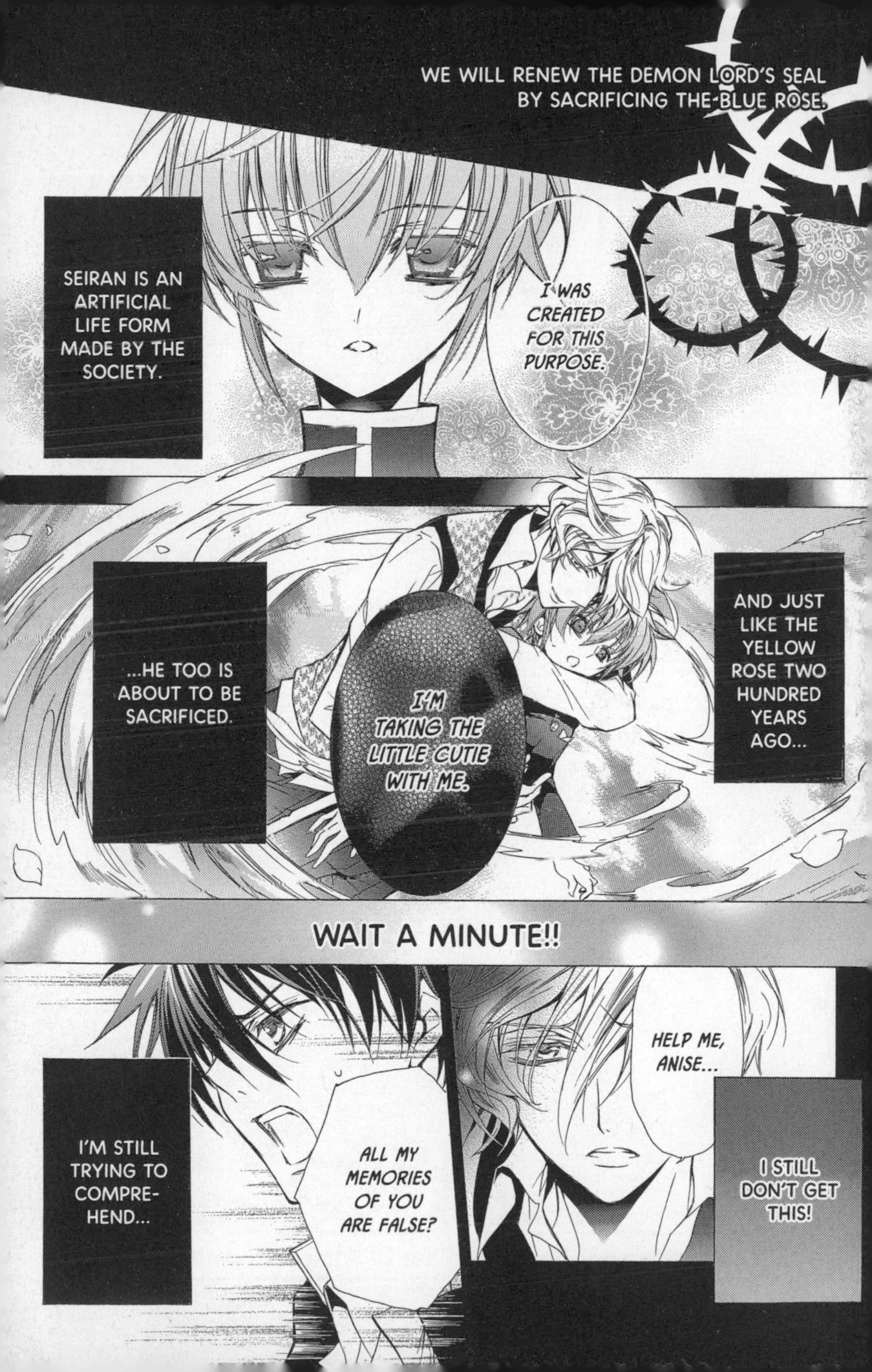
WE WILL RENEW THE DEMON LORD'S SEAL BY SACRIFICING THE BLUE ROSE.
I WAS CREATED FOR THIS PURPOSE.
SEIRAN IS AN ARTIFICIAL LIFE FORM MADE BY THE SOCIETY.
AND JUST LIKE THE YELLOW ROSE TWO HUNDRED YEARS AGO...
I'M TAKING THE LITTLE CUTIE WITH ME.
...HE TOO IS ABOUT TO BE SACRIFICED.
WAIT A MINUTE!!
HELP ME, ANISE...
I STILL DON'T GET THIS!
ALL MY MEMORIES OF YOU ARE FALSE?
I'M STILL TRYING TO COMPRE-HEND...

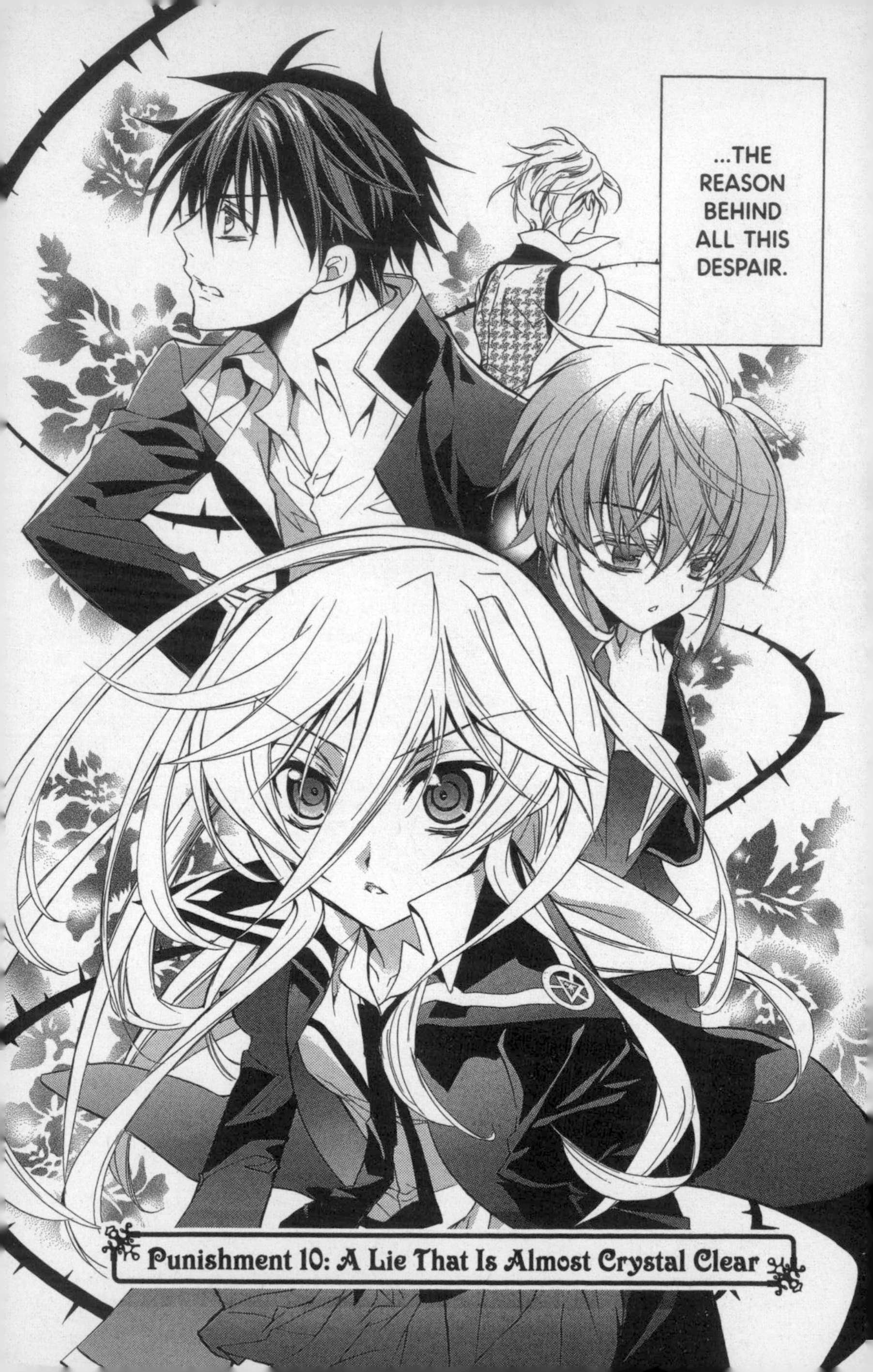
...THE REASON BEHIND ALL THIS DESPAIR.
Punishment 10: A Lie That Is Almost Crystal Clear

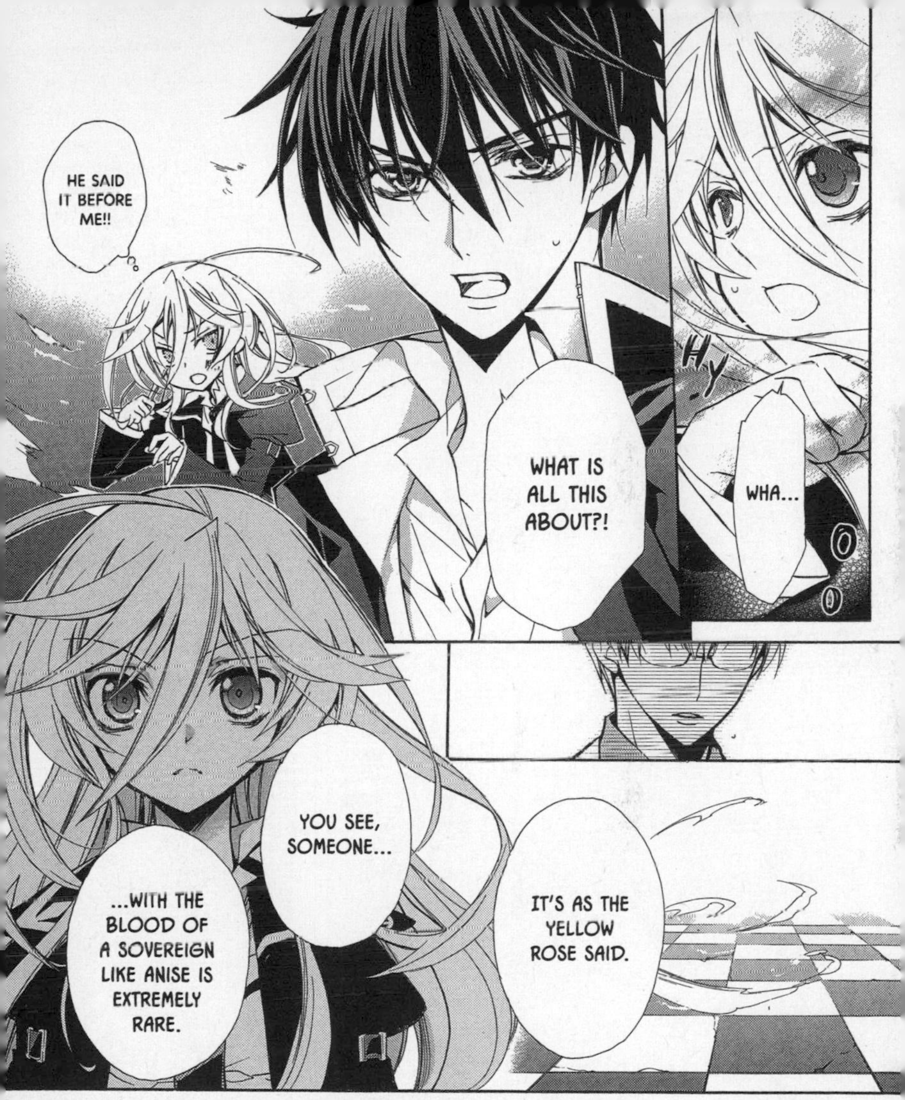
WHA...
WHAT IS ALL THIS ABOUT?!
HE SAID IT BEFORE ME!!
IT'S AS THE YELLOW ROSE SAID.
YOU SEE, SOMEONE...
...WITH THE BLOOD OF A SOVEREIGN LIKE ANISE IS EXTREMELY RARE.

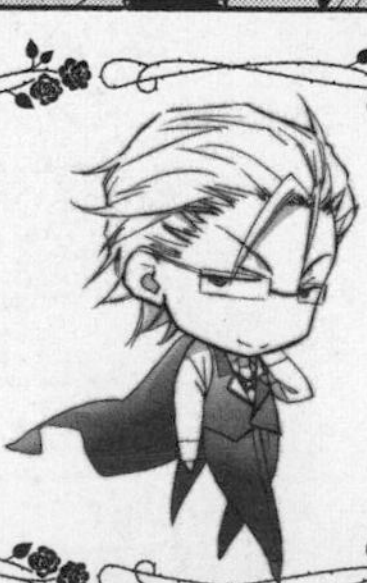

Schwarz Yamamoto

Daddy... Your first and last name don't go together... He probably has the family name of Anise's mother. He married into his wife's family. Kinda cute, huh? He is Anise's father, so he's relatively old, but his age remains a mystery. He will make a spectacle of himself in the next volume, so please look forward to it!! Sleep in terror!

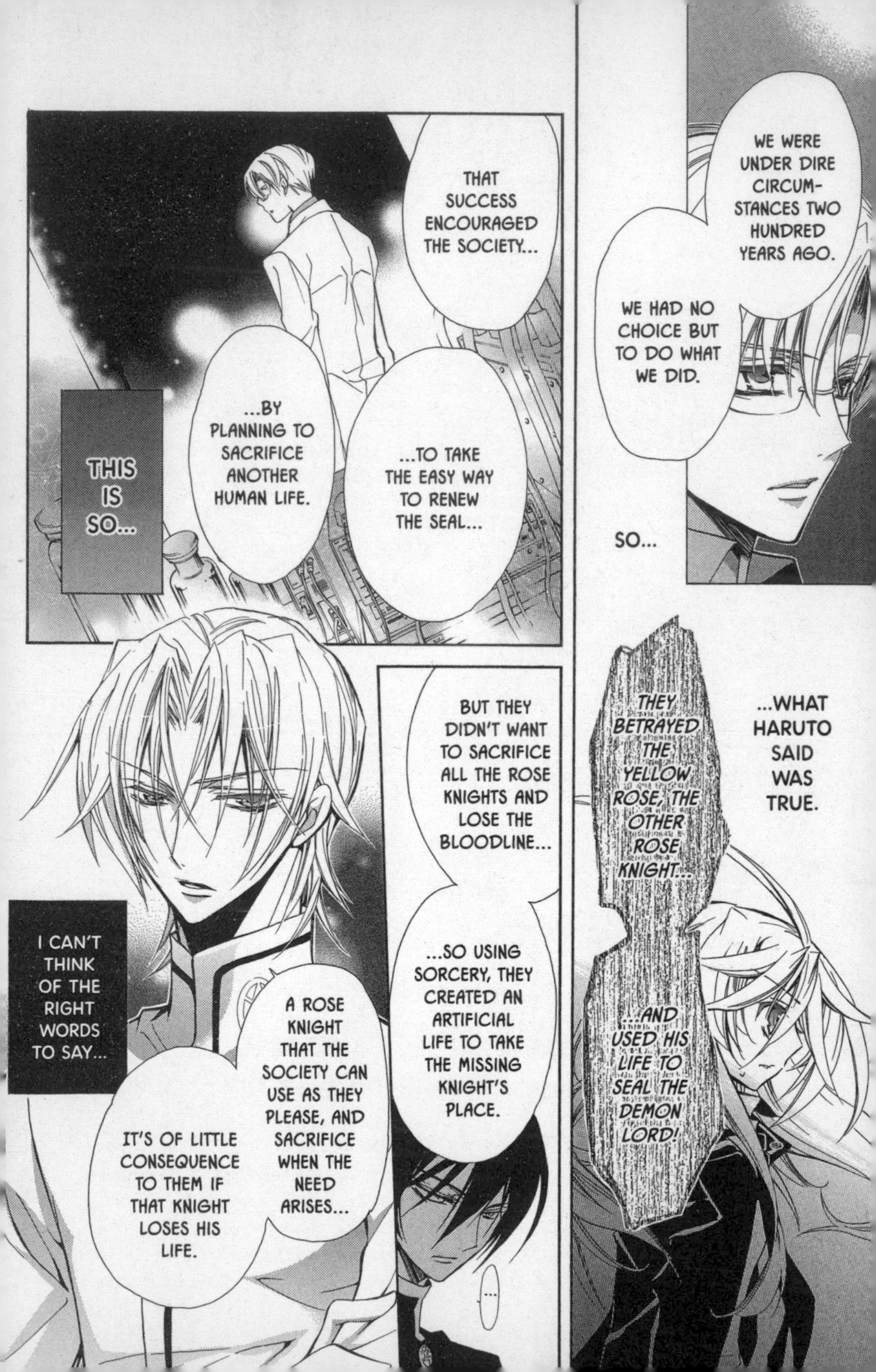
WE WERE UNDER DIRE CIRCUM-STANCES TWO HUNDRED YEARS AGO.
WE HAD NO CHOICE BUT TO DO WHAT WE DID.
SO...
...WHAT HARUTO SAID WAS TRUE.
THEY BETRAYED THE YELLOW ROSE, THE OTHER ROSE KNIGHT...
...AND USED HIS LIFE TO SEAL THE DEMON LORD!
THAT SUCCESS ENCOURAGED THE SOCIETY...
...TO TAKE THE EASY WAY TO RENEW THE SEAL...
...BY PLANNING TO SACRIFICE ANOTHER HUMAN LIFE.
THIS IS SO...
BUT THEY DIDN'T WANT TO SACRIFICE ALL THE ROSE KNIGHTS AND LOSE THE BLOODLINE...
...SO USING SORCERY, THEY CREATED AN ARTIFICIAL LIFE TO TAKE THE MISSING KNIGHT'S PLACE.
A ROSE KNIGHT THAT THE SOCIETY CAN USE AS THEY PLEASE, AND SACRIFICE WHEN THE NEED ARISES...
IT'S OF LITTLE CONSEQUENCE TO THEM IF THAT KNIGHT LOSES HIS LIFE.
I CAN'T THINK OF THE RIGHT WORDS TO SAY...
...

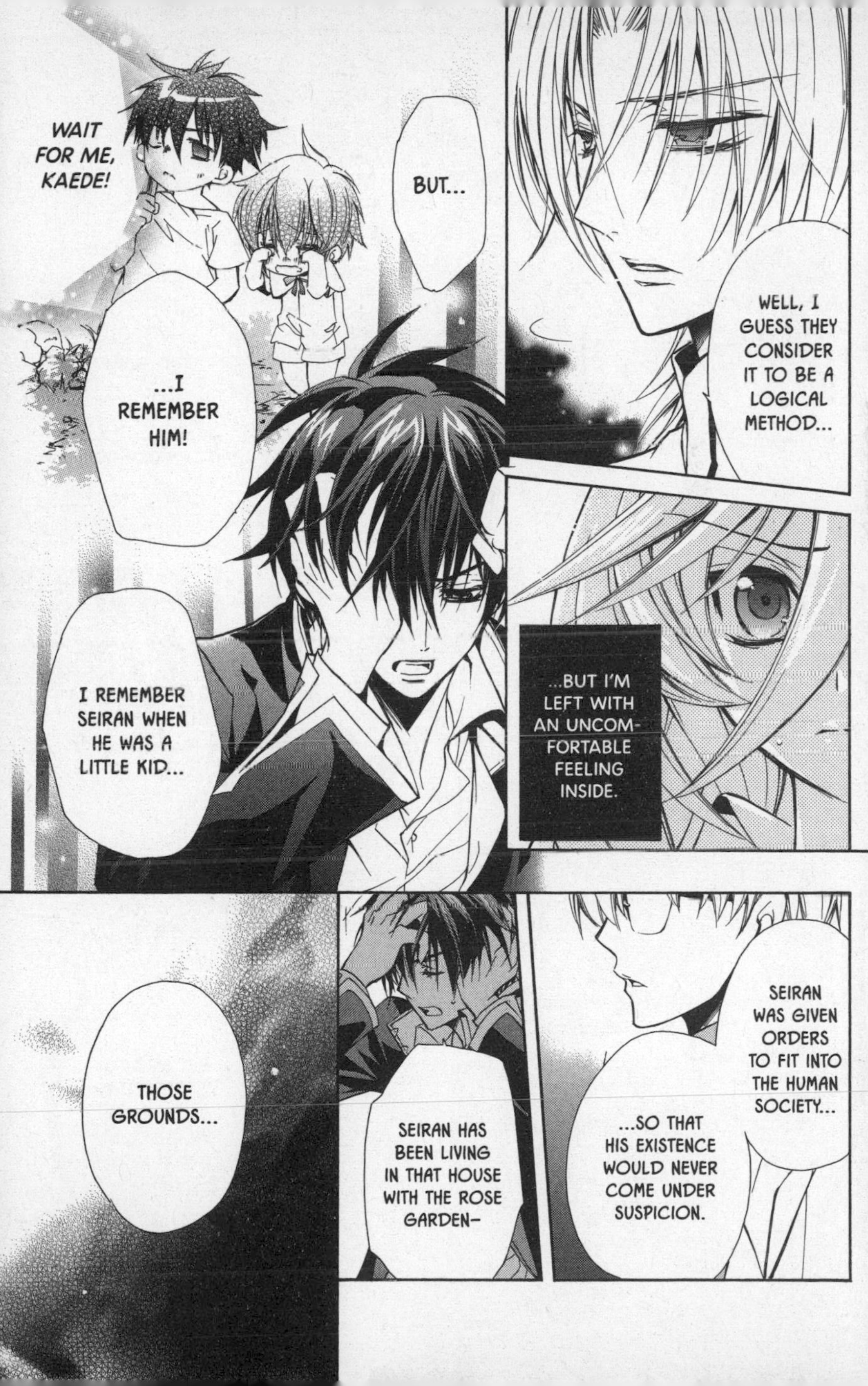
WELL, I GUESS THEY CONSIDER IT TO BE A LOGICAL METHOD...
...BUT I'M LEFT WITH AN UNCOM-FORTABLE FEELING INSIDE.
BUT...
WAIT FOR ME, KAEDE!
...I REMEMBER HIM!
I REMEMBER SEIRAN WHEN HE WAS A LITTLE KID...
SEIRAN WAS GIVEN ORDERS TO FIT INTO THE HUMAN SOCIETY...
...SO THAT HIS EXISTENCE WOULD NEVER COME UNDER SUSPICION.
SEIRAN HAS BEEN LIVING IN THAT HOUSE WITH THE ROSE GARDEN–
THOSE GROUNDS...

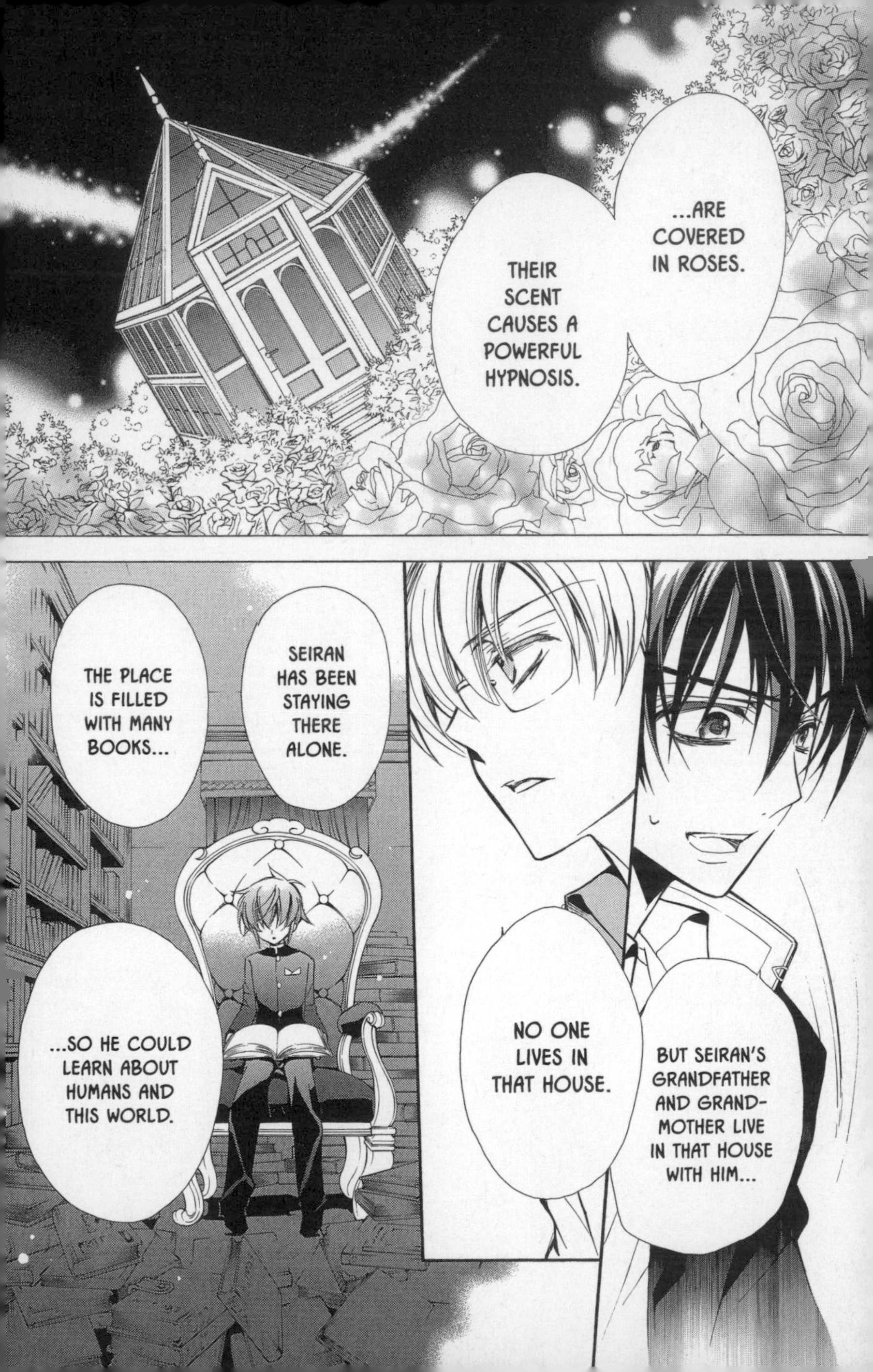
...ARE COVERED IN ROSES.
THEIR SCENT CAUSES A POWERFUL HYPNOSIS.
BUT SEIRAN'S GRANDFATHER AND GRAND-MOTHER LIVE IN THAT HOUSE WITH HIM...
NO ONE LIVES IN THAT HOUSE.
SEIRAN HAS BEEN STAYING THERE ALONE.
THE PLACE IS FILLED WITH MANY BOOKS...
...SO HE COULD LEARN ABOUT HUMANS AND THIS WORLD.

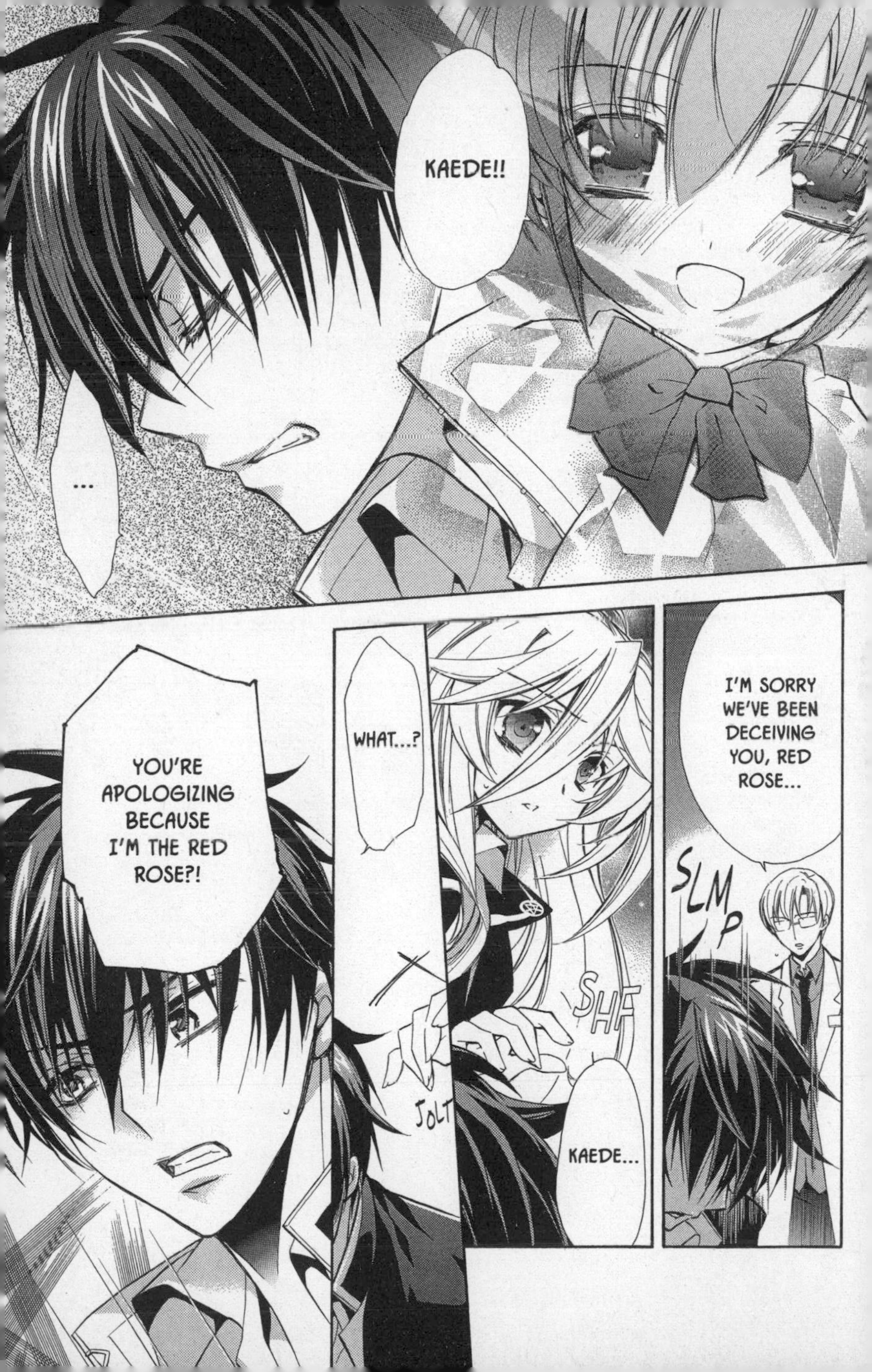
KAEDE!!
...
I'M SORRY WE'VE BEEN DECEIVING YOU, RED ROSE...
SLMP
SHF
KAEDE...
WHAT...?
JOLT
YOU'RE APOLOGIZING BECAUSE I'M THE RED ROSE?!

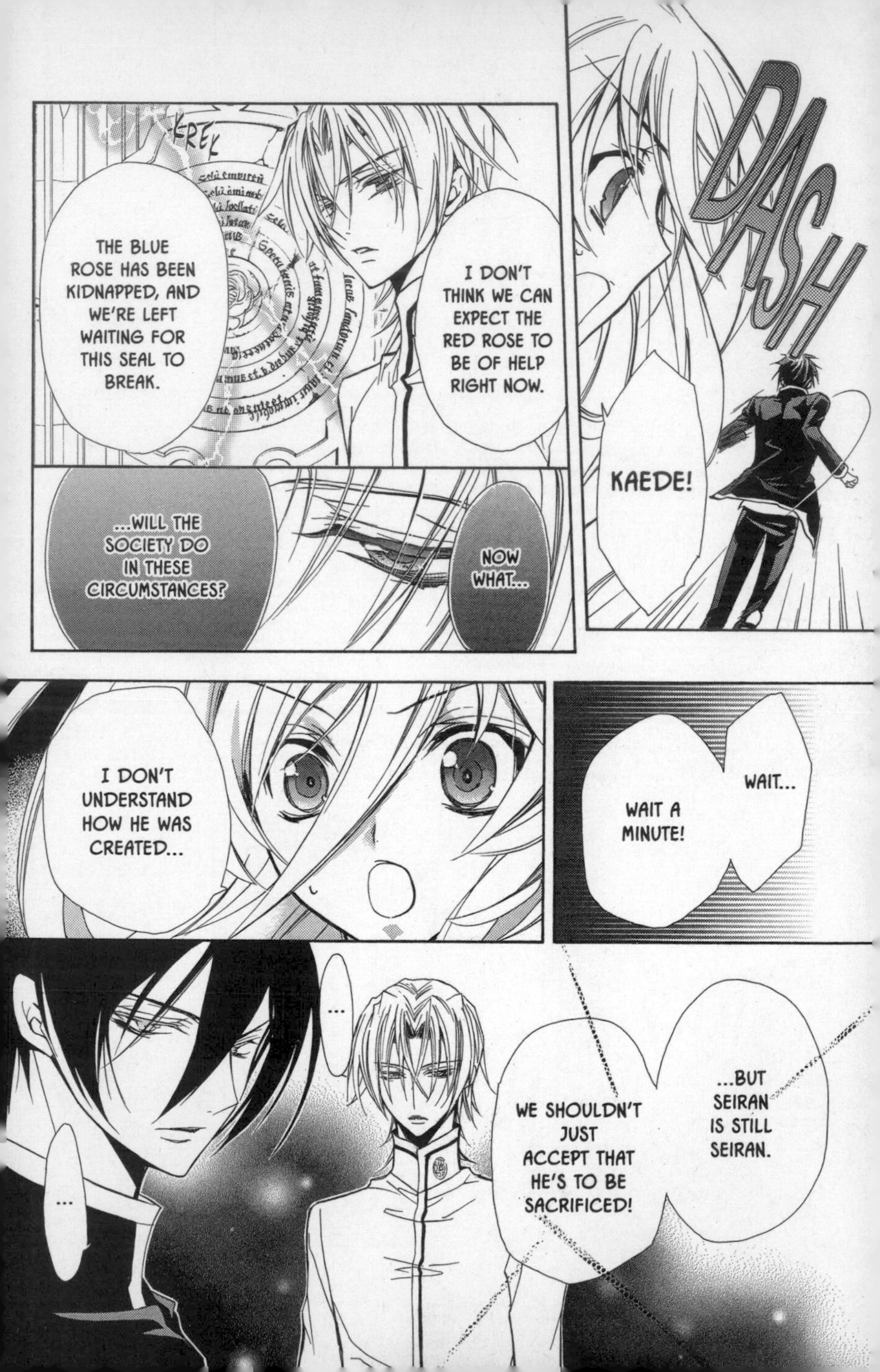
DASH
KAEDE!
I DON'T THINK WE CAN EXPECT THE RED ROSE TO BE OF HELP RIGHT NOW.
KREK
THE BLUE ROSE HAS BEEN KIDNAPPED, AND WE'RE LEFT WAITING FOR THIS SEAL TO BREAK.
NOW WHAT...
...WILL THE SOCIETY DO IN THESE CIRCUMSTANCES?
WAIT...
WAIT A MINUTE!
I DON'T UNDERSTAND HOW HE WAS CREATED...
...BUT SEIRAN IS STILL SEIRAN.
WE SHOULDN'T JUST ACCEPT THAT HE'S TO BE SACRIFICED!
...
...

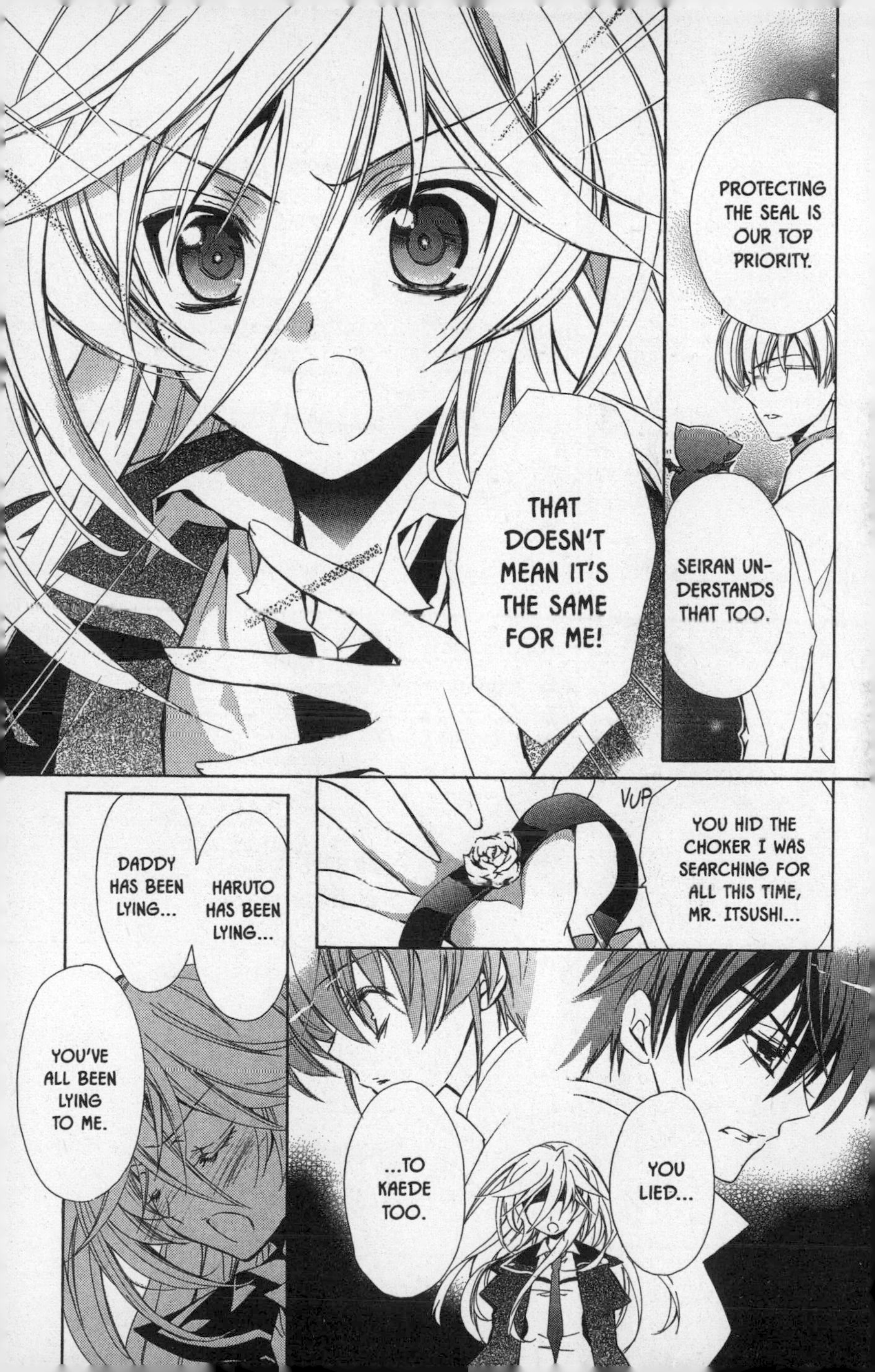
PROTECTING THE SEAL IS OUR TOP PRIORITY.
SEIRAN UN-DERSTANDS THAT TOO.
THAT DOESN'T MEAN IT'S THE SAME FOR ME!
VUP
YOU HID THE CHOKER I WAS SEARCHING FOR ALL THIS TIME, MR. ITSUSHI...
YOU LIED...
...TO KAEDE TOO.
HARUTO HAS BEEN LYING...
DADDY HAS BEEN LYING...
YOU'VE ALL BEEN LYING TO ME.

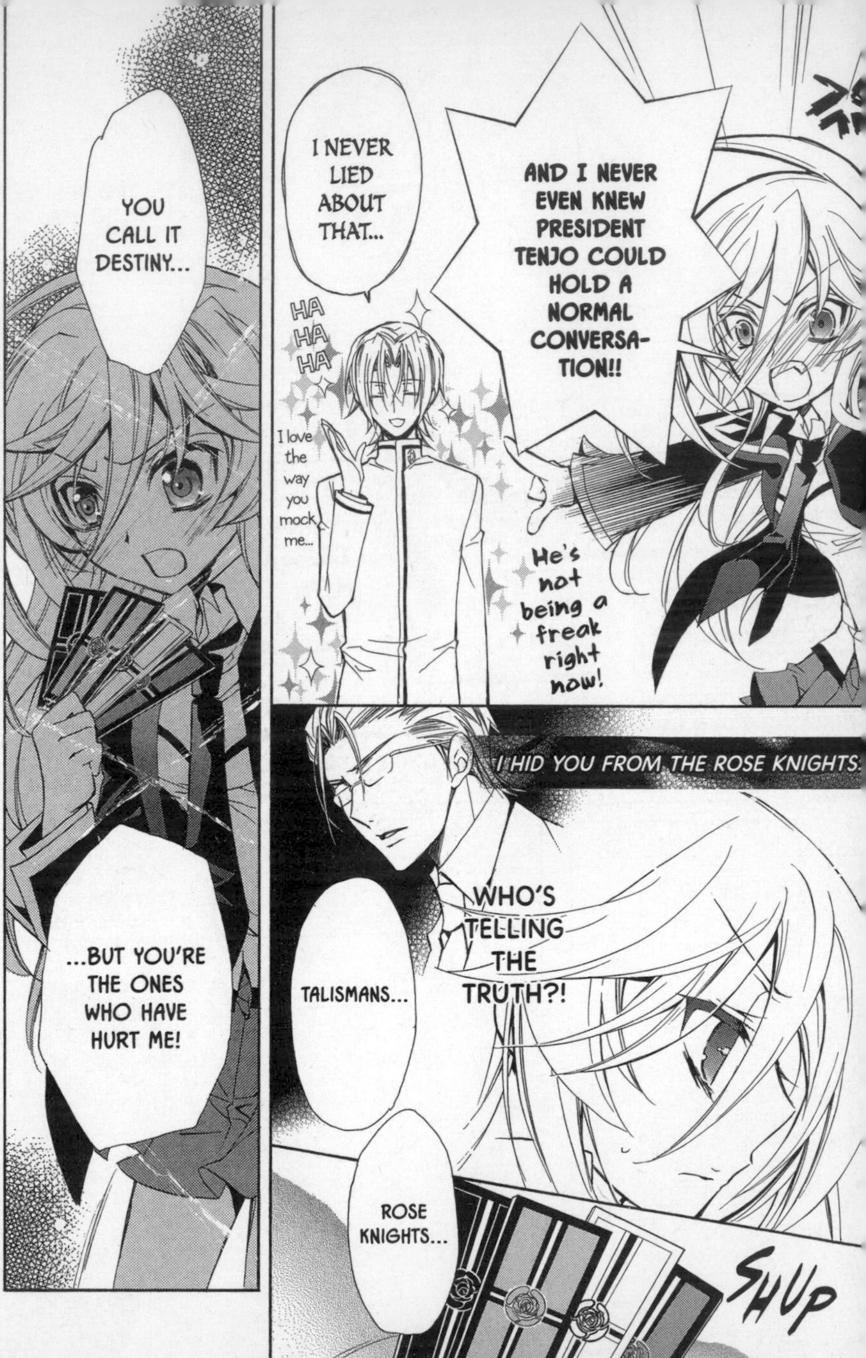
AND I NEVER EVEN KNEW PRESIDENT TENJO COULD HOLD A NORMAL CONVERSA-TION!!
He's not being a freak right now!
I NEVER LIED ABOUT THAT...
HA HA HA
I love the way you mock me...
I HID YOU FROM THE ROSE KNIGHTS.
WHO'S TELLING THE TRUTH?!
TALISMANS...
ROSE KNIGHTS...
SHUP
YOU CALL IT DESTINY...
...BUT YOU'RE THE ONES WHO HAVE HURT ME!

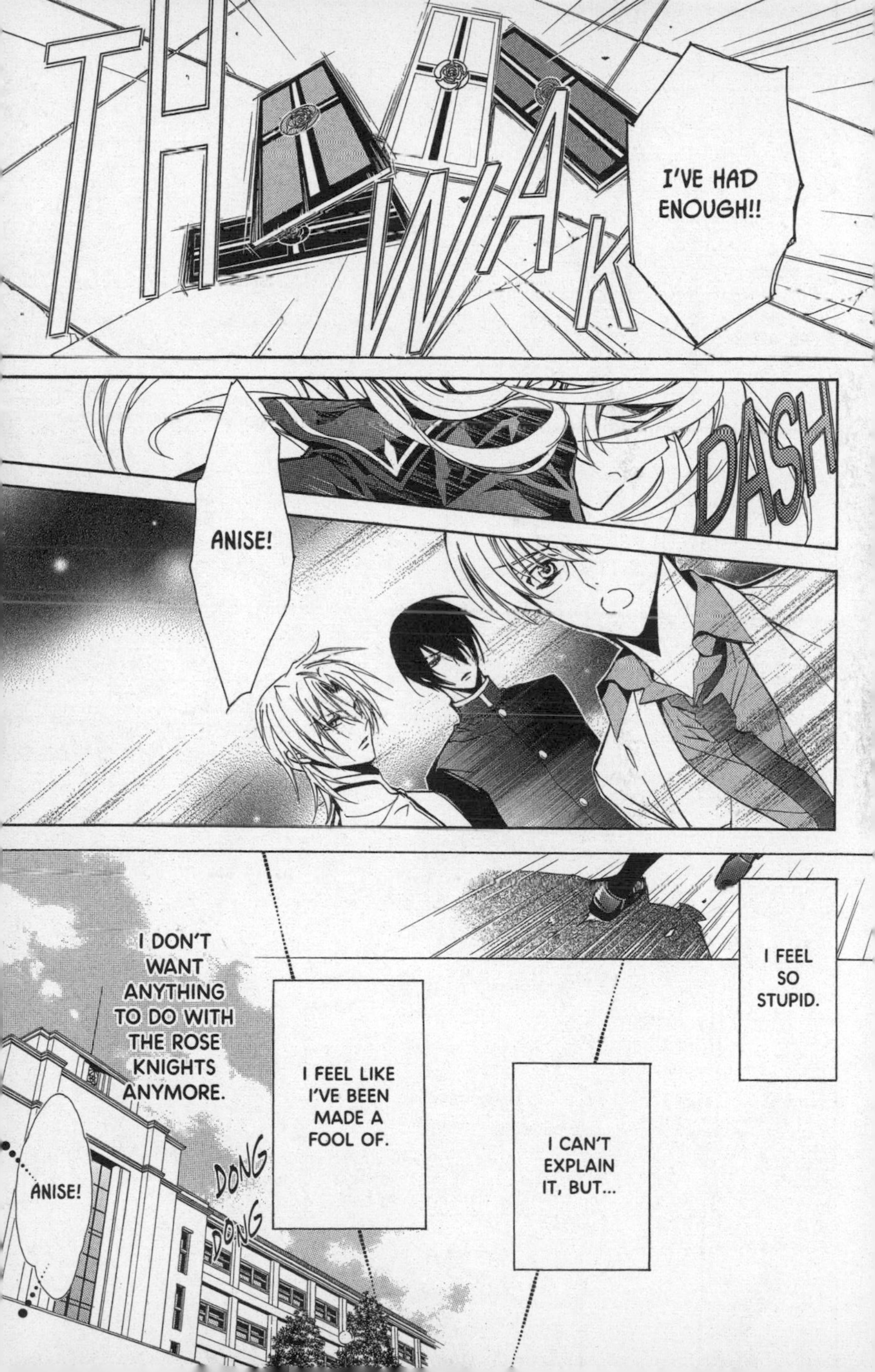
I'VE HAD ENOUGH!!
THWAK
DASH
ANISE!
I FEEL SO STUPID.
I CAN'T EXPLAIN IT, BUT...
I FEEL LIKE I'VE BEEN MADE A FOOL OF.
I DON'T WANT ANYTHING TO DO WITH THE ROSE KNIGHTS ANYMORE.
DONG
DONG
ANISE!

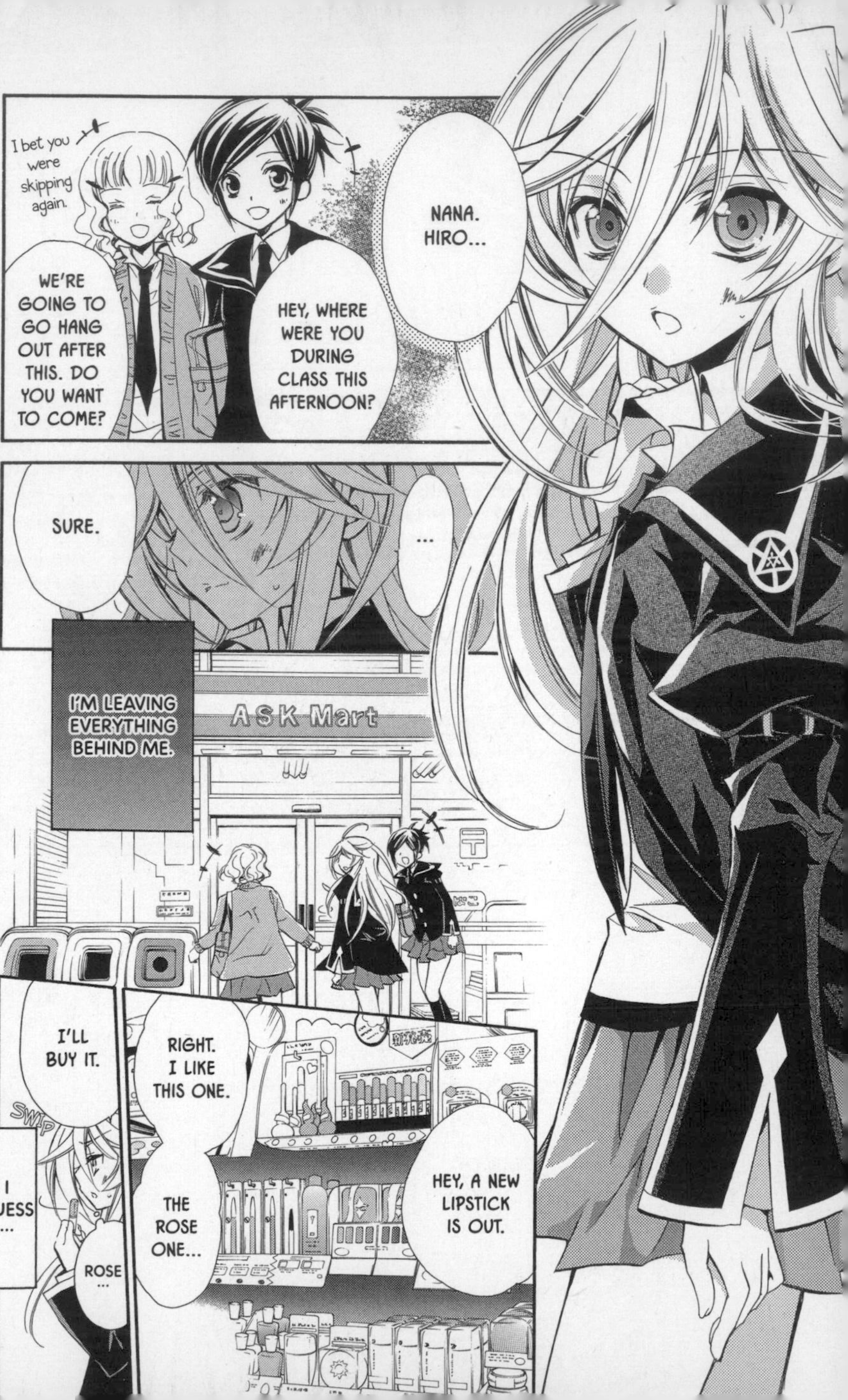
NANA. HIRO...
HEY, WHERE WERE YOU DURING CLASS THIS AFTERNOON?
WE'RE GOING TO GO HANG OUT AFTER THIS. DO YOU WANT TO COME?
I bet you were skipping again.
...
SURE.
I'M LEAVING EVERYTHING BEHIND ME.
ASK Mart
HEY, A NEW LIPSTICK IS OUT.
RIGHT. I LIKE THIS ONE.
THE ROSE ONE...
ROSE...
I GUESS...
SWIP
I'LL BUY IT.

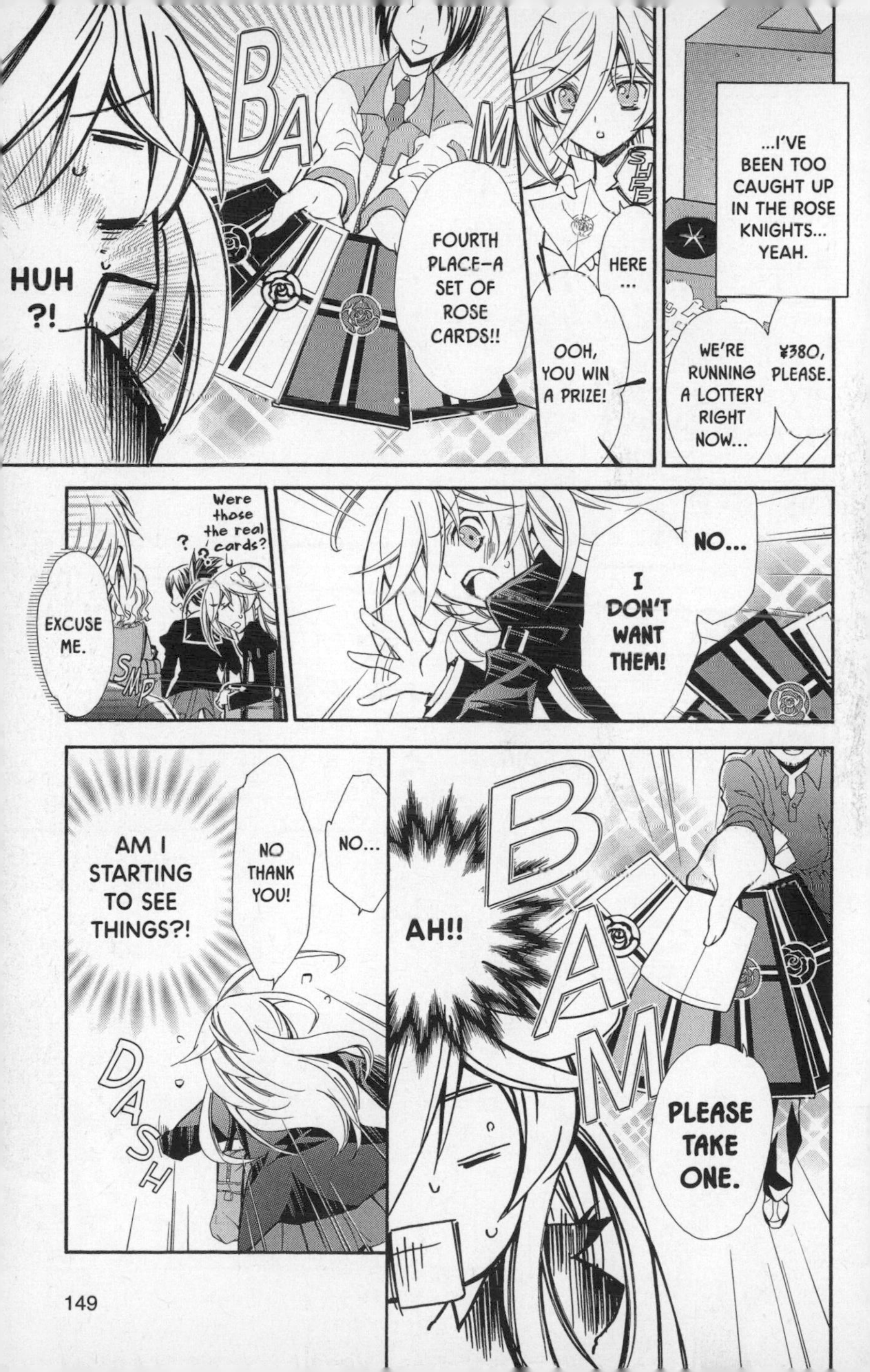
...I'VE BEEN TOO CAUGHT UP IN THE ROSE KNIGHTS... YEAH.
¥380, PLEASE.
WE'RE RUNNING A LOTTERY RIGHT NOW...
HERE ...
OOH, YOU WIN A PRIZE!
SHFF
BAM
FOURTH PLACE—A SET OF ROSE CARDS!!
HUH ?!
NO... I DON'T WANT THEM!
Were those the real cards?
EXCUSE ME.
SMP
BAM
AH!!
PLEASE TAKE ONE.
NO...
NO THANK YOU!
AM I STARTING TO SEE THINGS?!
DASH

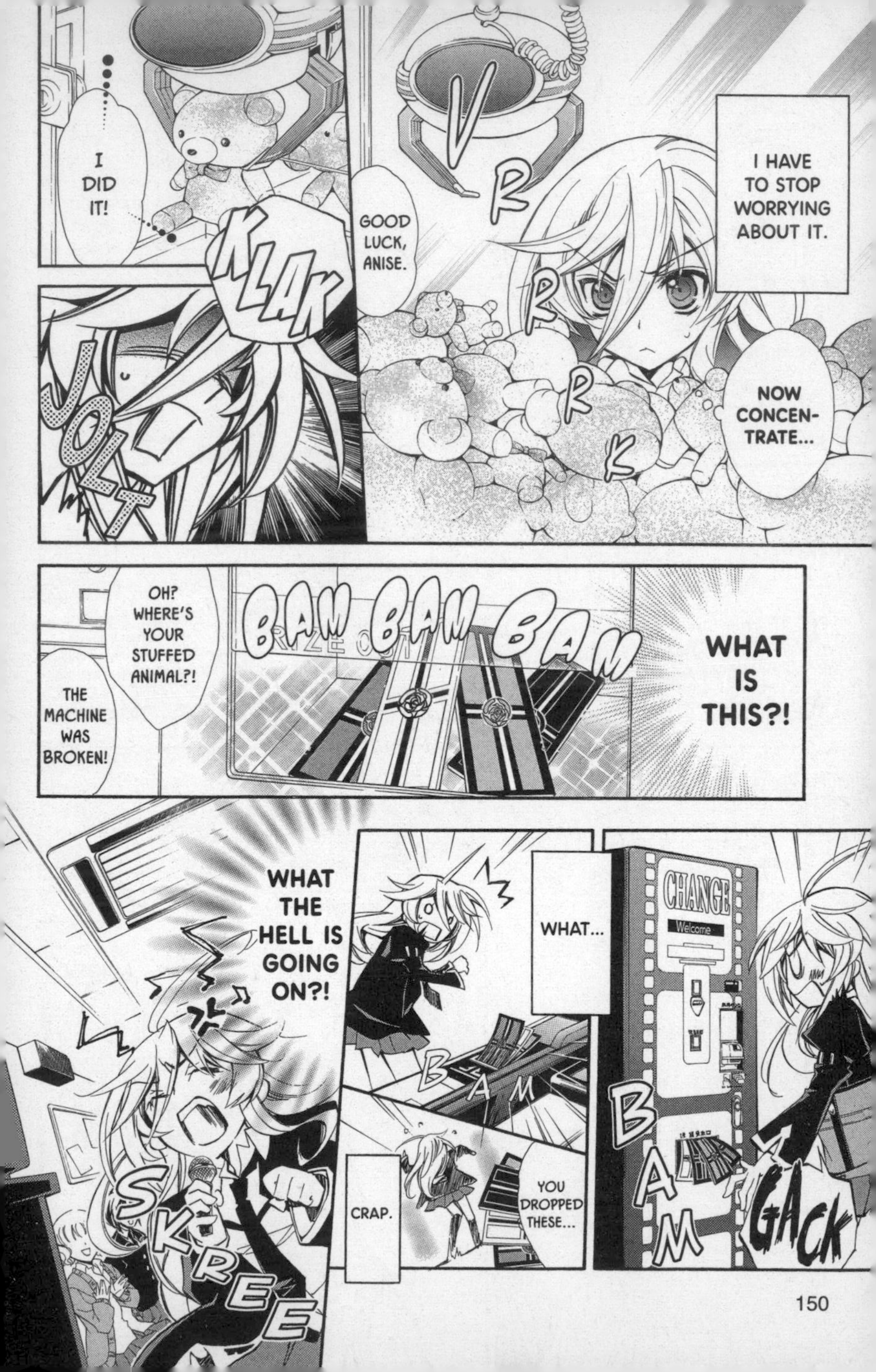
I HAVE TO STOP WORRYING ABOUT IT.
GOOD LUCK, ANISE.
VRRRRK
NOW CONCENTRATE...
I DID IT!
KLAK
JOLT
WHAT IS THIS?!
BAM BAM BAM
OH? WHERE'S YOUR STUFFED ANIMAL?!
THE MACHINE WAS BROKEN!
BAM
GACK
WHAT...
BAM
YOU DROPPED THESE...
CRAP.
WHAT THE HELL IS GOING ON?!
SKREEE

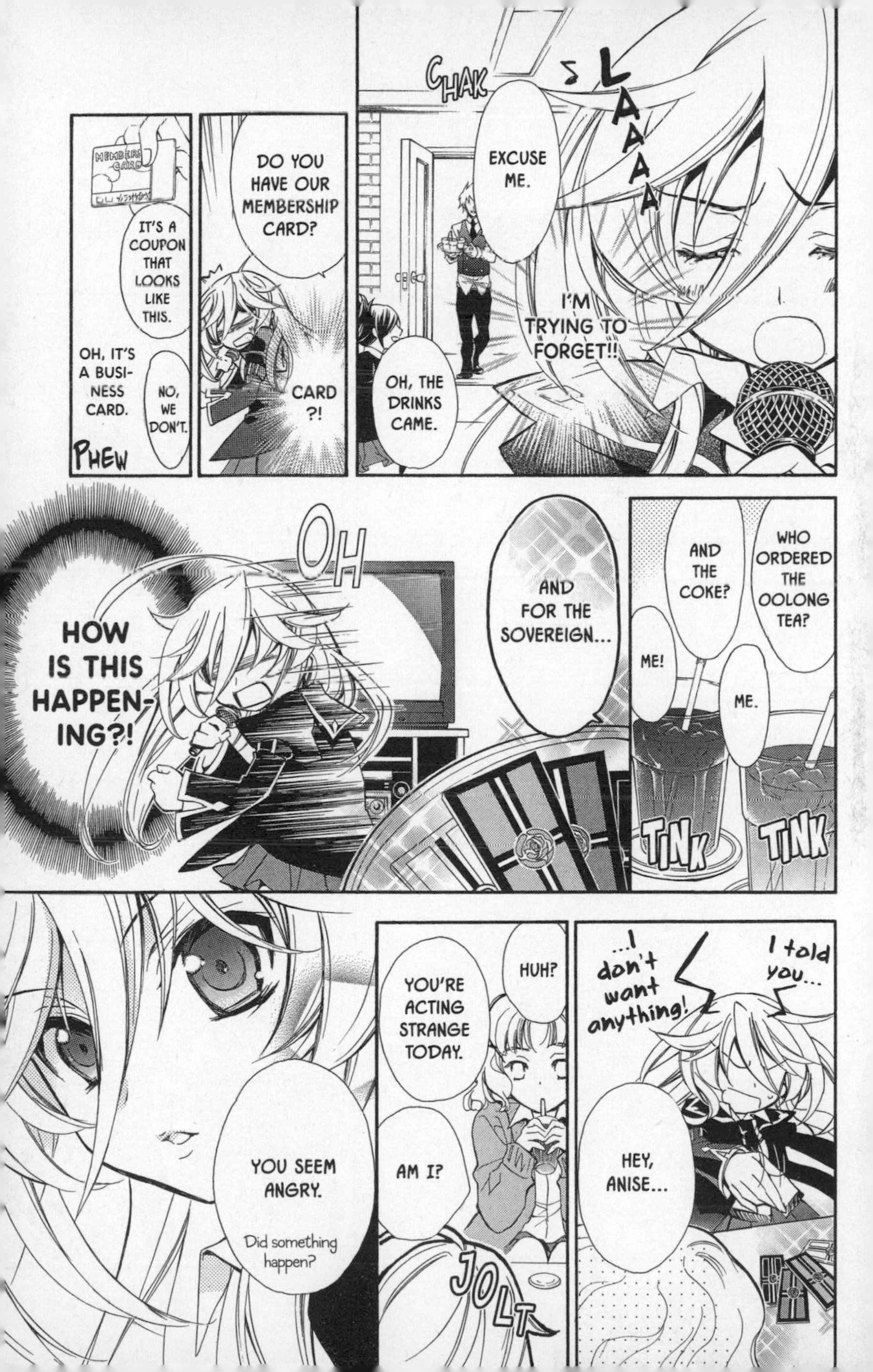
SLAAAA
I'M TRYING TO FORGET!!
EXCUSE ME.
CHAK
OH, THE DRINKS CAME.
DO YOU HAVE OUR MEMBERSHIP CARD?
CARD?!
NO, WE DON'T.
MEMBERS CARD
IT'S A COUPON THAT LOOKS LIKE THIS.
OH, IT'S A BUSINESS CARD.
PHEW
WHO ORDERED THE OOLONG TEA?
AND THE COKE?
ME.
ME!
TINK
TINK
AND FOR THE SOVEREIGN...
OH
HOW IS THIS HAPPENING?!
I told you...
...I don't want anything!
HEY, ANISE...
HUH?
YOU'RE ACTING STRANGE TODAY.
AM I?
JOLT
YOU SEEM ANGRY.
Did something happen?

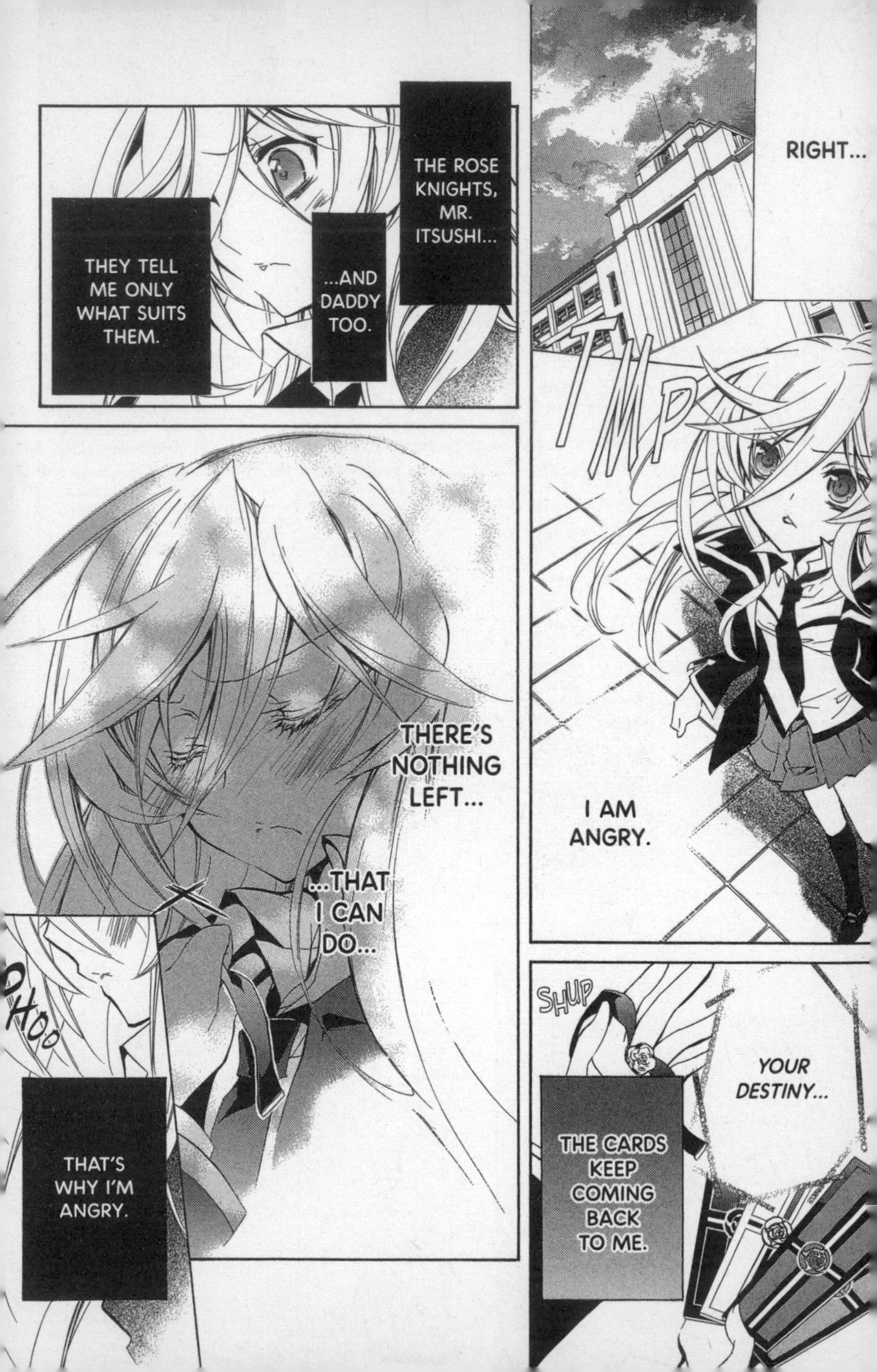
RIGHT...
TMP
I AM ANGRY.
SHUP
YOUR DESTINY...
THE CARDS KEEP COMING BACK TO ME.
THE ROSE KNIGHTS, MR. ITSUSHI...
...AND DADDY TOO.
THEY TELL ME ONLY WHAT SUITS THEM.
THERE'S NOTHING LEFT...
...THAT I CAN DO...
THAT'S WHY I'M ANGRY.

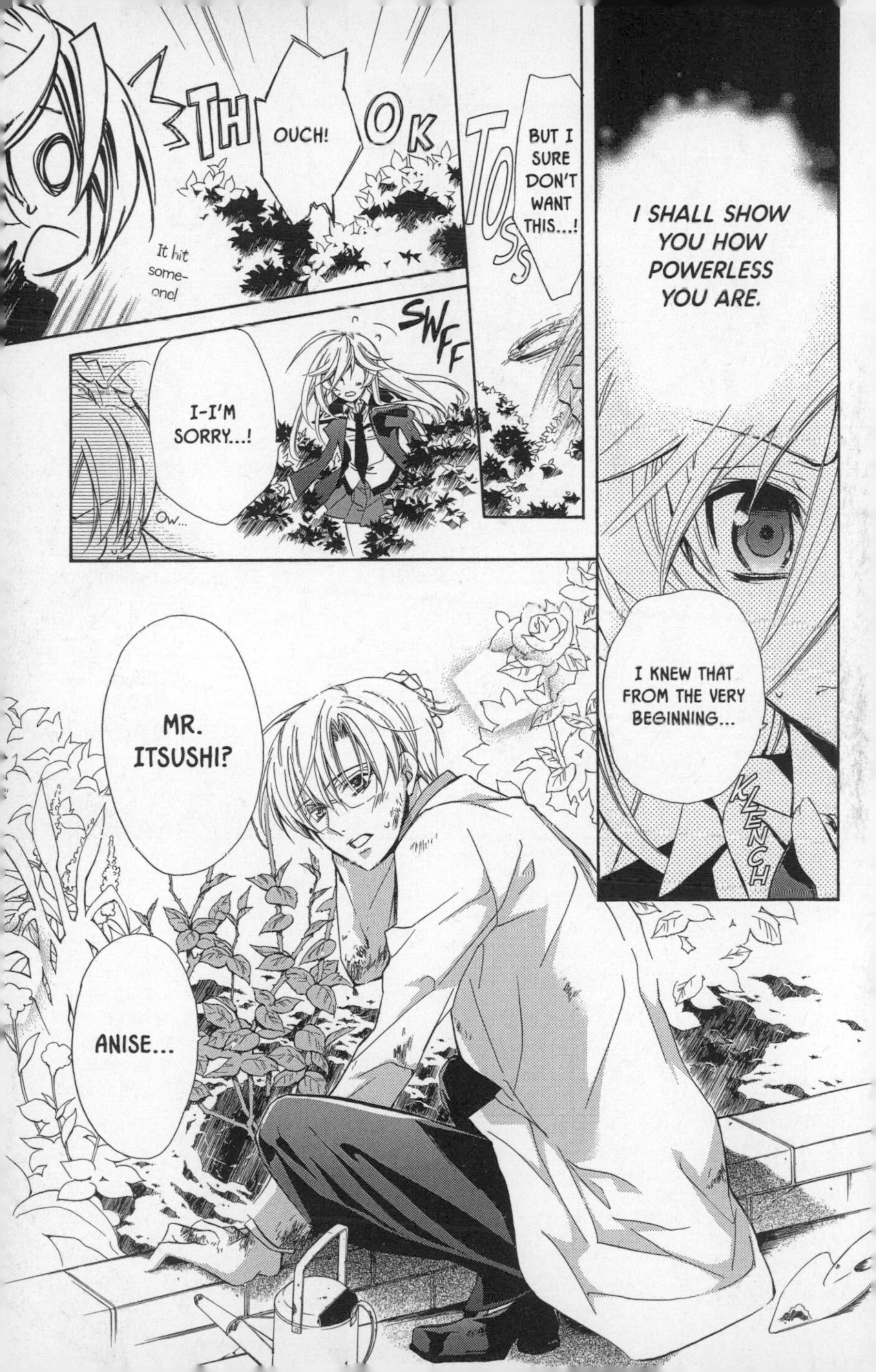
I SHALL SHOW YOU HOW POWERLESS YOU ARE.
I KNEW THAT FROM THE VERY BEGINNING...
KLENCH
BUT I SURE DON'T WANT THIS...!
TOSS
THOK
OUCH!
It hit some-one!
SWFF
I-I'M SORRY...!
Ow...
MR. ITSUSHI?
ANISE...

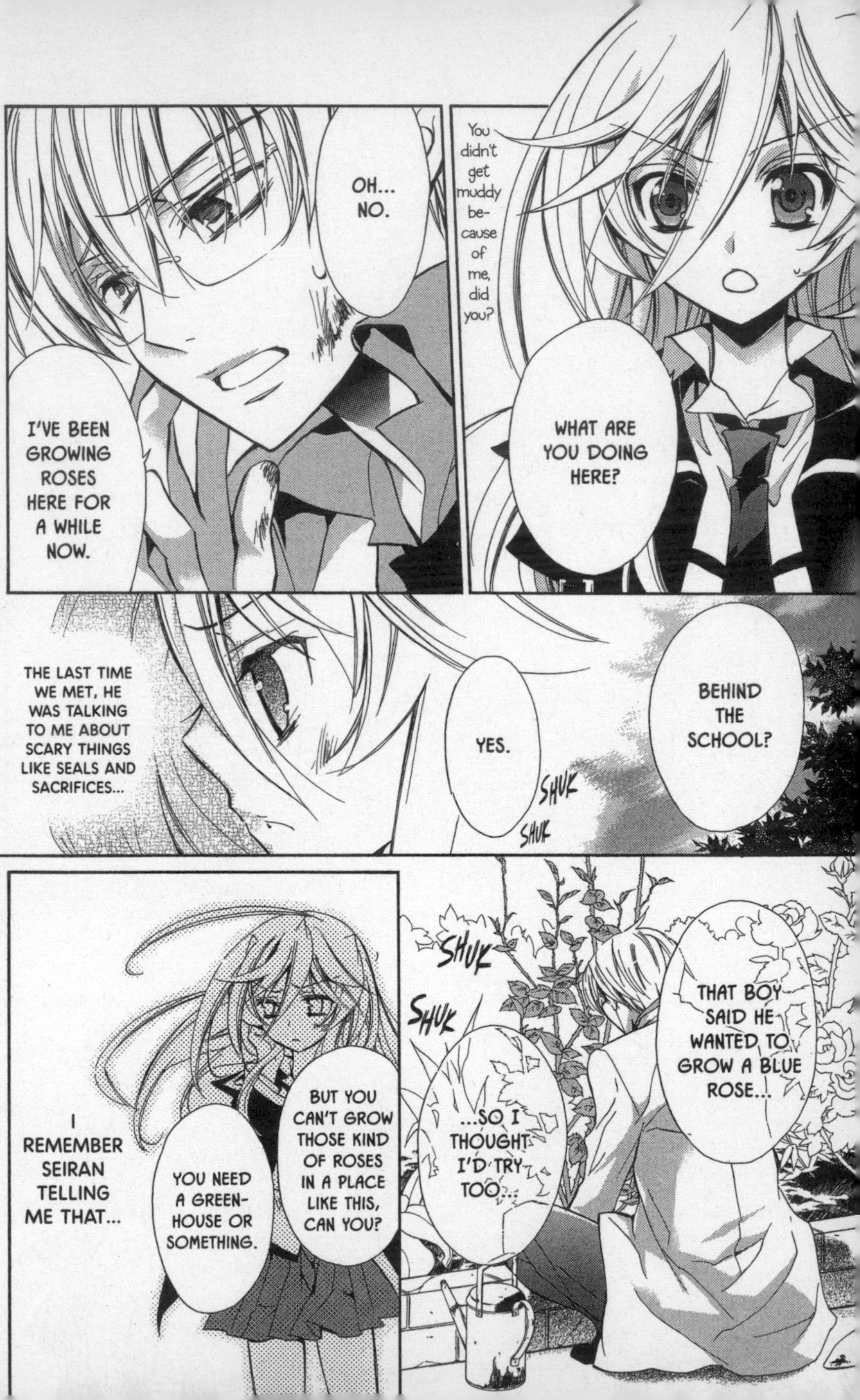
You didn't get muddy be-cause of me, did you?
WHAT ARE YOU DOING HERE?
OH... NO.
I'VE BEEN GROWING ROSES HERE FOR A WHILE NOW.
BEHIND THE SCHOOL?
YES.
SHUK
SHUK
THE LAST TIME WE MET, HE WAS TALKING TO ME ABOUT SCARY THINGS LIKE SEALS AND SACRIFICES...
THAT BOY SAID HE WANTED TO GROW A BLUE ROSE...
SHUK
SHUK
...SO I THOUGHT I'D TRY TOO...
BUT YOU CAN'T GROW THOSE KIND OF ROSES IN A PLACE LIKE THIS, CAN YOU?
YOU NEED A GREEN-HOUSE OR SOMETHING.
I REMEMBER SEIRAN TELLING ME THAT...

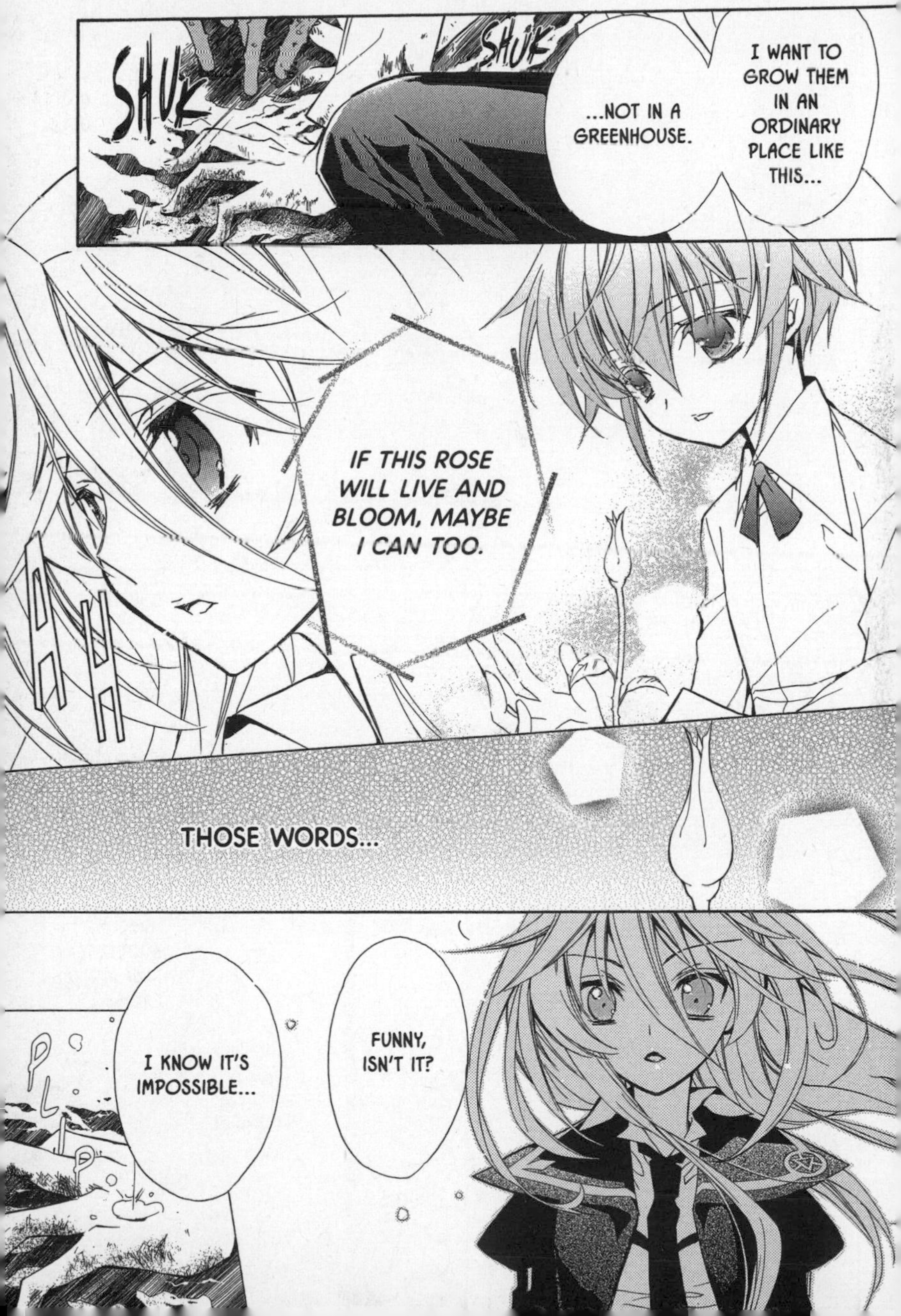

I WANT TO GROW THEM IN AN ORDINARY PLACE LIKE THIS...
...NOT IN A GREENHOUSE.
SHUK
SHUK
IF THIS ROSE WILL LIVE AND BLOOM, MAYBE I CAN TOO.
THOSE WORDS...
FUNNY, ISN'T IT?
I KNOW IT'S IMPOSSIBLE...
PLIP

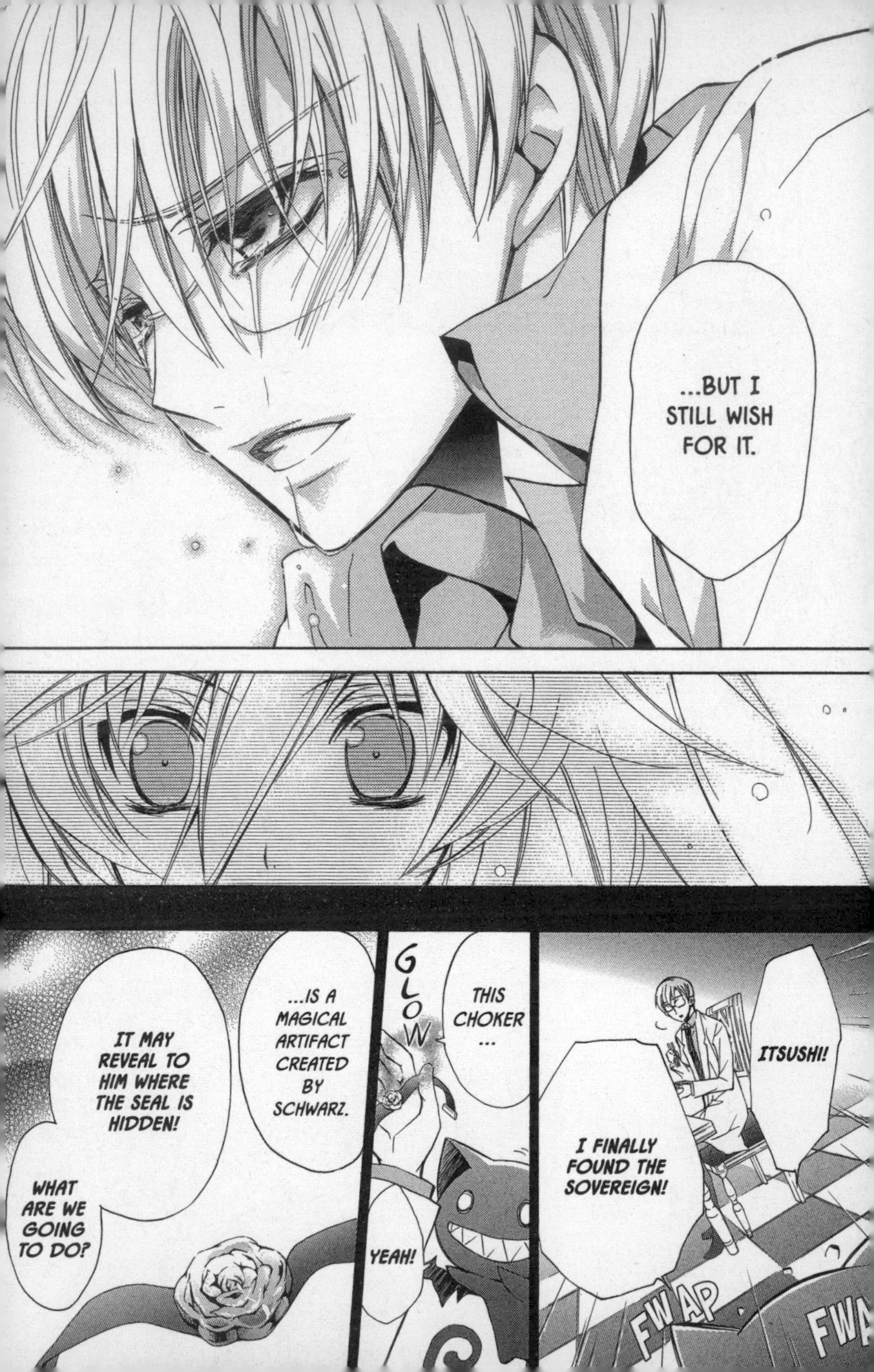
...BUT I STILL WISH FOR IT.
ITSUSHI!
I FINALLY FOUND THE SOVEREIGN!
FWAP
FWA
THIS CHOKER ...
GLOW
YEAH!
...IS A MAGICAL ARTIFACT CREATED BY SCHWARZ.
IT MAY REVEAL TO HIM WHERE THE SEAL IS HIDDEN!
WHAT ARE WE GOING TO DO?

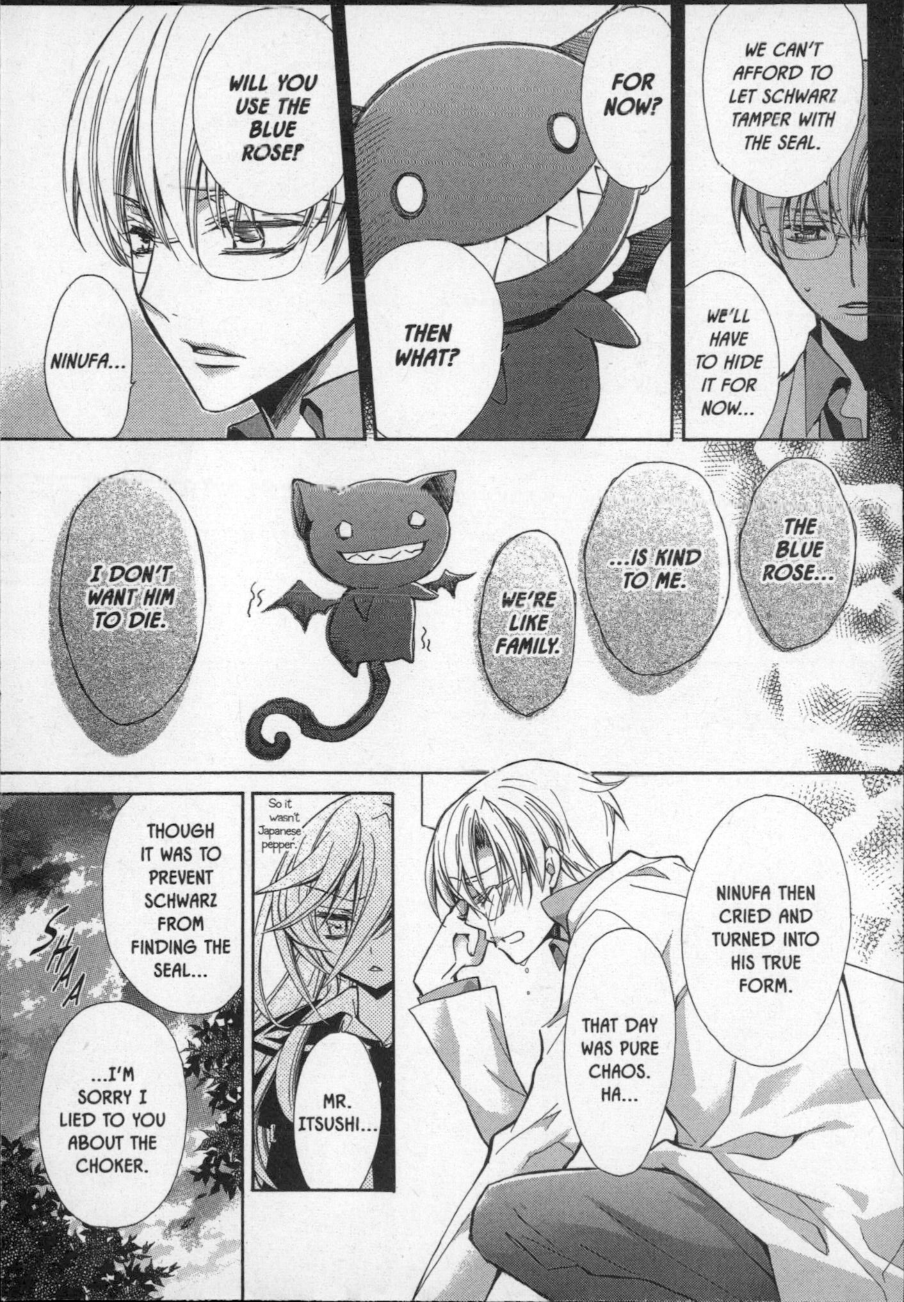
WE CAN'T AFFORD TO LET SCHWARZ TAMPER WITH THE SEAL.
WE'LL HAVE TO HIDE IT FOR NOW...
FOR NOW?
THEN WHAT?
WILL YOU USE THE BLUE ROSE?
NINUFA...
THE BLUE ROSE...
...IS KIND TO ME.
WE'RE LIKE FAMILY.
I DON'T WANT HIM TO DIE.
NINUFA THEN CRIED AND TURNED INTO HIS TRUE FORM.
THAT DAY WAS PURE CHAOS. HA...
So it wasn't Japanese pepper.
MR. ITSUSHI...
THOUGH IT WAS TO PREVENT SCHWARZ FROM FINDING THE SEAL...
SHAA
...I'M SORRY I LIED TO YOU ABOUT THE CHOKER.

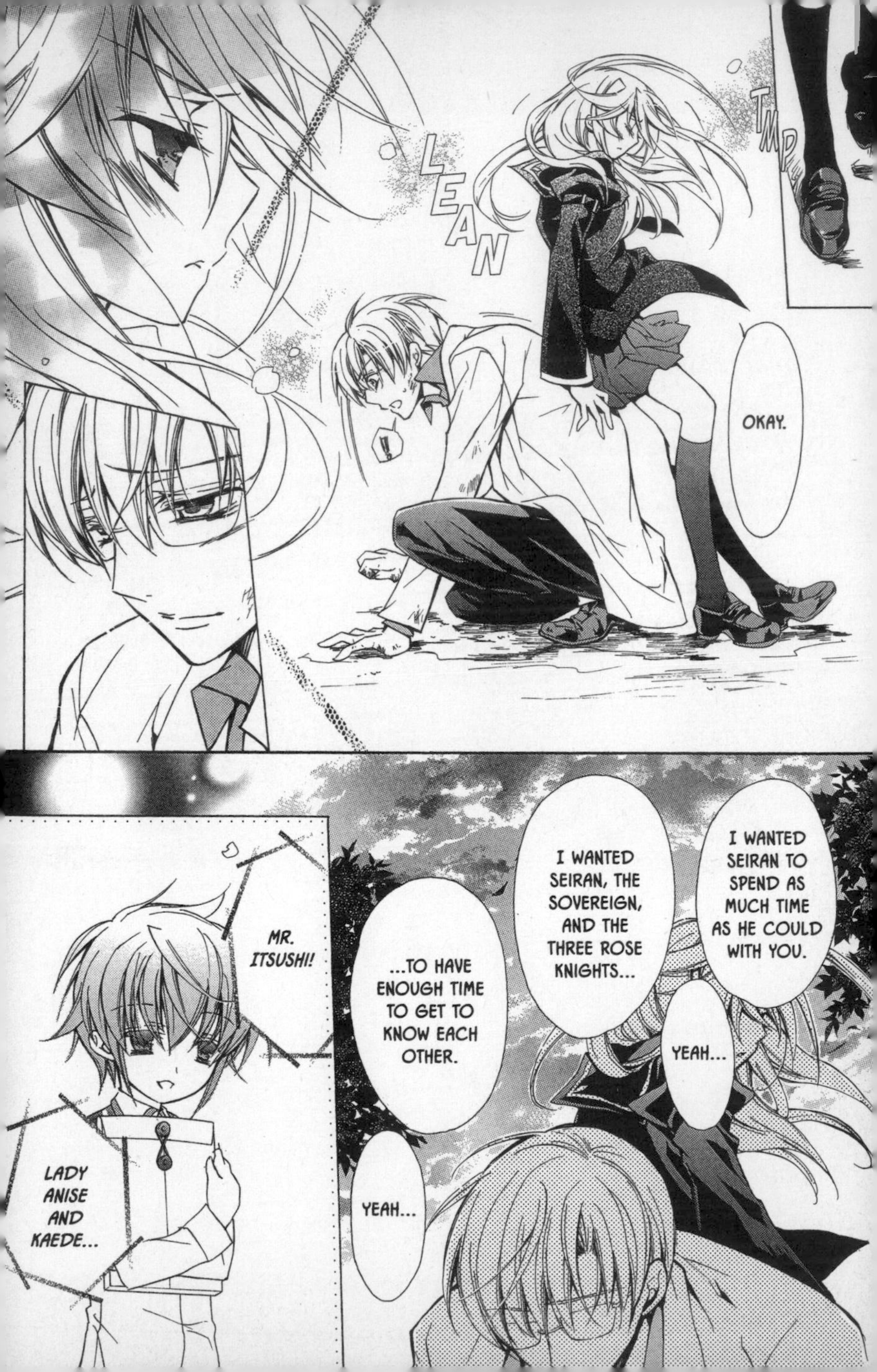
TMP
LEAN
OKAY.
!
I WANTED SEIRAN TO SPEND AS MUCH TIME AS HE COULD WITH YOU.
I WANTED SEIRAN, THE SOVEREIGN, AND THE THREE ROSE KNIGHTS...
YEAH...
...TO HAVE ENOUGH TIME TO GET TO KNOW EACH OTHER.
YEAH...
MR. ITSUSHI!
LADY ANISE AND KAEDE...

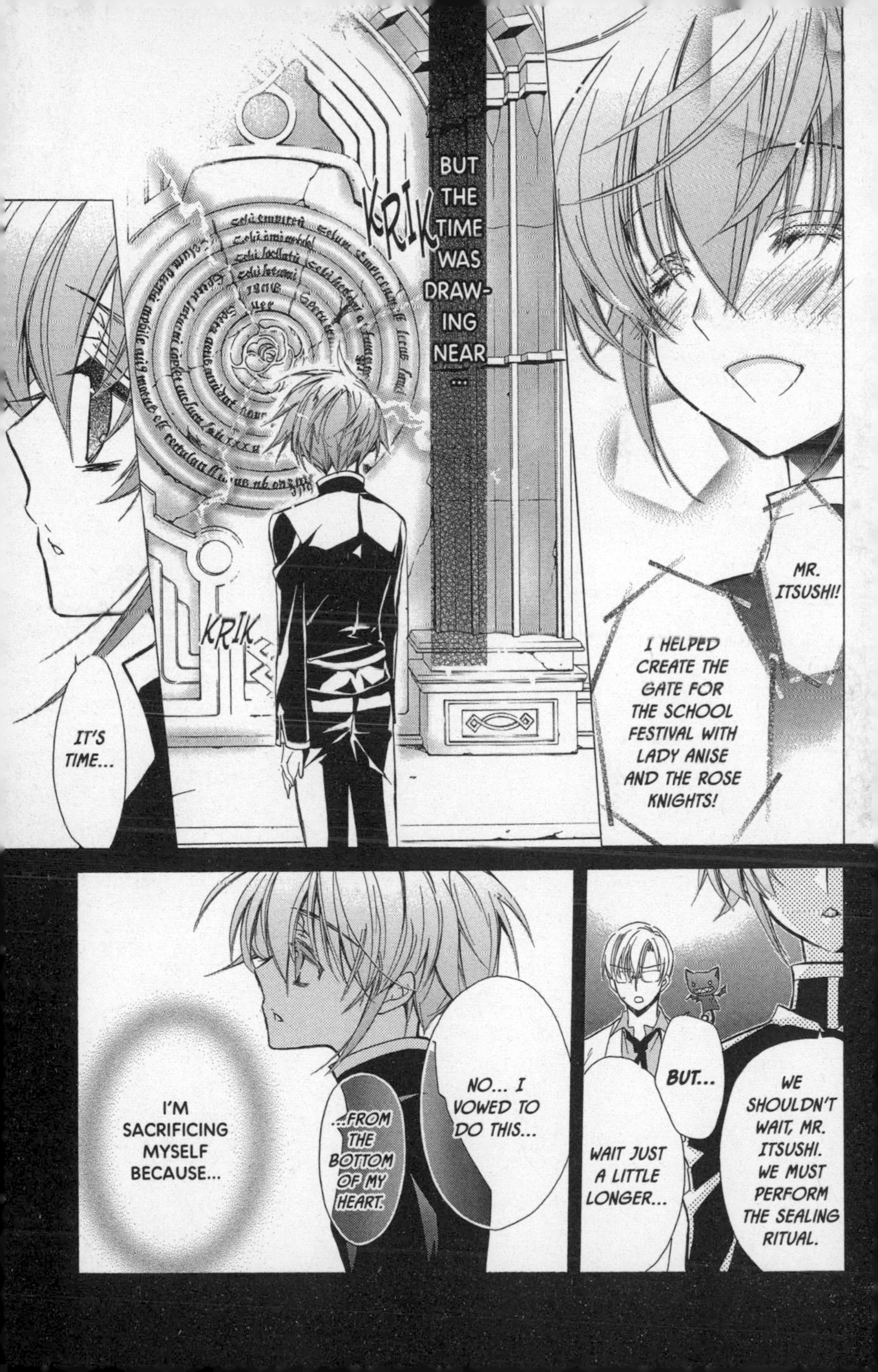
BUT THE TIME WAS DRAWING NEAR...
K-RIK
MR. ITSUSHI!
I HELPED CREATE THE GATE FOR THE SCHOOL FESTIVAL WITH LADY ANISE AND THE ROSE KNIGHTS!
KRIK
IT'S TIME...
WE SHOULDN'T WAIT, MR. ITSUSHI. WE MUST PERFORM THE SEALING RITUAL.
BUT...
WAIT JUST A LITTLE LONGER...
NO... I VOWED TO DO THIS...
...FROM THE BOTTOM OF MY HEART.
I'M SACRIFICING MYSELF BECAUSE...

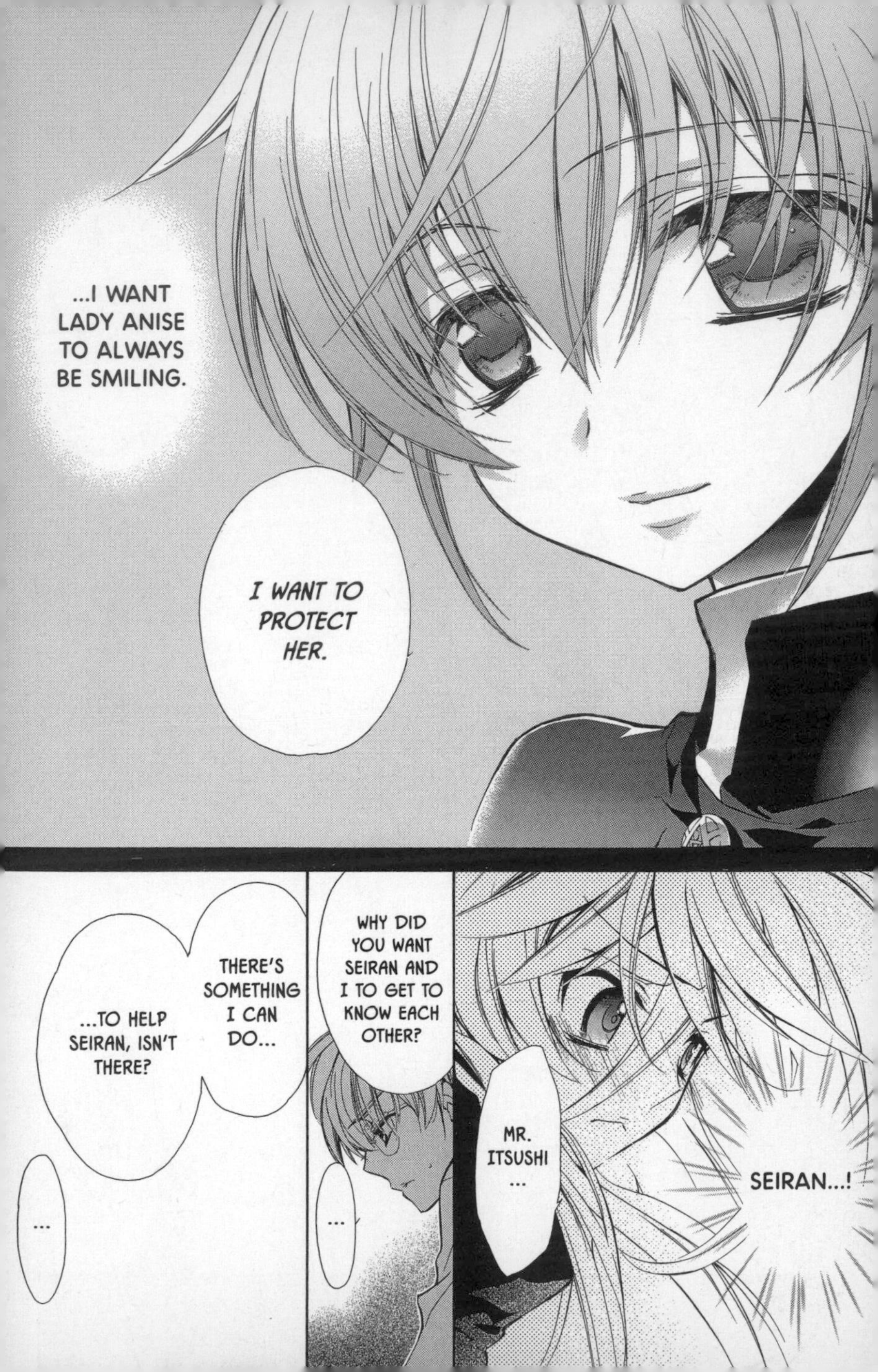
...I WANT LADY ANISE TO ALWAYS BE SMILING.
I WANT TO PROTECT HER.
SEIRAN...!
MR. ITSUSHI ...
WHY DID YOU WANT SEIRAN AND I TO GET TO KNOW EACH OTHER?
...
THERE'S SOMETHING I CAN DO...
...TO HELP SEIRAN, ISN'T THERE?
...

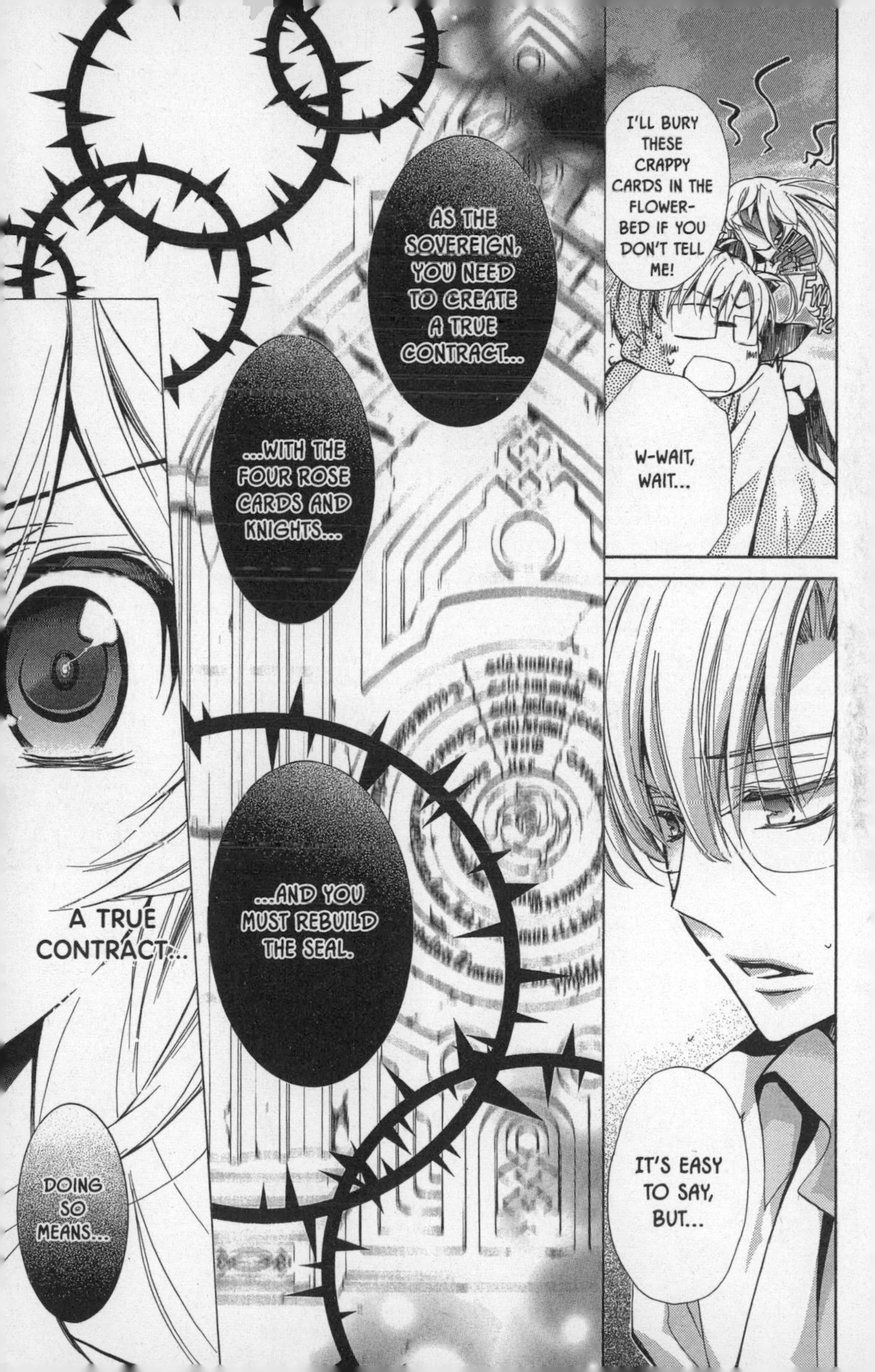
I'LL BURY THESE CRAPPY CARDS IN THE FLOWER-BED IF YOU DON'T TELL ME!
Fwik
W-WAIT, WAIT...
IT'S EASY TO SAY, BUT...
AS THE SOVEREIGN, YOU NEED TO CREATE A TRUE CONTRACT...
...WITH THE FOUR ROSE CARDS AND KNIGHTS...
...AND YOU MUST REBUILD THE SEAL.
A TRUE CONTRACT...
DOING SO MEANS...

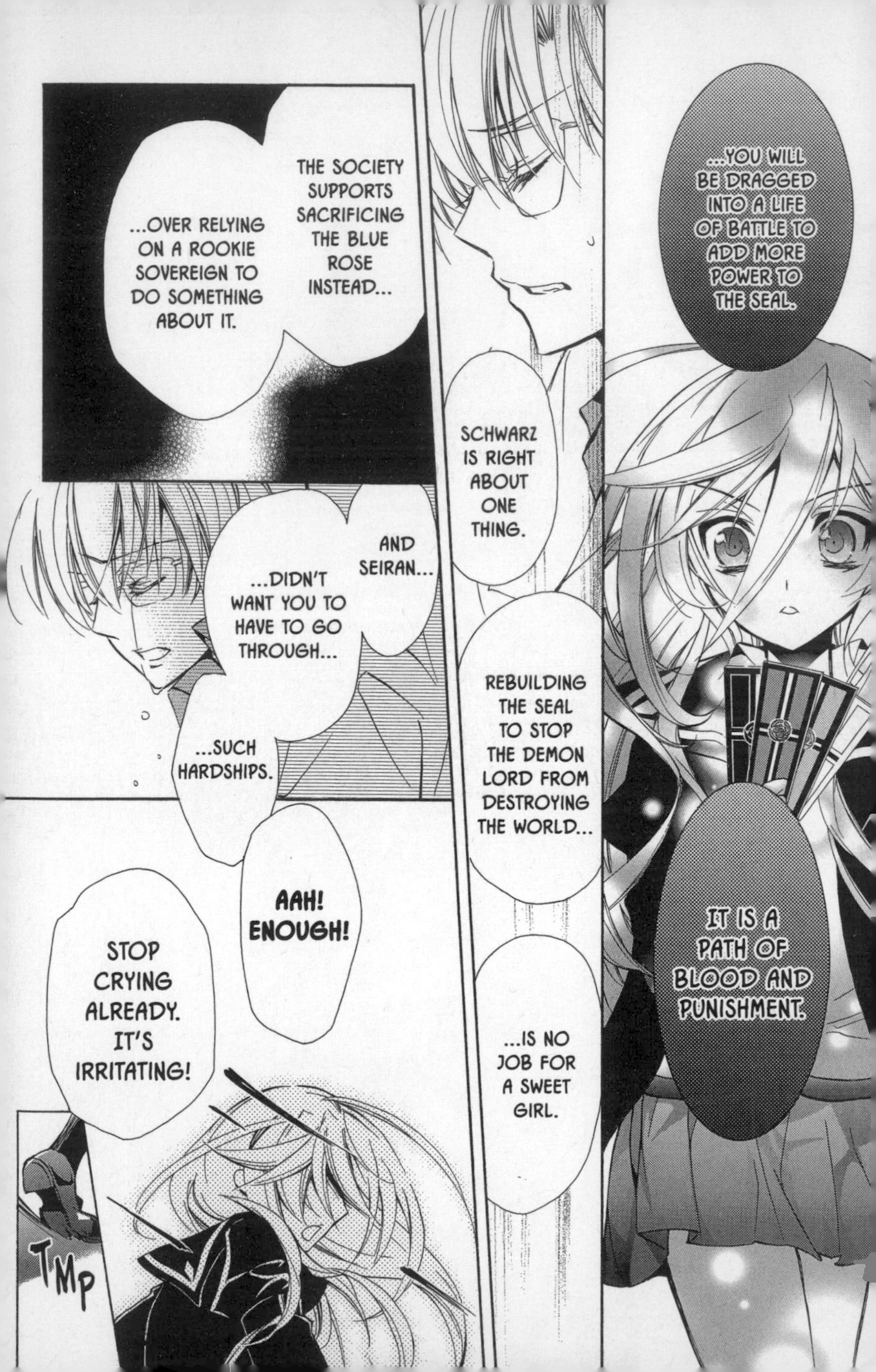
...YOU WILL BE DRAGGED INTO A LIFE OF BATTLE TO ADD MORE POWER TO THE SEAL.
IT IS A PATH OF BLOOD AND PUNISHMENT.
SCHWARZ IS RIGHT ABOUT ONE THING.
REBUILDING THE SEAL TO STOP THE DEMON LORD FROM DESTROYING THE WORLD...
...IS NO JOB FOR A SWEET GIRL.
THE SOCIETY SUPPORTS SACRIFICING THE BLUE ROSE INSTEAD...
...OVER RELYING ON A ROOKIE SOVEREIGN TO DO SOMETHING ABOUT IT.
AND SEIRAN...
...DIDN'T WANT YOU TO HAVE TO GO THROUGH...
...SUCH HARDSHIPS.
AAH! ENOUGH!
STOP CRYING ALREADY. IT'S IRRITATING!
TMP

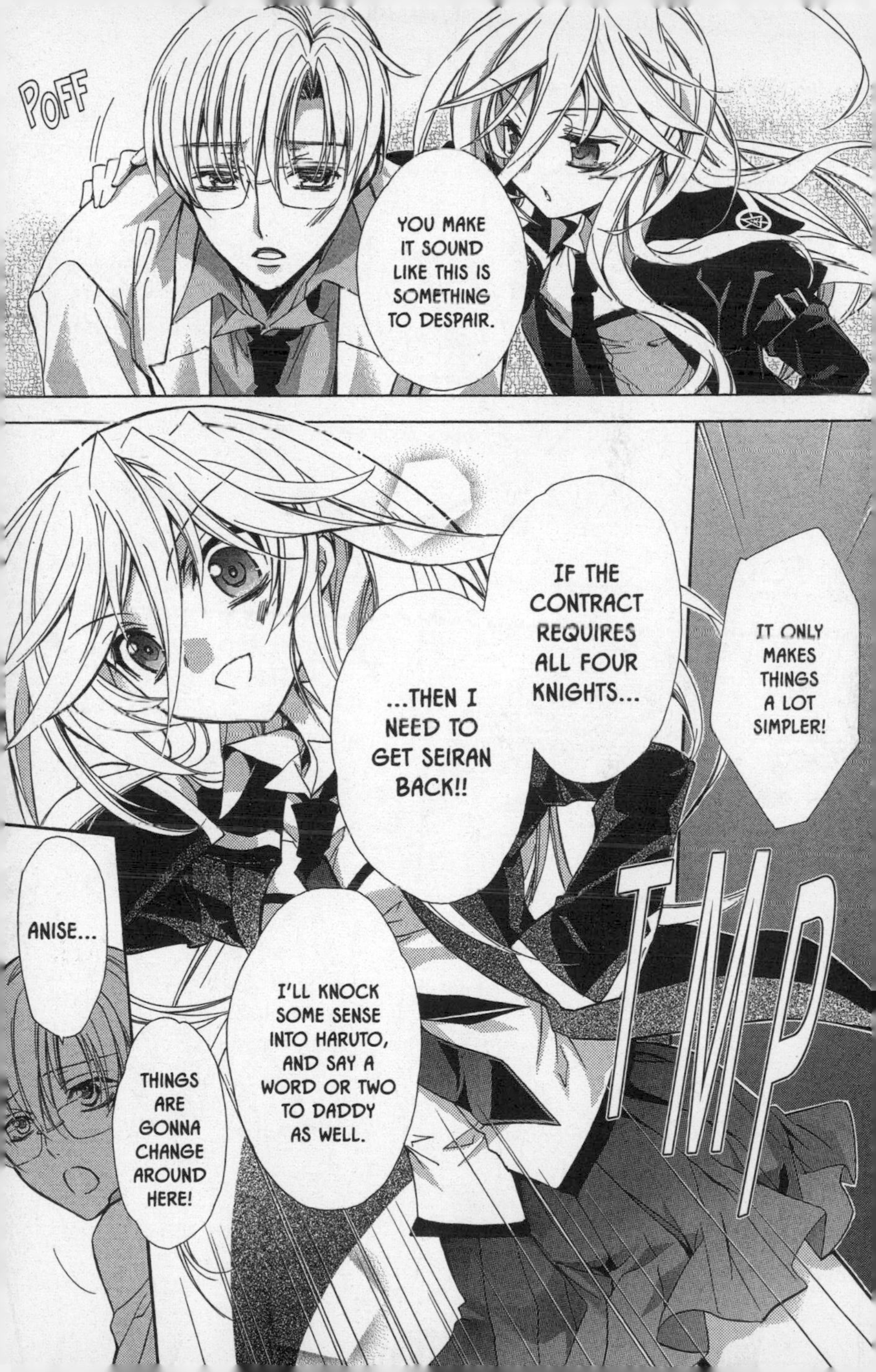
POFF
YOU MAKE IT SOUND LIKE THIS IS SOMETHING TO DESPAIR.
IT ONLY MAKES THINGS A LOT SIMPLER!
IF THE CONTRACT REQUIRES ALL FOUR KNIGHTS...
...THEN I NEED TO GET SEIRAN BACK!!
TMP
I'LL KNOCK SOME SENSE INTO HARUTO, AND SAY A WORD OR TWO TO DADDY AS WELL.
THINGS ARE GONNA CHANGE AROUND HERE!
ANISE...

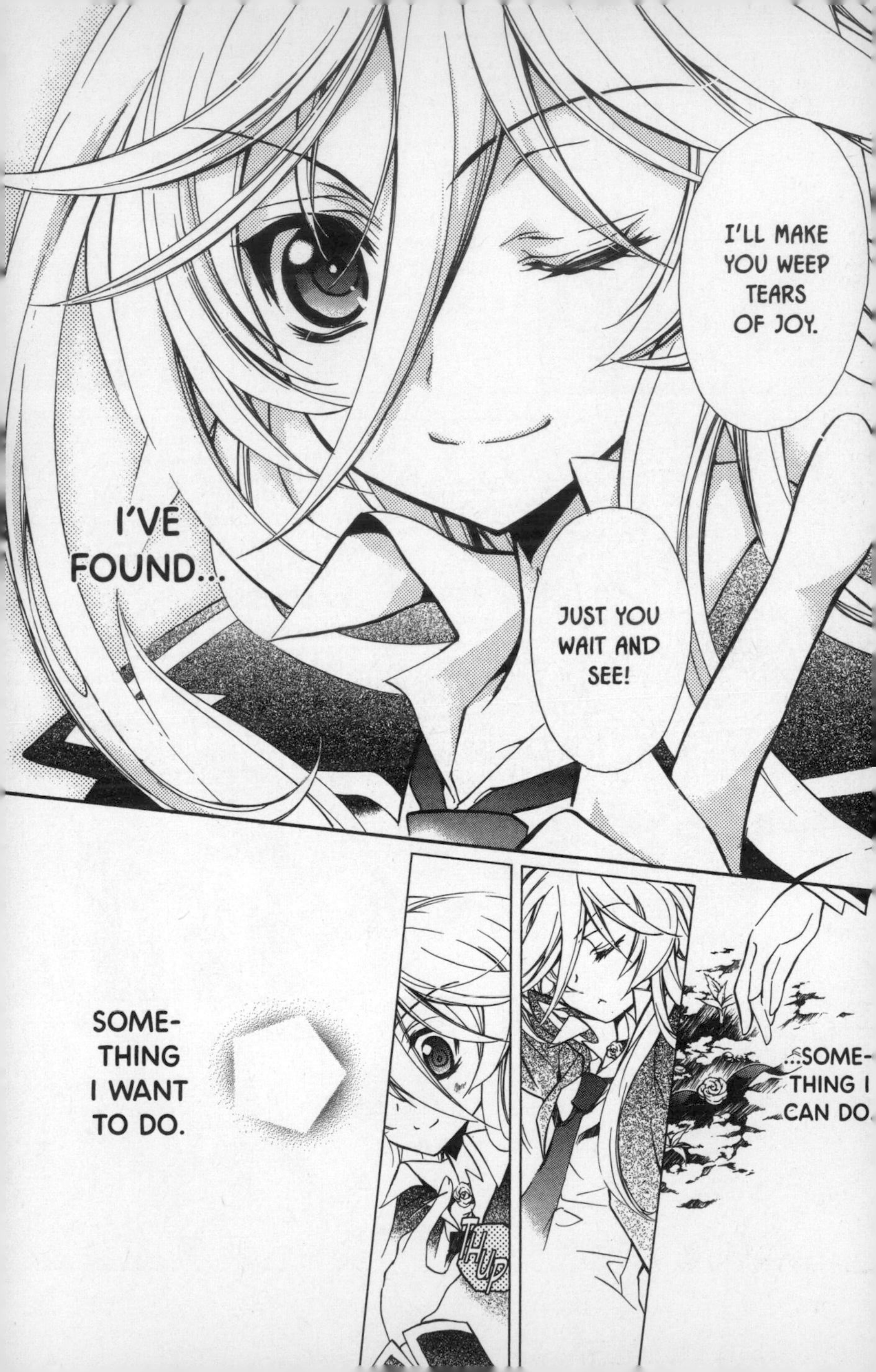
I'LL MAKE YOU WEEP TEARS OF JOY.
JUST YOU WAIT AND SEE!
I'VE FOUND...
...SOME-THING I CAN DO.
THUP
SOME-THING I WANT TO DO.

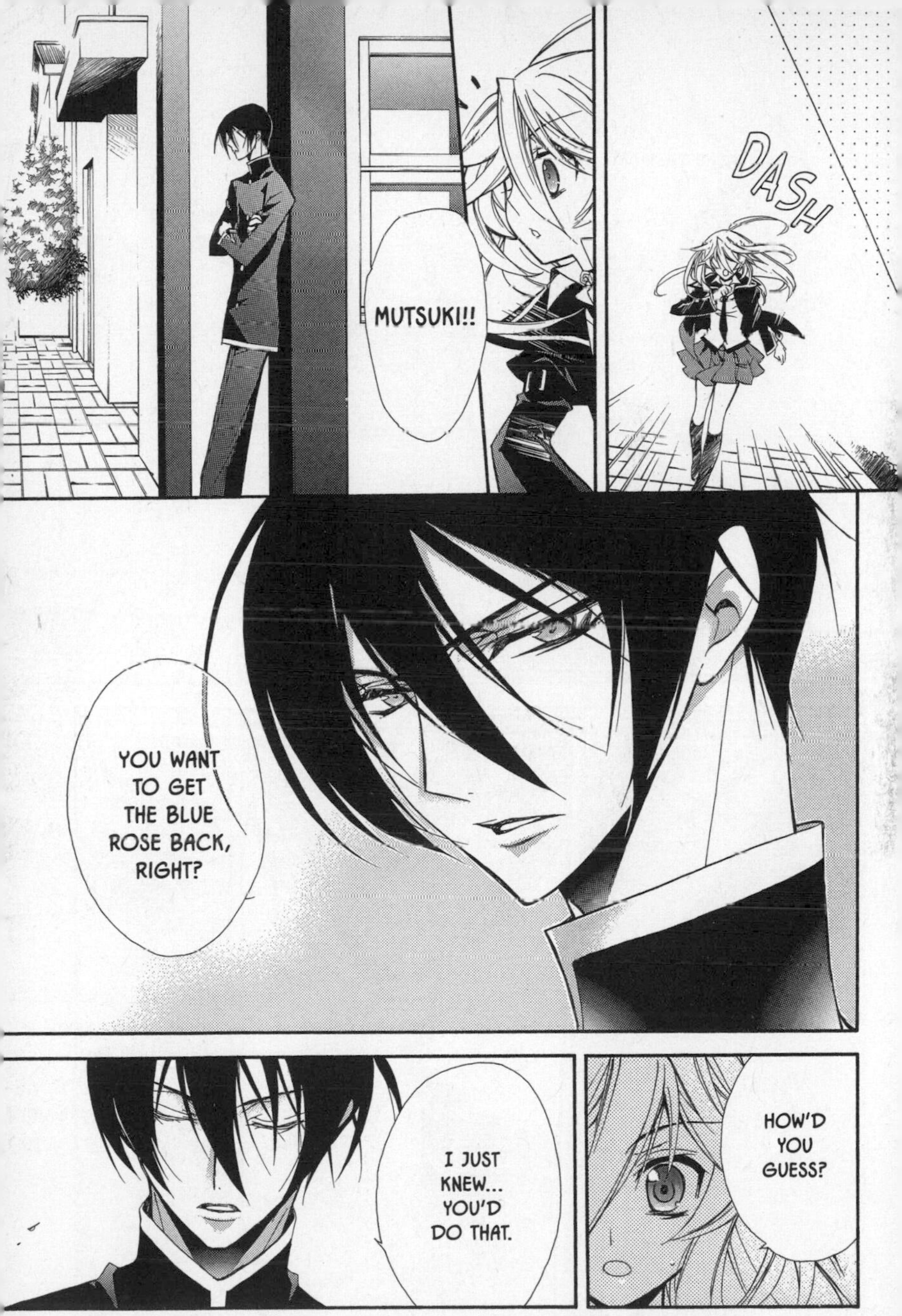
DASH
MUTSUKI!!
YOU WANT TO GET THE BLUE ROSE BACK, RIGHT?
HOW'D YOU GUESS?
I JUST KNEW... YOU'D DO THAT.

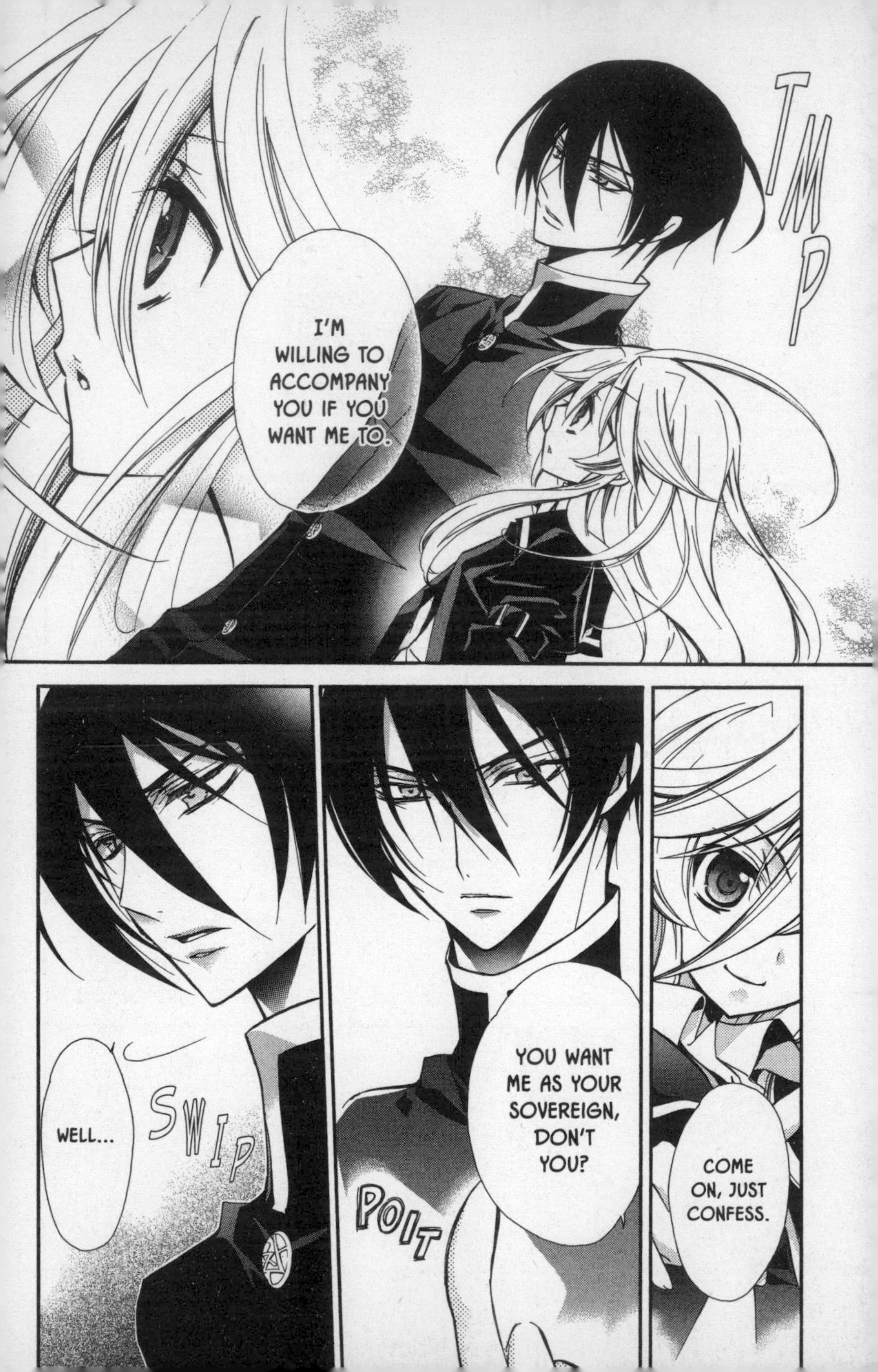
TMP
I'M WILLING TO ACCOMPANY YOU IF YOU WANT ME TO.
COME ON, JUST CONFESS.
YOU WANT ME AS YOUR SOVEREIGN, DON'T YOU?
POIT
SWIP
WELL...

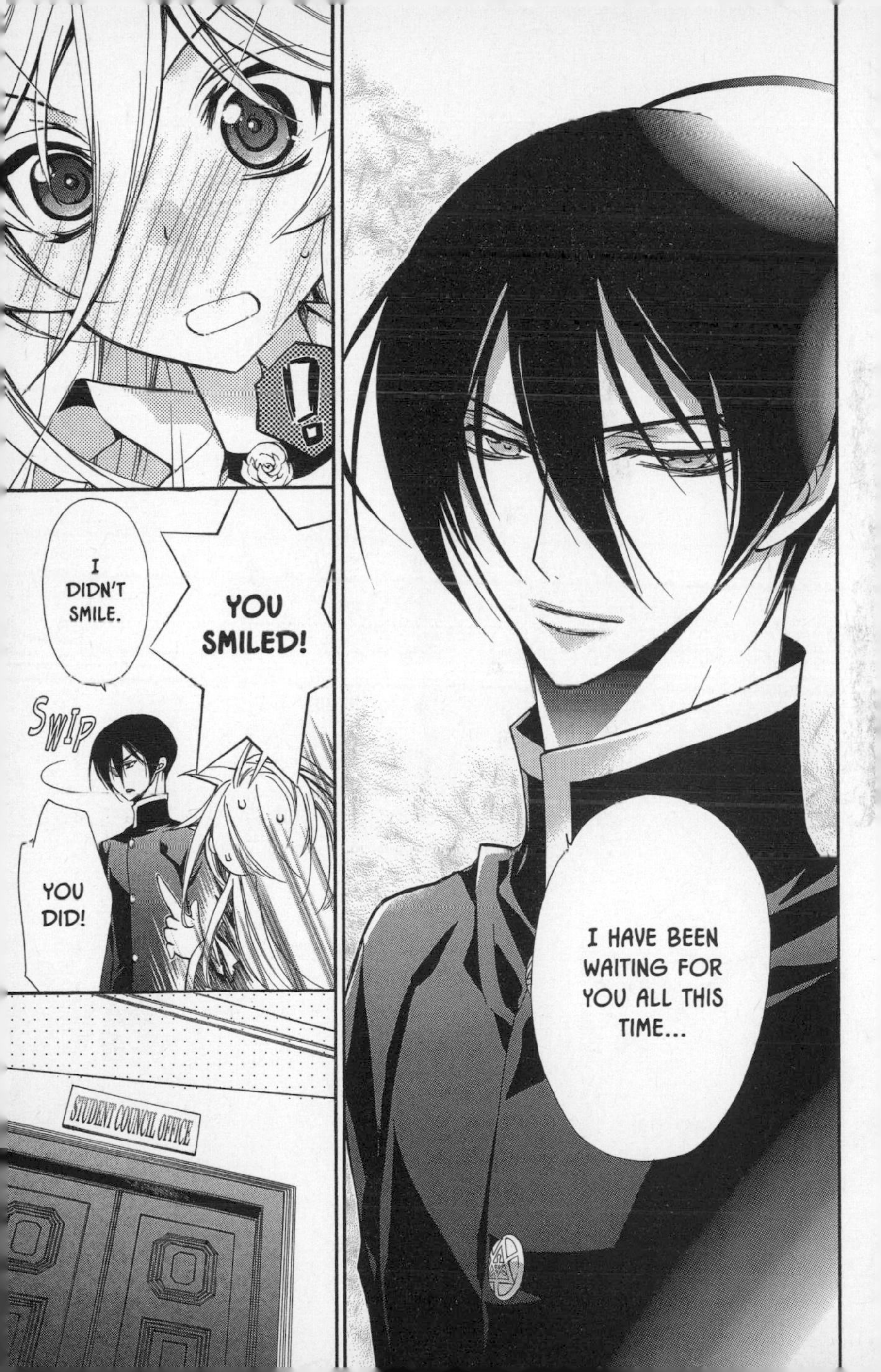
I HAVE BEEN WAITING FOR YOU ALL THIS TIME...
YOU SMILED!
I DIDN'T SMILE.
SWIP
YOU DID!
STUDENT COUNCIL OFFICE

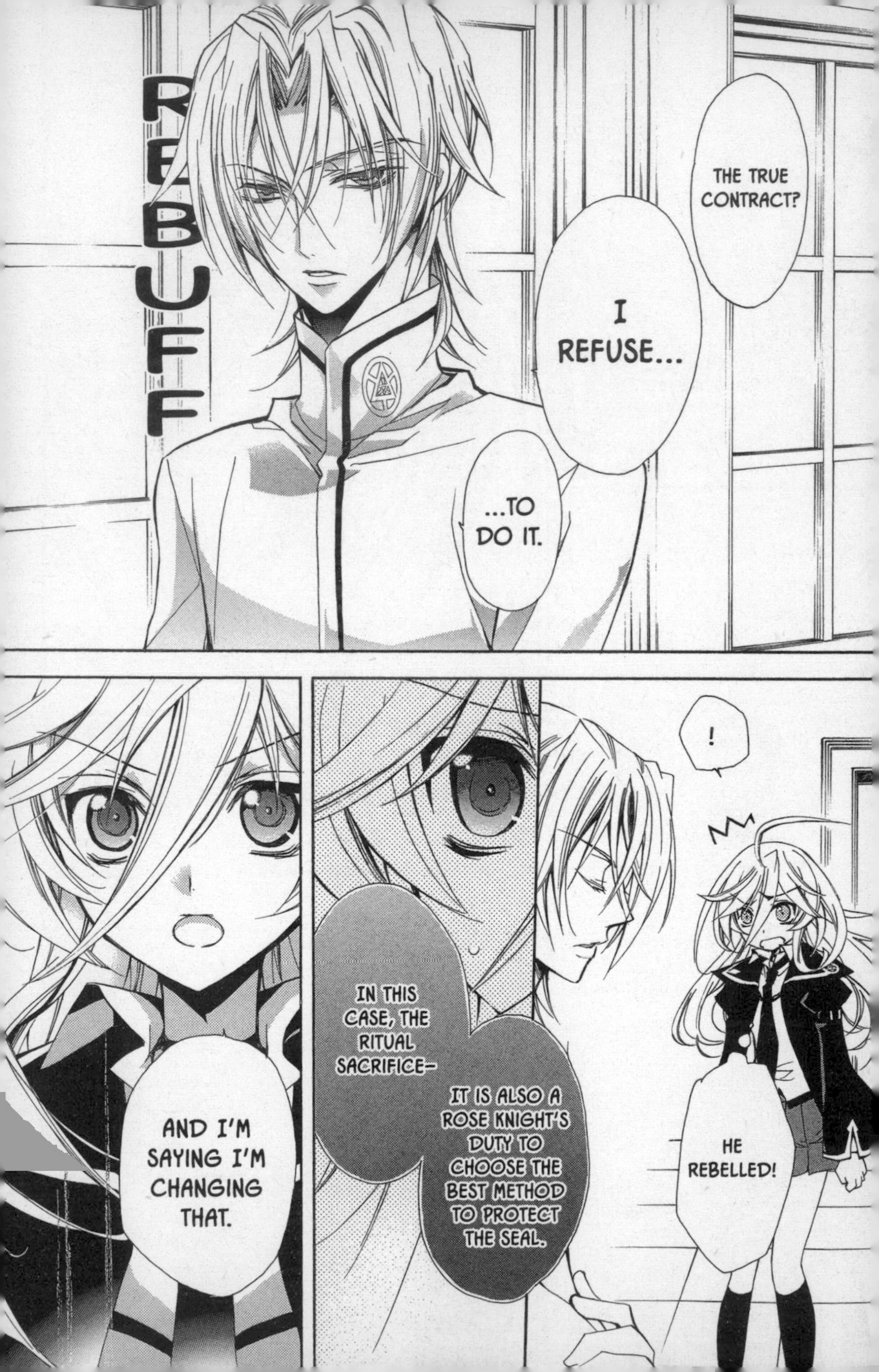
THE TRUE CONTRACT?
I REFUSE...
...TO DO IT.
REBUFF
!
HE REBELLED!
IN THIS CASE, THE RITUAL SACRIFICE–
IT IS ALSO A ROSE KNIGHT'S DUTY TO CHOOSE THE BEST METHOD TO PROTECT THE SEAL.
AND I'M SAYING I'M CHANGING THAT.

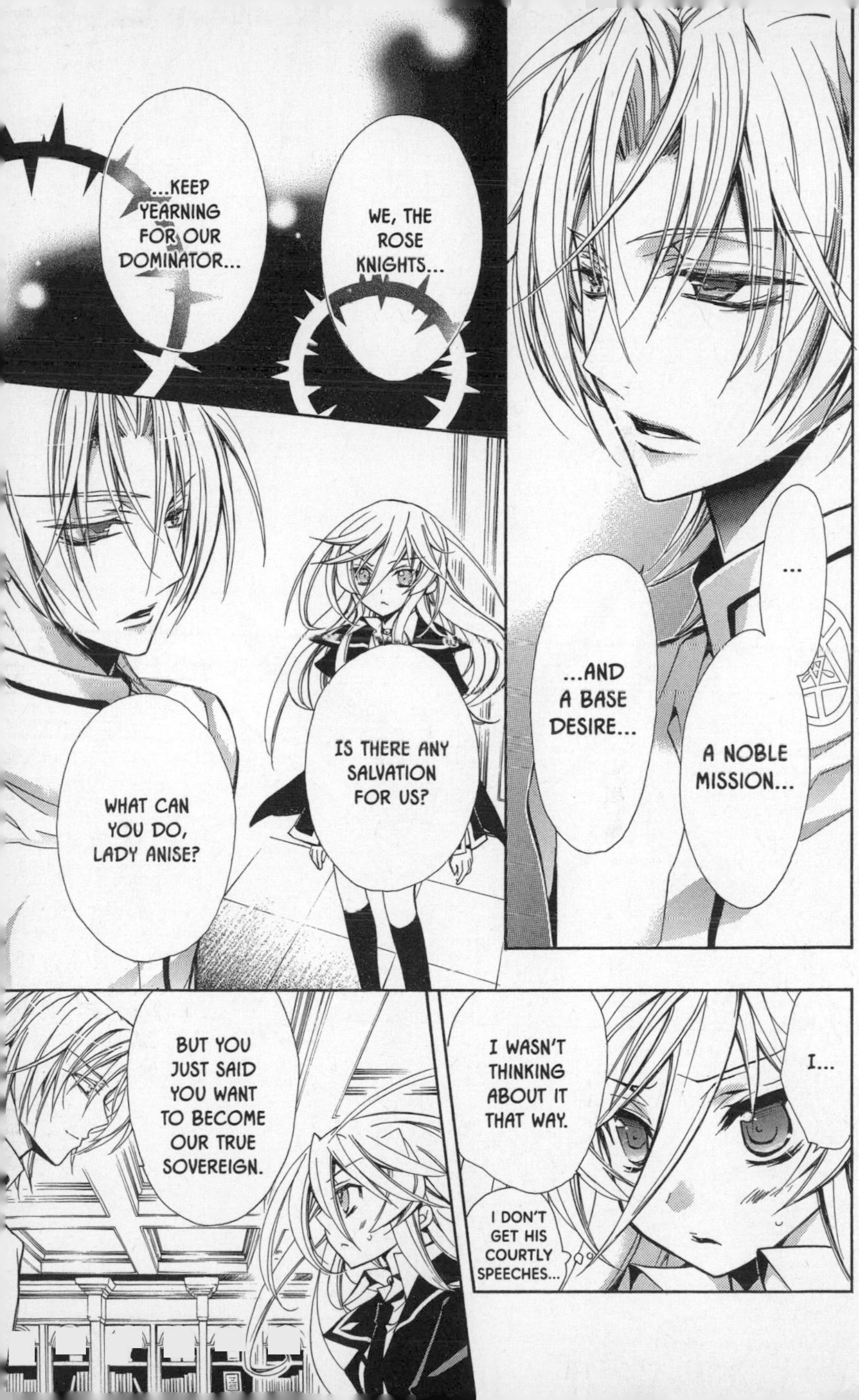
...
A NOBLE MISSION...
...AND A BASE DESIRE...
WE, THE ROSE KNIGHTS...
...KEEP YEARNING FOR OUR DOMINATOR...
IS THERE ANY SALVATION FOR US?
WHAT CAN YOU DO, LADY ANISE?
I...
I WASN'T THINKING ABOUT IT THAT WAY.
I DON'T GET HIS COURTLY SPEECHES...
BUT YOU JUST SAID YOU WANT TO BECOME OUR TRUE SOVEREIGN.

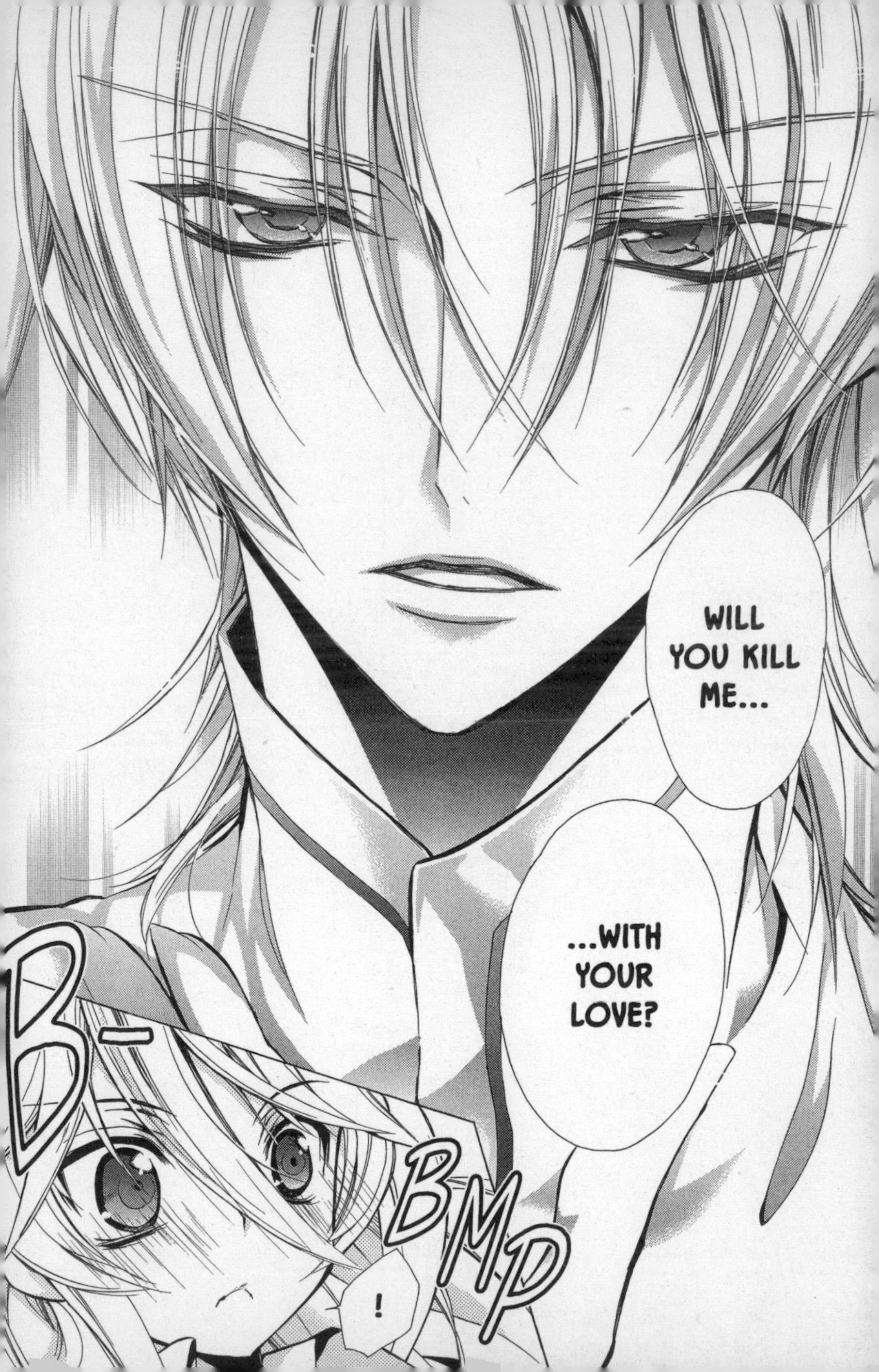
WILL YOU KILL ME...
...WITH YOUR LOVE?
B-BMP
!

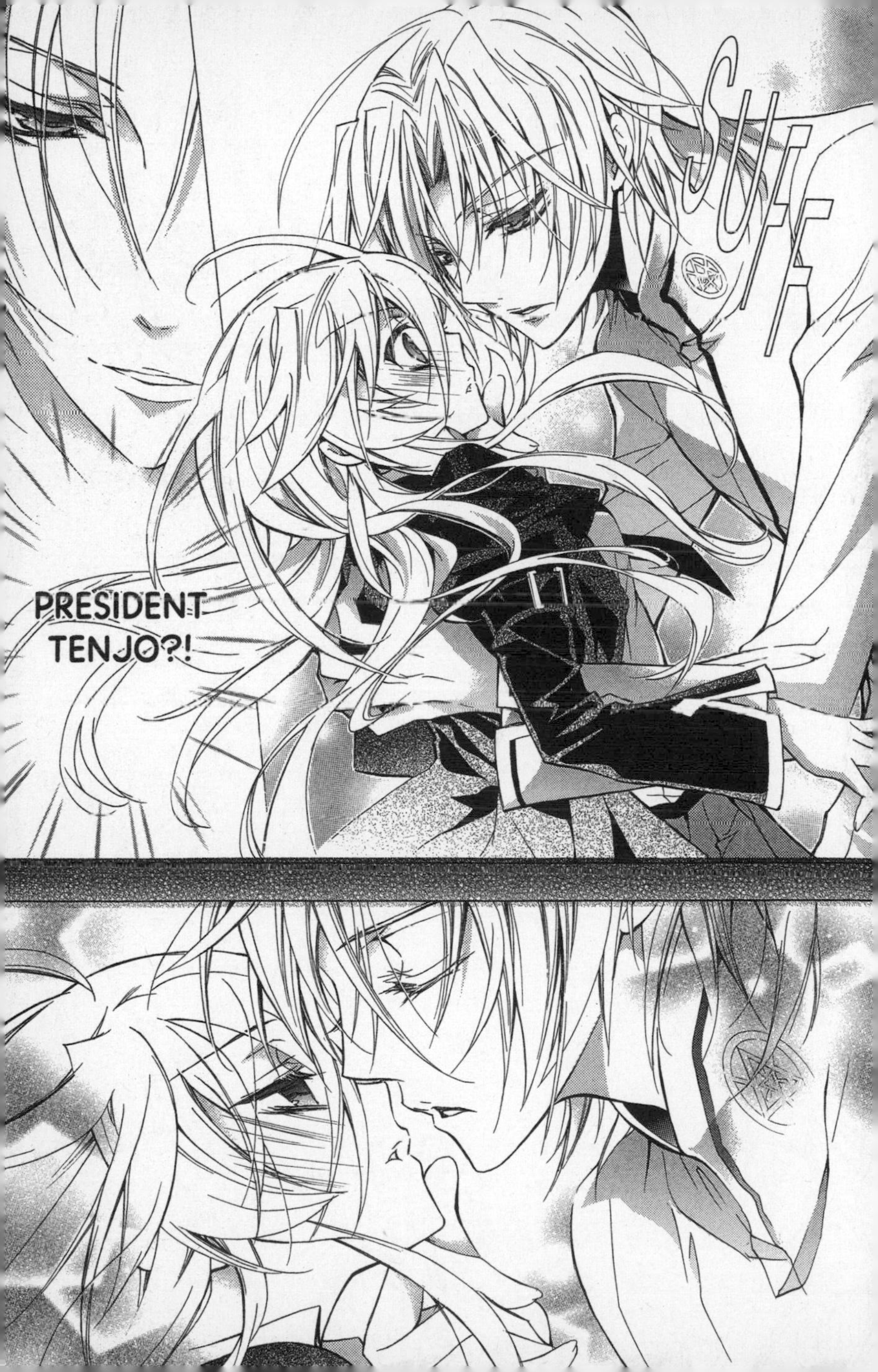
SUFF
PRESIDENT TENJO?!

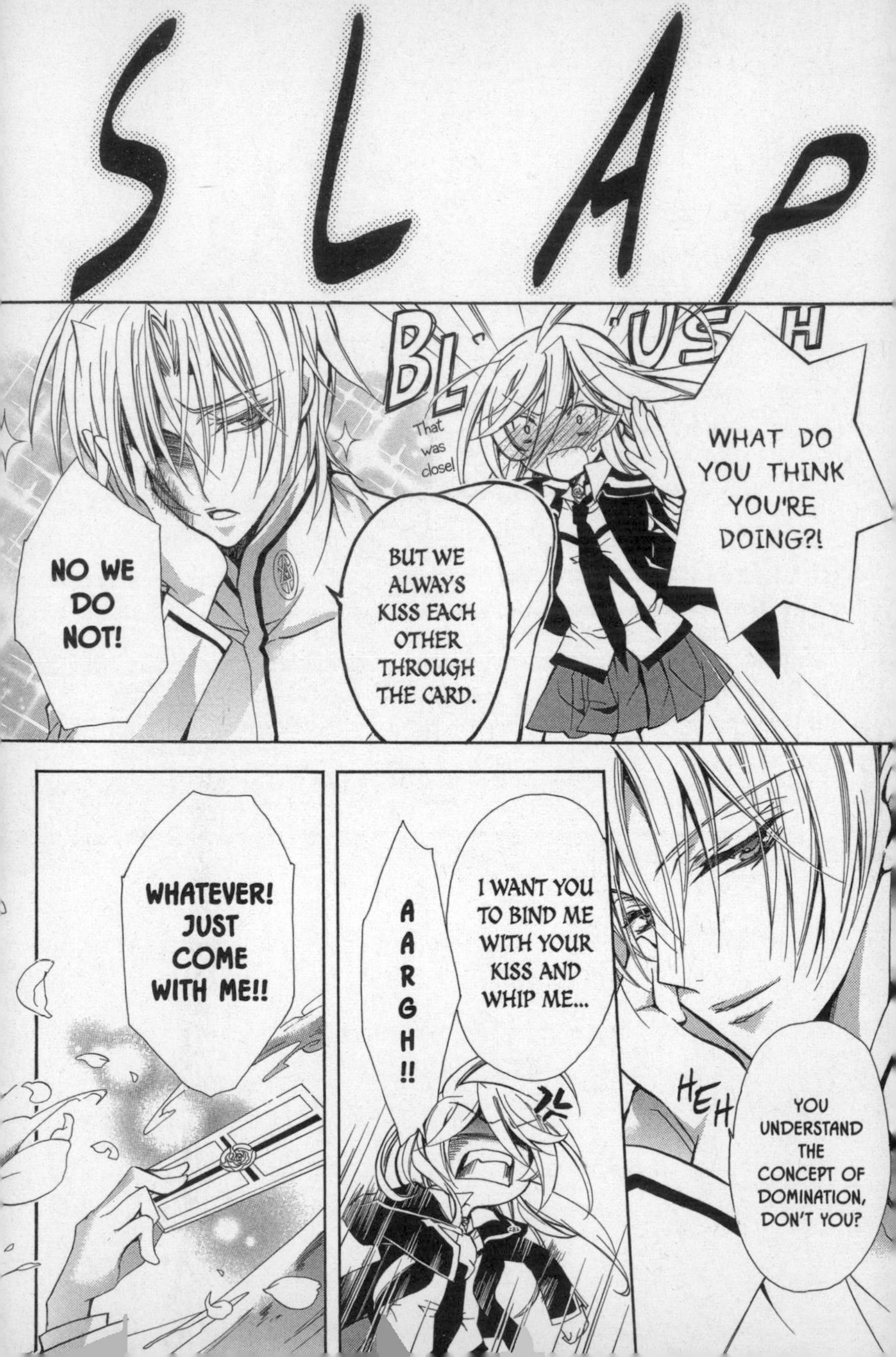
SLAP
BLUSH
WHAT DO YOU THINK YOU'RE DOING?!
That was close!
BUT WE ALWAYS KISS EACH OTHER THROUGH THE CARD.
NO WE DO NOT!
HEH
YOU UNDERSTAND THE CONCEPT OF DOMINATION, DON'T YOU?
I WANT YOU TO BIND ME WITH YOUR KISS AND WHIP ME...
AARGH!!
WHATEVER! JUST COME WITH ME!!

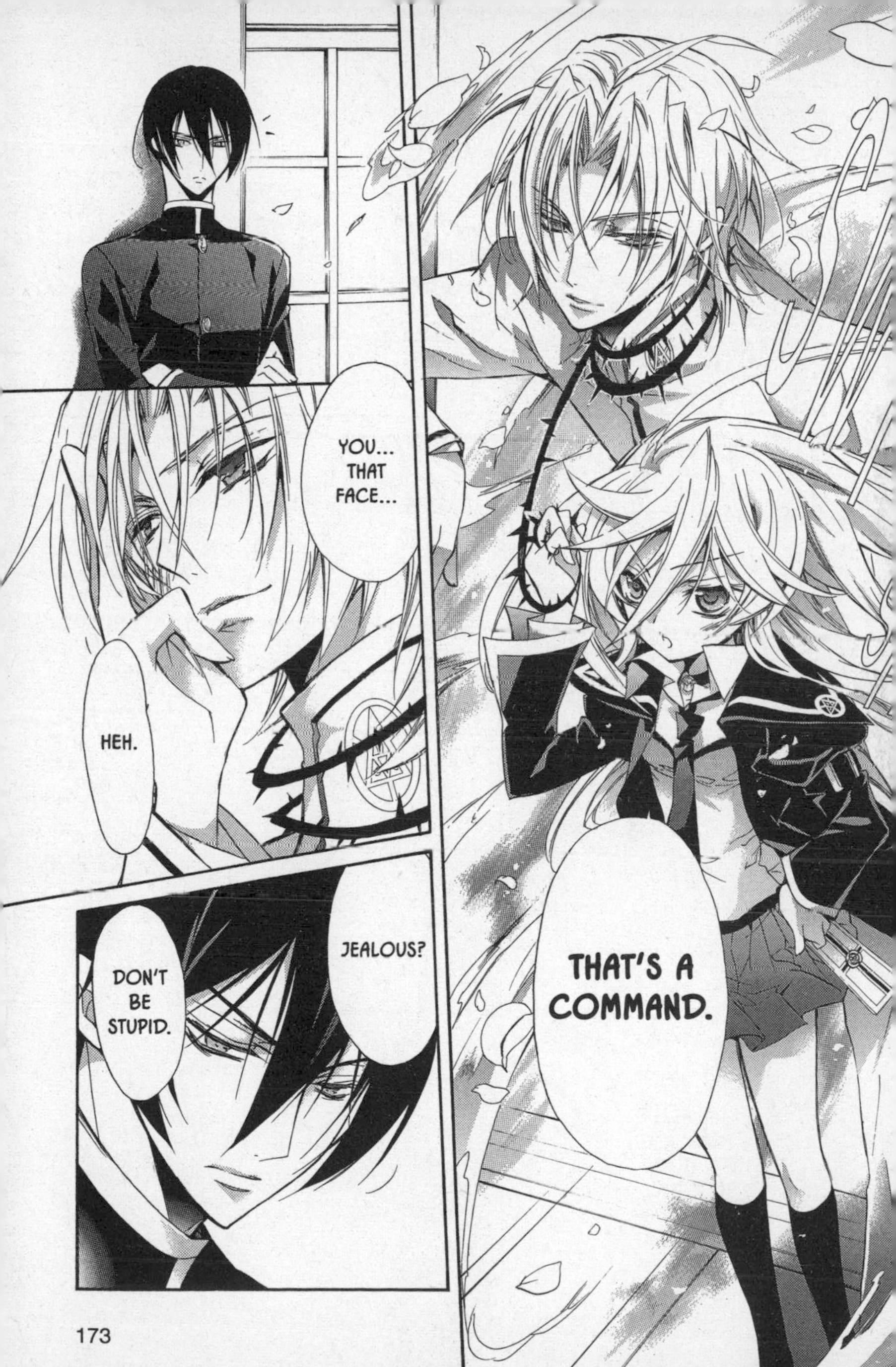
THAT'S A COMMAND.
YOU... THAT FACE...
HEH.
JEALOUS?
DON'T BE STUPID.

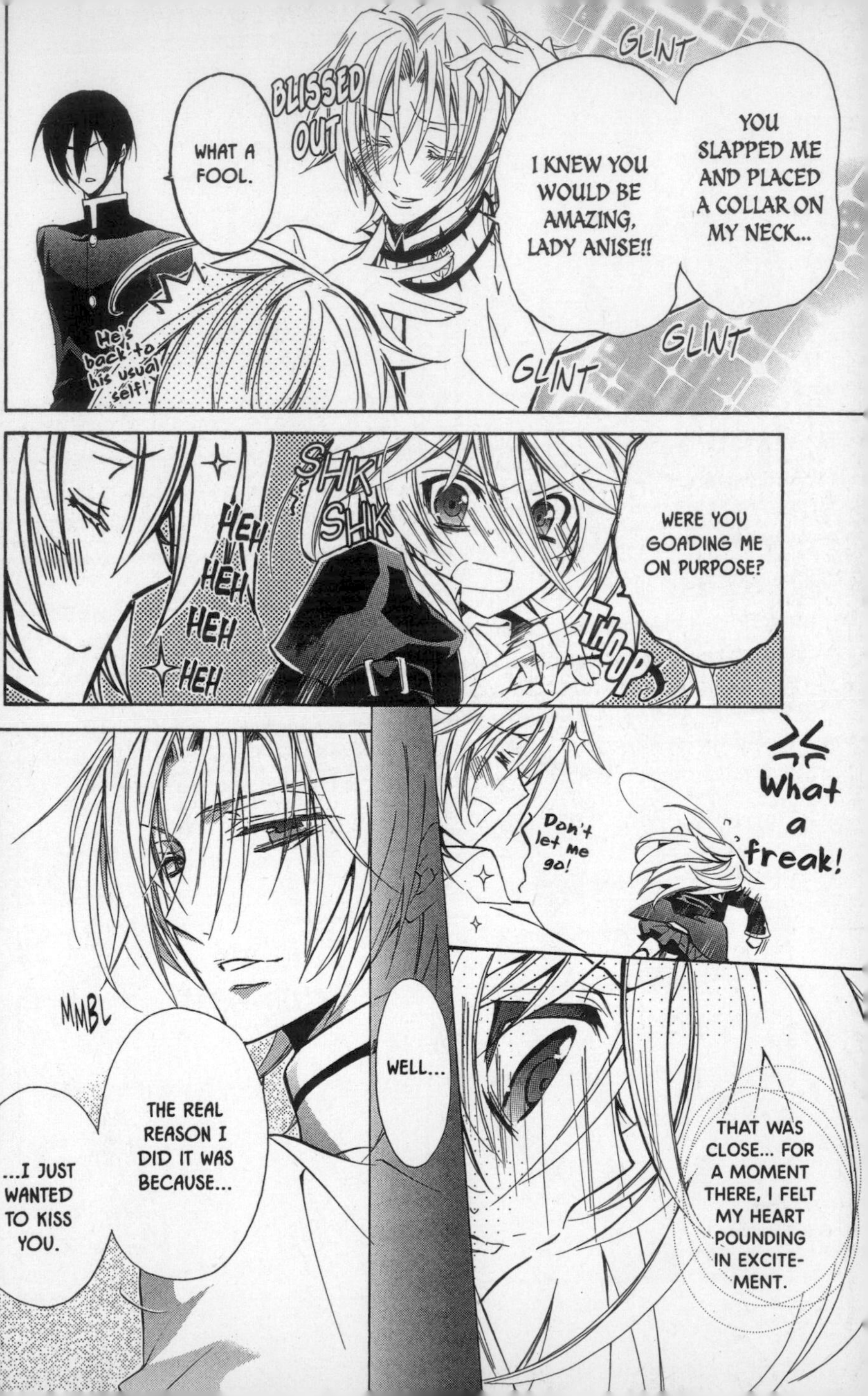
GLINT
YOU SLAPPED ME AND PLACED A COLLAR ON MY NECK...
I KNEW YOU WOULD BE AMAZING, LADY ANISE!!
BLISSED OUT
WHAT A FOOL.
GLINT
GLINT
He's back to his usual self!
WERE YOU GOADING ME ON PURPOSE?
THOOP
SHK SHK
HEH HEH HEH HEH
What a freak!
Don't let me go!
THAT WAS CLOSE... FOR A MOMENT THERE, I FELT MY HEART POUNDING IN EXCITEMENT.
WELL...
MMBL
THE REAL REASON I DID IT WAS BECAUSE...
...I JUST WANTED TO KISS YOU.

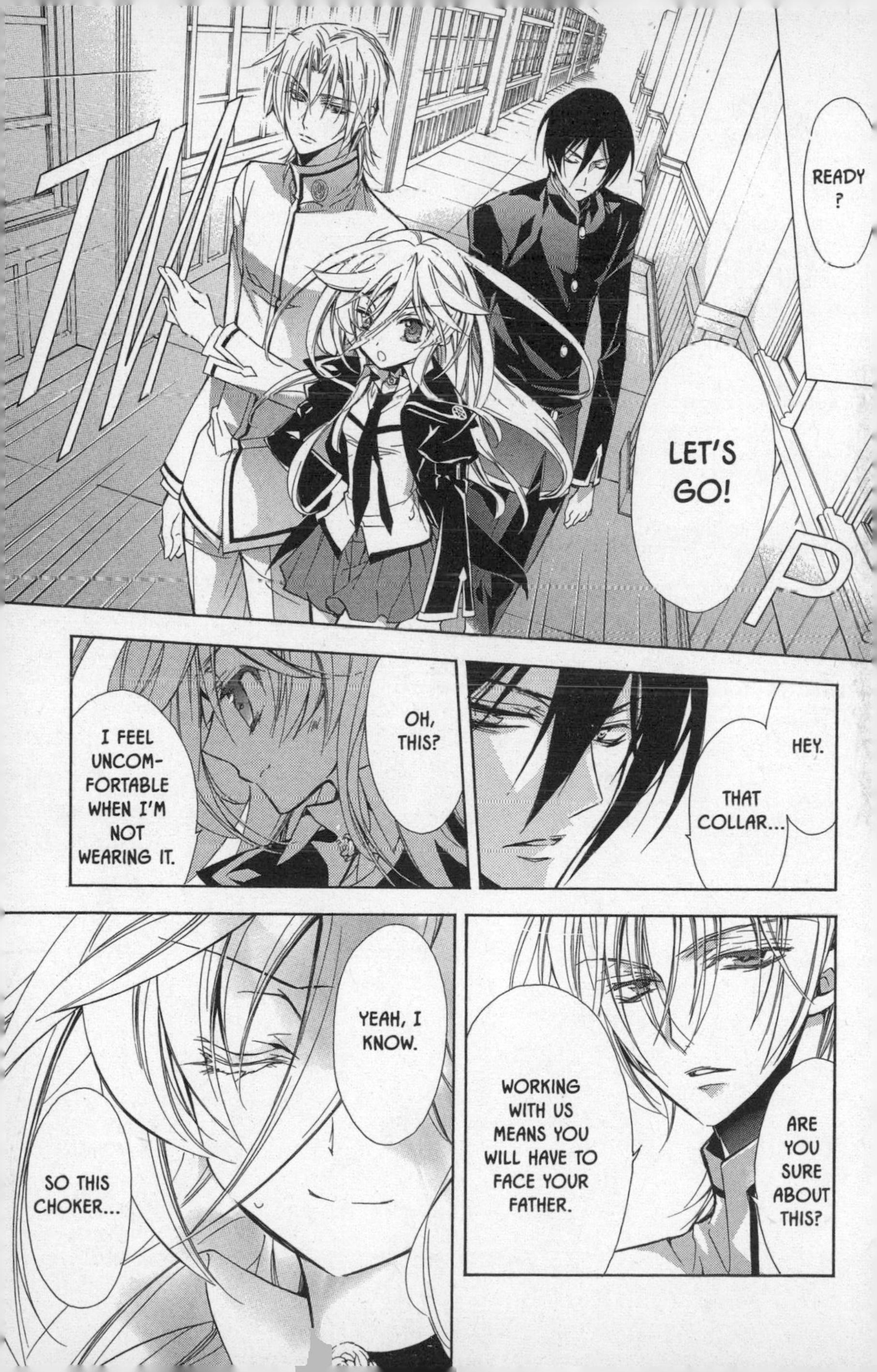
READY?
LET'S GO!
HEY.
THAT COLLAR...
OH, THIS?
I FEEL UNCOM-FORTABLE WHEN I'M NOT WEARING IT.
ARE YOU SURE ABOUT THIS?
WORKING WITH US MEANS YOU WILL HAVE TO FACE YOUR FATHER.
YEAH, I KNOW.
SO THIS CHOKER...

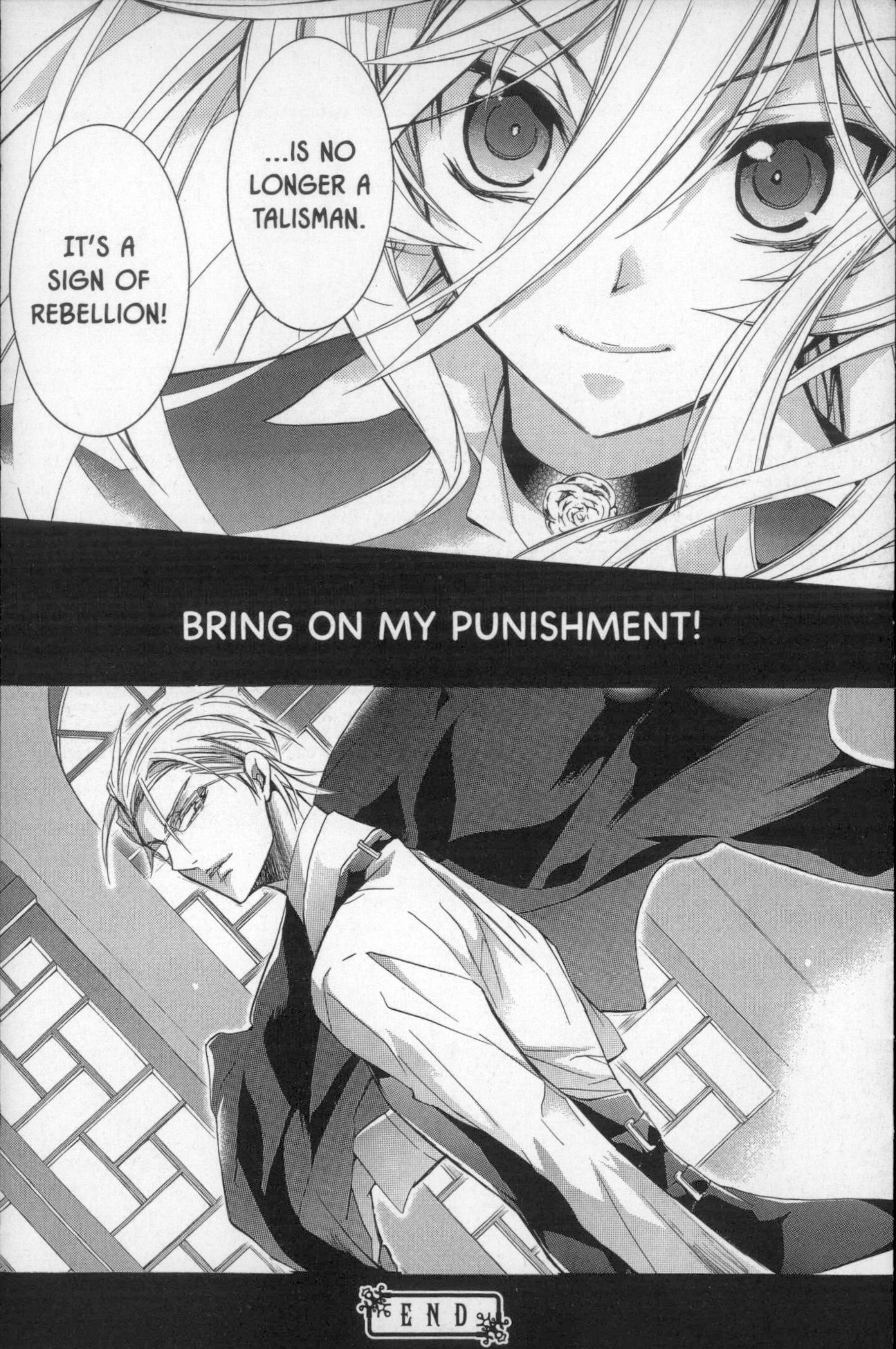
...IS NO LONGER A TALISMAN.
IT'S A SIGN OF REBELLION!
BRING ON MY PUNISHMENT!
END

Kiss
of the
R🌹se
Princess

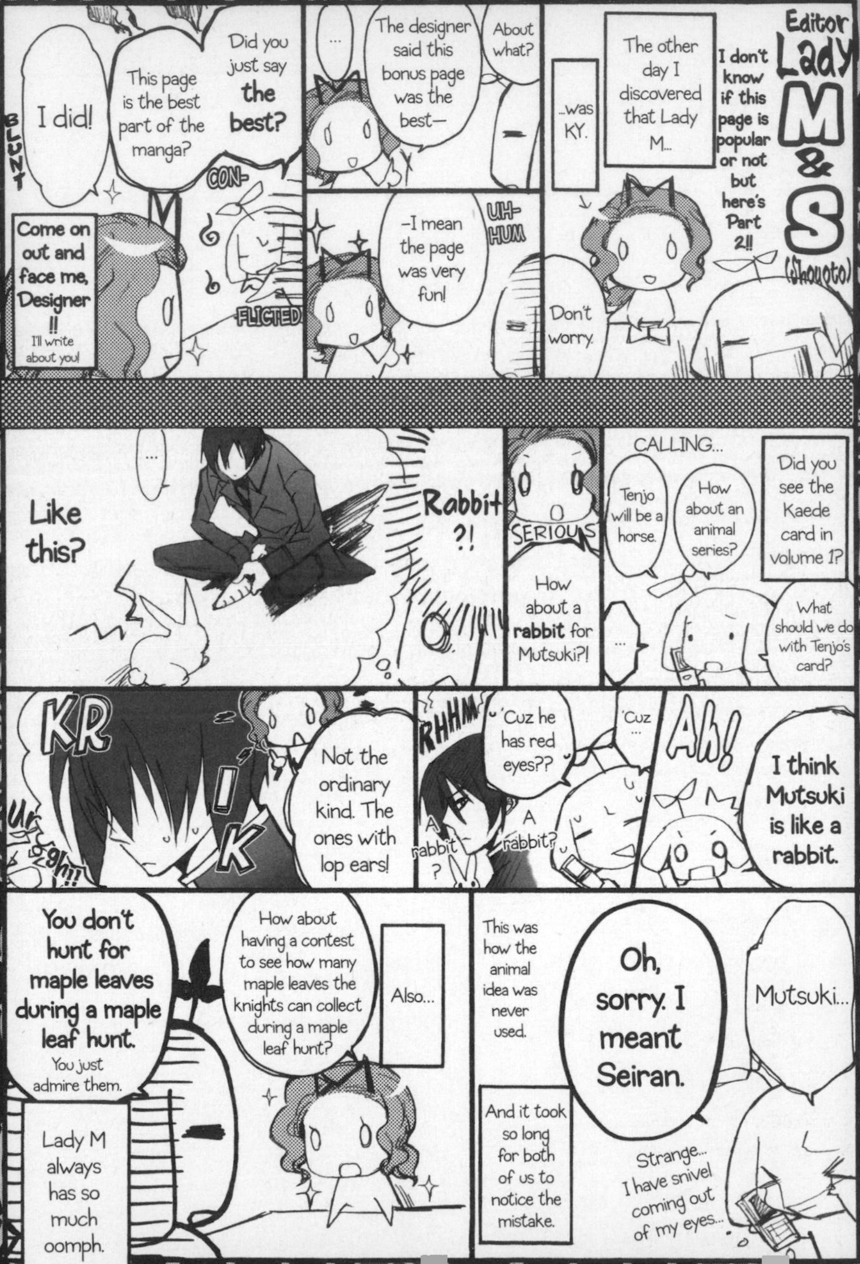

Editor Lady M & S (Shouoto)
I don't know if this page is popular or not but here's Part 2!!
The other day I discovered that Lady M...
...was KY.
Don't worry.
About what?
The designer said this bonus page was the best—
...
UH-HUM
–I mean the page was very fun!
Did you just say the best?
This page is the best part of the manga?
I did!
BLUNT
CON-FLICTED
Come on out and face me, Designer!!
I'll write about you!
Did you see the Kaede card in volume 1?
CALLING...
How about an animal series?
Tenjo will be a horse.
What should we do with Tenjo's card?
...
SERIOUS
How about a rabbit for Mutsuki?!
Rabbit?!
...
Like this?
I think Mutsuki is like a rabbit.
Ah!
'Cuz...
'Cuz he has red eyes??
A rabbit?
RHHM
A rabbit?
Not the ordinary kind. The ones with lop ears!
KRIK
Urggh!!
Mutsuki...
Oh, sorry. I meant Seiran.
This was how the animal idea was never used.
And it took so long for both of us to notice the mistake.
Strange... I have snivel coming out of my eyes...
Also...
How about having a contest to see how many maple leaves the knights can collect during a maple leaf hunt?
You don't hunt for maple leaves during a maple leaf hunt.
You just admire them.
Lady M always has so much oomph.

BONUS★

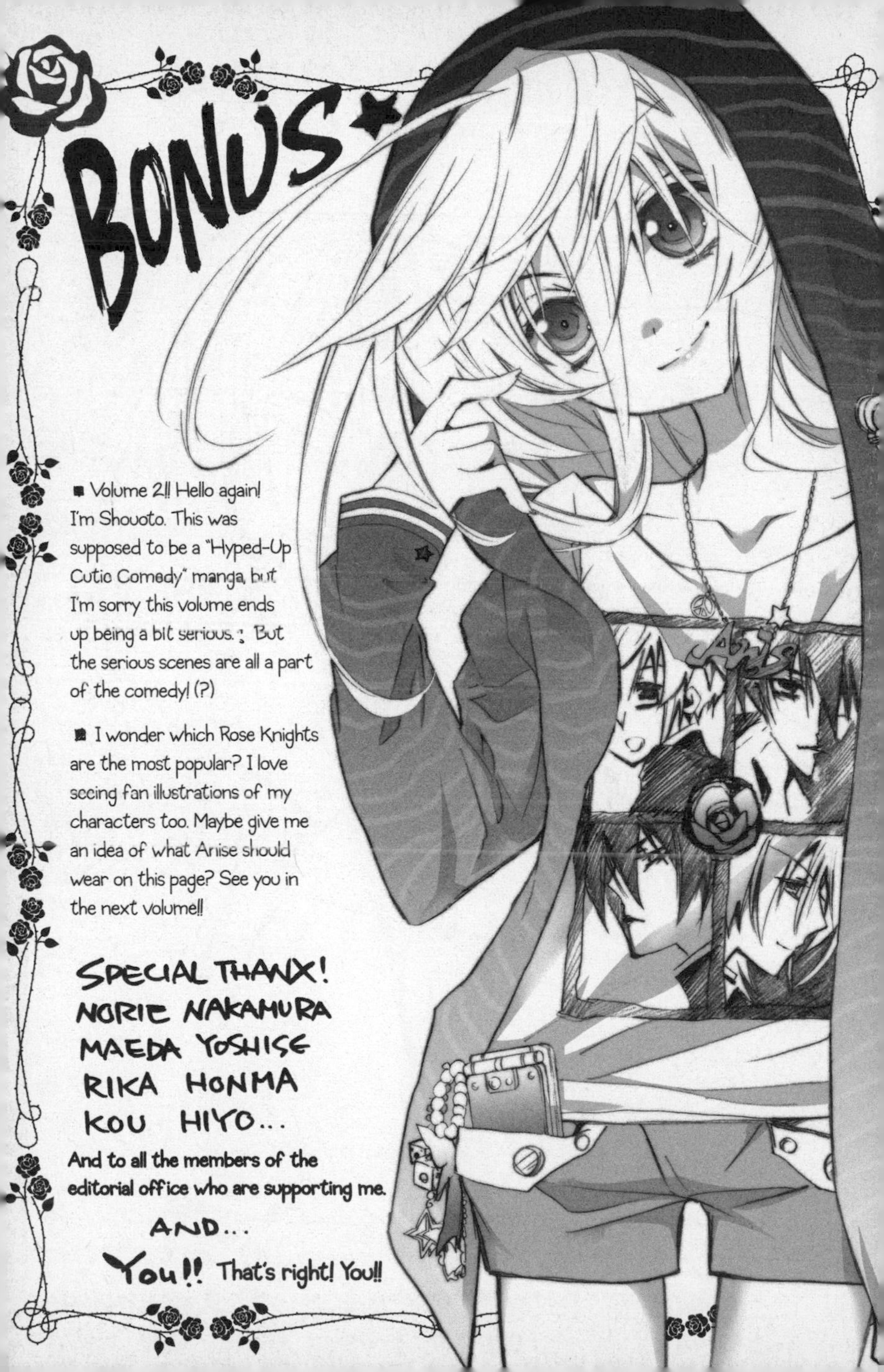

■ Volume 2!! Hello again! I'm Shouoto. This was supposed to be a "Hyped-Up Cutie Comedy" manga, but I'm sorry this volume ends up being a bit serious. ; But the serious scenes are all a part of the comedy! (?)

■ I wonder which Rose Knights are the most popular? I love seeing fan illustrations of my characters too. Maybe give me an idea of what Anise should wear on this page? See you in the next volume!!

SPECIAL THANX!
NORIE NAKAMURA
MAEDA YOSHISE
RIKA HONMA
KOU HIYO...
And to all the members of the editorial office who are supporting me.
AND...
You!! That's right! You!!

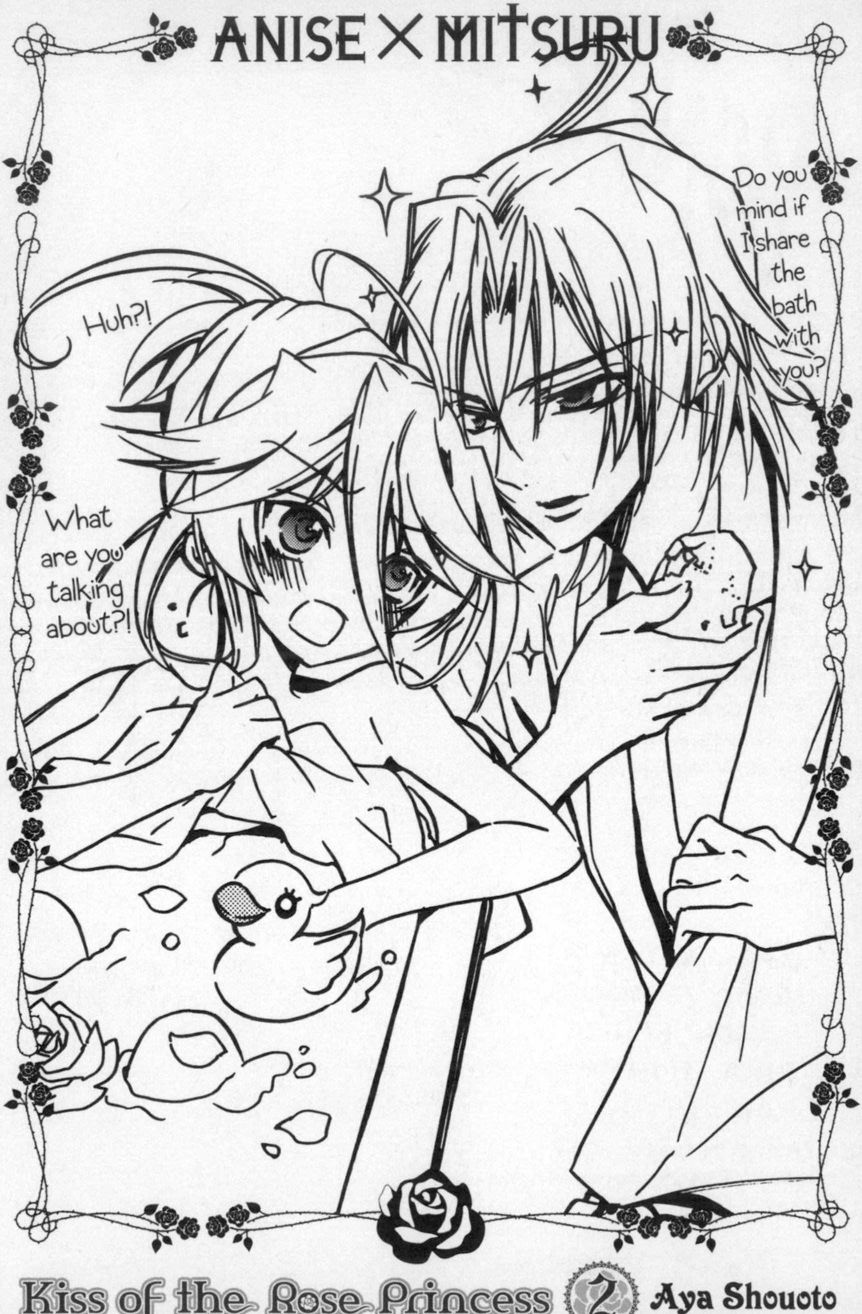
ANISE × MITSURU
Do you mind if I share the bath with you?
Huh?!
What are you talking about?!

Kiss of the Rose Princess 2 Aya Shouoto

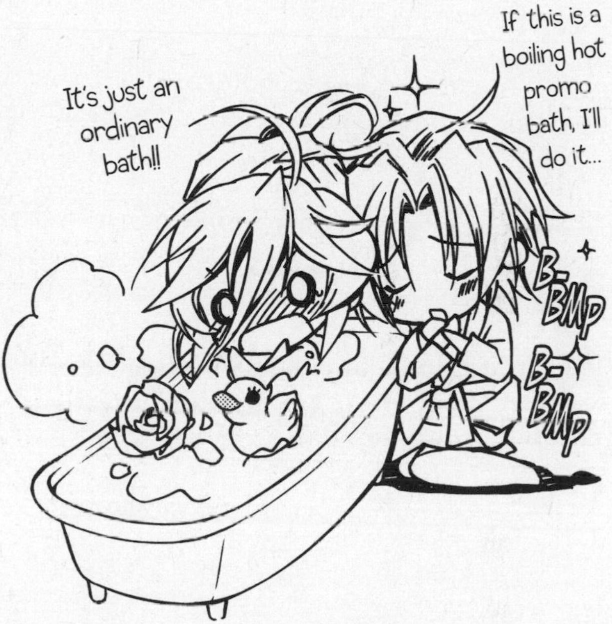
If this is a boiling hot promo bath, I'll do it...
It's just an ordinary bath!!
B-BMP
B-BMP

THE BATH OF THE ROSE PRINCESS

AYA SHOUOTO

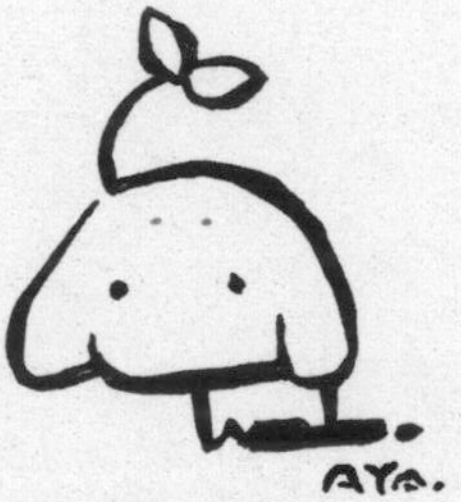
AYA.

I love decorations, but the only thing I can get myself to decorate are my nails. I really want to decorate my PSP...

-Aya Shouoto

Aya Shouoto was born on December 25. Her hobbies include traveling, staying at hotels, sewing and daydreaming. She currently lives in Tokyo and enjoys listening to J-pop anime theme songs while she works.

Kiss of the Rose Princess

Volume 2
Shojo Beat Edition

STORY AND ART BY
AYA SHOUOTO

Translation/Tetsuichiro Miyaki
Touch-up Art & Lettering/Inori Fukuda Trant
Design/Yukiko Whitley
Editor/Nancy Thistlethwaite

KISS OF ROSE PRINCESS Volume 2
© Aya SHOUOTO 2009
Edited by KADOKAWA SHOTEN
First published in Japan in 2009 by KADOKAWA CORPORATION, Tokyo.
English translation rights arranged with KADOKAWA CORPORATION, Tokyo.

Printed in the U.S.A.

Published by VIZ Media, LLC
P.O. Box 77010
San Francisco, CA 94107

10 9 8 7 6 5 4 3 2 1
First printing, January 2015

www.viz.com

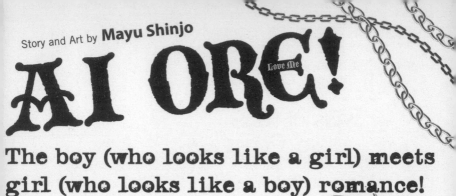

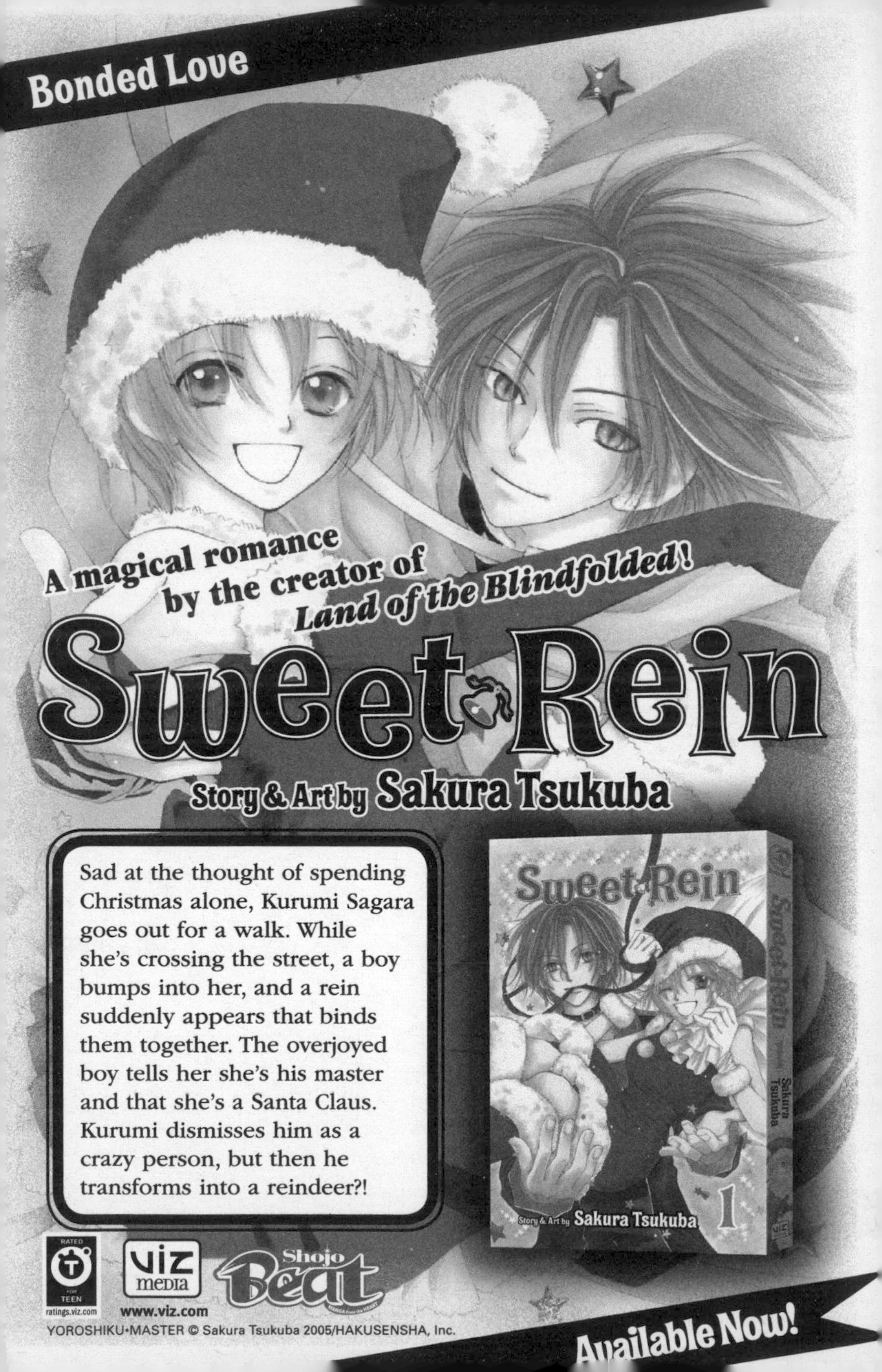
Bonded Love
A magical romance by the creator of Land of the Blindfolded!
Sweet Rein
Story & Art by Sakura Tsukuba
Sad at the thought of spending Christmas alone, Kurumi Sagara goes out for a walk. While she's crossing the street, a boy bumps into her, and a rein suddenly appears that binds them together. The overjoyed boy tells her she's his master and that she's a Santa Claus. Kurumi dismisses him as a crazy person, but then he transforms into a reindeer?!
Sweet Rein
Story & Art by Sakura Tsukuba
1
Sakura Tsukuba
RATED T FOR TEEN
ratings.viz.com
VIZ media
Shojo Beat
www.viz.com
YOROSHIKU•MASTER © Sakura Tsukuba 2005/HAKUSENSHA, Inc.
Available Now!

UIZMANGA

Read manga anytime, anywhere!

From our newest hit series to the classics you know and love, the best manga in the world is now available digitally. Buy a volume* of digital manga for your:

- iOS device (iPad®, iPhone®, iPod® touch) through the **VIZ Manga app**
- Android-powered device (**phone or tablet**) with a browser by visiting VIZManga.com
- **Mac or PC computer** by visiting VIZManga.com

VIZ Digital has loads to offer:

- 500+ ready-to-read volumes
- New volumes each week
- FREE previews
- Access on multiple devices! Create a log-in through the app so you buy a book once, and read it on your device of choice!*

To learn more, visit www.viz.com/apps

* Some series may not be available for multiple devices. Check the app on your device to find out what's available.

Aiwo Utauyori Oreni Oborero! Volume 1 © Mayu SHINJO 2010
DEATH NOTE © 2003 by Tsugumi Ohba, Takeshi Obata/SHUEISHA Inc.
NURARIHYON NO MAGO © 2008 by Hiroshi Shiibashi/SHUEISHA Inc.

This is the last page.

In keeping with the original Japanese comic format, this book reads from right to left, so action, sound effects, and word balloons are completely reversed. This preserves the orientation of the original artwork. Check out the diagram below to get the hang of things, then turn to the other side of the book to get started!

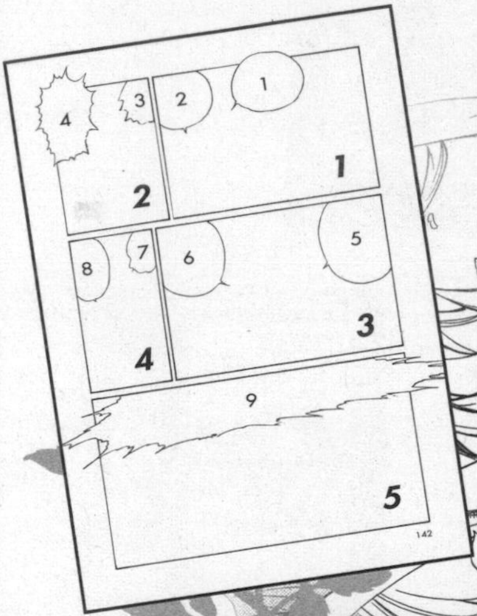

1
2
3
4
1
2
5
6
7
8
3
4
9
5
142

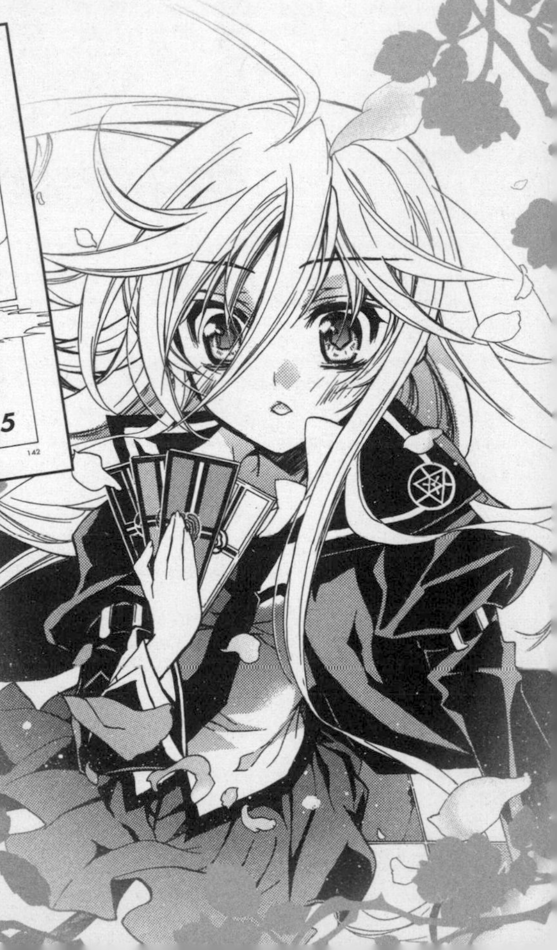